Basic
Microsoft™ BASIC
for the Macintosh™

Basic Microsoft™ BASIC for the Macintosh™

James S. Coan
Louisa Coan

Hayden Book Company
A DIVISION OF HAYDEN PUBLISHING COMPANY, INC.
HASBROUCK HEIGHTS, NEW JERSEY / BERKELEY, CALIFORNIA

Acquisitions Editor: MICHAEL VIOLANO
Production Editor: ALBERTA BODDY
Cover Design: JIM BERNARD
Cover Photo: LOU ODOR
Composition: ART, COPY, & PRINT COMPANY
Printed and bound by: COMMAND WEB OFFSET, INC.

Library of Congress Cataloging in Publication Data

Coan, James S.
    Basic microsoft BASIC for the Macintosh.

    Includes index.
    1. Macintosh (Computer)—Programming. 2. Basic (Computer program language) I. Coan, Louisa. II. Title.
QA76.8.M3C6   1985   001.64'2   85-6837
ISBN 0-8104-6558-2 (pbk.)

Copyright © 1985 by Hayden Book Company. All rights reserved. No part of this book may be reprinted, or reproduced, or utilized in any form or by any electronic, mechanical, or other means, now known or hereafter invented, including photocopying and recording, or in any information storage and retrieval system, without permission in writing from the Publisher.

Microsoft is a registered trademark of Microsoft Corporation. Macintosh is a trademark licensed to Apple Computer, Inc. MacPaint, MacWrite, QuickDraw, Imagewriter, and FatBits are trademarks of Apple Computer, Inc.

Printed in the United States of America

1	2	3	4	5	6	7	8	9	
85	86	87	88	89	90	91	92	93	YEAR

Preface

The material in this book is based on version 2.00 of Microsoft BASIC for the Macintosh. This version is dramatically different from the earlier versions 1.00 and 1.01. Microsoft BASIC, developed by Microsoft Corporation, is in use on vast numbers of computers today. Therefore, if you learn Microsoft BASIC, you will be able to use many computers. In addition, learning BASIC will be a good foundation for programming in other versions of BASIC and other computer languages everywhere.

This book is about programming in Microsoft BASIC using a Macintosh computer by Apple Computer, Inc. This BASIC is interpretive and highly interactive; that is, we can get at all parts of the program quickly and easily. We can instantly test the programs we write and see results without waiting for some long intermediate process to take place. This interactive nature of BASIC has been a primary reason for its tremendous popularity. We can write programs and instantly command the computer to execute them for us. We can even command the computer to execute individual BASIC statements directly from the keyboard. Our mistakes and typing errors are often pointed out to us in plain English rather than in undecipherable code.

This exciting version of BASIC is designed to take advantage of many of the unique features of the Macintosh—from using the mouse to speed program editing to inclusion of very fast and flexible graphics. Microsoft BASIC for the Macintosh introduces us to the world of programming in BASIC without line numbers. Instead, we may use optional line labels or numbers. Many structures are available to minimize the number of line references required. Even the Macintosh mouse cursor, windows, dialog boxes, buttons, and menus can be controlled by BASIC programs.

Problems included at appropriate points in the book make it suitable for the classroom as well as for the individual who wants to learn BASIC. Features of BASIC are generally introduced as they are appropriate for solving a task. Nearly one hundred programs are presented and discussed. The general approach is to begin with small programs to solve real problems and build them up into larger programs as required. One goal is to break programming tasks into segments that can be programmed in a single screen. The list of tasks is organized in such a way that even before we write any BASIC program statements, each item of the list becomes one of the remarks that forms the program documentation. Larger programs are developed by first writing a control routine that will manage a collection of subroutines, and then writing the subroutines. Sometimes the subroutines have already been written to solve earlier programming problems.

We learn now to use the Command, List, and output windows and get started with simple calculations and printed messages in Chapter 1. Chapter 2 introduces numeric and string variables. Here we also look at modular arithmetic and integer division. The loop concept comes up in Chapter 3, with the formal introduction of FOR and NEXT in Chapter 4. We learn about numeric and string functions, subroutines, and subprograms in Chapter 5. Chapter 6 introduces some of the impressive displays and user interaction possible with windows, buttons, menus, and related features. Chapter 7 presents numeric and string arrays. An alphabet game rounds out the work with string arrays. With many programming concepts and BASIC features in hand, a few interesting applications are considered in Chapter 8: a calendar program, the sieve of Eratosthenes, and different base numbering systems. Chapter 9 explores the Microsoft BASIC graphics statements, with LINE, CIRCLE, PSET, PRESET, POINT, PUT, and GET. Chapter 10 discusses the famous Macintosh QuickDraw ROM Routines as accessed through Microsoft BASIC. Chapters 11, 12, and 13 take us from a simple sequential access file to a workable mailing list program. The use of devices as sequential files is discussed in Chapter 11.

Appendix A covers use of the Microsoft BASIC menu bar. The keyboard commands for maintaining programs on the disk are presented in Appendix B. A chart of ASCII codes and an example in the Chicago font of codes from 128 to 216 are in Appendix C. Appendix D is an alphabetically arranged reference of all Microsoft BASIC functions. A listing of programs in the text appears in Appendix E. Appendix F contains solution programs for the even-numbered problems.

James S. Coan
Louisa Coan

To the Reader

Learning to program a computer can be very exhilarating. The thrill of seeing your first apparently complicated idea implemented in a clear, simple program is wonderful. People with a diverse range of interests will find that the Macintosh and Microsoft BASIC are especially well suited for learning to program. There is no need to be concerned about any external detail. You can skip operating systems, interfaces, drivers, prompts, PC boards, slots, and a host of other things, and get right to the job without having to learn other things. All you need to be able to do is move the mouse to make the little arrow point at the thing you want to do next, press the button on the mouse, and use a typewriter keyboard. The Macintosh and the Imagewriter printer offer an excellent facility to display quality results on paper for permanent records.

Everything that the computer does is explainable and predictable. Take care to evaluate the results that the computer produces. Do not blindly accept computer results as faultless. Under normal conditions, the computer will execute your instructions exactly. That means that mistakes or unexpected program results are usually due to inaccuracy in the program, not to the computer's failure to follow directions. A thorough check of the program almost always turns up a rational explanation for the problem.

No one need fear the computer. This is especially true when it comes to learning. When you learn to ride a bicycle or drive a car, someone is bound to notice all your mistakes. This need not be the case with the computer. You can work with it in total privacy and your errors are reported to you alone. The computer will keep its secret if you will keep yours. With truly infinite patience, the computer never raises its voice or becomes exasperated—not ever. Later, with practice and experience, you may confidently demonstrate your skill in public.

Learning to program a computer is not so complicated. You will probably find that an iterative process works best. Read a small section of the book, try it on the computer, and then go back to read some more. There are certain things that you cannot possibly know without being told and some things that just make sense based on what you already know. You will find that reading this book will help with writing the next program, and writing and executing each program will help with reading the book.

A program consists of a set of instructions that causes the computer to perform a particular task. The process of writing those instructions for the computer is called programming. Programs do an amazing variety of things, from the simplest of arithmetic calculations to the most complex of mathematical manipulations. You can write programs to interact with the user. You may want to do this to make the computer play a game or fill out a tax return. You can write a computer program to solve an algebra homework problem, display a graphics design project, or organize a directory of names and addresses. You may even be programming a computer just for the fun of it.

We hope that you are soon stimulated by your work in programming to bring to the computer your new and intriguing problems to be solved. Above all, to be successful, you will have to be an active participant. Experiment! Try variations on the programs presented in the text and challenge yourself with the problems. Actually write programs and execute them. Then try to see how what you have learned fits into the picture of the BASIC language and programming in general.

While nearly every feature of the language is discussed in this book, you are challenged to fit them together in new ways to work for you.

Contents

Chapter 1	**Getting Started**	1

	1-1. Our First Instructions	3
	1-2. Calculations	18
	1-3. Using the Printer	22

Chapter 2	**Adding Features**	25

	2-1. More Calculations	25
	2-2. Additional Arithmetic Operators	39
	2-3. More Messages	42

Chapter 3	**Writing a Program**	49

	3-1. Do It Again	49
	3-2. Do It Again (When We Don't Know How Many)	60
	3-3. Some Handy Tools	70

Chapter 4	**Loops**	**75**
	4-1. Counting with FOR and NEXT	**75**
	4-2. More Bounce to FOR and NEXT	**83**
	4-3. Let's Explore	**88**
	4-4. Nested Loops	**91**
	4-5. WHILE and WEND	**95**
Chapter 5	**Packages in BASIC: Functions, Subroutines, and Subprograms**	**101**
	5-1. Introduction to Numeric Functions	**102**
	5-2. String Functions	**106**
	5-3. Miscellaneous Functions	**114**
	5-4. Programmer-Defined Functions (DEF FN)	**119**
	5-5. Variable Typing and Precision	**124**
	5-6. Subroutines (GOSUB and RETURN)	**125**
	5-7. Subprograms (CALL and SUB)	**129**
Chapter 6	**Picture Windows: Using Macintosh Features**	**135**
	6-1. Windows	**135**
	6-2. Pictures	**141**
	6-3. Menus	**148**
	6-4. Buttons	**155**
	6-5. Event Trapping	**160**
Chapter 7	**Pigeonholes Galore (Arrays)**	**163**
	7-1. Numbers, Numbers, and More Numbers (Numeric Arrays)	**163**
	7-2. A Simple Sort	**171**
	7-3. Array Sizes and Shapes (DIM)	**173**
	7-4. Words, Words, and More Words (String Arrays)	**180**
	7-5. An Alphabet Game	**182**

Chapter 8	**Miscellaneous Applications**	**195**
	8-1. A Calendar Program	**195**
	8-2. The Sieve of Eratosthenes	**202**
	8-3. Number Bases	**204**

Chapter 9	**Graphics**	**213**
	9-1. Getting Started	**214**
	9-2. A Graphic Example (Drawing Dice)	**223**
	9-3. Drawing from DATA	**228**
	9-4. More Graphics Features	**235**
	9-5. Graphs from Formulas	**243**
	9-6. Polar Graphs	**247**

Chapter 10	**Using Macintosh QuickDraw Graphics Routines**	**251**
	10-1. Controlling the Mouse Cursor	**252**
	10-2. Drawing Lines (LINE and LINETO)	**259**
	10-3. Controlling the Graphics Pen	**259**
	10-4. Drawing with Rectangles, Ovals, Arcs, and Polygons	**268**
	10-5. Controlling Text	**281**

Chapter 11	**Files**	**289**
	11-1. Sequential Files	**291**
	11-2. A Program is a File, Too!	**300**
	11-3. Updating a Sequential File	**305**
	11-4. Miscellaneous Features and Techniques	**307**

Chapter 12	**Random-Access Files**	**315**
	12-1. Some Tools	**316**
	12-2. A Sample Random-Access File	**319**
	12-3. Some More Tools	**324**
	12-4. Mixed Access Files	**332**

Chapter 13   **Random-Access Address List**   **333**

13-1. Design the System   **333**
13-2. Write the Programs   **337**
13-3. Enhancing the Data Entry Program   **347**

Appendixes

Appendix A The Microsoft BASIC Menu Bar   **375**
Appendix B Using the Disk   **363**
Appendix C ASCII and Special Character Chart   **369**
Appendix D Microsoft BASIC Functions   **371**
Appendix E Listing of Programs   **379**
Appendix F Solution Programs for Even-Numbered Problems   **385**

Index   **423**

Basic
Microsoft™ BASIC
for the Macintosh™

CHAPTER

Getting Started

With some things, it is best to jump in with both feet. The objective is to get to the point where you can write programs and see results as quickly as possible. The proliferation of computers has made programming available to the masses. The Macintosh computer is a major contribution to that process. It is becoming easier for all of us to use and know about computers. At the same time, it is becoming more and more important for all of us to do just that.

We are going to write programs in the version of Microsoft BASIC that is available for the Macintosh computer. We need a Macintosh computer and a disk with "Microsoft Basic Interpreter for Apple Macintosh." It is important to make a copy of this disk to work on and experiment with. Then, if anything happens to the copy, you always have the original in a safe place to copy again. Directions are in the Macintosh manual.

There are two Microsoft BASICs on the version 2.0 disk. They are labeled (b) and (d), for binary and decimal. They are also represented by different symbols; version (b) displays the Greek letter π, and the decimal version displays a dollar sign ($). The two are distinguished by the way they handle noninteger numbers. The binary version allows for faster calculations and is used for scientific and engineering work. The decimal version eliminates round-off errors in calculations and is designed for financial and business applications. As suggested in the Microsoft BASIC manual, it is a good idea to prepare two disks—one for each version. In this book, we will work with the decimal version and refer to the binary version only to discuss differences.

To get started, turn on the machine and insert the Microsoft BASIC disk into the disk drive. When the desktop appears, we want to "Open" the Microsoft BASIC disk; that is, we want to display the contents of the disk in a window on the screen. To do this, click the mouse twice in rapid succession on the picture of the disk, called the "disk icon." Once the window is displayed, if you click on the little square in the title bar, the window disappears into the disk icon. Double-click again on the disk icon and the window reappears.

You are working with the "Finder," which will "find" Microsoft BASIC and other programs for you. The bar across the top of the desktop contains the names of several "pull-down menus." Any action initiated through these menus will be applied to whatever is highlighted on the screen. Select an icon to be highlighted by positioning the arrow on it and clicking once. To see what choices the menus offer, point to a title with the mouse and hold down the mouse button. To select any item on the menu, drag the arrow downward until your choice is highlighted, and then release the mouse button. The disk window can also be opened using this method: Make sure the disk icon is selected by clicking on it once, and then choose "Open" from the File menu. The various pull-down menus are discussed later. The desktop with the Microsoft BASIC disk window opened resembles Figure 1-1.

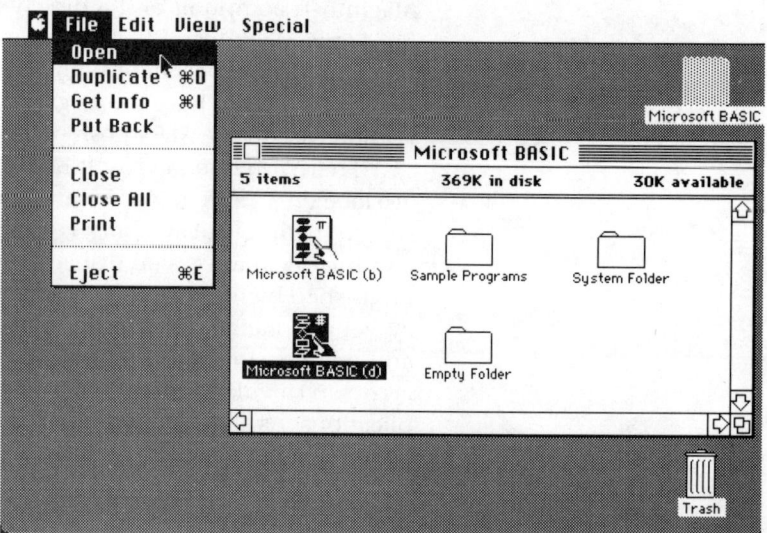

Figure 1-1. A disk window containing Microsoft BASIC icons.

So in order to use Microsoft BASIC, you may open it by either method. It is entirely up to you. Either select the corresponding icon and choose Open from the File menu, or double-click the mouse on the Microsoft BASIC icon and you're there. Since you have already placed the mouse arrow on the Microsoft BASIC icon and clicked once to select it, you might just as well click again and skip the menu. If there is too much time between the first and second clicks, you'll have to double-click again. The allowable time between clicks to qualify for a double-click can be adjusted with the Macintosh Control Panel.

You also have a choice of how to get out of BASIC and back to the Finder. If you have written a program and want to save it to work with some other time, choose "Save As..." from the File menu. A box will appear for you to name the program so it can be retrieved later on. "Save" in the File menu is a shortcut for saving a program with the current name. Appendix A describes this. Also, see Appendix B for more details about managing programs on disk. When you are ready to leave BASIC, choose "Quit" from the File menu. Typing "SYSTEM" in the Command window or including it in a program also causes the Macintosh to leave BASIC and return to the desktop. This takes you back to the Finder. It is a good idea to eject the disk before you turn the Macintosh off. With the disk icon selected, you can either choose "Eject" from the File menu or press ⌘-E. It just depends on whether your hand is on the mouse or the keyboard. (The Command key is just to the left of the space bar, and is labeled with a figure that resembles a four-leaf clover—⌘.) Hold down the Command key while you press "E". When you are finished, eject the disk, put it away, and turn the machine off. We are ready to begin.

1-1. Our First Instructions

Programming is the process of writing instructions to control a computer. Each programming language has its list of available instructions and rules about how to put the instructions together. BASIC is easy to learn because many o. the instructions use English words. We print messages with PRINT; we instruct the computer that we are at the end of the program with END; we tell the computer to stop everything right there with STOP; and so on. It is the programmer's job to select the most appropriate instructions from among those available and put them together in a sensible and efficient fashion to solve the problem at hand.

In order to be assured that the computer has actually done something for us, we should always include some instructions to display a message. Therefore, we start with the PRINT statement.

PRINT Messages

Here is a complete program:

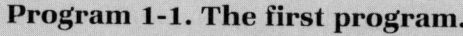

Program 1-1. The first program.

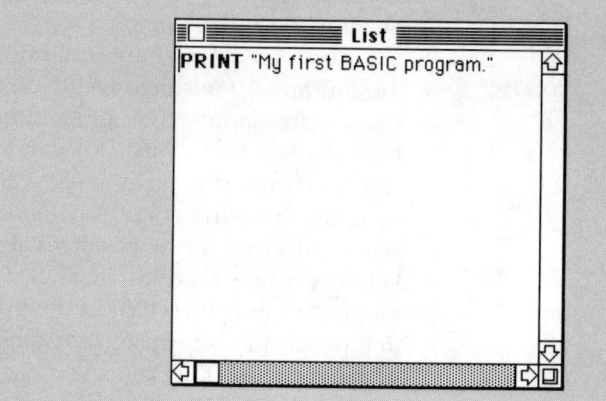

This is just a one-liner. It causes the computer to "PRINT" the message contained within quotation marks. It will last until it is pushed out of the window with additional messages. When we want to get the message printed on paper for more permanent use, we can make a few simple adjustments to have the display go to the printer instead of the screen. See Section 1-5.

We may display any message by enclosing it within quotation marks in a PRINT statement. The words inside quotation marks are not instructions to BASIC. They remain exactly as we type them. Normally, any instruction must have a space before and a space after for BASIC to properly recognize it. Further, there must not be any spaces within the word itself. Note that "P RINT" with the space will not be recognized and you will have to change the line. Microsoft BASIC preserves the spacing just as we type it. Typing a question mark is a shortcut for typing PRINT. When the Return key is pressed at the end of the line, BASIC converts it to the word PRINT.

RUN a Program

If we just type this one program statement into the computer, there will be no action. The line is simply displayed in the List window. After typing in a line, the next thing that we must do is press the Re-

5 Our First Instructions

turn key. Then, everything we have just typed is accepted by BASIC; this is signified by the conversion of all the BASIC instruction words, called keywords, to boldface uppercase letters. This makes programs very easy to read. All BASIC keywords stand out and are higly visible. This also gives a clue to potential errors. If something you thought was a keyword doesn't "light up" when you press Return, there must be an error. Still, our program does not do anything until we get BASIC to "Run" it. Do this by using the mouse to select "Start" from the Run menu at the top of the screen, or do it directly from the keyboard by typing ⌘-R, for "Run."

When the Macintosh carries out the instructions of this little program, the results are displayed in the output window. It looks like Figure 1-2:

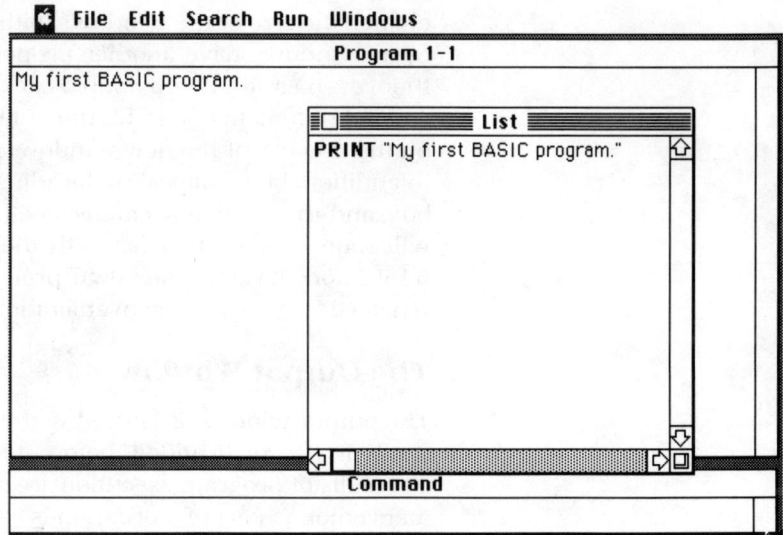

Figure 1-2. Program 1-1 Listed and RUN.

Although we can easily see the actual message as it appears in quotation marks in the List window, BASIC programming allows us to have the computer do something with that message when we RUN the program. In this case our short message is printed in the output window. As we go through the process of learning to program, we will be able to use the powerful resources of BASIC to manipulate words and numbers to solve complex problems and produce interesting games and diversions. First, we need to get a feel for how to utilize the BASIC workspace.

The BASIC Windows

BASIC provides four windows to work with: the output window, the Command window, and two List windows. One is called the List window and the other is the Second List window. You can use the mouse to drag windows around the desktop, and you can change the size of the windows with the size box. In BASIC, moreover, windows have another property that makes working with them even easier. If you double-click on its title bar, a window will expand automatically to fill the entire screen. If you double-click on the title bar of the new window, it reverts to its original shape. In addition, both shapes can be adjusted individually with the size box, and the automatic changes will use the adjusted shapes. You will soon become familiar with the mechanics of working with BASIC and develop your own preferences. Use these features in whatever way is most convenient for you.

The Output Window

The output window is labeled with the name of the program currently in use, or "Untitled" before it has been Saved. This is where all results of program execution are shown. Nothing that programmers enter as part of a program is registered here.

The Command Window

The Command window at the bottom of the screen is just the opposite of the output window. The computer never displays messages in it. Instead, we use it to communicate instructions directly to BASIC. For instance, to Run a program, activate the Command window by choosing "Show Command" from the Windows menu or clicking once anywhere in the Command window itself with the mouse. Then type "R", "U", "N" at the keyboard and press Return. The instructions of the program will be carried out just as if you typed ⌘-R or chose Start from the Run menu. We can also execute statements with keywords like PRINT by typing the statement in

7 Our First Instructions

the Command window. Just enter the line and when you press Return, the instruction is carried out instantly. This is called "immediate" execution. When we type a line into the List window, it is called a "deferred" instruction. Execution is deferred until the program is RUN. Thus, BASIC commands can be issued in two ways: The Command window is used for immediate execution and the List window is used to develop programs for deferred execution.

Editing in the List Window

The window used to write programs is the List window. The window itself can be manipulated in the same ways as the other windows. To put it away temporarily, click on the close box (go-away box) in the title bar. For many programs, you will want to do this to keep the List window from covering the display after the program is done. To retreive it, choose "Show List" from the Windows menu or type ⌘-L. You can even type "list" in the Command window.

The List window is where program statements are typed in and edited as we go along to develop our programs. Most of the Macintosh MacWrite editing capabilities are available in Microsoft BASIC, so it is very convenient to use the mouse to help make changes in lines that have already been typed in.

Try it! You will benefit greatly from actual experience on the computer. Sit down in front of a Macintosh now and type in Program 1-1. Type the program exactly as it appears. If you make a typing error, there are lots of ways to correct it. You can press Backspace as many times as it takes to fix the mistake, or you can hold down the Command key and press H to achieve the same effect. Now suppose you have a line that is too messed up to fix this way. No problem: Just use the mouse to select the entire line. Place the pointer at either end of the line and hold down the mouse button while you move the pointer to the other end. Release the button when everything to be erased has been highlighted. Then this highlighted area behaves as if it were a single point, so if you press the Backspace key once, the entire line is eliminated. The line is canceled and you can begin again. At the end of the line, press the Return key—nothing will happen until Return is pressed.

The process of selecting characters in the List window for editing will soon become automatic. Click on one end of the segment and drag over everything you want to select.The selected text is highlighted. Release the mouse button and BASIC waits for Cut, Copy, Paste, or typed characters. This will become a familiar routine. This works for a single character or a thousand. If the other end is off the screen, that's ok—just drag over the top or bottom of the List window and BASIC will scroll more lines into view, selecting as they go. Occasionally you may want to select a large segment of a program, maybe a couple of windowfuls. This is easy to do with shift-click. First, click and release at one end of the desired segment. Then, move the mouse to the other end (using the scroll bar if necessary) and shift-click (click the mouse button while holding the shift key). This selects everything in between.

All of the editing features are available in both list windows. When you are working with very long programs, this can speed things up. Two entirely different parts of a program can be listed in the two list windows—not two *programs*, just two *parts* of the same program. You can Cut from one window and Paste into the other.

If the computer talks back to you with an error box and a bell, it is probably because you typed something wrong. If this happens when you run a program or type something in the Command window, simply click the mouse on the OK in the box or press the Return key once more. Then type the correct thing in the Command window or use the mouse to edit the line in the List window. Don't let this be upsetting. Soon we will cover more ways to correct errors. You can't hurt the computer with program instructions. This is one of the nice things about programming: No error can damage the computer. On the other hand, if you were to experiment with the electronics hardware, any little flaw or error could damage or destroy your machine. Your attitude should always be that you are determined to control the computer, and not the other way around. Don't be put off by anything the computer does.

Now, back to our program. RUN it. Now type in Program 1-2.

9 Our First Instructions

Program 1-2. A two-line program.

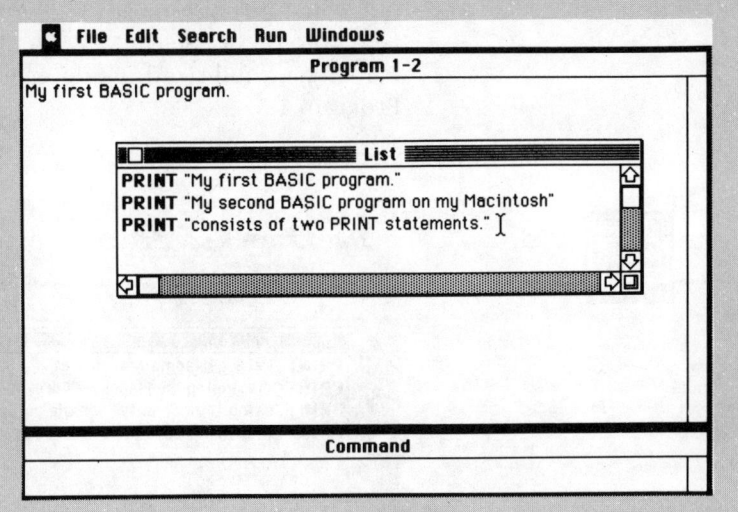

Typing more statements simply adds more lines to the original program. Choose RUN again, and we will see the two messages faithfully displayed on three lines in the output window. This was actually intended to be an entirely new program, so we should erase the earlier line. Later we will see programs of many lines. It is impractical to eliminate entire programs with Backspace. Therefore, BASIC provides the keyword "NEW".

NEW

NEW is used only when we wish to eliminate an entire program. It can be chosen with the mouse from the File menu or typed into the Command window. Once NEW has been selected, any program that we had in the List window is gone forever. For this reason, BASIC checks whether the current program is saved. If it is not saved, a dialog box reports that the program is not saved and allows you to save it if you want to. If you want to be able to retrieve a program, save it before using NEW. Then, to use the program, choose Open from the File menu and when the dialog box appears, select the name under which it was saved. Whenever we desire to begin a new programming project, we should use the NEW keyword. Otherwise, the new program will just be added onto the old one. It is important to begin with a clean slate.

Cut, Copy, and Paste

Let's consider some longer messages. What we are going to do here will come through more vividly if you can follow along by typing right into BASIC. Select NEW, double-click on the List window title bar to get a full-sized window, and then type in the four lines of Program 1-3.

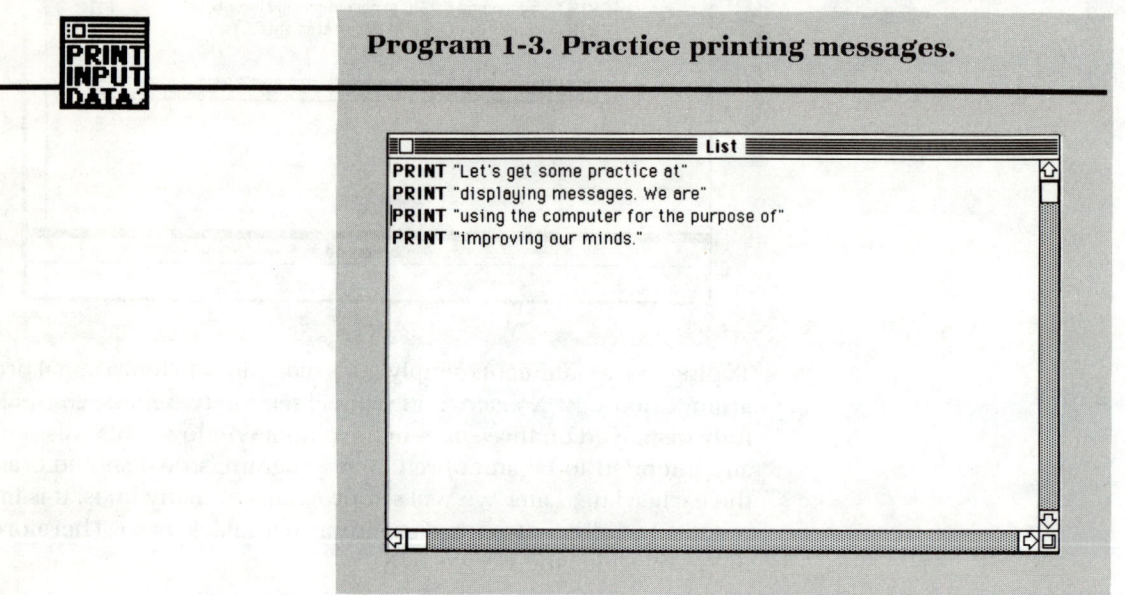

Program 1-3. Practice printing messages.

Executing this program will produce the messages in quotation marks as typed in the program. Double-click the title bar of the List window again and run the program.

11 Our First Instructions

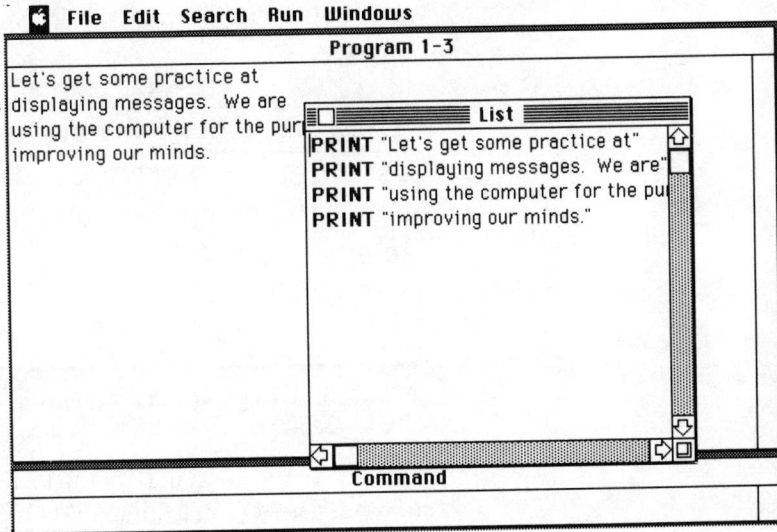

Figure 1-3. Execution of Program 1-3.

Once again, we see the List window ready for work. Next, let's tinker with our little program. Let's eliminate the second line by dragging over the line with the mouse to select it. Then choose "Cut" from the Edit menu or type ⌘-X at the keyboard, which accomplishes the same thing, and press Backspace. Now check the Listed program again.

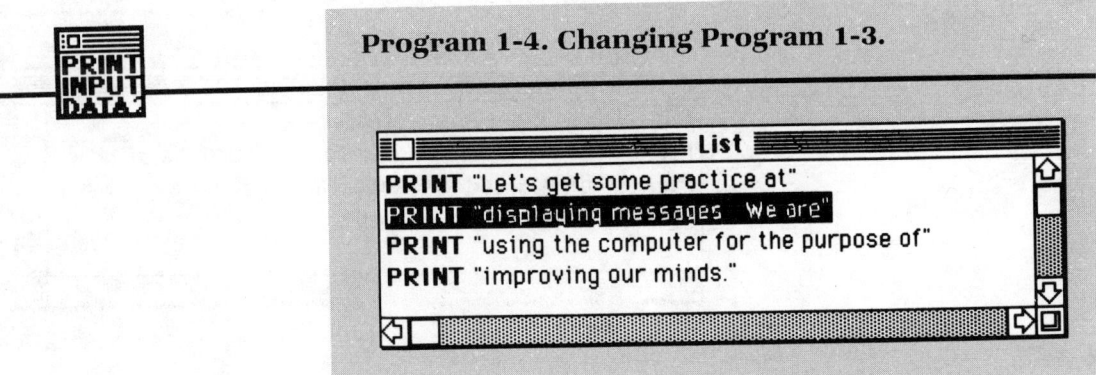

Program 1-4. Changing Program 1-3.

12 Chapter 1: Getting Started

When we execute this new program, the corresponding message is displayed.

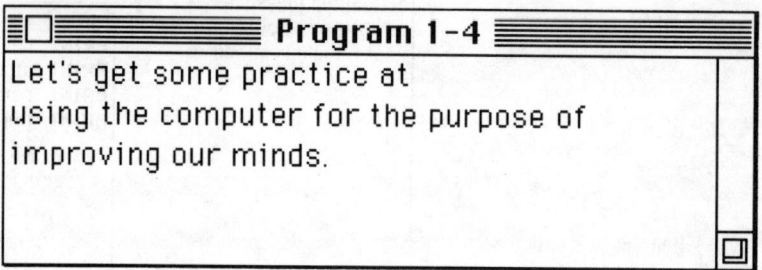

Figure 1-4. Execution of Program 1-4.

Now move the insertion point to the beginning of the last line, choose "Paste" (⌘-V) from the Edit menu, and press Return. The insertion point is where the next character typed at the keyboard will appear on the screen and is indicated by the blinking vertical bar. The insertion point can be moved with the mouse. Simply move the mouse until the little I-beam is located where you want to type next and click the mouse. The blinking vertical bar should move to that point. Now we have used the cut-and-paste features of Microsoft BASIC to produce Program 1-5.

Program 1-5. Paste the line somewhere else.

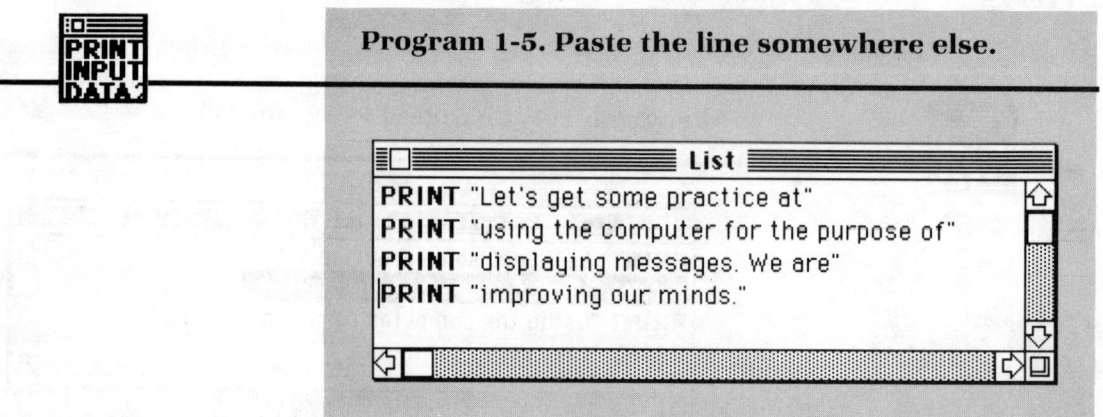

13 Our First Instructions

We are getting a little experience here at simply manipulating a program. We could easily restore the original program by rearranging these two lines again. We can Cut or Copy several lines at a time as well. Click at the beginning of the first line and drag vertically until the desired lines are highlighted. Release and Cut or Copy as required. See Program 1-6.

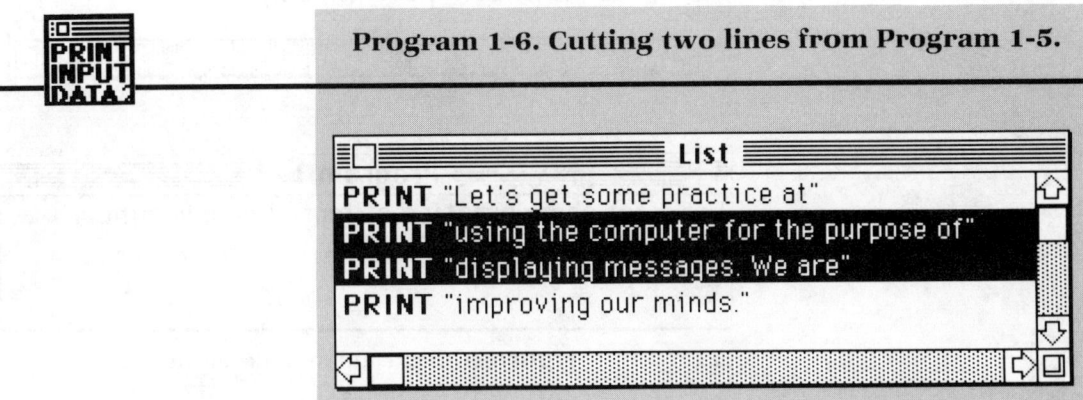

Program 1-6. Cutting two lines from Program 1-5.

Only the selection most recently Cut or Copied is stored to be Pasted. Be sure to Paste each selection before going on to Cut or Copy another one.

The Semicolon

Let's make one more change in our message-printing program. As written, the program displays its message on two separate lines. It would be nice to have it produce a one-line display. In BASIC, that is very easy: We place a semicolon at the end of the first line. To do this, use the mouse to position the pointer just after the closing quotation mark and click once to move the insertion point to this spot. Now whatever you type is inserted at this point. Simply type in the semicolon—but don't press the Return key. That would create an entirely new line. In this case, to get the new line accepted by BASIC, click the pointer anywhere in the List window outside that line. You can also just RUN the program, regardless of where the insertion point is. See Program 1-7 and Figure 1-5.

Program 1-7. Two PRINT statements displayed on a single line.

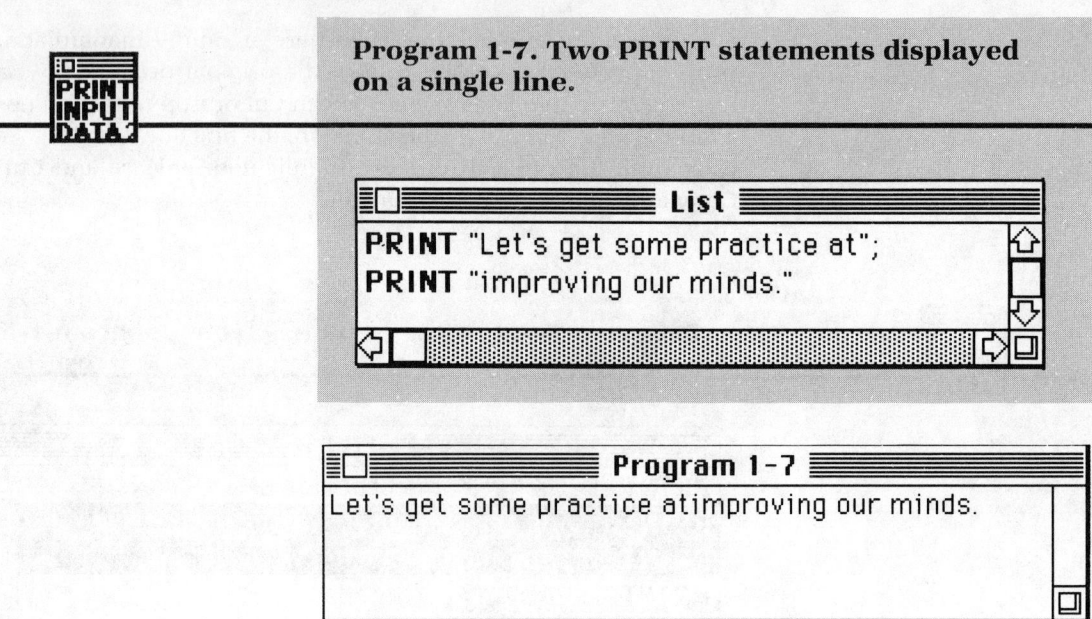

Figure 1-5. Execution of Program 1-7.

The semicolon at the end of the PRINT statement is an instruction to BASIC to continue further printing on the same display line. Oops! We really want a space between "at" and "improving." If we want a space, then we must include it in our instructions to the computer. Since anything enclosed within quotation marks is displayed as typed, all we need to do is include a space at the appropriate spot. Move the insertion point again by moving the arrow to the right place and clicking the mouse button twice—once to make the List window active and again to move the blinking vertical bar. This is done in Program 1-8.

Program 1-8. Include the space this time.

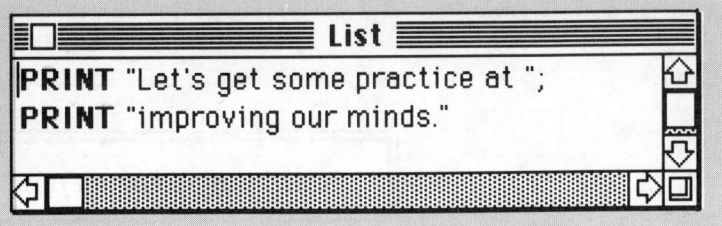

Now RUN it.

Use the mouse to move the insertion point whenever you need to correct a typing mistake, change a word or two in a program, or add a new line. Once you have moved the insertion point around to correct mistakes, you will need to move it to the end of the program again to add more lines. Suppose you want to insert a statement at the beginning or the middle of the program instead of the end. Move the insertion point to the beginning of the line you want the new statement to precede. Press Return to get a new empty space, and move the mouse again to the beginning of that clear line. Another way to do it is to move the insertion point to the beginning of a line and just begin typing the new line, pushing the one already there out to the right. At the end of the new statement, just type Return, and each statement is on its own line again. For instance, try adding a title to the final message of Program 1-8:

PRINT "My Third BASIC program on my Macintosh."

These exercises should give you a good idea of how to do some of the beginning things in BASIC. We have entered a program, RUN it, and modified it for further execution. These procedures will soon become second nature.

At the Keyboard

If you have been following along with these exercises, there is a fair chance that you have seen some disapproving message from BASIC. You may have witnessed the

| Undefined subprogram | OK |

error box. Suppose we type something like:

   pront "This is a sample error"

in the List window. Nothing happens—until we execute the program. At that time, BASIC detects the problem and gently responds with a soft tone (how soft is controlled with the Control Panel), the error box, and a box outlining the line in question in the List window. When BASIC encounters the beginning of a line in the List window that it does not recognize as a BASIC keyword, it interprets the line as a subprogram label and delivers the "Undefined subprogram" error box. Subprograms will be described in Chapter 5. For now, just click the OK button or press Return and edit the mistake with a few moves of the mouse. Perhaps you typed "rin" in the Command window, intending to RUN a program; "ruin" is a favorite—that doesn't work either; or perhaps you typed "lost" instead of list.

Another common error is the Syntax error. "Syntax" simply refers to form. Everything we enter into the computer must have a correct form or syntax. If we enter an incorrect form, BASIC cannot determine what action to take. Thus, it reports a "Syntax error." Typing "PRINT RUN" will do it. No harm has been done. Simply click the OK button or press Return, type the instruction correctly, and proceed.

Summary

When we turn on the Macintosh and insert a disk with Microsoft BASIC on it, we may need to double-click on the disk icon to open the disk window. Once we can see what is on the disk, we double-click on the Microsoft BASIC icon to begin. When we are done, we should Save our programs and choose Quit from the File menu to go back to the Finder.

We have spent some time here becoming familiar with BASIC by causing the computer to display word messages. This has given us a chance to see how to build programs in the List window and make changes in them. Programs are built up by typing instructions having a syntax or form that we know BASIC can analyze and act upon. We change an existing program line by using the mouse to move the insertion point so we can Backspace over the error and type in the new text.

There are certain words that we may use in BASIC to instruct the computer. We have seen the keywords PRINT, RUN, LIST, and NEW. We have used Start, New, Show Command, Show List, Cut, Copy, and Paste from the pull-down menus.

We may display messages by enclosing them within quotation marks in a PRINT statement. On a printed line, we may combine messages by using semicolons in PRINT statements. The computer will carry out the instructions of our program when we enter the RUN instruction (Start from the Run menu and ⌘-R). We may examine our entire program with the LIST instruction (Show List from the Windows menu or ⌘-L). We erase a program from the computer with the keyword NEW.

Problems for Section 1-1

Don't limit yourself to the problems listed here. As you begin to understand BASIC and programming, you will want to draw on problems of special interest to you. The process of learning to program a computer is unique in that the computer will provide you with some measure of your success. You don't need a teacher or an answer book to give important feedback on your progress. It is especially satisfying to be able to formulate your own problems, program their solutions, and verify the result—all on your own.

1. Think up any message that you would like the computer to display—for example, "Now is the time for all good people to come to the aid of their country." RUN the program. Try other messages.

18 Chapter 1: Getting Started

2. Write a program to display the message, "Programming is fun. The computer will solve problems for us." Use two PRINT statements—one for each sentence. Have the message displayed on a single line.

1-2. Calculations

The ability to display messages is crucial to good programming. Well thought-out messages and labels for program results are very important. Every computer program should display some message.

The message is not the only thing. Often it is the ability of the computer to perform calculations with lightning speed that makes it so useful. Even if our real interest lies in graphics, games, voice, learning systems, word processing, or any other seemingly non-mathematical application, it is the arithmetic power of the computer that makes it perform so many different tasks. For this reason, it is important for us to learn how to direct it to calculate for us.

We can calculate an important number with a simple program such as Program 1-9.

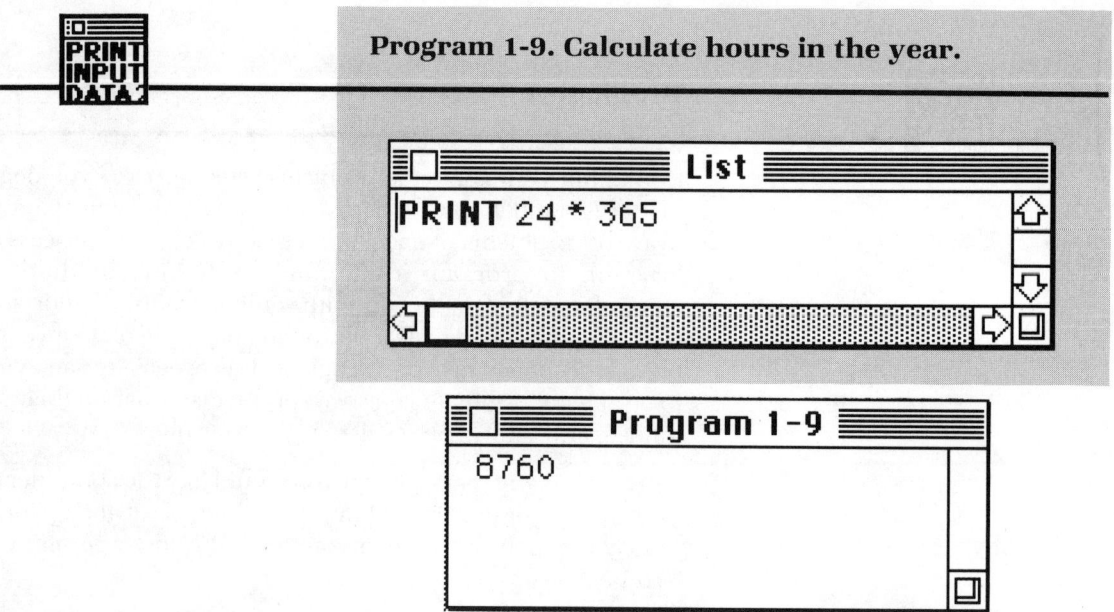

Program 1-9. Calculate hours in the year.

```
PRINT 24 * 365
```

Program 1-9

```
8760
```

Figure 1-6. Execution of Program 1-9.

19 Calculations

We can easily direct the computer to perform calculations right in the PRINT statement with no quotation marks. We have used the asterisk symbol (*) to indicate multiplication. We might even want to use immediate execution to display such a simple result.

We really ought to dress up our program a little by including a label to tell us what that number is. All we have to do is add a quoted message. Program 1-10 does the job.

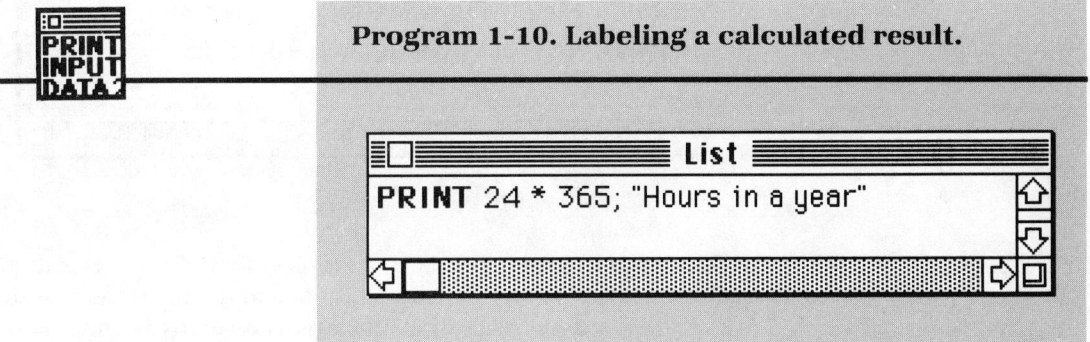

Program 1-10. Labeling a calculated result.

```
PRINT 24 * 365; "Hours in a year"
```

Here we have used the semicolon to place the message right on the same line as the calculated result. Look carefully at the execution of Program 1-10.

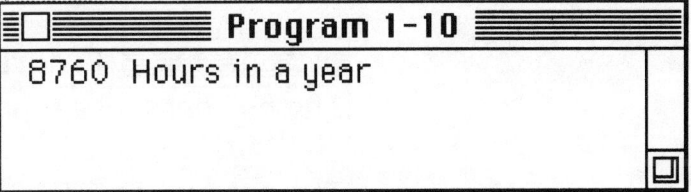

```
8760 Hours in a year
```

Figure 1-7. Execution of Program 1-10.

Note that we got a space between the 0 in 8760 and the H in Hours. BASIC always inserts a space following the display of a numeric value.

Program 1-11 is a simple program to demonstrate multiplication, addition, subtraction, and division of two numbers.

Program 1-11. Demonstrate simple calculations.

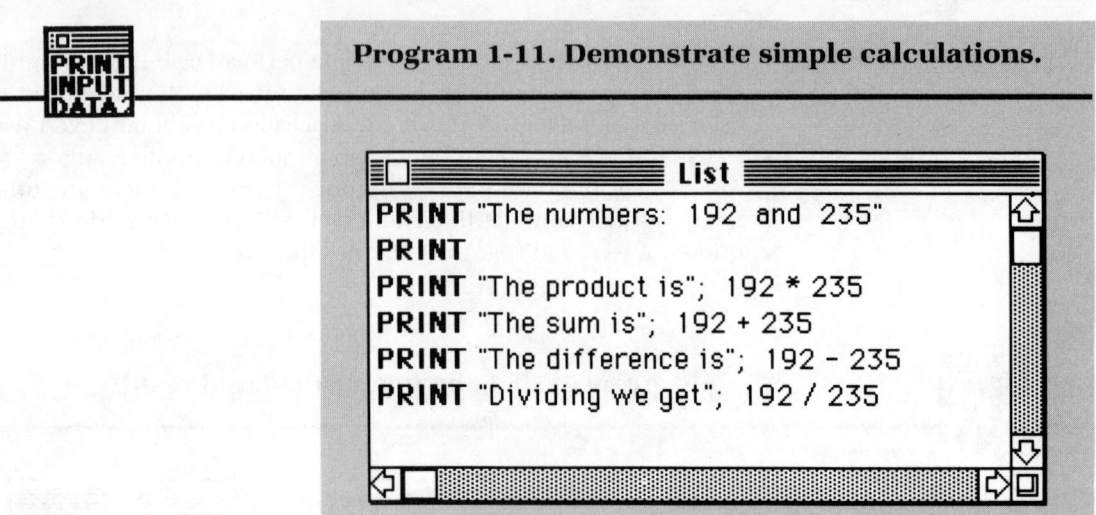

We can see in Program 1-11 that *is used to multiply, + is used to add, − is used to subtract, and / is used to divide. Here, one short program has done several calculations. How many we might direct the computer to perform is limited only by the number of statements we are willing to type. Note that we used a blank PRINT statement in the second line to improve the appearance of the program display. This simply prints an empty line in the output window.

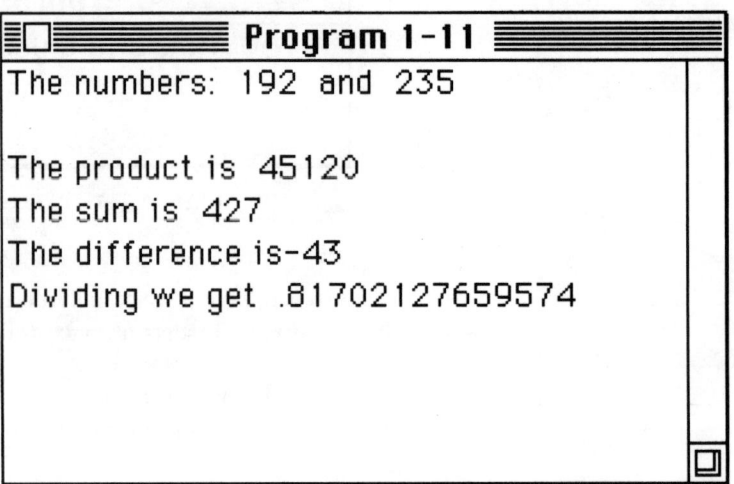

Figure 1-8. Execution of Program 1-11.

21 Calculations

That decimal value for the division is necessarily approximate. If we do that problem out "all the way," we find a 46-digit repetition. In this case, BASIC rounded the result off to 14 digits. That will be enough for many applications. We may even prefer fewer digits. The binary version of Microsoft BASIC would display the result of 192/235 as .8170213. This is the major difference between the two versions. Each uses different precisions for calculations. Note that the three positive results are preceded by a space, while the negative value is indicated in the conventional manner.

We may direct the computer to perform arithmetic in any order by using parentheses. The expression 2 + 3 * 4 evaluates to 14, while (2 + 3) * 4 equals 20.

It is important to realize that very soon we will see more convenient ways to perform calculations on the computer. Right now we are trying to approach the learning of programming with a minimum of new detail at each step along the way. As each idea becomes familiar, we will be ready to tackle the next feature or programming technique. It will be very satisfying to learn to write programs by progressing from the known to the unknown.

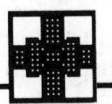

Summary

So now we have the ability to display messages and perform arithmetic calculations in PRINT statements. We even have the ability to produce an empty line for nice display using the blank PRINT. BASIC uses the asterisk (*) to indicate multiplication, and plus (+), minus (−), and slash (/) are used for addition, subtraction, and division, respectively. The decimal version of BASIC provides 14-digit precision without any special action on the programmer's part. The binary version of BASIC provides 7-digit precision without any special action on the programmer's part.

Problems for Section 1-2

1. Write a program to calculate the sum of the counting numbers from 1 to 10.
2. Write a program to find the average of 78, 89, and 82.
3. Write a program to calculate the number of days since you were born.
4. Write a program to calculate the number of hours since you were born.
5. Write a program to find the simple interest at 11.98% on $4949 for one year.
6. Add 283.4, 658, 385.8, and 17.

1-3. Using the Printer

So far we have only been using the Macintosh screen for displays we have produced. To have messages printed on paper, first a printer must be attached, have paper in it, and be turned on. The Apple Imagewriter produces excellent results. The programs written for display on the screen can be converted for display on paper with a change in only one keyword. If we replace every occurrence of the keyword PRINT with LPRINT, then the display goes to the lineprinter. These changes are easily made with the options available in the Microsoft BASIC Search menu. Choose "Replace" and have the computer do all the substitution work.

The other keyword that specifies display on the printer is LLIST. Typing LLIST in the Command window will produce a listing of the program just as it is shown in the List window, except in smaller type and without reproducing the boldface style for the BASIC keywords. To have an exact replica of the contents of the List window, choose "Print . . ." from the File menu.

Another way of reproducing the images on the screen is to type LCOPY in the Command window. This will print on paper an exact copy of the contents of the entire screen, including windows and menu titles. The same effect can be achieved by typing ⌘-4 with both the Shift key and Caps Lock down. The advantage of doing it this way from the keyboard is that the screen is not changed by the process of typing the keyword LCOPY. There is also a keyboard shortcut for printing a picture of the window that is currently active. Hold down the Shift key while typing ⌘-4 but without Caps Lock. All of these require an Imagewriter printer.

Using The Printer

If the lines overlap on the Imagewriter, you have probably used a program that sets the printer up for graphic display. You will need to reset the printer. One way to do this is to turn the printer off and back on again. Another method is to control the printer by sending special codes through the program. Include the following line as part of the program:

LPRINT CHR$(27); CHR$(99)

or just type the line in the Command window. For other codes see the Imagewriter manual. For more information on CHR$, see Chapter 5.

CHAPTER 2

Adding Features

Now that we have written a few programs and are familiar with the computer and Microsoft BASIC, it is time to add some simple but powerful features. We will learn how to supply values for our programs to work on in a much more general way than we did in Chapter 1. The ability to store values using numeric and string variables will be revealed. We'll be doing more with calculations and displaying messages.

2-1. More Calculations

It is your job to buy the eggs this week. That's not so tough: Just go to the grocery store and buy some eggs. But you are also asked to get the best buy. So you read the paper and learn that extra large eggs cost $1.00, large eggs are priced at $.95, medium eggs go for $.87, and small eggs sell for $.72 a dozen. Which should you buy? How do you decide which is the best buy? You probably want the lowest cost per ounce. So you want to know the weight per dozen. That is easy: Look at the egg cartons. There you will find that the four sizes of eggs listed above weigh 27, 24, 21, and 18 ounces per dozen, respectively. It is also easy to determine the price in cents per ounce. The problem is solved for us by Program 2-1.

Program 2-1. Calculate egg values.

PRINT 100/27; 95/24; 87/21; 72/18

Here we have a one-line program to tell us which size eggs to buy to get the most egg for the money. It produces the report shown in Figure 2-1.

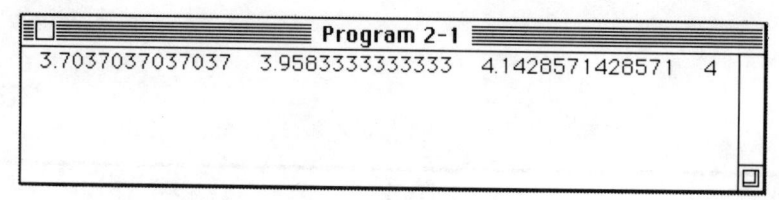

```
╔══════════════ Program 2-1 ══════════════╗
  3.7037037037037   3.95833333333333   4.14285714285714   4
```

Figure 2-1. Execution of Program 2-1.

From this we can see that we get the lowest price per ounce by purchasing the extra large eggs. If the store is out of them, then large eggs are the ones to get.

Program 2-1 may have solved a problem for us. It listed four numbers. By remembering that the sizes are listed decreasing from left to right, we can interpret the results. However, it is a very primitive program. At the very least, we should have the computer label each of the values for us. One way to do this is to write four separate PRINT statements as shown in Program 2-2.

Program 2-2. Label egg values.

```
PRINT "Extra large";    100/27
PRINT "      Large";     95/24
PRINT "     Medium";     87/21
PRINT "      Small";     72/18
```

It is always a good idea to arrange programs and program output so that things are easy to read. The leading spaces within quotation marks will help produce a nicely arranged report. The extra spaces following the semicolons on those same lines help to make the program itself easier to read. Be careful with Macintosh's proportional spacing. It may not always be possible to line the columns up exactly, since different characters require different amounts of space. The standard character width is the width of any of the numerals, 0 through 9. Spaces are only half as wide as the standard width, so we usually include two for every regular digit space. Microsoft BASIC leaves in any extra spaces we type for clarity (or even by accident). This feature gives us a chance to insert lots of space to make programs more readable. This is all for your benefit—the computer doesn't care.

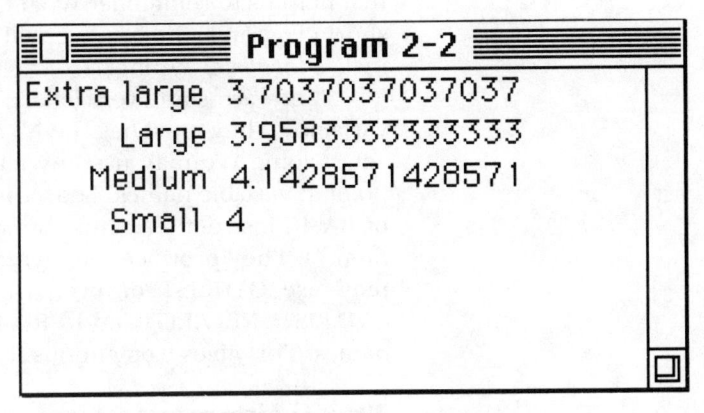

```
▣▬▬▬▬▬ Program 2-2 ▬▬▬▬▬▬
Extra large  3.7037037037037
      Large  3.9583333333333
     Medium  4.1428571428571
      Small  4
```

Figure 2-2. Execution of Program 2-2.

It might be nice to insert a line at the beginning to display a message announcing "Egg prices in cents per ounce" or something such as that.

Calculating cents to the nearest ten trillionth isn't relevant to our problem. One of the things we will be looking for a little later on is a way to round off numeric results.

Number Pigeonholes (Numeric Variables)

We can program the computer to perform many useful and interesting calculations using just the arithmetic available in PRINT statements. That gives us a hand-held calculator for the price of a computer. Tremendous additional problem-solving power is unleashed with each new programming feature available in BASIC. Thus far we have been using our screen display or a piece of paper to save any results produced by a program.

BASIC contains the ability to save results within a program without having to display them. We simply think of a nice name for a value and tell the computer to remember a number by that name.

Computer people call it a variable. If we want to save a number, 765, representing a person's wages, then we might well ask the computer to use a variable called WAGES. We will have to remember that it is a measure of money. The computer won't do that for us. So, in a program, if we need to calculate a 2.4% wage tax, we would use an expression such as

    WAGES * .024

And we could have the computer remember that value in another variable—perhaps TAX, or WAGETAX. We should select names that help us to remember what the number represents. For quick, short programs, though, we will often use just a single letter. This makes for faster typing.

There are some restrictions on what names we may use for variables. They must begin with a letter and may be up to 40 characters long. We may use any letters, any digits, and the decimal point in variable names. The variable name must not be a keyword or BASIC instruction. Thus, names like NEW, PRINT, and LIST are no-no's. They produce the "Syntax error" error box. However, we may use OLDLIST or even NEWLIST if it suits our purpose. OLD.LIST, NEW.LIST, and PRINT.LIST are all legitimate variable names. This gives tremendous flexibility.

The Assignment Statement (LET)

BASIC has a special statement that allows us to direct it to remember values. It is called the LET statement and can be used as follows:

    LET WAGES = 765

And to retain the value for taxes in TAX, we would use a statement such as

    LET TAX = WAGES * .024

The LET statement is referred to as the *assignment statement* because it causes the computer to assign a value to the variable named on the left of the equal sign.

Next, we might want to know how much is left and save that value in NPAY or even NET.PAY.

    LET NET.PAY = WAGES−TAX

Finally, we ought to have the program display the result.

    PRINT "Net pay is:"; NET.PAY

Putting these together, we get Program 2-3.

Program 2-3. First program with variables.

```
LET WAGES = 765
LET TAX = WAGES * .024
LET NET.PAY = WAGES − TAX
PRINT "Net pay is:"; NET.PAY
```

RUNning this program produces the output of Figure 2-3.

```
program 2-3
Net pay is: 746.64
```

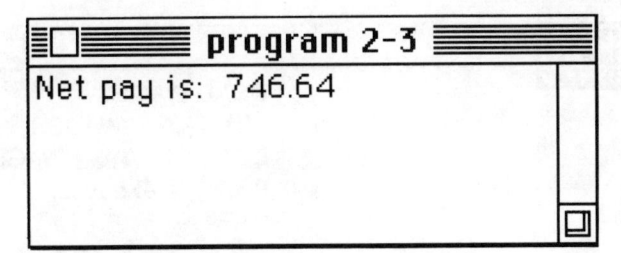

Figure 2-3. Execution of Program 2-3.

We have created a program that consists of a sequence of instructions leading to a problem solution. This program may be saved and used again with another value for WAGES. By making a slight change in the program, we may solve the same problem for any wages figure we like. To find the net pay for a person having wages of 635, simply replace the first line in Program 2-3 with

LET WAGES = 635

and RUN the program. The LET statement is probably one of the most frequently used statements in BASIC.

Optional LET

The use of the LET keyword itself is optional. We may use the statement

WAGES = 635

to assign the value 635 to the variable WAGES. This is still called an assignment statement and will perform in exactly the same manner as the equivalent LET statement. Many people strongly encourage the beginner to continue using the LET keyword until he or she is quite comfortable with programming. For this reason, we will use LET for a little while longer in this book.

We may also cause the computer to READ values stored elsewhere in the program as DATA.

READ and DATA

Earlier in our wages program, we changed the value of WAGES by replacing the old figure in the LET statement with the new one. We can simplify this process a little by using READ and DATA. Consider Program 2-4.

Program 2-4. Introduce READ and DATA.

READ WAGES
LET TAX = WAGES * .024
LET NET.PAY = WAGES−TAX
PRINT "Net pay is:"; NET.PAY
DATA 765

This program will produce exactly the same result as our first wages program. The action of the first line—READ WAGES—is to search the program for a DATA statement. Upon finding it, READ assigns the value found there to the variable named in the READ statement. Thus the statement pair

READ WAGES
DATA 765

does exactly the same job as the statement

LET WAGES = 765

Furthermore, as we will see shortly, the READ and DATA combination is used to supply many values for variables during the execution of a program. In the meantime, we will look at a third method for assigning values to variables.

So far, we have the LET statement and the READ and DATA combination. Both techniques require that all values be stored as part of the program and be known before the program is executed. The third method allows us to enter values at the keyboard while the program is actually running.

Entering Values From the Keyboard (INPUT)

We often find that a program solves a problem based on just a few items of information, such as wages. In addition, we would like to create programs that nonprogrammers can run with ease. Sometimes when we RUN a program we don't even know what numbers to enter until we see some results from another part of the program. In situations like this, we may use the INPUT statement of BASIC.

INPUT WAGES

is another way to assign a value to a variable. The INPUT statement provides the program operator with an opportunity to type values at the keyboard. After the Return key is pressed, the typed value is assigned to the variable named in the INPUT statement, in this case WAGES. This means that we do not have to edit a program to solve the problem with different values. With this capability, people who are not programmers can feel confident using our programs to solve their own problems. It is a good idea to display a label to describe the value that is to be entered. See Program 2-5.

Program 2-5. Demonstrate the INPUT statement.

```
PRINT "Enter wages";
INPUT WAGES
LET TAX = WAGES * .024
LET NET.PAY = WAGES−TAX
PRINT "Net pay is:"; NET.PAY
```

Notice that this program uses three different BASIC statements: INPUT, LET, and PRINT. Programming is the process of putting together those statement types required to solve the problem at hand. Now the program may be used to solve the net-pay problem for many values of wages without changing the program itself. It is this kind of capability that makes the computer such a useful machine. When this program RUNs, it will display the message in quotes in the first line, followed by a question mark. That is the signal for us to enter a number. See Figure 2-4.

```
╔═══════ Program 2-5 ═══════╗
Enter wages? 635
Net pay is: 619.76
```

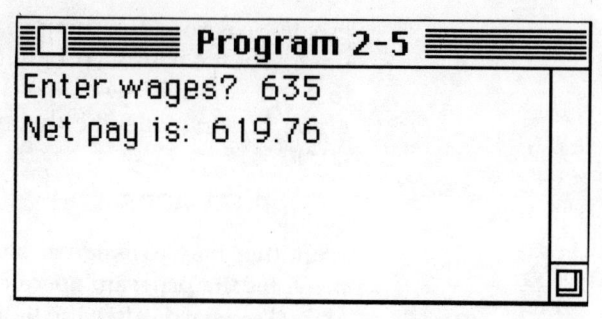

Figure 2-4. Execution of Program 2-5.

When we executed Program 2-5, we typed the value 635 and the program displayed everything else. Notice that we got the question mark on the same line as our message by using a semicolon in the PRINT statement.

If you should happen to press the Return key without entering a value, BASIC will take the value to be zero. In the event that you happen to lean on the keyboard and enter more than 63 digits, BASIC will cough. Two messages will be displayed in the output window, followed by another question mark.

Overflow
?Redo from start
?

That means just what it says: The number you entered is too large. Reenter your value.

Now we have three methods for providing values for a program to work on. They are LET, READ and DATA, and INPUT. LET assigns a value according to the expression following an equal sign. READ and DATA may be combined to supply values right in the program itself for use during execution. INPUT assigns a value entered from the keyboard.

PRINT USING

Suppose in Program 2-5 we respond with 777, then what? Let's try it. See Figure 2-5.

More Calculations

```
┌─────────── Program 2-5 ───────────┐
│ Enter wages? 777                  │
│ Net pay is: 758.352               │
│                                   │
└───────────────────────────────────┘
```

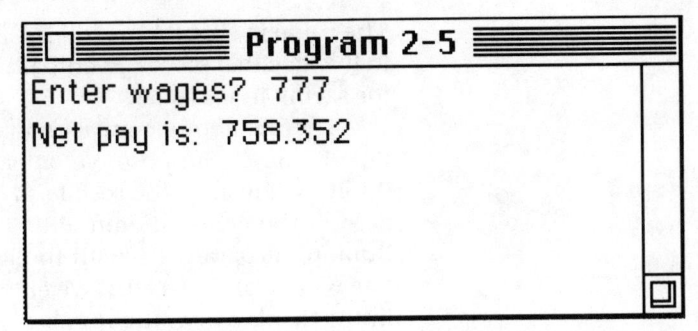

Figure 2-5. Try a different value for wages in Program 2-5.

It is difficult to spend .352 dollars. We would like to have our results in this calculation rounded to the nearest cent. That is easy to do with PRINT USING. PRINT USING allows us to lay out the form we would like to see for the display. We may use number signs (#) to describe how we want the results to look. To allow for three digits to the left of the decimal and two to the right, we use the following statement:

PRINT USING "###.##"; NET.PAY

When our program executes this line, BASIC will use only the spaces occupied by the number signs for digits. Further, we may include our descriptive label in the quotation marks. Now it looks like this:

PRINT USING "Net pay is: ###.##"; NET.PAY

Including this new line in Program 2-5 produces the display of Figure 2-6.

```
┌─────────── Program 2-5 ───────────┐
│ Enter wages? 777                  │
│ Net pay is: 758.35                │
│                                   │
│  ┌─────────── List ───────────┐   │
│  │ PRINT USING "Net pay is:###.##"; NET.PAY │
│  └──────────────────────────────┘ │
└───────────────────────────────────┘
```

Figure 2-6. Program 2-5 with PRINT USING.

The value in NET.PAY is still 758.352, but the display is rounded off to two decimal places. Eventually, we will see how to round values for saving in variables.

There is another situation in which it would be nice to employ PRINT USING. Suppose we enter 800 when we run Program 2-5. BASIC will display the result as 780.8. It would be nice to show the zero in the cents column. PRINT USING is just the ticket for this. Running Program 2-5 with the latest version of the PRINT USING line will display 780.80. If we enter a value that calls for more digits in the display than the number signs allow to the left of the decimal, the program displays a percent sign (%) to the left of the result. So it is a good idea to allow plenty of space.

```
Program 2-5
Enter wages? 7778
Net pay is:  %7591.33
```

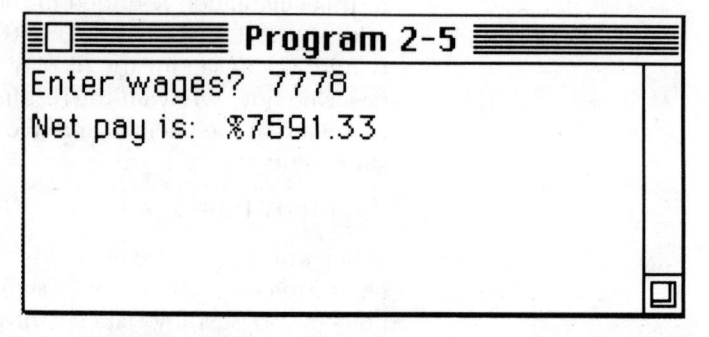

Figure 2-7. Percent sign indicates excess output.

Since Program 2-5 talks about money, let's get PRINT USING to include a dollar sign ($) in the display. Use

PRINT USING "Net pay is: $###.##"; NET.PAY

to produce the results of Figure 2-8.

```
Program 2-5
Enter wages? 777
Net pay is: $758.35

List
PRINT USING "Net pay is: $###.##"; NET.PAY
```

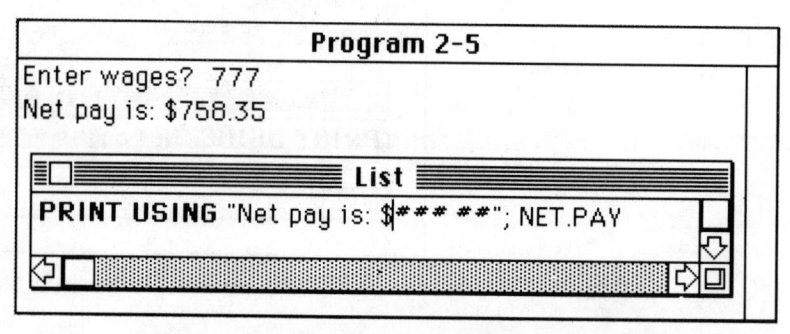

Figure 2-8. A dollar sign in PRINT USING.

We may include one or two dollar signs there. In either case, only one will be displayed. A second one acts just like a number sign—it holds a space for a digit if needed. If only one dollar sign is used, then it will be displayed in the column where it appears in the PRINT USING statement. For two dollar signs, BASIC places a dollar sign right up against the figure in the display.

There are some additional features of PRINT USING that we will look at later.

Multiple INPUT and Multiple READ

The INPUT statement is powerful enough just as we have seen it. In addition, we may easily enter several values using a single INPUT statement. We simply list all of the variables we wish to assign following the keyword INPUT, separating them with commas. While we may list many variables in a single INPUT statement, it is a good idea to limit the number to three or four at the most. It is difficult to type a very long list of numbers on one line without getting lost somewhere. Two to three is ideal.

When the program runs, the user must type the values separated with commas. So, to enter the four eggs prices from our earlier program, we may use

INPUT PE, PL, PM, PS

where PE stores Price Extra large. The READ statement may be used in the same way.

READ WE, WL, WM, WS

Here we store Weight Extra large in WE. It makes sense to use READ and DATA for the egg weights per dozen since they will never change. It makes sense to use INPUT to assign values for egg prices because they often change. We next supply some sensible messages and display the cents per ounce as before, and the program is done. This time we have a program that may be used by anyone. See Program 2-6.

Program 2-6.   Making the eggs program more flexible.

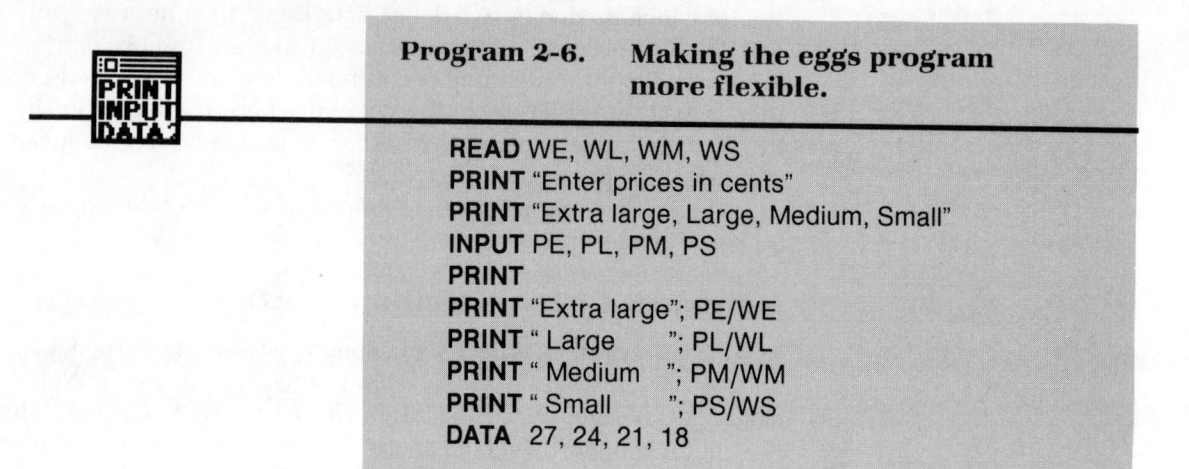

```
READ WE, WL, WM, WS
PRINT "Enter prices in cents"
PRINT "Extra large, Large, Medium, Small"
INPUT PE, PL, PM, PS
PRINT
PRINT "Extra large"; PE/WE
PRINT " Large     "; PL/WL
PRINT " Medium    "; PM/WM
PRINT " Small     "; PS/WS
DATA 27, 24, 21, 18
```

Notice that we have blended the use of INPUT and READ nicely in the same program. READ is appropriate for values that seldom change and INPUT is used for values that usually change.

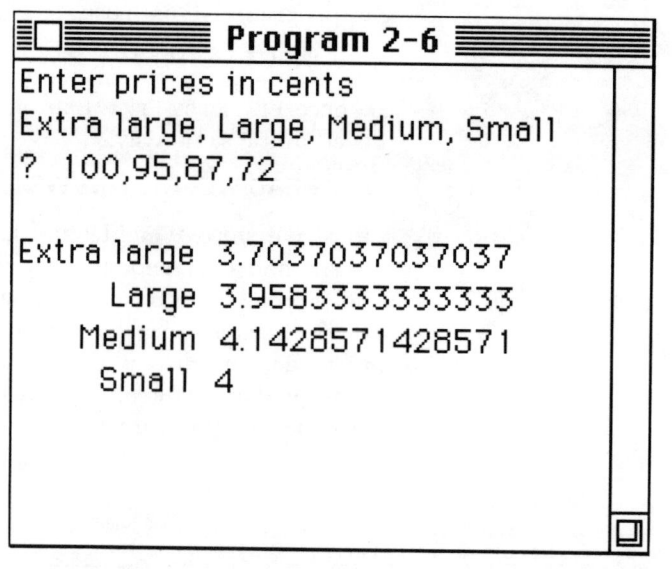

```
═══════════ Program 2-6 ═══════════
Enter prices in cents
Extra large, Large, Medium, Small
? 100,95,87,72

Extra large  3.7037037037037
      Large  3.9583333333333
     Medium  4.1428571428571
      Small  4
```

Figure 2-9. Execution of Program 2-6.

An INPUT statement requesting a single value will accept Return and set the variable to zero. An INPUT statement requesting several

More Calculations

values will insist that we enter the appropriate number of values. If we enter fewer or more, we get the

    ?Redo from start

error message in the output window.

By using the multiple value capability of READ and INPUT, we have gotten the equivalent of eight LET statements into one READ, one INPUT, and one DATA. The number of values possible here is limited only by the line length limit (255 characters) and the readability of the program.

RESTORE

Occasionally, we would like to READ DATA more than once. Normally, if the program runs out of data, BASIC delivers the

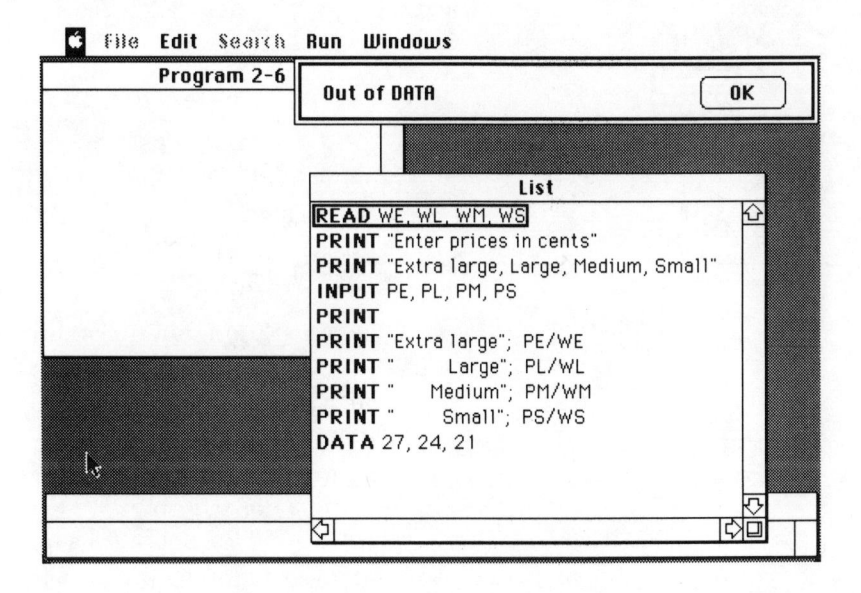

```
 File  Edit  Search  Run  Windows
┌──────────Program 2-6──────────┐
│           Out of DATA     OK  │
│                               │
│           ┌────── List ──────┐│
│           │READ WE, WL, WM, WS││
│           │PRINT "Enter prices in cents"│
│           │PRINT "Extra large, Large, Medium, Small"│
│           │INPUT PE, PL, PM, PS│
│           │PRINT             ││
│           │PRINT "Extra large"; PE/WE│
│           │PRINT "    Large"; PL/WL│
│           │PRINT "   Medium"; PM/WM│
│           │PRINT "    Small"; PS/WS│
│           │DATA 27, 24, 21   ││
│           └──────────────────┘│
└───────────────────────────────┘
```

error box and execution terminates. The bold outline locates the line in the program where the READ statement appears. We can change that with the

    RESTORE

statement. All DATA is restored to the program and the next item read by a READ statement will be the very first item in the first DATA statement.

Summary

We have seen the use of numeric variables. Numeric variables store numeric values within a program. Values are stored in numeric variables using LET, READ, and INPUT. The LET statement assigns the value on the right of an equal sign to the variable named on the left. READ copies values from DATA statements to variables. INPUT looks to the keyboard for its source of information.

Both READ and INPUT may be used for several variables by separating them with commas. We may reread DATA by using RESTORE to restore all data.

We can display results rounded off and with a dollar sign. We just put the pattern we want in quotation marks in a PRINT USING statement.

Problems for Section 2-1

1. What will the following program display?
   LET WAGES=432
   LET TAXES=WAGES * .022
   PRINT WAGES

2. Write a program to request three numbers from the keyboard and calculate the average.

3. Write a program to read three numbers from data and calculate the average.

4. Program the computer to request an interest rate in percent and a dollar amount. Have your program display the interest and the amount for simple interest for one year.

5. Read three digits into three variables. Then display all possible arrangements in six PRINT statements. The first PRINT will be

   PRINT A; B; C

6. Modify Program 2-6 to display the cents per ounce with dollar signs, rounded off to thousandths of a cent.

2-2. Additional Arithmetic Operators

We have become used to working with the conventional arithmetic operations of addition, subtraction, multiplication, and division. Three more operations are available to us. We may raise a value to a power using an exponent. We may also command BASIC to perform modular arithmetic and integer division. These operations may be programmed with extra statements, but it is very nice to have them directly accessible.

Order of Operations

BASIC does addition, subtraction, multiplication, and division exactly the way we would do them on paper. Multiplication and division are done first, followed by addition and subtraction. We may also use parentheses to change that order just as we would in mathematical expressions. Thus, if we need to divide 7 by the sum of 6 and 9, we might type the following:

PRINT 7 / (6 + 9)

It doesn't take long to get used to writing all these things on a single line. It's just like using an electronic calculator.

Raising to a Power

We can easily square a number by multiplying it by itself. For higher powers, this may not be the best way, and for decimal powers, this technique doesn't help us. Since we cannot write X cubed by writing a superscript, BASIC uses the ^ symbol to indicate "to the power." This is found at "Shift-6" on the Macintosh keyboard. So, we write X cubed as

X^3

Raising to the power is carried out before addition, subtraction, multiplication, and division, just as we ordinarily do it. An expression like:

$$\frac{x^2 + y^2}{x^2 - y^2}$$

is written in BASIC as

(X^2 + Y^2) / (X^2 − Y^2)

MODular Arithmetic

Many calculations are cyclic in nature. One common example is the reckoning of time of day. We keep track of time in 12-hour segments. Some institutions use a 24-hour clock. This is a modular process. When we add some number of hours to a given time, we determine the resulting time using modular arithmetic. The days of the week rotate in a modular fashion.

For days of the week, we think of a seven day rotation. Using modular arithmetic, we would label the days from zero through six inclusive. Thus if we choose to designate Sunday as day zero, then Thursday becomes day four, and Saturday becomes day six. In this situation, we say the modulus is seven. Using the MOD operation of BASIC, it becomes a simple matter to determine the day of the week that is 17 days from a Tuesday. We simply write a statement such as

PRINT (17 + 2) **MOD** 7

and the computer will promptly report a five, which corresponds to a Friday. As with other operations, we should be aware of the order in which the computer will do things. Note that we surrounded an expression with parentheses. This is because the MOD operator has a higher priority than addition. Without the parentheses in that statement, the computer would display 19 because it would take 2 MOD 7 first and then add 17. The priority of the MOD operator comes after multiplication and division, and before addition and subtraction.

The MOD operator expects values in the range -32768 to 32767, or we will get an "Overflow" error message.

Integer Division

Integer division simply ignores any remainder after division. While 18 / 7 is 2.5714285714286, the result of integer division is 2. The symbol for this new operation is the backslash (\). It is found just above the Return key.

PRINT 18 \ 7

produces the desired result. The -32768 to 32767 limit applies here, too.

Additional Arithmetic Operations

Table 2-1 shows the order in which BASIC carries out the various arithmetic operations. As we have already seen, we may use parentheses to alter that order in any expression in our program.

Table 2-1. Order of operations in BASIC.

Symbol	Name	Example
^	Exponentiation	X ^ 3
*, /	Multiplication and Division	X * Y
\	Integer division	A \ B
MOD	Modular Arithmetic	A MOD B
+, −	Addition and Subtraction	X+Y, X−Y

Problems for Section 2-2

1. Write a program to print a value for

$$\frac{\frac{1}{2} + \frac{1}{3}}{\frac{1}{4} - \frac{3}{5}}$$

Do this by assigning values as follows: A=1, B=2, C=3, D=4, and E=5.

2. Write a program to print a value for

$$\frac{\frac{2}{3} + \frac{3}{4}}{\frac{5}{6} + \frac{2}{3}}$$

Assign variables as follows: A=2, B=3, C=4, D=5, and E=6.

3. Write a program to calculate

$$\frac{(17.45 - 6.92)^4}{6.98^3 - 96.2^2}$$

4. Write a program to request two numbers. Have the program print the first number MOD the second. Experiment with a variety of values.

5. Write a program to request two numbers. Print the result of integer division of the first number divided by the second one. Experiment with a range of values.

2-3. More messages

We have been displaying messages by enclosing them in quotation marks in PRINT statements. Sometimes the message depends on the program results. For example, we might be looking for the day of the week with the highest temperature or the lowest sales volume. Or we might want to do something as simple as programming the computer to display someone's name to attract attention. BASIC has many features for handling nonnumeric values with ease.

Word Pigeonholes (String Variables)

We may assign a message to a variable. Such a variable is different from a numeric variable, and so we need to use a special kind of variable name. Any variable name that ends with a dollar sign ($) may be used for this purpose. Variables of this type are usually called "string variables" because they may store a string of characters. Let's see an example. Look at Program 2-7.

Program 2-7. Demonstrate a string variable.

```
LET MYNAME$ = "Alice"
PRINT MYNAME$; " is nice."
```

This little program simply assigns a string value to the string variable MYNAME$ in the first line, and then displays the contents with a little message in the second line. That's all.

```
Program 2-7
Alice is nice.
```

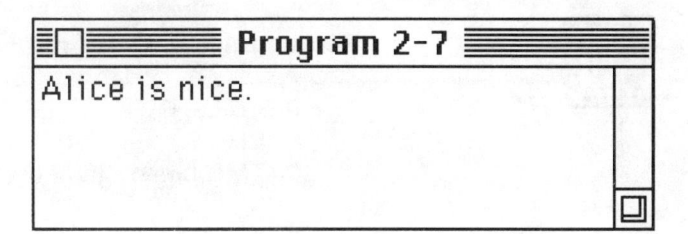

Figure 2-10. Execution of Program 2-7.

Suppose we try using NAME$ as a variable name.

LET NAME$="Alice"

Execution of this statement will bring forth an unexpected result. BASIC uses NAME as a keyword. NAME is used to change the name of a disk file. (See Appendix B.) So trying to use NAME as a variable is an error. RUNning a program with this line will bring forth a notification of a Syntax error. Since you won't know all keywords in advance, this will occasionally happen. We solved this problem in Program 2-7 by using MYNAME$. We could just add a period to the end of any keyword to obtain a legal variable name. So we might also use NAME.$ in this case.

Chapter 2: Adding Features

We may work with string variables in many of the ways in which we work with numeric variables. For instance, any of the following statements may appear in a program:

LET	A$ —"First"
READ	A$
INPUT	A$
PRINT	A$

String variables may store from 0 to 32767 characters at any time. In order to READ A$, we must provide a corresponding DATA statement. If we want to include a comma in the string, then we must enclose the string in quotation marks. Without the use of quotation marks, any comma is interpreted as the end of the current DATA item. Since string variables may be used with INPUT and READ as well, we could easily change the message in quotes in Program 2-7 and get the computer to say something nice to our friends.

Program 2-8 is a little demonstration of reading more than one data string.

Program 2-8. Demonstrate string READ.

READ L$, F$
PRINT F$; " "; L$
DATA Tubman, Harriet

The first line reads the first string into L$ and the next string into F$. See Figure 2-10.

```
Program 2-8
Harriet Tubman
```

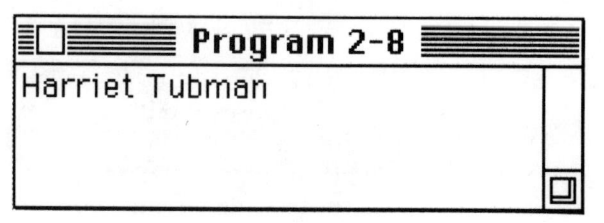

Figure 2-11. Execution of Program 2-8.

Suppose we really want to store "Tubman, Harriet" in a string variable. We simply use quotation marks, as mentioned earlier. It looks like Program 2-9.

Program 2-9. READ a comma into a string variable.

READ NAME.$
PRINT NAME.$
DATA "Tubman, Harriet"

More INPUT features

We can use an option in the INPUT statement to display a prompt without a separate PRINT statement.

INPUT "Year and Month"; YEAR, MONTH

first displays the message followed by a question mark, and then waits for two numeric values. This enables us to do the work of a PRINT statement and an INPUT statement in a single INPUT statement. Replacing the semicolon above with a comma causes BASIC to omit the question mark in the display.

Placing a semicolon immediately following INPUT allows us to keep the next display on the same line.

INPUT; "   Year"; YEAR
INPUT; "   Month"; MONTH
INPUT; "   Day"; DAY

allows us to request all three values on the same line, but one at a time.

Entering a comma requires special treatment. We can use quotation marks, but that is an unnecessary inconvenience. LINE INPUT accepts all characters typed up to the Return key.

LINE INPUT "Enter City and State"; ADDRESS$

will accept responses such as: Chicago, Illinois. The other INPUT statement options are available here, too.

Adding Strings (Concatenation)

Sometimes we want to build up one string from other strings. We can attach strings with the plus sign (+). Plus will not mean numeric addition, but "putting together" or concatenation. We might want to use a person's name in a variety of ways in a program. We might want to use the first name sometimes and the full name at other times. Consider Program 2-10.

Program 2-10. String concatenation.

```
READ L$, F$
LET FULL$=F$ + L$
PRINT "First name"; F$
PRINT "Last name"; L$
PRINT " Full name"; FULL$
DATA Lincoln, Abraham
```

Here is what it does:

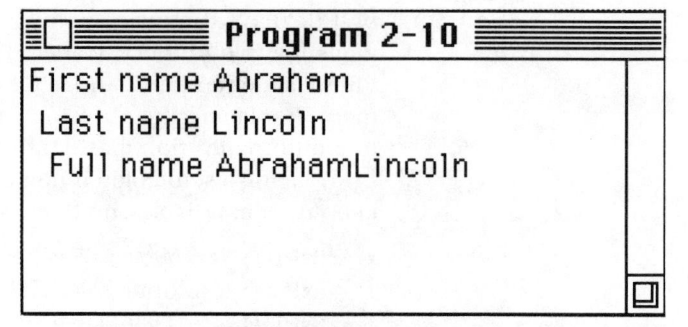

```
╔═══════════ Program 2-10 ═══════════╗
First name Abraham
Last name Lincoln
 Full name AbrahamLincoln
```

Figure 2-12. Execution of Program 2-10.

Oops! We must change the third line in Program 2-10 to read

　LET FULL$=F$ + " " + L$

Now we will get a space between Abe's first and last names. We may use the plus sign to join strings as long as we wish until we use up all available memory or the string contains more than 32767 characters, whichever comes first. If the 32767 character limit is exceeded, we will see the

```
String too long                          [ OK ]
```

error box.

Don't get carried away with string operations. If we try to subtract strings, we will evoke another error message from BASIC. The line

    C$=B$−D$

will produce the following:

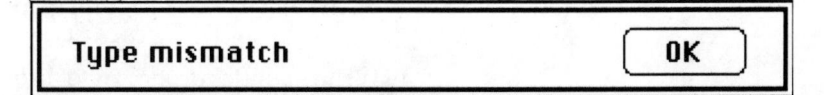

```
┌─────────────────────────────────────────────┐
│  Type mismatch                    [  OK  ]  │
└─────────────────────────────────────────────┘
```

It just isn't defined. Minus is for numbers, not strings. BASIC allows two data types: strings and numerics. We will get the same response for a statement such as:

    LET A$=65.45

We simply can't indiscriminantly mix strings and numerics.

We will be adding more string capabilities to our repertoire as time goes on, but direct subtraction and direct arithmetic will not be among them. To get the characters 65.45 stored in string variable A$, just enclose them in quotation marks.

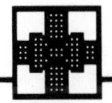

    LET A$="65.45"

Summary

String variables may be used to store nonnumeric data. We may use strings with LET, INPUT, READ and DATA, and PRINT statements. Two strings may be joined using a plus sign. To include a comma in a string, it is necessary to surround the string data with quotation marks.

Problems for Section 2-3

1. Rewrite Program 2-6 to read the egg size names from DATA along with the weight per dozen.
2. Write a program to read the days of the week into seven variables and display them.
3. Write a program to request a person's name from the keyboard. Have your program respond with "Hello there 'your name.' "
4. Write a little program to request a single string using INPUT and display the string variable with PRINT. Experiment. Enter a string with and without a comma. Verify that you can get a comma into the string by using quotation marks. Work with this until you are comfortable with string INPUT.
5. Write a program to request a person's name in two strings, first name first. Display the name in the form last name, comma, first name. For example, for "Jane, Jones" entered at the keyboard, display as "Jones, Jane".

CHAPTER 3

Writing a Program

This chapter will continue to introduce new features of BASIC. We will see how to use BASIC to repeat procedures and make decisions. Here we will begin to develop the habit of describing the program as part of the programming process. As we write longer programs, it will become clearer that we should do some planning before we begin typing any program lines. This will provide a good framework on which to hang many interesting and powerful programming tools.

3-1. Do it Again

Many, if not most, computer applications involve repetitious operations. Often that requires counting of some kind. Counting is one of the earliest mathematically oriented skills learned in life. If we can teach the computer to count, then we will be well on the way to managing repetitious calculations of all kinds.

Think about counting. We set up at 1. Then we get to 2 by adding 1. Then we get to 3 by adding 1. We always get to the next number in line by adding 1. We are ready to write a program to count.

Our First Counting Program

We easily set up at 1 with a simple assignment statement.

```
COUNT = 1
```

Then we get to the next number by adding 1.

```
TEMP  = COUNT + 1
COUNT = TEMP
```

If we were limited to the statements offered so far, then we would have to use another pair of statements:

```
TEMP  = COUNT + 1
COUNT = TEMP
```

and another and another... That would lead to very long programs. We would like the computer to execute those statements over and over again without having to type them into the program over and over again. This is easily done with two new features of BASIC.

Line Labels and GOTO

BASIC provides the ability to give any line of a program a label. Such a label may be any sequence of letters or digits. A line label can either be a number in the range 0 to 65529 or else any combination of characters that begins with a letter and ends with a colon. Nonnumber labels may be up to 40 characters long. Labels that begin with a letter may contain periods. They may be alone on a line or on the same line with program statements. It makes sense to select labels that say something about what is going on in the program. Delay:, Mortgage.Setup:, ScoringRoutine:, 10, 212, 30, and 100: are examples of line labels. If we forget to end a line label with a colon or inadvertently use a space in the middle of one, BASIC responds with an "Undefined subprogram" error box—unless putting the space in the label creates a keyword. For example, EndPrint: might become END PRINT:, and that becomes a "Syntax error." (We'll get to subprograms later.) Labels like Step1:, Label:, and Abc: give no clue about the purpose of the statements in the program. If we select good line labels, then our programs will read like a book. People will be able to figure out what a program does just by reading the line labels, variables, and BASIC language statements. Mysterious programs are not useful; clear ones are.

Line labels provide some program editing features. Program lines can be deleted with statements of the following form:

DELETE Begin
DELETE One−Last

DELETE Begin removes the line from the program. DELETE One—Last removes all lines from One to Last inclusive. Once deleted, the lines are gone; they are not on the Clipboard.

LIST Begin

simply makes Begin the first line in the window. LIST always applies to the List window rather than the Second List window.

The GOTO statement is used to direct the computer to execute the statement of our choice. We may use a line label and GOTO to execute our two program lines above again and again for counting as follows:

```
Counting:
   TEMP  = COUNT + 1
   COUNT = TEMP
   GOTO Counting
```

We have used GOTO to form a loop that will continuously repeat statements just processed. The complete program is shown as Program 3-1.

Program 3-1. Our first counting program.

```
COUNT = 1
Counting:
   TEMP  = COUNT + 1
   COUNT = TEMP
   GOTO Counting
```

You should be a little suspicious of Program 3-1. What makes it stop? Certainly nothing in the program conveys the idea that it will end. And it won't—until you select Stop (⌘-.) from the Run menu or pull the plug. ⌘-. and Stop in the Run menu are emergency procedures that will halt execution of any program regardless of the instructions in the program. We don't want to create an emergency! This is a classic endless loop. Not only that, the program never tells us where it is. It counts to itself. So we're not done yet! Let's make it count "out loud." But first a comment about the use of GOTO.

Many articles have been written about the evils of the GOTO statement in BASIC (and some other programming languages). Indeed, the beginning programmer is likely to overuse it. Programs that have a lot of GOTOs are very difficult to read. We like to read programs and segments of programs pretty much from top to bottom. Too many GOTOs interrupt this natural way of reading. Thus, after three or four detours to follow GOTOs, we begin to become confused. It is hard to determine whether or not we have read the whole program, and even lose track of what the program is supposed to do. As we plan programs, we will use GOTO sparingly. Indeed, the BASIC we are using is ideally suited to minimizing the need for GOTO. We will use it very little. There are some programming situations, however, where GOTO provides a simple solution to the problem. We will use it for those situations.

Now let's make the counting program display each number as it counts. All we have to do is include a PRINT statement in the right place and make sure that it is executed for all values of COUNT. That place is after the statement COUNT = 1 and before the program adds 1. The result is Program 3-2.

Program 3-2. Counting "out loud" this time.

```
COUNT = 1
Counting:
  PRINT COUNT
  TEMP  = COUNT + 1
  COUNT = TEMP
  GOTO Counting
```

The PRINT statement was inserted immediately following the label Counting:. That is all it takes. Now we are ready to tell the counting program where to stop. Let's have it count from 1 to 7.

We need the ability to stop the counting process once the value of COUNT has been set to 7 and displayed. For this we will use the IF statement of BASIC.

IF. . . THEN

The IF statement may be used to divert execution from the usual sequential progression through a program depending on some condition. For our counting example we may use the following statement:

IF COUNT > 7 **THEN** EndCount

where EndCount is the label of the line to be executed when the counting process is finished. We can have our program display a little message at that point. Here the symbol > is used to represent "greater than." We have six options in an IF statement:

<	less than
<=	less than or equal to
=	equal to
<>	not equal to
>	greater than
>=	greater than or equal to

These symbols are called *relational operators*. Any BASIC expression may appear on either side of a relational operator.

The IF statement above will transfer the flow of execution of the program to EndCount as soon as the value of COUNT passes 7. At EndCount, a PRINT statement will display a simple message.

The resulting program simply counts "out loud" from 1 to 7. See Program 3-3.

Program 3-3. Counting from 1 to 7.

```
COUNT = 1
Counting:
    IF COUNT > 7 THEN EndCount
    PRINT COUNT
    TEMP = COUNT + 1
    COUNT = TEMP
    GOTO Counting
EndCount:
    PRINT "Done"
```

It is important to note that the value of COUNT actually overshoots by 1. So, when this program terminates, the value of COUNT will be 8.

The two lines

TEMP = COUNT + 1
COUNT = TEMP

deserve some discussion. Those lines were used to increase the value of the variable COUNT by 1, using TEMP as an intermediate variable. We really want the variable COUNT to take on the value COUNT + 1. In an assignment statement in BASIC, the equal sign implies exactly that.

COUNT = COUNT + 1

is perfectly legal and proper in a computer program. In this situation, the equal sign does not declare an equivalence as in algebra, but describes an action for the computer to carry out. Think of the equal sign as a little arrow pointing to the left when it is used in this way. The computer must calculate the value of COUNT + 1 defined on the right and store it in the variable COUNT named on the left. By using this simplified method of adding 1 to COUNT, we have shortened our program by one line. Whenever we can shorten a program without making it any harder to read, it is a good idea. In this case, it seems like a good idea. See Program 3-4.

Program 3-4. Counting from 1 to 7 with COUNT = COUNT + 1.

COUNT = 1
Counting:
 IF COUNT > 7 **THEN** EndCount
 PRINT COUNT
 COUNT = COUNT + 1
 GOTO Counting
EndCount:
 PRINT "Done"

```
┌─────────────────────────────────────────┐
│ ▤□▬▬▬▬▬ Program 3-4 ▬▬▬▬▬▬ │
│ 1                                       │
│ 2                                       │
│ 3                                       │
│ 4                                       │
│ 5                                       │
│ 6                                       │
│ 7                                       │
│ Done                                    │
│                                         │
└─────────────────────────────────────────┘
```

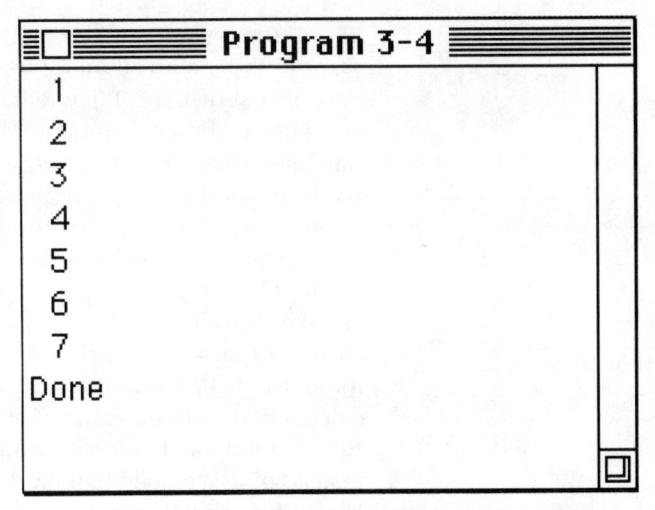

Figure 3-1. Execution of Program 3-4.

Program 3-3 and Program 3-4 produce the same results.

Our counting program has four distinct components. These four ingredients play a part in all program loops.

1. The counting variable is initialized.
2. The value of the counter is tested to determine whether to recycle or exit the repetition.
3. Some action is programmed. In our example, we display the current value of the counter.
4. Increment the counter, and loop to step 2.

Later on we will be taking advantage of an automatic "loop maker" in BASIC. We have designed our first loop program to perform in exactly the same way as the automatic feature of BASIC does.

With our loop maker it is easy to make small changes to alter how the program will count. The line COUNT = 1 can easily be edited to begin the count at any number we like. We can change the IF statement to end the count anywhere. The statement COUNT = COUNT + 1 can be altered to count by twos or sixes or nines or whatever. We could have our program count backwards by subtracting instead of adding. To do that we need to make the final value less than the initial value.

Usually we have some higher purpose in mind for counting than merely displaying the value of the counter. We want to scan the days of the week, or the months of the year, or the years of the life of a mortgage, or the names on a customer list. Or we might want to flip a coin so many times. Maybe we want to roll so many dice or just display "I like Mac" nine times.

For our first counting application, let's study the behavior of a hard steel ball bouncing on a hard surface. How high and how many times it bounces depends on the elasticity of the material. Suppose the ball recovers nine-tenths of its height on each bounce. If we drop such a ball from ten meters, it will bounce to 9 meters on the first bounce and 8.1 meters on the second. It is not hard to develop a formula to calculate the height after any number of bounces, but it is also not hard to write a program to simulate the bouncing of the ball. It will then be very easy to modify that program to calculate additional values for us. Let's bounce the ball five times. All we need for that is to change our counting program to stop at 5 instead of 7. We need to include a statement that calculates the new height for every bounce. We need a PRINT statement to display the number of bounces and the height. It would be nice to include a PRINT statement to label the two columns of figures. See Program 3-5.

Program 3-5. Bouncing a steel ball.

```
PRINT "Bounce Height"
HEIGHT = 10
COUNT = 1

Bouncing:
   IF COUNT > 5 THEN AllDone
   HEIGHT = HEIGHT * .9
   PRINT COUNT; "        "; HEIGHT
   COUNT = COUNT + 1
   GOTO Bouncing

Alldone:
   PRINT "Done"
```

```
┌─────────────────────────────────┐
│ ▣  ▤▤▤ Program 3-5 ▤▤▤          │
├─────────────────────────────────┤
│ Bounce Height                   │
│    1       9                    │
│    2       8.1                  │
│    3       7.29                 │
│    4       6.561                │
│    5       5.9049               │
│ Done                            │
│                                 │
└─────────────────────────────────┘
```

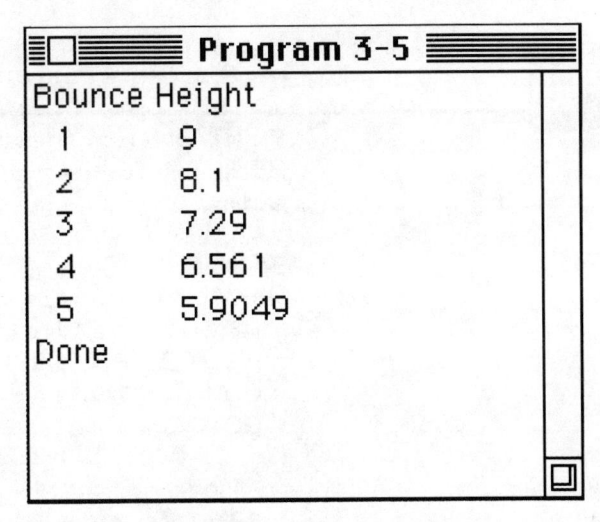

Figure 3-2. Execution of Program 3-5.

Look at the line PRINT COUNT; "   "; HEIGHT in Program 3-5. It takes some effort to include the right amount of space within the quotation marks in conjunction with semicolon to produce a nice display. In this particular program, the results are lined up only because all the values in the first column have the same number of digits. If that changes, then the second column will not be so straight.

Comma Spacing

If we use commas to separate items in a PRINT statement, BASIC automatically forms columns 14 digits wide. Program 3-5 can quickly be changed by editing the following two lines:

PRINT "Bounce Height"
PRINT COUNT; "   "; HEIGHT

to look like this:

PRINT "Bounce" , "Height"
PRINT COUNT, HEIGHT

See Program 3-6.

Program 3-6. Program 3-5 with comma spacing.

PRINT "Bounce" , "Height"
HEIGHT = 10
COUNT = 1

Bouncing:
 IF COUNT > 5 **THEN** Alldone
 HEIGHT = HEIGHT * .9
 PRINT COUNT, HEIGHT
 COUNT = COUNT + 1
 GOTO Bouncing

Alldone:
 PRINT "Done"

```
Program 3-6
Bounce          Height
  1                9
  2                8.1
  3                7.29
  4                6.561
  5                5.9049
Done
```

Figure 3-3. Execution of Program 3-6.

For many purposes it is quite satisfactory to use comma spacing. This feature allows us to quickly produce a nicely arranged display without the bother of having to count spaces and go to extra trouble to line things up. BASIC does it for us.

Summary

We have learned to count in this section; rather, we have learned how to make the computer count. This is done using the GOTO and IF statements in conjunction with line labels. Line labels may be selected that identify a location in a program and add meaning for the reader.

Names up to 40 characters long may be used to label lines of BASIC programs. GOTO is used to unconditionally divert the order in which the statements of the program are executed. The IF statement has been used to conditionally determine which statement will be executed next. We have seen that the assignment statement (LET statement) in BASIC may name the same variable on both sides of the equal sign. This causes the result of the calculation on the right to be assigned to the variable on the left. A comma may be used to separate items in a PRINT statement. This sets up the display screen into columns that are 14 digits wide.

Problems for Section 3-1

1. Write a program to display "I like my Macintosh." eight times.
2. Modify Program 3-4 to count from 1 to 19.
3. Modify Program 3-4 to count from 1 to 7 by 2's.
4. Modify Program 3-4 to count from 1 to 100 and calculate the sum of the numbers in the sequence. You might not want to display all 100 values of the counting variable.
5. Modify Program 3-4 to count from 2 to 42 by 2's.
6. Modify Program 3-4 to count backward from 10 to -10.

3-2. Do it Again (When We Don't Know How Many)

It is easy to tell the computer to do something a certain number of times when we know how many times we want, but that is not always the case. In fact, we might want the program to perform a certain calculation until some point is reached, and then report how many times it took. We might want to know how many bounces the steel ball makes before it bounces less than half the original height. We might want to have a program keep asking for values from the keyboard until a special value is entered as an instruction to stop requesting values.

How about a program to calculate test averages? One person might enter three test scores while another person might wish to enter five test scores. For this we need to know the total of the scores entered and the number of scores. How will the program "know" when the person has entered all the scores? Let's choose a special value to signal that. How about -1? If someone enters -1, the computer should proceed to the average calculating statements of the program. If someone enters any positive score, then the program should add that score to the current sum and ask for a new test score.

A Little Planning

This program is shaping up to be a little more involved than those we've done up to this point. So this is an opportunity to work on the process of program development. There are really three things this program ought to do.

1. Tell the user what the program does.
2. Request test scores from the keyboard.
3. Calculate and display the average.

Once the programmer understands the problem and what steps are involved in the solution, it is a good idea to define these steps right in the program itself. We could put the three steps listed above in PRINT statements, but that might not be appropriate for the running program. It is usual to have messages in the program for programmers alone. In BASIC this is done with the REM statement.

REMark

Whatever follows on the line after REM in a program statement will be ignored by BASIC. Thus, what we type acts as a "remark" to anyone reading our program, rather than an instruction to the computer to perform any action. This is a part of what is called *program documentation*.

Good REM statements are brief and succinct. It takes a little skill to develop good remarks in a program. REMarks like "Increment J1" and "Subtract NUMBER from OLDNUMBER" are quite uninformative. We could better see those actions from the program statements themselves. Such REMarks actually make a program harder to read. On the other hand, REMarks like "Initialize accumulated mileage" or "Terminate on negative INPUT" describe the intended action and are helpful to anyone reading our program. Indeed programs that are crystal clear to us right now will be foggy and mysterious a few weeks from now. So REMs ought to be an integral part of the program from the beginning. A lot of people write their programs and then go back to insert REMs. Some people write the REMs first and then write the program. Let's do the latter.

Taking the three segments of our average calculating program above, let's write the REMs.

1. Tell the user what the program does. This is really the instructions. We will do that with a few PRINT statements.

   REM ** Instructions

   The stars tend to set this statement off a little. If the remark runs over to several lines, we will omit the stars after the first line.

2. Request test scores from the keyboard. This is where we request data, add the scores to a summing variable, and recycle to the INPUT statement using GOTO.

   REM ** Request test scores and keep running totals

   That ought to do it.

3. Calculate and display the average. And finally, we need to report the results to the program user.

   REM ** Calculate and display average

Using this method of program planning is very beneficial. We have separated the programming job into little tasks that are relatively easy to do one at a time. We have created some program documentation in advance. All too often programmers, being human, work feverishly until the program performs the desired task. Then it is very difficult to be disciplined enough to go back and produce good documentation. After all, the program is done, isn't it?

Doing it our way, when the program is done, at least part of the documentation is done, too. At this point we have headings for the three parts of the program.

> **REM** ** Instructions
> **REM** ** Request test scores and keep running totals
> **REM** ** Calculate and display average

We can use these REMs as our program outline during the process of writing the BASIC program statements. The finished program will also contain descriptive line labels. This combination will result in highly readable programs.

Now we can easily write program statements for each of the three parts without having to think about any of the other parts because we have an outline to refer to as we go along. This segmenting of the program simplifies things for clear thinking. It is time to write the program . . .

First, the instructions:

Program 3-7a. Instructions segment.

```
REM ** Instructions
PRINT "Test score averaging"
PRINT
PRINT "Enter test scores, one at a time"
PRINT "Enter -1 after last score"
PRINT
```

We have tried to say what the program does and what the user should do in Program 3-7a. It is important to write short and easy-to-read instructions. It is worth the effort to produce clear, succinct displays for the user. Long instructions that fill the screen are difficult to read. Long, hard-to-read REMs are also not good.

Next is the keyboard entry segment. Two labels are required in this segment: one to repeat the request for a score from the keyboard and one for an IF statement to use when -1 is entered as the signal to move to the next segment of the program. See Program 3-7b.

Do It Again (When We Don't Know How Many)

Program 3-7b. Keyboard entry segment.

```
REM ** Request test scores and keep running totals
NUMBER = 0
SUM    = 0

RequestScores:
  PRINT "Score"; NUMBER + 1;
  INPUT SCORE
  IF SCORE = -1 THEN PrintAverage
  SUM    = SUM + SCORE
  NUMBER = NUMBER + 1
  GOTO RequestScores
```

And finally, the calculation of average and the display are done as shown in Program 3-7c.

Program 3-7c. Program segment to calculate and display average.

```
REM ** Calculate and display average
PrintAverage:
  AVG = SUM / NUMBER
  PRINT
  PRINT "Average ="; AVG
```

It is important to remember to use the line label PrintAverage in Program 3-7c since that is the label we chose for the IF statement that directs the computer to proceed with the average calculation and display.

We have developed a program in three parts. This allowed us to concentrate on one piece of the program at a time. Each part may be saved as a program on a disk. When all of the pieces are finished, we can collect them into a single program by using LOAD or OPEN to bring in the first part, and using MERGE to attach succeeding segments.

MERGE

The statement

> **MERGE** "Program 3-7b"

entered in the Command window causes Program 3-7b to be appended to the end of whatever program is currently in memory. For how to deal with more than one disk, see MERGE in Appendix B. MERGE may be used any number of times to gather any number of program pieces into a single program. Program 3-7 can be created by merging Programs 3-7a through 3-7c.

Program 3-7. Calculate test score average.

```
REM ** Instructions
PRINT "Test score averaging"
PRINT
PRINT "Enter test scores, one at a time"
PRINT "Enter -1 after last score"
PRINT

REM ** Request test scores and keep running totals
NUMBER = 0
SUM    = 0

RequestScores:
  PRINT "Score"; NUMBER + 1;
  INPUT SCORE
  IF SCORE = -1 THEN PrintAverage
  SUM    = SUM + SCORE
  NUMBER = NUMBER + 1
  GOTO RequestScores

REM ** Calculate and display average
PrintAverage:
  AVG = SUM / NUMBER
  PRINT
  PRINT "Average ="; AVG
```

All that remains is to RUN it. See Figure 3-4.

```
╔═══════════ Program 3-7 ═══════════╗
Test score averaging

Enter test scores, one at a time
Enter -1 after last score

Score 1 ? 100
Score 2 ? 91
Score 3 ? 71
Score 4 ? -1

Average = 87.333333333333
```

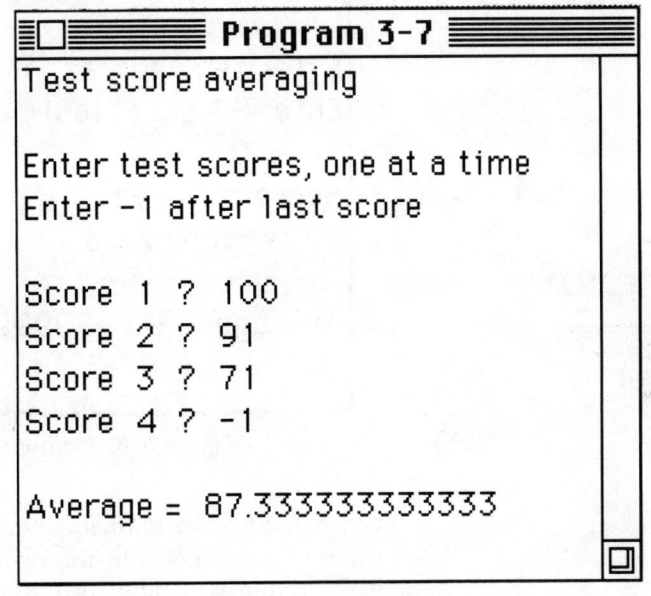

Figure 3-4. Execution of Program 3-7.

We get the 14 digits of the decimal version of Microsoft BASIC here. The binary version would display the average as 87.33334. Although we get 7 digits in this case, clearly the seventh digit suffers from round-off error. In either version of BASIC, we might want to take advantage of PRINT USING here. This would allow us to round off results to suit our purpose.

PRINT USING "Average = ##.#"; AVG

rounds off to the nearest tenth. It is easy to do and greatly improves the appearance of program results. It is good to have control over how many digits a program displays.

There is another little wrinkle in Program 3-7 that deserves some more attention. Suppose someone runs this program and then decides not to enter any scores. Or suppose someone enters -1 as the first score by accident. When execution arrives at the line AVG = SUM / NUMBER, the value of NUMBER is zero. That's bad news. Let's see what BASIC does with it.

```
┌─────────────────────────────────────────────┐
│ ▤□ ▥▥▥▥▥▥▥ Program 3-7 ▥▥▥▥▥▥▥ │
│ Test score averaging                        │
│                                             │
│ Enter test scores, one at a time            │
│ Enter -1 after last score                   │
│                                             │
│ Score 1 ? -1                                │
│ Division by zero                            │
│                                             │
│ Average = 9.9999999999999D+62               │
│                                             │
└─────────────────────────────────────────────┘
```

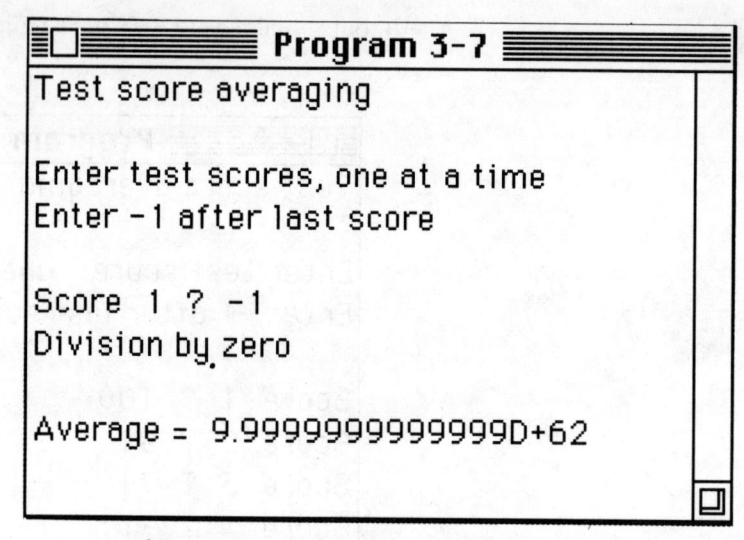

Figure 3-5. Demonstrate division by zero.

When BASIC tries to divide by zero, it assigns the largest possible value and proceeds. In the decimal version, the largest possible value requires a new format to display. The "D" indicates "D-format." D-format is used to display values that cannot be expressed in 14 digits. The binary version would produce 3.402824E+38, using an "E" to indicate "E-format," which represents Exponential notation. The "E" is used for single precision and the "D" is used for double precision.

An important goal for computer programmers is to never subject the person who uses our programs to errors of the kind displayed in Figure 3-5. Just before the line AVG = SUM / NUMBER, the program should determine whether or not the value of NUMBER is zero. If the value of NUMBER is zero, then we want to divert execution away from the calculation. We used the line label All-Done for this in Program 3-5 and Program 3-6. At AllDone, those programs displayed the message "Done." That works just fine, but suppose we don't want a message like that? There are other options. We could use a blank PRINT statement, or even a labeled line with nothing following. Such techniques, while they might produce the desired result, will be confusing to anyone reading our program. We can eliminate that confusion by using the END statement of BASIC.

END

Up to this point, we have allowed our programs to terminate by simply "running off the end." We may be more explicit with the END instruction. END says "go no further." It is an orderly way for a program to terminate. We may follow the labeled line AllDone with END to create the following program segment:

```
REM ** Calculate and display average
PrintAverage:
IF NUMBER = 0 THEN AllDone
  AVG = SUM / NUMBER
  PRINT
  PRINT "Average ="; AVG
Alldone:
  END
```

There is yet another way to do this. It turns out that the IF statement has several options.

IF... THEN Revisited

We have been using only the feature of the IF statement that transfers control to a labeled line in the program. IF... THEN may also be used to execute any BASIC statement—even another IF. Thus,

```
IF X = 5 THEN GOTO Clean.up
```

produces the same effect as

```
IF X = 5 THEN Clean.up
```

But, more to the point, we may use statements such as any of the following:

```
IF TOTAL > 99999 THEN PRINT "Limit exceeded"
IF PLAYER = 1 THEN PRINT "Hello "; P1$
IF VALUE = 201 THEN VALUE = 1
IF STATUS = 0 THEN READ NEWVALUE
```

Using this new concept, all that is needed in Program 3-7 is the following statement immediately after PrintAverage:

```
IF NUMBER = 0 THEN END
```

It's that simple.

STOP

We may use STOP to terminate program execution. STOP is a statement in BASIC that causes the computer to stop executing the program. The Macintosh bell is sounded and a message, "Program Stopped," is flashed in the upper right corner of the Macintosh screen. The message disappears as soon as a key is pressed or the mouse is moved. The STOP statement in a program causes a significantly different sequence of events from Stop (⌘-.) in the Run menu. While the latter simply halts program execution, STOP in a program also causes the List window to scroll to the part of the program where it is located and to display a box around the statement itself. If the List window is not visible, choose Show List or press ⌘-l. This is considered an abnormal situation. It can be used, however, as an important aid to program development. We may insert STOP statements at points in a program where we suspect a problem. When the program halts, we may display values of variables at that point with PRINT in the Command window and use the results to help us figure out what is going on. Once the program is performing properly, we should remove all unwanted STOP statements. Find. . . in the Search menu will help us do that.

There are other aspects of our average calculation program that we ought to think about. What happens if we enter a negative score other than -1? It is summed right in with the others. We could easily include an IF test to see if a negative score other than -1 is entered. A nice touch would be to display a message saying that the score entered is out of range and requesting a value again. Well-written programs verify response from the keyboard. Values absolutely out of range are refused and the user is required to enter another value. For the averaging problem, we might exclude all scores above 100 as well. This is left as an exercise.

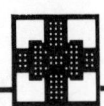

Summary

The REM statement has been introduced. Programmers use REM statements to include messages in BASIC programs. These messages may provide the human reader with information that is not obvious from reading the BASIC program statements. Well-written REMs make it clear what is going on in the program. REMs have no effect upon the execution of a running program. Programmers can use REM statements judiciously to help organize their thoughts prior to actually writing BASIC program statements. The combination of good REMs and well-chosen line labels contribute greatly to producing readable programs.

The END statement may be used for an orderly program termination. In addition to changing the order in which the computer executes program statements, IF...THEN has the ability to execute any statement that follows THEN on the same program line. The STOP statement halts program execution.

Problems for Section 3-2

1. Modify Program 3-6 to determine how many times the ball bounces before it recovers less than half the original height.
2. In Problem 1, calculate the total distance traveled by the steel ball. Remember that it travels down one distance and up another.
3. Modify Program 3-7 so that the user cannot enter any negative score other than -1. Also reject any score above 100.
4. Write a program to convert money into coins. For example: 99 U. S. cents becomes
   Enter cents:? 99
     1 Half dollars
     1 Quarters
     2 Dimes
     4 Pennies

Place the coin values and names in DATA statements.

3-3. Some Handy Tools

Let's develop a program to display the passing of the hour. It will just repeat 1 through 12 over and over again, displaying as it goes. The primary consideration is that whenever HOUR reaches 12, we reset it to 1 and continue. Counting repeatedly from 0 to 11 behaves exactly like modular addition, so we simply add 1 to each value to obtain the 1-to-12 sequence required for a clock.

Think about displaying the hours. If we just use a PRINT statement, the numbers will first form a column on the screen and then scroll out of sight. It would be nice to imitate a digital clock. The PTAB function will help us do just that.

PTAB

PTAB(X) in a PRINT statement places the next item in the output window according to the value of X, which is reckoned in a measure called pixels. Normal digits require a width of 8 pixels. A line in the normal output window is 491 pixels wide, allowing us to use a value of X in the range from 0 to 490. If the value is greater than 490, the display falls outside the output window. For the clock we need to allow for three characters because PRINT inserts a space in front of a number and we want to display two digits. This means we could use up to 466 pixels. The positioning is absolute; that is, we may first display at 100 and then at 20. The printing pen can be moved forward or backward with PTAB.

Since we are developing a clock, it would make sense to think about timing. If we simply display the hour and GOTO the point in the program that calculates a new hour, the display will change too fast to be seen. We need to provide a delay between successive displays. This is easy to do with a little loop that does nothing but count. Once the program works, displaying the correct sequence of hours, we could experiment with an upper limit on the counting loop to leave each value on the screen for an hour. See Program 3-8.

Program 3-8. An hourly digital clock.

```
REM ** Display passing hours
HOUR = 12

SetHour:
  HOUR = HOUR MOD 12 + 1
  PRINT PTAB(466); HOUR;

  X = 1
Delay:
  X = X + 1
  IF X < 200 THEN Delay
  GOTO SetHour
```

Type Program 3-8 into the computer and try it.

IF...THEN...ELSE

Look at the two lines

    IF X < 200 **THEN** Delay
    GOTO SetHour

The IF statement allows us to program two alternative actions like this right in the IF...THEN itself. The action for true follows THEN, while the action for false follows ELSE. The two lines above may be represented as follows:

    IF X < 200 **THEN** Delay **ELSE GOTO** SetHour

Just as any BASIC program statement may follow THEN, any statement may follow ELSE. BASIC even allows just a line label following ELSE. Using this idea, the line becomes

    IF X < 200 **THEN** Delay **ELSE** SetHour

There is one more interesting feature of BASIC that will help us in this program.

Multiple Statements on One Line (:)

In BASIC we may separate two or more statements on the same line by using a colon. Thus we may use lines like

X = 5 : Z = 18

It is very nice to be able to place statements that belong together on the same line. Use this with caution, however. Don't make program lines too long; they may become difficult to read. Getting back to our clock: There are two places where we might try this new idea of putting two or more statements on the same line. See Program 3-9.

Program 3-9. Program 3-8 with added features.

```
REM ** Display passing hours
HOUR = 12

SetHour:
  HOUR = HOUR MOD 12 + 1 : PRINT PTAB(466); HOUR;

  X = 1
Delay:
  X = X + 1 : IF X < 200 THEN Delay ELSE SetHour
```

Logical Operators (AND, OR, and NOT)

We can gain tremendous flexibility in an IF statement using logical operators. A statement such as

IF X > 0 AND X < 7 THEN Rollem

causes the program to Rollem only if X is in the range 1 to 6. Both conditions must be true. OR is used to cause the statements following THEN to execute if at least one of the conditions is true. NOT reverses the truth of a relational test in an IF statement. Thus,

IF NOT X < 25000 THEN PRINT "New tax bracket"

displays "New tax bracket" only for values of X greater than or equal to 25000. AND, OR, and NOT, when used this way, behave just as the use of the words in English suggests.

Summary

PTAB allows us to specify any position on a line for the next PRINT position. This position is measured in pixels and is independent of where the last item appears on the line. The IF... THEN statement allows us to program two options in the same statement using the ELSE keyword. The logical operators AND, OR, and NOT may be used in an IF statement. We may use a colon to separate BASIC statements on a single program line.

Problems for Section 3-3

1. Extend the digital clock of Program 3-9 to show minutes and seconds.
2. Set up a digital clock to display hours on a 24-hour clock alongside a 12-hour clock designating A.M. and P.M.
3. Do Problem 2 and include minutes and seconds.

CHAPTER 4

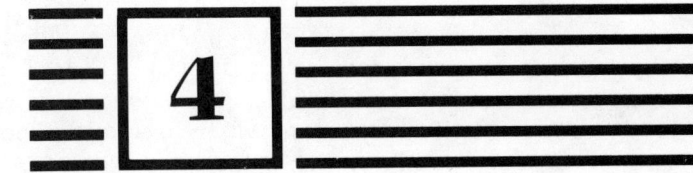

Loops

In the last chapter, we developed the idea of looping in programs. Many computing situations involve repetitious operations. The counting process pervades computer programming to such an extent that it makes sense to automate the instructions. In this chapter, we will use BASIC control structures for loops. The FOR and NEXT statements allow us to set values for beginning and ending limits as well as an interval for a repetition. WHILE and WEND are used to control a repetition in which the endpoint depends on conditions other than those in the counting process itself.

4-1. Counting with FOR and NEXT

Program 3-4 counts from 1 to 7. Program 4-1 does the same thing using FOR and NEXT.

Program 4-1. Counting with FOR and NEXT.

```
FOR COUNT = 1 TO 7
  PRINT COUNT
NEXT COUNT
PRINT "Done"
```

A FOR statement in BASIC is used to set the beginning and ending values for a selected variable, COUNT in this case. COUNT is called the *loop variable.* All statements between here and a matching NEXT statement will be executed as long as the selected variable is within the range indicated. NEXT COUNT automatically adds 1 to the value of COUNT and causes program execution to recycle to the statement immediately following the corresponding FOR statement. When COUNT exceeds 7, the statement following the NEXT statement will be processed. Thus, in our little program, the word "Done" will be displayed and the value of COUNT will be 8.

Suppose we write a routine such as

FOR COUNT= 7 **TO** 3
 PRINT COUNT
NEXT COUNT

What will happen when it runs? Nothing. The program produces no display because BASIC cannot get from 7 to 3 by adding a series of 1s.

BASIC allows the programmer to drop the variable name in the NEXT statement. You may see programs written that way. This may be confusing to read, because you have to check carefully to be sure which FOR statement is matched with this particular NEXT statement. It is much easier to visually match NEXT COUNT with a statement that begins with FOR COUNT. This becomes more important with longer programs that have more FOR . . . NEXT loops.

STEP

The STEP feature of the FOR statement allows us to specify an increment. If we want to count by twos, we can do it easily with FOR, NEXT, and STEP. See Program 4-2 and Figure 4-1.

Program 4-2. Counting by twos with STEP.

FOR COUNT= 2 **TO** 10 **STEP** 2
 PRINT COUNT
NEXT COUNT

```
┌─────────────── Program 4-2 ───────────────┐
│ 2                                         │
│ 4                                         │
│ 6                                         │
│ 8                                         │
│ 10                                        │
└───────────────────────────────────────────┘
```

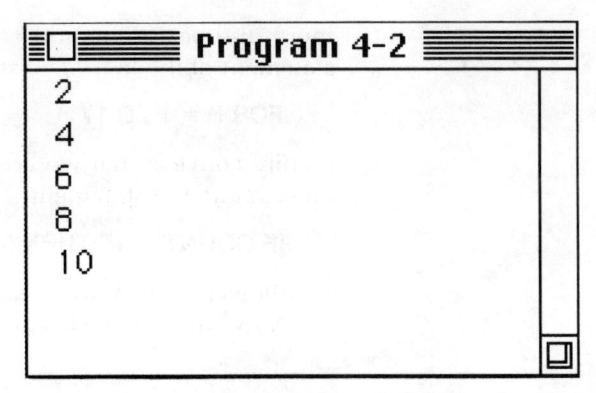

Figure 4-1. Execution of Program 4-2.

Of course, the value of COUNT will be 12 following execution of Program 4-2. If we ever want the value of a FOR variable that was the last one actually used in the loop, then we should use a statement such as

TEMP = COUNT

immediately following the FOR statement. Then we are assured that the variable TEMP has saved the last value of COUNT, no matter how execution exits the loop.

With STEP we can easily count backwards. Just use a negative STEP value and be sure that the limits in the FOR statement are correct. So to get from 7 to 3 by 1's, we just use

FOR COUNT = 7 TO 3 STEP −1

The values in the FOR statement may be variables or even expressions.

FOR PERIOD = YEAR TO YEAR + N STEP N/T

is perfectly legal.

FOR and NEXT are widely used in programs. They constitute a good shorthand. When we encounter the need to count in a program for any purpose it is easy to think in terms of FOR and NEXT. We don't have to think about initializing a variable, incrementing it, and testing it to see if we are through. All this is done automatically and painlessly, so the programmer's mind remains uncluttered and free to consider the higher purposes of the program.

In addition, FOR and NEXT are very helpful to us when reading existing programs. When we see FOR, we know that a repeated process follows, ending with a matching NEXT statement. Furthermore, the beginning and ending values appear right in the first statement of the loop. The statement

FOR K = 1 **TO** 17

readily conveys that we are going to count from 1 to 17. On the other hand, the statement

IF COUNT > 17 **THEN** Next.Operation

could mean other things besides the end of a loop process.

Now suppose we begin a loop with

J = 1

and then inadvertently signify the end with

NEXT J

Mercifully, BASIC will tell us what happened. The message "NEXT without FOR" will appear in an error box, and inside the List window a box will outline the NEXT statement. Similarly, BASIC will report a missing NEXT statement with "FOR without NEXT". These messages are very helpful to us when we are testing our programs. We simply click on the OK button or press Return and then fix it. Of course, one of our objectives is to never allow these messages to appear. It is possible to write programs that work the first time, but we will occasionally bring forth error messages despite our best efforts to prevent them.

Semicolons, Commas, and WIDTH

With loops, it is just as easy to generate 50 values as it is to generate 7. If we simply change the upper limit in the FOR statement of Program 4-1 to 50, what happens? Most of the display is scrolled out of the output window at the top, leaving only a few visible values. Remember what happens when a semicolon is placed at the end of a PRINT statement? The next display is placed on the same line of the output window. This is done in Program 4-1a.

Program 4-1a. Displaying 1 to 50 with semicolon in PRINT.

```
FOR COUNT = 1 TO 50
    PRINT COUNT;
NEXT COUNT
```

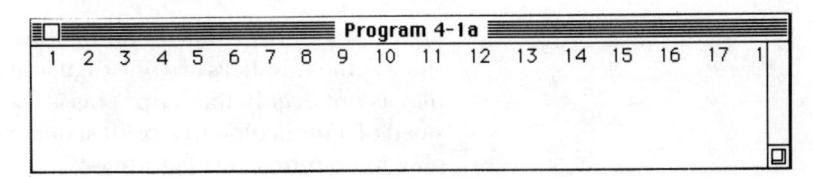

```
Program 4-1a
1  2  3  4  5  6  7  8  9  10  11  12  13  14  15  16  17  1
```

Figure 4-2. Execution of Program 4-1a.

Figure 4-2 demonstrates that it is possible to cause the display to disappear outside the output window at the right edge. Although this can happen, it is important to avoid situations like this. When BASIC is first invoked, the printed line is infinitely long. This is the default condition.

The default is what happens if a program does not explicitly specify other conditions. This concept allows us to ignore limits until we have a situation that requires us to control a specific feature of the language. Numerous features have built-in defaults. The windows have default locations and sizes. The decimal version uses double precision 14-digit variables as the default. The binary version uses single precision 7-digit variables as the default. The list goes on and on. We can change the line length from the default.

The statement

WIDTH N

sets the width of the display line to the width of N normal digits. Later, we will see how to change the width of the output window. Remember that the width of a normal digit is 8 pixels and the width of the normal output window is 491, so the maximum width is 61 digits. Let's set the width to 60 in Program 4-1a. See Figure 4-3.

Program 4-1a

```
 1  2  3  4  5  6  7  8  9 10 11 12 13 14 15 16 17
18 19 20 21 22 23 24 25 26 27 28 29 30 31 32
33 34 35 36 37 38 39 40 41 42 43 44 45 46 47
48 49 50
```

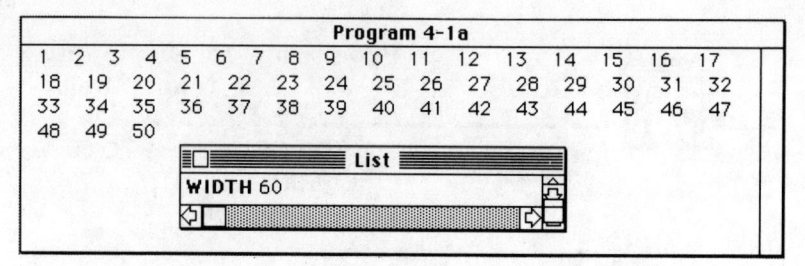

List
WIDTH 60

Figure 4-3. Execution of Program 4-1a with WIDTH 60.

Figure 4-3 shows that none of the display is missing. However, since some numbers are one digit and others are two digits, the display is not evenly lined up. This is a good place to use a comma instead of a semicolon in a print statement in order to arrange the display in columns. See Figure 4-4.

Program 4-1a

1	2	3	4
5	6	7	8
9	10	11	12
13	14	15	16
17	18	19	20
21	22	23	24
25	26	27	28
29	30	31	32
33	34	35	36
37	38	39	40
41	42	43	44
45	46	47	48
49	50		

List
WIDTH 60
FOR COUNT = 1 TO 50
 PRINT COUNT,
NEXT COUNT

Figure 4-4. Execution of Program 4-1a with WIDTH 60 and comma in PRINT.

We can see in Figure 4-4 that the results are displayed nicely in uniform columns. Remember, BASIC automatically establishes columns of 14 digits for commas in PRINT. Ah ha! Another default. This one can be changed, too.

The WIDTH statement also allows us to set the width of the columns for comma spacing. In the statement

WIDTH N, C

the value of C is the number of 8-pixel digits that may be displayed in a single column or print zone.

WIDTH 40, 5

allows print zones 5 standard digits wide on an output line 40 digits wide. See Figure 4-5.

Program 4-1a						
1	2	3	4	5	6	7	8
9	10	11	12	13	14	15	16
17	18	19	20	21	22	23	24
25	26	27	28	29	30	31	32
33	34	35	36	37	38	39	40
41	42	43	44	45	46	47	48
49	50						

```
WIDTH 40,5
FOR COUNT = 1 TO 50
   PRINT COUNT,
NEXT COUNT
```

Figure 4-5. Displaying 1 to 50 with WIDTH 40, 5 and comma in PRINT.

If we want to change comma spacing without changing the line length, we simply omit the first value in the WIDTH statement as follows:

WIDTH ,20

Now comma spacing is set to 20 characters. Once WIDTH has changed line width or comma spacing, it stays changed until another WIDTH statement is executed.

Command-S or Suspend

With loops it is just as easy to display 1000 values as it is to display 7 or 50. In spite of our best efforts to avoid it, occasionally a program may cause the display to disappear off the top of the output window before we can get a good look at it—some loop going from 1 to 10000, for example. We can freeze the display with ⌘-S. Or we may select Suspend in the Run menu. Now we can relax to study the screen. Press any key except another ⌘-S or ⌘-. to continue program execution. Selecting Continue in the Run menu will also continue program execution. We should take great care that our final programs control the output window in such a way that the user does not have to frantically lunge at the keyboard searching for ⌘-S.

Summary

FOR, NEXT, and STEP are revealed as the way to set up repeated operations when we know where we want to start and end. FOR COUNTER = FIRST TO LAST STEP JUMP begins the loop. NEXT COUNTER closes the loop. The WIDTH statement is used to control the display line width and the width of print zones for a comma delimiter in PRINT statements. ⌘-S or Suspend may be used to suspend a running program. The program will continue if we press any other key except ⌘-.. Continue in the Run menu also causes the program to resume execution.

> **Problems for Section 4-1**
>
> 1. Write a FOR ... NEXT loop to count from 10 to 20.
>
> 2. Write a FOR ... NEXT loop to count from 93 to 80 by twos.
>
> 3. Write a program to display "I like BASIC." six times.
>
> 4. Write a program to display the integers from 1 to 15 paired with their reciprocals.
>
> 5. Write a program to display decimal values for sevenths. That is, display 1/7, 2/7, ... 6/7, and 7/7.
>
> 6. Do Problem 5 for elevenths.
>
> 7. Write a program to calculate the sum of the counting numbers from 1 to 100. (You probably don't want the computer to display the values of the loop variable in this one.)

4-2. More Bounce to FOR and NEXT

In Programs 4-1 and 4-2 we simply displayed the FOR variable to demonstrate that the structure performs as advertised. We are usually interested in other things.

Let's pursue the bouncing steel ball of Chapter 3 a little more. By writing a routine to simulate the actual bouncing, we can supplement it to calculate more information. For example, suppose we want to learn the total distance the ball travels from the point we release it to the top of the eighth bounce. First, we write the bouncing simulation with FOR and NEXT. See Program 4-3.

Program 4-3. Bouncing a steel ball with FOR and NEXT.

```
REM ** Simulate a bouncing steel ball
PRINT "Bounce" , "Height"
HEIGHT=10

REM ** Bounce here
FOR BOUNCE = 1 TO 8
   HEIGHT = HEIGHT * .9
   PRINT BOUNCE, HEIGHT
NEXT BOUNCE
PRINT "Done"
```

Program 4-3 simply uses FOR and NEXT to perform the job of our earlier ball-bouncing program (Program 3-6).

Now it is a simple matter to incorporate the logic needed to calculate the total distance traveled. We simply initialize DISTANCE to zero outside the FOR . . . NEXT loop and add in the length of the downward path and the length of the upward path. On the downward path the ball travels the old height, and on the upward path the ball travels the new height. Just insert two distance-adding statements—one before the HEIGHT is calculated and one after the HEIGHT is calculated. Next, it would be a good idea to display the distance along with the bounce number and the height. This is done in Program 4-4.

Program 4-4. Calculate the distance for a bouncing ball.

```
REM ** Simulate a bouncing steel ball
PRINT "Bounce", "Height", "Total Distance"
HEIGHT = 10
DISTANCE = 0

REM ** Bounce here
FOR BOUNCE = 1 TO 8
   DISTANCE = DISTANCE + HEIGHT 'Add downward path
   HEIGHT = HEIGHT * .9
   DISTANCE = DISTANCE + HEIGHT 'Add upward path
   PRINT BOUNCE, HEIGHT, DISTANCE
NEXT BOUNCE
PRINT "Done"
```

The Apostrophe

Look at the following two lines from Program 4-4:

```
DISTANCE = DISTANCE + HEIGHT 'Add downward path
DISTANCE = DISTANCE + HEIGHT 'Add upward path
```

We have used a new feature of BASIC to document those statements. The apostrophe may be used just like a REM statement. The apostrophe is especially convenient where we want to comment on the purpose of a single line. Everything following an apostrophe on a line is ignored during program execution. Here it is clear what those two lines do. Techniques of this sort may be used to make programs ever more readable. Anything that makes programs more readable makes them easier to work with.

```
┌─────────────────────────────────────────────┐
│ ▤▢▬▬▬▬▬▬▬▬▬ Program 4-4 ▬▬▬▬▬▬▬▬▬▬          │
│ Bounce          Height           Total Distance │
│    1              9                 19          │
│    2              8.1               36.1        │
│    3              7.29              51.49       │
│    4              6.561             65.341      │
│    5              5.9049            77.8069     │
│    6              5.31441           89.02621    │
│    7              4.782969          99.123589   │
│    8              4.3046721         108.2112301 │
│ Done                                            │
└─────────────────────────────────────────────┘
```

Figure 4-6. Execution of Program 4-4.

Once again, we might want to pretty up our program display. Look at the two PRINT statements in Program 4-4. Let's replace them with:

PRINT "Bnce   Height   Total Distance"
PRINT USING "##   ##.##   ###.##"; BOUNCE, HEIGHT, DISTANCE

Now see the display in Figure 4-7.

Program 4-4a

Bnce	Height	Total Distance
1	9.00	19.00
2	8.10	36.10
3	7.29	51.49
4	6.56	65.34
5	5.90	77.81
6	5.31	89.03
7	4.78	99.12
8	4.30	108.21

Done

List

```
PRINT "Bnce   Height   Total Distance"
PRINT USING "##      ##.##    ###.##"; BOUNCE, HEIGHT, DISTANCE
```

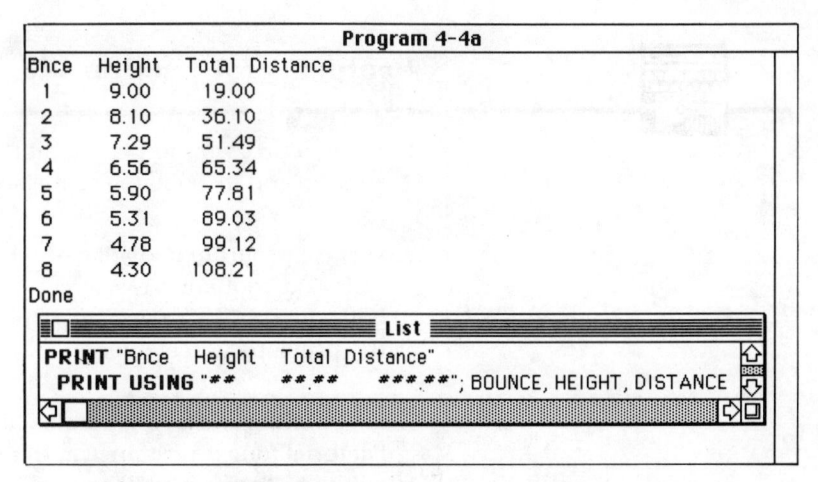

Figure 4-7. Execution of Program 4-4 with PRINT USING.

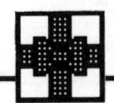

Summary

We have used a program simulating a bouncing ball to demonstrate FOR and NEXT. In this program we are interested in several quantities besides the value of the loop variable. The apostrophe has been introduced as an alternative vehicle for including comments within a BASIC program. This is especially desirable when we would like to comment on the purpose of a single line in a program.

Problems for Section 4-2

1. Write a program to print a table containing a number, its square, and its cube for values in a range from 1 to 20.

2. Write a program to display the first 20 Fibonacci numbers. This is a sequence for which the first two elements are both ones and succeeding values are obtained by adding the previous two elements.

3. Factorials are used a great deal in probability calculations. Factorial four is written 4! and is calculated by multiplying all the counting numbers from 1 to 4. That is
   $$4! = 4 * 3 * 2 * 1$$

   Write a program to display the factorial of a value entered using an INPUT statement. Note: 0! is defined as 1.

4. In the song "The Twelve Days of Christmas," gifts are given to the singer according to a progression of numbers. On the first day she got a partridge in a pear tree. On the second day she got two turtle doves and a partridge in a pear tree. On the last day she received 12 + 11 + ... + 2 + 1 gifts. Write a program to display the total number of gifts she received. If she had to return one each day, on what day would she return the last gift?

4-3. Let's Explore

Interest

Interest is paid for the use of money. It is a kind of rent. Simple interest is paid on an annual basis. For example, simple interest at 18% on a thousand dollars comes to $180 for the year. Compound interest is calculated and added to the principal at intervals. With the proliferation of computers, daily compounding has become commonplace. If interest is compounded daily, the interest is added to the principal daily. The annual percentage is prorated. That is, an 18% annual interest rate comes to 18/365 or about .049315068493151% per day. Although there is a formula for this, we can easily calculate compound interest using a FOR loop. See Program 4-5.

Program 4-5. Calculate compound interest.

```
PRINT "Calculate compound interest."
PRINT

INPUT "   Principal"; P
INPUT "Annual rate"; AR
PRINT
AR = AR / 100
DR = AR / 365 'Daily Rate
FOR DAY = 1 TO 365
  INTEREST = P * DR
  P = P+ INTEREST
NEXT DAY
PRINT USING "$$####.##   After one year"; P
```

```
≣□≣≣≣≣≣≣ Program 4-5 ≣≣≣≣≣
Calculate compound interest.

   Principal? 1000
Annual Rate? 18

 $1197.16  After one year
```

Figure 4-8. Execution of Program 4-5.

We see that we pay an extra $17.16 for compounding instead of using simple interest. Of course, if we are doing the lending, that looks pretty good. Let's look at a different application.

Fibonacci Numbers

Fibonacci numbers describe many natural phenomena and are of interest to mathematicians. A sequence of numbers is involved. The first two numbers in the sequence are both 1. Following this, each number in the sequence is the sum of the previous two values. So, the third element is 1 plus 1 or 2. Let's write a little program to display a few Fibonacci numbers. See Program 4-6.

Program 4-6. Display Fibonacci numbers.

```
PRINT "Fibonacci numbers:"
B = 0 : FIB = 1

FOR J = 1 TO 10
   PRINT FIB;
   A = B : B = FIB
   FIB = A + B
NEXT J
```

Here we save the last two elements in the sequence in variables A and B at all times. To get the sequence going we artificially set them both to 0. The variable B begins with 0 in the assignment statement B = 0, and the variable A begins with 0 when the statement A = B is executed for the first time.

```
Program 4-6
Fibonacci numbers:
 1  1  2  3  5  8  13  21  34  55
```

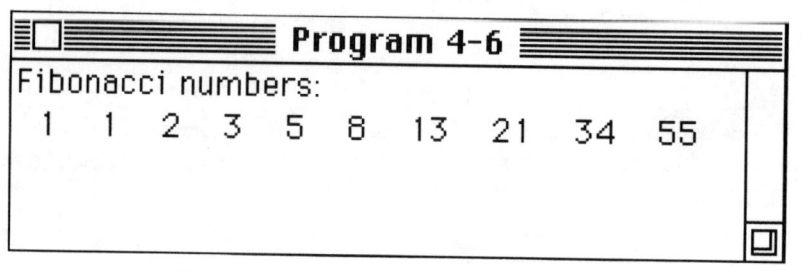

Figure 4-9. Execution of Program 4-6.

Problems for Section 4-3

1. Compare the interest on $1000 for one year at 18% with the interest at 12%.
2. Modify Program 4-6 to display the square of an element in the sequence and the product of the elements immediately before and immediately after. Also display the result of subtracting one from the other.
3. How many Fibonacci numbers can be expressed with six or fewer digits?

4-4. Nested Loops

Nested loops resemble sets of child's blocks that fit one within another or nest together. Any inside loop must fall entirely within an outside loop. Nested loops help us deal with charts and tables of all kinds having figures in rows and columns, and simulate numerous phenomena. The passing of time is a perfect example.

A Digital Clock

Let's take another look at a digital clock. Hours loop from 1 to 12, while minutes loop from 0 to 59 during every hour. So the guts of a digital clock can be simulated with nested loops as follows:

```
FOR HOUR = 1 TO 12
  FOR MINUTE = 0 TO 59
  NEXT MINUTE
NEXT HOUR
```

When HOUR equals 1, MINUTE goes through an entire cycle from 0 to 59 until execution exits the inner loop. When HOUR is incremented to 2, the inner loop does its thing once more, and so on. It is now a simple matter to display the time with PTAB and PRINT USING. Remember that PTAB in a PRINT statement sets the absolute pixel position on the current line for printing. See Program 4-7.

Program 4-7. Digital clock with nested loops.

```
FOR HOUR = 1 TO 12
  FOR MINUTE = 0 TO 59
    PRINT PTAB(200);
    PRINT USING "##:##"; HOUR, MINUTE
  NEXT MINUTE
NEXT HOUR
```

Program 4-7 could be enlarged to include other units of time. A loop going from 1 to 2 surrounding the HOUR loop would make it simulate a 24-hour day. A seconds loop would go within the MINUTE loop.

Notice in Program 4-7 that NEXT MINUTE is followed immediately by NEXT HOUR. If several FOR loops have a common end point, the end point may be designated with a single NEXT statement that names each loop variable. For example,

NEXT MINUTE, HOUR

Although this works for BASIC, it may not be as clear to the human reader. It is a good idea to use separate NEXT statements and consistent indenting to convey as much meaning as possible in the program listing.

Another Look at Compound Interest

Suppose we need to calculate compound interest over several years. This is another example of the passing of time. Let's display the compound amount each year on $1000 for five years. We can easily do this by enclosing the yearly interest calculation of Program 4-5 within a FOR loop that enumerates the years. See Program 4-8.

Program 4-8. Compound interest for several years.

```
PRINT "Calculate compound interest."
PRINT

INPUT "    Principal"; P
INPUT "Annual rate"; AR
PRINT
AR = AR / 100
DR = AR / 365 'Daily Rate
FOR YEAR = 1 TO 5
  FOR DAY = 1 TO 365
    INTEREST = P * DR
    P = P + INTEREST
  NEXT DAY
  PRINT USING "$$####.## After # years"; P, YEAR
NEXT YEAR
```

Beginning with Program 4-5, we simply added the lines

    FOR YEAR = 1 **TO** 5
    NEXT YEAR

to carry the calculation through five years using a FOR loop with YEAR as the variable, and we replaced the PRINT USING statement with one containing a more appropriate message.

See Figure 4-10 for the display from Program 4-8.

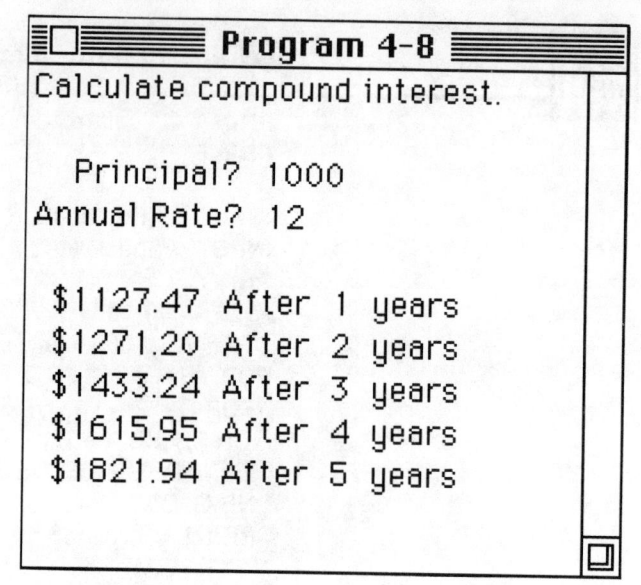

```
╔═════════════ Program 4-8 ═════════════╗
Calculate compound interest.

    Principal? 1000
 Annual Rate? 12

 $1127.47  After  1  years
 $1271.20  After  2  years
 $1433.24  After  3  years
 $1615.95  After  4  years
 $1821.94  After  5  years
```

Figure 4-10. Execution of Program 4-8.

Problems for Section 4-4

1. Here is a formula for compound interest:
   $$A = P(1 + I)^N$$

   where

   A = compound Amount
   P = Principal
   I = Interest rate per interest period
   N = Number of interest periods

   Write a program to calculate interest using this formula.

2. Write a program to display a multiplication table. Select an upper limit so that you can produce a nice display on the screen. Use nested loops and PRINT USING.

4-5. WHILE and WEND

FOR loops are nearly indispensible. Whenever the end point of a loop is a definite value, a FOR loop is the way to go. Whenever the end point of a loop is determined by some other calculation, however, a WHILE loop might be more appropriate.

Pythagorean Triples

There is an interesting set of right triangles with sides whose lengths are integers. These triangles provide us with our next example. Any three integers that can represent the sides of a right triangle are referred to as a *Pythagorean triple*. If we label sides of a right triangle as LEG1, LEG2, and HYP, then the Pythagorean Theorem states that the square of the hypotenuse equals the sum of the squares of the two legs, or

$$HYP^2 = LEG1^2 + LEG2^2$$

Suppose we want to find all Pythagorean triples with either leg up to 25. Let's first write this program using FOR loops and then incorporate a WHILE loop, so that we can compare FOR with WHILE. A program to find these sets of values is based on the following nested FOR loops:

```
FOR LEG1 = 1 TO 25
  FOR LEG2 = 1 TO 25
    FOR HYP = 1 TO 50
    NEXT HYP
  NEXT LEG2
NEXT LEG1
```

Loops are nested three deep in this program fragment. That's perfectly okay, but we should be a little cautious about this process. Even though computers are fast, it is surprisingly easy to program a task that will take too long for the computer to do. We have programmed 31250 steps. Although this is not much of a challenge for the computer, there will be a noticeable wait for the full results. It is worthwhile for us to study the problem with an eye toward eliminating as many steps as possible. By examining the upper and lower limits on the loop variables, we can decide how to reduce the number of steps without missing any of the triples.

If we let values for both legs range from 1 to 25, then we will get 3, 4, 5 and 4, 3, 5 in the result. We can easily eliminate duplication by changing FOR LEG2 = 1 to 25 so that the value of LEG2 begins with the current value of LEG1, or even LEG1 + 1.

FOR LEG2 = LEG1 + 1 **TO** 25

That saves a lot of unnecessary steps for the computer.

Now look at FOR HYP = 1 TO 50. Certainly we do not have to make the computer use values for the hypotenuse beginning with 1. We could safely begin with LEG2. The hypotenuse must be at least as long as the longer leg. So we may replace that line with

FOR HYP = LEG2 **TO** 50

For each set of three numbers, the program must compare the square of the hypotenuse with the sum of the squares of the two legs. If the square of the hypotenuse is less than the sum of the squares of the legs, then try a larger value for the hypotenuse. If the square of the hypotenuse is greater than the sum of the squares of the legs, then we have overshot on the hypotenuse and it is time to try a new value for LEG2. If they are equal, display the three lengths and proceed to the next value for LEG2. See Program 4-9.

Program 4-9. Display Pythagorean triples using FOR loops.

```
PRINT "Pythagorean triples:"
FOR LEG1 = 1 TO 25
  FOR LEG2 = LEG1 + 1 TO 25
    FOR HYP = LEG2 TO 50
      IF HYP^2 < LEG1^2 + LEG2^2 THEN More.HYP
      IF HYP^2 > LEG1^2 + LEG2^2 THEN More.LEG2
      PRINT LEG1; LEG2; HYP : GOTO More.LEG2
More.HYP:
    NEXT HYP
More.LEG2:
  NEXT LEG2
NEXT LEG1
```

Look at the HYP loop in Program 4-9. Notice that there are three line label references in three successive program lines. Also notice that FOR HYP = LEG2 TO 50 suggests that the upper limit on the HYP loop is 50. In reality the upper limit is determined by the next line in the program:

IF HYP^2 < LEG1^2 + LEG2^2 **THEN** More.HYP

A WHILE loop may be used to eliminate that confusion. WHILE causes all statements between it and a WEND statement to be executed as long as a condition in the WHILE statement is true. See Program 4-10.

Program 4-10. Display Pythagorean triples using WHILE.

PRINT "Pythagorean triples:"
FOR LEG1 = 1 **TO** 25
  FOR LEG2 = LEG1 + 1 **TO** 25
    HYP = LEG2
    WHILE HYP^2 < LEG1^2 + LEG2^2
      HYP = HYP + 1
    WEND
    IF HYP^2 = LEG1^2 + LEG2^2 **THEN PRINT** LEG1; LEG2; HYP
  NEXT LEG2
NEXT LEG1

In Program 4-10 the two lines

HYP = LEG2
WHILE HYP^2 < LEG1^2 + LEG2^2

establish the beginning value of HYP and the ending condition of the WHILE loop. We can't state such an ending condition in a FOR statement. This program makes good use of both FOR and WHILE. Sometimes it is better to use FOR and sometimes WHILE. Clearly

FOR LEG1 = 1 **TO** 25
NEXT LEG1

is better than the following equivalent using WHILE:

```
LEG1 = 1
WHILE LEG1 <= 25
    LEG1 = LEG1 + 1
WEND
```

The results are shown in Figure 4-11.

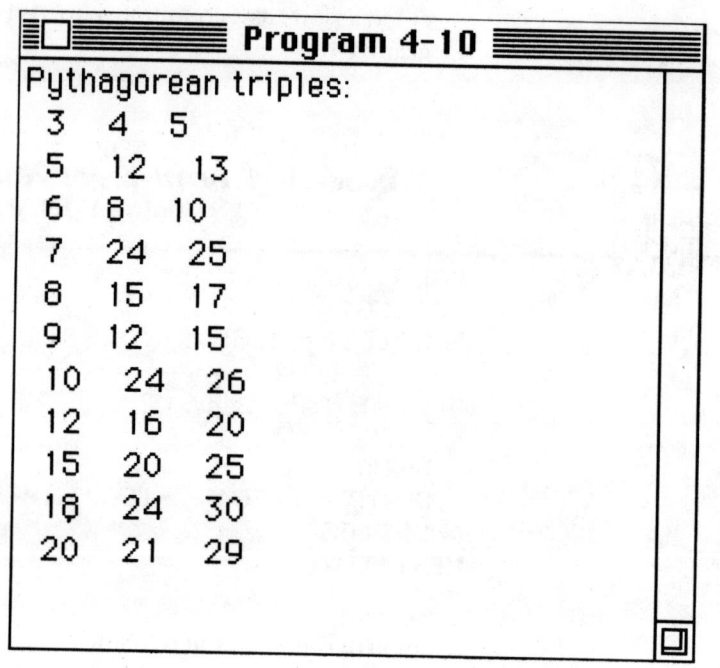

```
Program 4-10
Pythagorean triples:
 3    4    5
 5   12   13
 6    8   10
 7   24   25
 8   15   17
 9   12   15
10   24   26
12   16   20
15   20   25
18   24   30
20   21   29
```

Figure 4-11. Execution of Program 4-10.

TAB

We could line up those columns nicely with comma spacing and WIDTH. Or we could use TAB in the PRINT statement. TAB(X) causes the next printed item to begin in the column numbered X. The first column is numbered 1. While the PTAB(X) statement positions absolutely on the line, TAB(X) cannot back up on the line. An attempt to do so results in the display moving to the next line. The other difference between PTAB(X) and TAB(X) is that while PTAB(X) positions are measured in pixels, TAB(X) positions correspond to standard character widths. We can use this line to get the nicely spaced display of Figure 4-12:

IF HYP^2 = LEG1^2 + LEG2^2 **THEN PRINT** LEG1; **TAB**(5); LEG2; **TAB**(10); HYP

```
Program 4-10
Pythagorean triples:
 3   4   5
 5  12  13
 6   8  10
 7  24  25
 8  15  17
 9  12  15
10  24  26
12  16  20
15  20  25
18  24  30
20  21  29
                                            List
IF HYP^2 = LEG1^2 + LEG2^2 THEN PRINT LEG1; TAB(5);LEG2; TAB(10); HYP
```

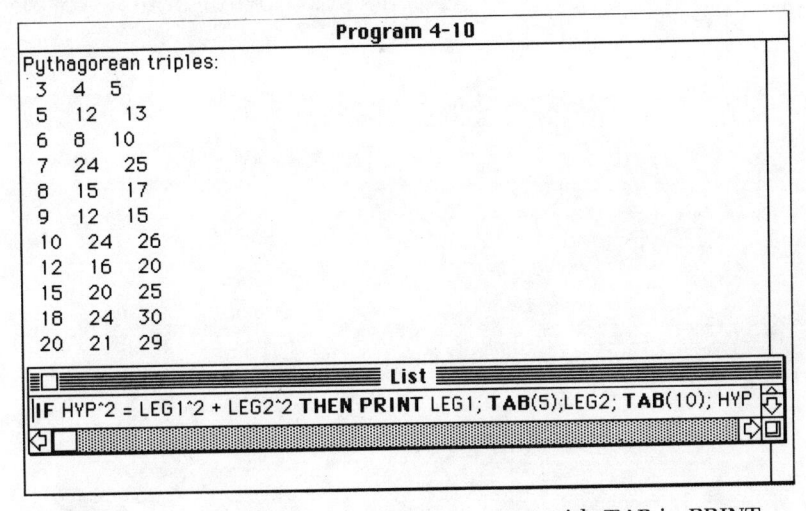

Figure 4-12. Execution of Program 4-10 with TAB in PRINT.

Notice that with TAB, columns are left justified. PRINT USING enables us to produce right-justified columns.

LOCATE

The LOCATE statement gives even more flexibility for placing display in the output window.

LOCATE Y, X

places the next character at the position X,Y. X and Y are measured in eight pixel characters. Note that Y comes first and X second.

Problems for Section 4-5

1. 9, 40, 41 and 12, 35, 37 are Pythagorean triples. They do not appear in the execution of Program 4-10. Find these and more additional Pythagorean triples by raising the upper limit on LEG2 to 50 or more.

CHAPTER 5

Packages in BASIC: Functions, Subroutines, and Subprograms

BASIC is made up of several kinds of features. There are the keywords and the loop structures. We have line labels, numeric variables, and string variables. Numerous arithmetic operations are available. In this chapter we are going to add a collection of tremendous tools to our programming repertoire. We are going to discuss many of the functions available. In addition, we are going to learn about subroutines and subprograms.

A function is a process that returns a value. For example, there is a function that returns the square root of a number. Although we could write the necessary BASIC routine to do that, it is desirable to have the programming language do it for us. Why should every user of BASIC have to write it? Another function returns the number of characters in a string variable. BASIC includes many such functions as features of the language. In addition, we may create our own programmer-defined functions.

A subroutine is like a mini-program. It is a segment of a program that we may isolate and utilize from anywhere else in our program. Subroutines are useful whenever we need the same calculation at many different places in a program. Furthermore, subroutines make it possible to partition the work of a big program into little jobs. This helps us to concentrate on a smaller programming task at any one time.

Subprograms are similar to subroutines except that variables named in subprograms may be local. Local variables are independent from variables in the rest of the program. So, BLUEONES in a

Chapter 5: Packages in BASIC

subprogram is not the same variable as BLUEONES in the main program. Of course, values can be passed to and retrieved from subprograms.

5-1. Introduction to Numeric Functions

SQR (Square Root)

We can easily write a little program to display the square roots of the integers from one to ten. The square root function is designated by SQR. The value for which we require the square root is enclosed in parentheses. The value in parentheses is called the "argument" of the function. See the PRINT statement in Program 5-1.

Program 5-1. Display some square roots.

```
FOR J = 1 TO 10
   PRINT J, SQR(J)
NEXT J
```

```
Program 5-1
1         1
2         1.4142135623731
3         1.7320508075689
4         2
5         2.2360679774998
6         2.4494897427832
7         2.6457513110646
8         2.8284271247462
9         3
10        3.1622776601684
```

Figure 5-1. Execution of Program 5-1.

Here we simply display the value. SQR(J) takes on many values during execution of Program 5-1. We may use those values in all of the ways that we use other values. The following statements demonstrate some of them.

    X = **SQR**(HEIGHT)
    SIDE = **SQR**(X^2 + Y^2)
    T = **SQR**(J) − 2∗T + 18∗R9

INT (Greatest Integer)

The INTeger function returns the largest integer not greater than the argument. So, INT(5.0) becomes 5 and INT(5.99) also becomes 5. INT(−6.5) becomes −7. The result won't be −6 because that is greater than −6.5. INT is not the same as doing integer division using the backslash (\). The difference shows up for negative results. INT(6 / −4) evaluates as −2 while 6 \ −4 works out to −1. This function is often used to round off values. Probably the most frequent application is in financial calculations.

We always round to the nearest hundredth of a dollar to express whole cents. All values half a cent or more we round up, and values less than half a cent we round down. So, first we multiply the dollar value by one hundred to get cents. Now, if we simply apply the INT function, the result is always rounded down. Since we only want to round down for values less than half a cent, we add half a cent first. This means that values of more than half a cent have been pushed up to the next whole cent, while values less than half a cent have not. Finally, applying the INT function produces the desired result.

    INT(DOLLARS ∗ 100 + .5)

represents the number of cents. Now all we need to do is divide by one hundred to get the decimal point back in. The final expression is

    INT(DOLLARS ∗ 100 + .5) / 100

If this evaluates to $54.40, BASIC will print without the trailing zero. And if it comes out to a whole dollar, no cents digits will appear at all. This is an ideal situation for PRINT USING to display trailing zeros as well as dollar signs.

FIX (Remove Decimal Digits)

The FIX(X) returns the result of simply cutting off any decimal portion of X. This is sometimes called truncation. FIX(C) produces the same results as INT(C) for positive values of C. But, FIX(−5.5) evaluates to −5 and INT(−5.5) equals −6.

Factors

Since we can now take the greatest integer of a value, we can also decide if one number divides evenly into another. If a value and INT of the value are equal, that implies that the value has no decimal part. So, statements of the form:

IF A/B = **INT**(A/B) **THEN PRINT** B 'B is a factor

may be used to identify factors. Note that if B is a factor of A, then A/B is, too. This makes finding factors of integers an ideal example. Factors occur in pairs. See Table 5-1.

Table 5-1. Factor pairs.

$$2 * 6 = 12$$
$$3 * 4 = 12$$
$$4 * 3 = 12$$
$$6 * 2 = 12$$

In fact, all pairs of factors occur twice, except in the case of a perfect square. Also, every factor greater than the square root is paired with a factor less than the square root. So, a program that tests all integers up to and including the square root of a number will find all integer factors. Study Program 5-2.

Program 5-2. Find factor pairs.

```
INPUT "Find factor pairs of"; N
FOR D = 2 TO SQR(N)
  Q = N / D
  IF Q = INT(Q) THEN PRINT D; Q
NEXT D
```

```
┌──────────── Program 5-2 ────────────┐
│ Find factor pairs of?  1001          │
│    7    143                          │
│   11     91                          │
│   13     77                          │
└──────────────────────────────────────┘
```

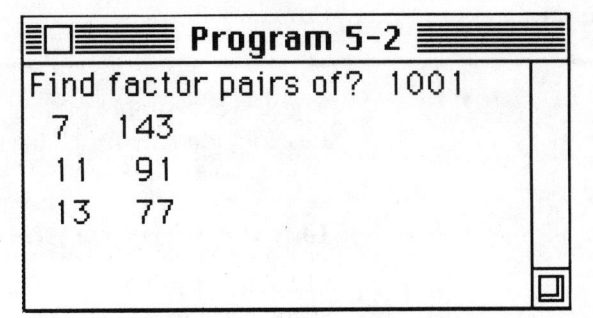

Figure 5-2. Execution of Program 5-2.

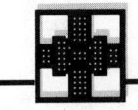

Summary

The SQR function returns the square root of the argument. The INT(Z) function returns the greatest integer in Z not greater than Z. The FIX(Z) function truncates Z.

Problems for Section 5-1

1. Write a program to display the square roots of integers from 1 to 20 rounded off to the nearest tenth.
2. Do problem 1, displaying the values with PRINT USING.
3. Modify Program 5-2 to find the smallest prime factor of an integer.
4. Write a program that requests a numeric date in the form YYMMDD. One of the reasons that we like to use this numeric yymmdd form for the date in a computer is that if we sort by that number, the result will be in chronological order. First, verify that it is a legal date within reason. Then display the date in the form YY MM DD. That is, 790121 becomes 79 1 21.

5-2. String Functions

There are a number of functions that will help us handle string values. Included are functions to determine the length of a string, pick strings apart, and generally simplify programming with strings.

LEN (Length of a String)

LEN(A$) returns the number of characters actually stored in the string variable A$. This value can range from 0 to 32767. Whenever we analyze a string character by character the LEN function is useful for determining how many characters to look at.

WIDTH (Width of a String)

WIDTH(A$) returns the number of pixels required to display the string A$ on the Macintosh. Letters of the alphabet range from 5 to 11 pixels in width, while digits all display in 8 pixels. A space is equal to 4 pixels. The pixel widths only apply to the characters displayed on the screen. All characters sent to the printer through LPRINT are printed in the same space.

ASC (ASCII Value)

The ASC function returns a number corresponding to the internal code that BASIC uses to represent characters. For example,

ASC("a")

has a value of 97. The ASCII value for z is 122. ASCII is the American Standard Code for Information Interchange. It is used by a great many computer systems. A partial table of ASCII values is presented in Appendix C. ASC(V$) returns the ASCII value associated with the first character in the string variable V$.

INKEY$

A$ = INKEY$

provides the opportunity for A$ to accept a single character from the keyboard. Program execution does not wait for a key to be struck. If no key has been pressed, the length of the string A$ is 0. Since ASC cannot evaluate a string of zero length, we must always provide for a length check before applying ASC. We often have a situation in a program where we want to provide the user an opportunity to examine an output window before going on to another phase in a program. The following line is ideal for this:

    CheckKey: **IF LEN(INKEY$)** = 0 **THEN** CheckKey

BASIC will stay on this line until a key is pressed.

INPUT$

    A$ = **INPUT$**(NUMBEROFCHARACTERS)

waits at the keyboard until NUMBEROFCHARACTERS are entered at the keyboard. Following this, the string A$ will contain the string returned by INPUT$. The string will accept any keyboard characters at all, except ⌘-. Even after the user presses the Return key, INPUT$ waits if more characters are needed to get up to NUMBEROFCHARACTERS.

CHR$ (Character Whose ASCII Code is Given)

The CHR$ function is the reverse of the ASC function. We give it an ASCII value and it returns the corresponding character. So,

    PRINT CHR$**(40), **CHR$(41)

returns

    (   )

since the left and right parentheses are represented by 40 and 41 in ASCII. We can easily have this function reveal the Macintosh special characters, including symbols, foreign characters, and fancy punctuation marks using the values 128 through 216. Try it!

STR$ (Convert Numeric to String)

The STR$ function converts a numeric value to string format. STR$(N) converts the internal binary code used to represent the numeric value of N into the ASCII code used for each of the digits. Let's examine the effect of a statement such as

    T$ = **STR$**(X)

While X stores a numeric value that we may use directly in arithmetic calculations, T$ stores the digits of the number as string characters. So, T$ permits us to manipulate the digits using string functions and techniques. T$ will begin with a space if X is positive, or a minus sign if X is negative. That is just the way it is.

VAL (Convert String to Numeric)

VAL is the reverse of STR$. VAL(N$) returns a numeric value. If N$ is a string of digits, VAL converts them into the binary format used for storing numbers. If the first character could not be part of a number, a zero is returned. If the function is successful in converting the beginning of a string, it continues to the end of the string or until it encounters an impossible character. Thus,

VAL("7 Days in the week")

will convert to

7

LEFT$, MID$, and RIGHT$ (String Segments)

The LEFT$, MID$, and RIGHT$ are among the most often used string functions. These functions return a string value. As the names imply, these functions work with the left, middle, and right parts of strings.

LEFT$(A$,5) returns the five leftmost characters in the string variable A$. If A$ contains fewer than five in this case, the LEFT$ returns whatever is there. RIGHT$ performs exactly the same duty on the right end of a string.

MID$ extracts characters from the interior of a string. Well, it doesn't remove them, it just obtains a copy of them. MID$(A$,9,4) refers to the four characters of A$ beginning with the ninth character. And MID$(A$,K,1) specifies the Kth character in the A$ string.

For RIGHT$ and LEFT$, arguments greater than 32767 or less than −32768 constitute an "Overflow" error, while values in the range −1 to −32768 will evoke the "Illegal function call" error box. The MID$ function has similar restrictions except that if the beginning character value is 0, it is considered an "Illegal function call".

The simple example of Program 5-3 enters some days of the week in a string and separates them for display.

Program 5-3. Demonstrate LEFT$, MID$, and RIGHT$.

```
WEEK$ = "MonTueWedThuFri"
PRINT LEFT$(WEEK$,3)
PRINT MID$(WEEK$,7,3)
PRINT RIGHT$(WEEK$,3)
```

```
┌─────────────────────────────────┐
│ ▢ ═══ Program 5-3 ═══           │
├─────────────────────────────────┤
│ Mon                             │
│ Wed                             │
│ Fri                             │
│                                 │
│                                 │
│                                 │
│                              ▢  │
└─────────────────────────────────┘
```

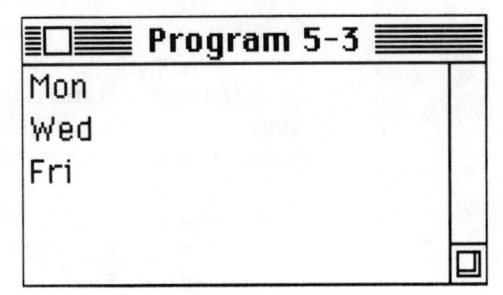

Figure 5-3. Execution of Program 5-3.

The expression LEFT$(WEEK$,3) represents the three leftmost characters in the character string WEEK$, or Mon. Similarly, RIGHT$(WEEK$,3) becomes the three rightmost characters in WEEK$, giving us Fri. MID$ is a little different. The expression MID$(WEEK$,7,3) represents 3 characters, beginning with the seventh character in the string WEEK$, which produces Wed.

We have used MID$ as a function here. MID$ may also be used as a statement to assign characters anywhere in a string variable. If X$ = "MonTueWed", and the following statement is executed:

**MID$**(X$,4,3) = "Feb"

then X$ will contain "MonFebWed".

INSTR (Find Substring)

Given two strings, INSTRing looks for an occurrence of the second string within the first string. INSTR(FIRST$,SECOND$) returns the position of the first character of the match. If no match is found, then INSTR returns 0. For example, suppose we need to enter the day of the week and have the program use the day number for further calculation. Program 5-4 is a little routine that will report the character position of the name of a day.

Program 5-4. Demonstrate INSTR.

```
REM ** What day is this?
WEEK$ = "SUNMONTUEWEDTHUFRISAT"
INPUT "Day"; DAY$
DAY$ = LEFT$(DAY$,3) 'Take 1st 3 characters to match
P = INSTR(WEEK$,DAY$)
PRINT "Found in position"; P
```

We have set up a string with the days of the week for the program to match against a day name entered from the keyboard. The LEFT$ function is used to isolate the first three characters of the entered day name. Note that we will have to enter all uppercase to obtain a match. (See UCASE$ below.)

```
▭▬▬  Program 5-4  ▬▬▬
Day? FRIDAY
Found in position  16

Day? friday
Found in position  0
```

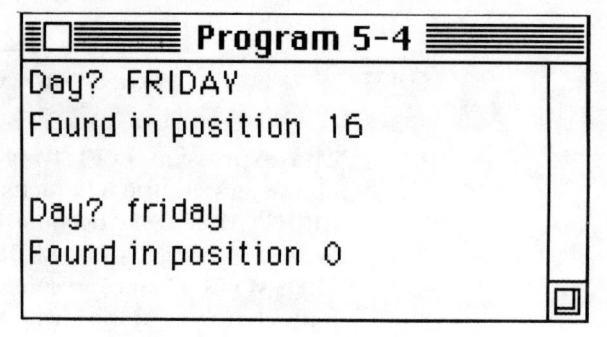

Figure 5-4. Execution of Program 5-4.

Although Program 5-4 found FRIDAY in position 16, we really would like to know which day number that is. It would be a good idea to first rule out illegal responses whenever INSTR returns 0. Now if we divide the position values returned in Program 5-4 by 3 and apply the FIX function, integer values 0 through 6 are produced. So, Sunday is day 0 and Saturday is day 6. This would also be a good place to use integer division indicated by a backslash (\).

INSTR also allows the search to begin anywhere in the sample string.

PRINT INSTR(4,"ABXDEFGHIJXK", "X")

produces the following response:

11

INSTR didn't report the X at position 3 because the search began with character number 4.

UCASE$ (Convert to Uppercase)

In Program 5-4 we noted that the day names had to be entered in all uppercase for the program to work. BASIC offers the UCASE$ function for just such situations. It returns all letters in a string in uppercase, and leaves other characters unchanged.

```
A$ = "AbCdEf123"
PRINT UCASE$(A$)
```

will display

```
ABCDEF123
```

There is no equivalent for lowercase.

STRING$ (String of Characters)

STRING$(1,J) simply returns the character whose ASCII value is J—just like CHR$. STRING$(K,J) returns K of them. STRING$(5,37) becomes five percent signs. This function is handy for filling in reports and dressing up program display in general. Values for J less than 0 or greater than 255 evoke an "Illegal function call," while values for K or J outside the range −32768 to 32767 cause an "Overflow." And if we allow the value of K to become very large, we might even get an "Out of memory" error box. Values for K in the range −1 to −32768 constitute an "Illegal function call."

STRING$ may also be used with a string argument to indicate the character to be repeated.

```
STRING$(10,"−")
```

will become ten dashes. This function can be used to put spaces in a display, but a special SPACE$ function is provided for this.

SPACE$ (String of Spaces)

SPACE$(15) becomes 15 spaces. SPACE$(X) becomes X spaces. This SPACE$ string can be used in general string assignment and display statements of all kinds.

DATE$

The DATE$ function returns the date in the form mm-dd-yyyy from the Macintosh calendar. January 30, 1997 would be displayed as 01-30-1997. We may display DATE$ directly in a PRINT statement or we may want to assign it to some string variable.

DATE$ may also be used as a statement to set the Macintosh calendar.

```
DATE$ = "1-21-17"
DATE$ = "02-28-2001"
DATE$ = "05/30/54"
DATE$ = "7/4/1918"
```

are all acceptable forms. Microsoft BASIC assumes 1900s if the century is left off.

TIME$

The TIME$ function returns the time in the form hh:mm:ss. That is, 21:40:24 is 9:40 pm and 24 seconds.

The time can also be assigned with TIME$.

TIME$ = "13"
TIME$ = "12:31"
TIME$ = "09:30:30"

are all forms that assign the time. Data left off is assumed to be dropped from the right. Thus, "12:31" is taken to be 12:31:00. TIME$ uses a 24 hour clock, so "13" represents 1:00 PM.

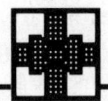

Summary

We have introduced LEN, WIDTH, ASC, INKEY$, INPUT$, CHR$, STR$, VAL, LEFT$, MID$, RIGHT$, INSTR, UCASE$, STRING$, SPACE$, DATE$, and TIME$. We may use all of the earlier string concepts here. Thus, expressions such as the following all perform sensibly:

B$ = B$ + **SPACE$**(3) + **MID$**(A$,J,2)
MID$**(A$,X,Y−1) = **STRING$(Y,91)
C$ = **RIGHT$**(C$,**LEN**(C$)−1)

MID$, besides being a function to isolate characters in a string, may be used to assign characters anywhere in a string. DATE$ and TIME$ may be used to assign the date and time.

Problems for Section 5-2

1. Write a program to display the contents of a string backwards.
2. Using PTAB and string features from this section, write a program that scrolls a message horizontally across the screen.
3. Write a program to request a name, last name first followed by a comma and the first name. Have your program search for the comma and rearrange the name in first-name-first format. Thus, Anthony, Susan B. will become Susan B. Anthony. Note: the response to INPUT will have to be enclosed in quotes to get the comma into the string. Or use LINE INPUT.
4. Modify Program 5-4 so that it displays the correct day number rather than the character position.
5. Use UCASE$ in Program 5-4 so that the user is not limited to uppercase.
6. In Program 5-4, incorporate a fixed string that contains the day names spelled out and beginning with capital letters. Use the position in WEEK$ to display the full name from your new string.
7. Write a program that requests a date in a string in the form YY/MM/DD. Note that dates in this form can be sorted to arrange in real chronological order. First verify that it is a legal date within reason. Then display the date in the form YY-Mmm-DD. That is, 79/02/21 becomes 79-Feb-21.
8. Write a program that requests a numeric date in the form YYMMDD. One of the reasons that we like to use this numeric YYMMDD form for the date in a computer is that if we sort by that number, the result will be in chronological order. First verify that it is a possible date. Then display the date in the form YY-Mmm-DD. That is, 790221 becomes 79-Feb-21.

5-3. Miscellaneous Functions

ABS (Absolute Value)

The ABSolute value function changes the sign of all negative arguments, so ABS(−10) is 10. ABS(X) returns zero for X equals zero, and gives X for positive values of X.

There is an interesting application that uses ABS. We can determine the minimum of A and B with the following:

MIN = (A + B − **ABS**(A − B)) / 2

A simple change makes this work for maximum. Alternatively, we could obtain the minimum with an IF test such as

MIN = A : **IF** A > B **THEN** MIN = B

And here is yet another way:

IF A > B **THEN** MIN = B **ELSE** MIN = A

Either one produces the desired value.

Suppose we are testing for X = Y in an IF statement. If both values are decimal numbers in the binary version of BASIC, we may be satisfied if they are within .0000001 of each other and we don't care which is larger. This is just the place for ABS.

IF ABS(X−Y) < .0000001 **THEN** match statements here

ABS will come in handy for calculating distances from coordinate pairs in the Cartesian coordinate system.

SGN (Sign)

The SiGN function returns 1, 0, or −1 according to whether the argument is positive, zero, or negative. It doesn't get much of a workout.

RND (Random Numbers)

One popular function is the random number generator. The ability of the computer to produce random numbers makes it easy to create programs that do different things each time they are run. The RND function returns double-precision random values in the range 0 to 1. Program 5-5 shows how this works.

Miscellaneous Functions

Program 5-5. Demonstrate random numbers.

```
FOR R = 1 TO 10
  PRINT RND
NEXT R
```

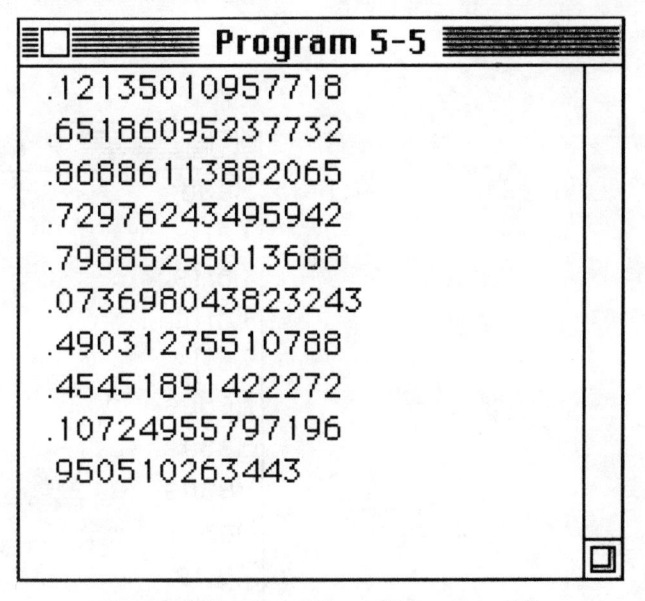

```
Program 5-5
.12135010957718
.65186095237732
.86886113882065
.72976243495942
.79885298013688
.073698043823243
.49031275510788
.45451891422272
.10724955797196
.950510263443
```

Figure 5-5. Execution of Program 5-5.

Values produced by RND may be assigned to variables and used in calculations of all kinds. We might want to use random numbers to simulate some activity. This could be as simple as flipping a coin or as complex as modeling the traffic on a proposed road bridge.

For our first example, let's flip a coin. A coin can come up either heads or tails. We could divide the random numbers evenly by splitting the interval from zero to one at the .5 mark. It is equally simple to multiply all values by two to make the interval become from zero to two. If we then apply the INT function, only two values are possible—zero and one. These two values are used in Program 5-6 to flip a coin ten times.

Chapter 5: Packages in BASIC

Program 5-6. Flip a coin ten times.

```
FOR C = 1 TO 10
  COIN = INT(2 * RND)
  IF COIN = 0 THEN PRINT "Heads"
  IF COIN = 1 THEN PRINT "Tails"
NEXT C
```

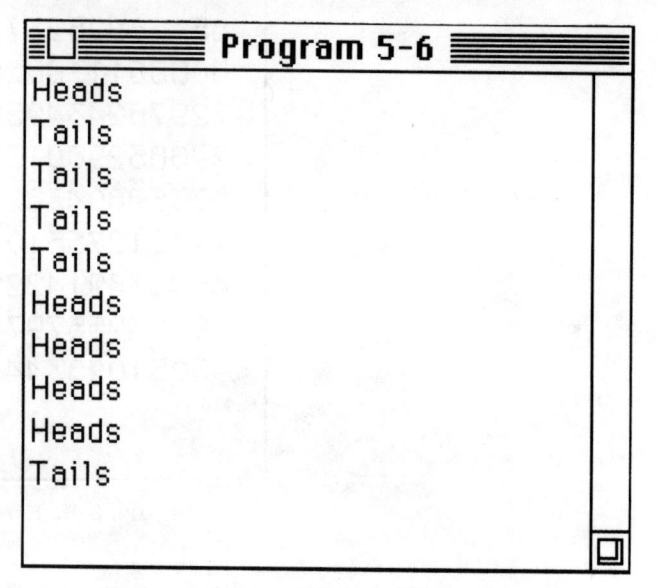

```
Program 5-6
Heads
Tails
Tails
Tails
Tails
Heads
Heads
Heads
Heads
Tails
```

Figure 5-6. Execution of Program 5-6.

The beauty of this concept is that it also applies easily to many other random events. To roll dice, we simply multiply by six to get integers from zero to five. In the case of the dice, we can then add one to obtain the six different faces. Here is the way to roll a die five times.

Program 5-7. Roll a die five times.

```
FOR D = 1 TO 5
  DIE = INT(6 * RND) + 1
  PRINT USING "Roll # : #"; D; DIE
NEXT D
```

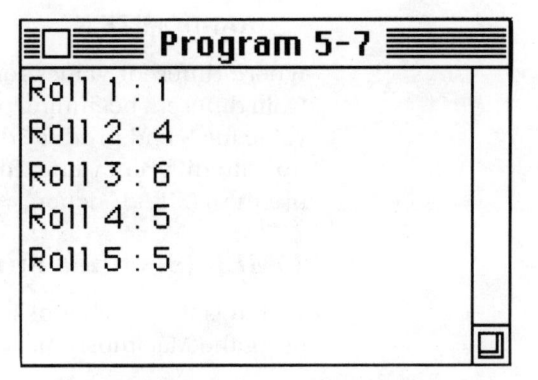

```
Program 5-7
Roll 1 : 1
Roll 2 : 4
Roll 3 : 6
Roll 4 : 5
Roll 5 : 5
```

Figure 5-7. Execution of Program 5-7.

Running Program 5-7 again will produce the same results. RND gives a sequence of numbers that is repeatable. The list is quite long so that it is useful for most purposes. To get a different roll of the dice, we need a way to start at a different place in the list every time the program is executed. BASIC offers two ways to do this: One is to place a value in parentheses to go with RND and the other is to use the RANDOMIZE statement.

RND(X)

RND(X) is affected by the value of X. For a given negative value of X we get the same value of RND(X). Each different negative value for X gives a different starting point. For X equals zero we get the most recently generated random value. And for X positive we get the same result as for RND without the argument.

RANDOMIZE

The RANDOMIZE statement permits us to enter a number from the keyboard that "seeds" the random number generator. Give it a different seed and get a different sequence. RANDOMIZE displays the following message:

Random Number Seed (−32768 to 32767)?

Simply enter a number off the top of your head.
RANDOMIZE also allows the following form:

RANDOMIZE N

where different values for N cause random values to be selected from different beginning points in the sequence. Choose a different value for N and produce different results. The easiest way to come up with different values for N each time a program is executed is to use the TIMER function.

TIMER (Seconds Since Midnight)

TIMER is the number of seconds that have elapsed since midnight, using the Macintosh Alarm Clock. So, the statement

RANDOMIZE TIMER

automatically gives different results for successive runs of the program. It may be important to find the fastest way to solve a problem or create a delay of exactly so much time. To use TIMER to measure elapsed time in a program, save its value at the beginning of a process and subtract from TIMER at the end of the process.

FRE (Free Memory)

FRE(X) returns information relating to memory. For X = −1 the value is the number of free bytes in the heap. The heap is a segment of Macintosh memory reserved by Microsoft BASIC to hold parts of BASIC itself and provide space for certain features of BASIC as workspace. For X = −2 the value is the number of bytes never used by the stack. The stack is used to keep track of things like nested loops for a running program. Any other value for X returns the number of bytes of memory available for our BASIC program and data. This is helpful to the programmer working on large programs. Running the program first will give a more realistic number. Each character requires one byte. An integer occupies two bytes. A single precision number takes up four bytes, while a double precision value uses eight bytes. Memory use is especially important to the programmer working with large arrays. (See Chapter 7.)

EXP (e to a Power)

EXP(X) returns e (2.718281828459...) raised to the X power. This may be useful for some mathematics oriented applications.

Trigonometric Functions

ATN(Z), COS(Z), SIN(Z), and TAN(Z) are the four trigonometric functions. In each case the value of Z is taken to be in radians rather than degree measure. Results are in double precision in the decimal version of Microsoft BASIC. Results are single precision or double precision according to the argument of the function in the binary version of Microsoft BASIC. Other trigonometric functions may be derived from these four.

Problems for Section 5-3

1. Write a little routine to request a person's name and use the number of characters in the name to seed the random number generator.
2. Flip a coin 200 times. Report on the number of Heads and Tails.
3. Roll a pair of dice ten times. Display each roll.

5-4. Programmer-Defined Functions (DEF FN)

Numeric Functions

Earlier we saw an expression to round off values to the nearest hundredth.

INT(DOLLARS * 100 + .5) / 100

Every time we want a rounded value, this expression must be repeated. Sometimes we would rather use such an expression once and refer to it whenever needed. The programmer-defined function capability exists for just this kind of situation. Once, usually early in the program, we use a statement such as the following:

DEF FN ROUND(X) = **INT**(X * 100 + .5) / 100

Then, wherever we need to round to the nearest hundredth, we simply incorporate FN ROUND(DOLLARS) as appropriate. The DEFined function statement must execute before any statement that refers to it. Failure to do this constitutes an "Undefined user function" error. It is a good idea to place all DEF statements at the very beginning of the program. Program 5-8 is a simple demonstration of a rounding function.

Program 5-8. Demonstrate rounding with DEF FN.

```
PRINT "ROUNDED", "UNROUNDED"
DEF FN ROUND(X) = INT(X * 100 + .5) / 100

Reading:
    READ DOLLARS
    IF DOLLARS = 0 THEN END
    PRINT FN ROUND(DOLLARS), DOLLARS
    GOTO Reading

DATA 1.091, -17.569, 100.999
DATA 17.569
DATA 0
```

```
================ Program 5-8 ================
ROUNDED         UNROUNDED
 1.09             1.091
-17.57           -17.569
 101              100.999
 17.57            17.569
```

Figure 5-8. Execution of Program 5-8.

Look at the following two lines from Program 5-8:

DEF FN ROUND(X) = **INT**(X * 100 + .5) / 100
PRINT FN ROUND(DOLLARS), DOLLARS

Note that while the variable used to define the function is X, when the computer gets to the PRINT statement it replaces X everywhere with DOLLARS. The computer simply matches up the variable in parentheses in the FN reference statement with whatever variable appears in parentheses in the function definition statement. The X used in this way is called a *dummy variable*. It simply serves to tell the computer where to use the value named in the referencing statement later on. If we happen to use X for some other purpose in our program, that is all right. The two uses of the variable X do not interact at all.

We can round values off and store the result in a variable using a rounding function such as this. Although we may also do rounding with PRINT USING, the results appear only in the display and are not stored in variables in the program.

Suppose we want to round to different degrees of precision at different points in a program. We could do a DEF FN for each precision, or we could do one DEF FN in terms of precision for the whole job. We would like to have two values go into the function: the figure to be rounded and the degree of precision. We could use the number of decimal places as the degree of precision. Thus for rounding to the nearest hundredth, we would use a 2. The following function does it.

DEF FN ROUND(X, Y) = **INT**(X * 10^Y + .5) / 10^Y

Now in a line such as:

PRINT FN ROUND(DOLLARS, P)

the computer will replace X with DOLLARS and replace Y with P. So, it will evaluate

INT(DOLLARS * 10^P + .5) / 10^P.

If the number of arguments in the reference to a function is different from the number of arguments in the definition, a syntax error results. We will see the same message if there is a syntax error in the DEF statement. Even though the error is in the DEF statement, BASIC will display a box around the referencing statement rather than the defining statement in the List window. So if you don't see anything wrong in the statement that refers to the function, go right to the DEF statement and look at it. You will save a lot of staring.

If we name a variable in the function definition that is not in the argument list in parentheses following DEF FN..., then the program will simply use that variable's actual value for the calculation.

String Functions

Occasionally we want to define our own string functions. For example, suppose we have a program in which the days of the week are numbered 0 through 6 using the ideas we developed in Section 5-2, and we want to use the day number to display the day name. First, enter the day names in a string. Wednesday requires 9 characters. If we just type one long string with the names of the days of the week, allowing 9 characters each, we will get a long line. BASIC is well equipped to handle this. The List window automatically moves right and left as necessary. However, here it will be done with two statements just to keep the presentation simple.

    WEEK$ = "Sunday   Monday   Tuesday Wednesday"
    WEEK$ = WEEK$ + "Thursday Friday   Saturday"

Day number 0 begins at 1, day number 1 begins at 10, and day number D begins at 9*D + 1. So, for a given day numbered D, the following expression would define the string segment containing the name of the day of the week:

    **MID$**(WEEK$, D*9 + 1, 9)

We can simplify this expression by using a programmer-defined function.

    DEF FN DAY$(D) = **MID$**(WEEK$, D*9 + 1, 9)

Once this function is defined, the mere mention of FN DAY$(N) produces the name of the day of the week numbered N. The defined function allows us to produce the correct day name by giving only the day number. There is no need to think about the string that contains the names or any of the calculations required to select the right segment for this particular day. The defined function does it automatically. Program 5-9 demonstrates the technique.

Program 5-9. Defined string function.

DEF FN DAY$(D) = **MID$**(WEEK$, D*9 + 1, 9)
WEEK$ = "Sunday   Monday   Tuesday Wednesday"
WEEK$ = WEEK$ + "Thursday Friday   Saturday"

INPUT "Enter day number"; N
PRINT "You selected"; FN DAY$(N)

Programmer-defined functions come in especially handy when a scientific or mathematic formula is used at several points in a program. Define it once and simply refer to it after that. It saves a lot of typing and energy that we would rather spend on other elements of the program.

Problems for Section 5-4

1. Define a function to convert centigrade to Fahrenheit. To get from centigrade to Fahrenheit, multiply by 9/5 and add 32.
2. Define a function to convert Fahrenheit to centigrade. To go from Fahrenheit to centigrade we subtract 32 and multiply by 5/9.
3. Define a function to return the average of three numbers.
4. If someone responds to the question in Program 5-9 with a decimal number such as 3.8, it produces strange results. Modify the function definition to avoid this.
5. If a day number greater than 6 is entered in Program 5-9, FN DAY$(N) is blank. Modify the function definition by applying modular arithmetic to the day number to eliminate the problem.

5-5. Variable Typing and Precision

DEFINT, DEFSNG, DEFDBL, DEFSTR

Up to this point we have had two types of variables: numeric and string. In the decimal version of Microsoft BASIC the default for numeric variables is 14-digit double precision. In the binary version of Microsoft BASIC the default for numeric variables is 7-digit single precision. The binary version is subject to round-off error. For example, we saw in Program 3-7 that the decimal version produced 87.333333333333, while the binary version came up with 87.33334. We can use DEFINT, DEFSNG, DEFDBL, or DEFSTR to assign other types to groups of variables.

Integers are whole numbers in the range -32768 to 32767. Integers are stored in two bytes in memory and are handled in the same manner in the decimal and binary versions. Many programs use only integers.

DEFINT A-Z

at the beginning of a program limits all numeric variables in a program to integers by declaring that variables beginning with letters in the range from A to Z are of type integer. A variety of beginning letters can be selected with a statement such as the following:

DEFINT A, F-H, X, Z

The program can still work with string variables using the familiar dollar sign.

Single-precision numbers are defined differently in the decimal and binary versions. Both versions store single precision numbers in 4 bytes. The decimal version allows up to 6 digits of precision for numbers in the range $-9.99999E+62$ to $9.99999E+62$ where "E+62" means "times 10 raised to the 62nd power." The binary version allows up to 7 digits of precision for numbers in the range $3.402824E+38$ to $-3.402824E+38$. This is the default precision. Following the statement:

DEFSNG A, C, T-W

all variables beginning with the letters named will be limited to single precision.

Double-precision numbers are also defined differently in the decimal and binary versions. Both versions store double-precision numbers in 8 bytes. The decimal version allows up to 14 digits of precision for numbers in the range $-9.9999999999999D+62$ to $9.9999999999999D+62$, where "D+62" means "times 10 raised to the 62nd power." This is the default condition for all calculations. The binary version allows up to 16 digits of precision for numbers in the range 1.797693134862316D+308 to −1.797693134862316D+308. The binary version offers a greater range of values, at the cost of some round-off error. Built-in functions in the binary version perform calculations in the precision of the argument of the function. DEFDBL declares a selection of letters for double precision variables.

For string variables, DEFSTR may be used to select a collection of letters. Each character stored in a string variable requires one byte of memory.

%, !, #, and $ Variable Type Indicators

We are familiar with the clear visual distinction between numeric variables and string variables made possible by the use of the dollar sign in string variable names. Using other special symbols will enable us to make the same clear distinction between the various types of numeric variables. The percent sign is for integers, the exclamation point is for single precision variables, and the number sign is for double-precision variables. These symbols prevail over a declaration made with a DEF . . . statement. You are encouraged to use these symbols when the variable type is important. All of the following statements make it clear what precision is in use:

```
NUMBEROFITEMS% = NUMBEROFITEMS% + 1
ROOT! = SQR(NUMBER!)
XCOORDINATE# = R# * SIN(THETA#)
STORENAMES$ = "GERTRUDE"
```

5-6. Subroutines (GOSUB and RETURN)

A subroutine is a side excursion. The program is diverted from what it is doing to execute program statements in another part of the program. Following this, it comes back to work on what it was doing when it took the excursion in the first place. We direct the computer to make the side excursion with the keyword GOSUB, and we signal the end of the excursion with the keyword RETURN.

Subroutines are useful whenever a particular process is required at various points in the same program. For example, a program might request dates entered from the keyboard. A subroutine could check the response to make sure that the numbers could be a real date. The same program might request part numbers in a special format in several places. A subroutine could check them all.

Defined functions are also useful for processes that are repeated within a program. But, while the work of a function must be accomplished with a single assignment statement, a subroutine may contain as many statements as are practical. And with a defined function, the function name itself takes on a value, which a subroutine cannot do.

The statement

GOSUB Special

causes the computer to begin executing program statements beginning at the line labeled Special. This is just like

GOTO Special

except that with GOSUB, BASIC remembers its place to return to.

For GOSUB to work properly, BASIC must encounter a RETURN statement. The program statements beginning with Special: and ending with the RETURN statement make up the subroutine. This makes a clearly defined package. Executing a RETURN without first executing a GOSUB constitutes a "RETURN without GOSUB" error. The way to avoid this error is to place subroutines at the end of the program and include an END statement just before the first subroutine in the program. BASIC does not check for GOSUB without RETURN. That is the programmer's responsibility. And, programming

GOSUB Trying

when there is no line label Trying: in the program will cause the "Undefined label" error box to appear.

Suppose we are writing a program that has a lot of yes–no questions in it. We can write a subroutine to handle this and use it from many places in the program. It is common practice to accept Y for yes and N for no and allow either uppercase or lowercase. See Program 5-10.

Program 5-10. Subroutine to process yes–no answers.

```
YesNo:
    REM ** Yes-No processor
    PRINT QUESTION$; : INPUT ANS$ : ANS$ = UCASE$(LEFT$(ANS$,1))
    IF ANS$ = "Y" THEN ANS = 1 : GOTO EndYesNo
    IF ANS$ = "N" THEN ANS = 0 : GOTO EndYesNo
    PRINT "Answer Yes or No, Please"
    PRINT
    GOTO YesNo
EndYesNo:
    RETURN
```

Now we have a subroutine that we can use from anywhere in our program with

    QUESTION$ = "Next menu" : **GOSUB** YesNo
    IF ANS = 1 **THEN** YesRoutine **ELSE** NoRoutine

This technique saves us from having to include the actual program statements to process input from the keyboard at numerous points in our program. It enables us to associate the whole idea of handling the keyboard with the simple statement

    GOSUB YesNo

Thus, we can concentrate on another portion of the program. For larger programming tasks, it is impossible to keep the entire solution in mind at any particular instant in time. So any device we can develop that helps to simplify what we have to think about at any one moment is desirable.

It often works out that subroutines we write for one program are useful in other programs. Once this begins to happen, it becomes worthwhile to develop more sophisticated routines than we might for just one application. For example, suppose we are working on a routine to accept the date from the keyboard. We might keep the year in the range 0 to 99, keep the month in the range 1 to 12, and keep the day in the range 1 to 31 and be done with it. At the next level of sophistication we might also check that for month number 2, the day is in the range 1 to 29. Finally, we might develop a routine that distinguishes the 30- and 31-day months and accounts for leap year. Once we have this routine fully tested, we may then use it in all future programs dealing with a calendar.

ON N GOSUB

GOSUB can be used to select one of a collection of subroutines

ON N **GOSUB** EnterData, EditAddress, DisplayStatus, CleanUp

selects one of the four subroutines listed in the statement according to the value of N. The subroutines are numbered 1 to 4, so values of N from 1 to 4 make sense for this statement. For N equals 0 and for N greater than the number of line labels in the list, BASIC simply proceeds to the next statement in sequence with no GOSUB diversion. Note that ON N GOTO can be used in exactly the same way to select from among a list of line labels to execute next according to a value.

As we accumulate a collection of useful subroutines, we can use MERGE to incorporate them into new programs. (See Appendix B.)

Problems for Section 5-6

1. From Program 5-2 (finding factor pairs), write a subroutine to find all prime factors of a value entered from the keyboard.

2. Write a subroutine to process a date in the form YY/MM/DD. Note that dates in this form can be sorted to arrange in real chronological order. Verify that it could be a real date with another subroutine. Then create a string holding that date in the form YY-Mmm-DD. For example: 75/12/25 becomes 75-Dec-25.

3. Write a subroutine to convert times entered at the keyboard to times on a 24-hour clock. First, verify that it could be a real time with another subroutine. Then hold the time in a string variable in the form hh:mm:ss.

5-7. Subprograms (CALL and SUB)

Subprograms are similar to subroutines in that they are both executed as a diversion from the execution of program statements that appear sequentially within a program and they both return to execute the statement immediately following the one that caused the diversion. However, variables named in a subprogram have no connection with the variables of the same name in the rest of the program. Variables within a subprogram are referred to as *local variables*. This means that we may develop subprograms to include in many different programs without any worry about coordinating variable names. BASIC provides a simple mechanism for transmitting values from the main program to a subprogram and back. Program 5-11 demonstrates a subprogram to process yes–no answers. We use this example to compare subroutines and subprograms.

Program 5-11. Subprogram to process yes–no answers.

```
REM ** Test Yes-No processing subprogram
BeginTest:
    QUESTION$ = "Do it - (Yes or No)"
    CALL ProcessYesNo(QUESTION$, ANSWER)
    PRINT "Numeric equivalent (1=Yes, 0=No)"; ANSWER
    GOTO BeginTest

SUB ProcessYesNo(A$, R) STATIC
YesNo:
    PRINT A$; : INPUT R$ : R$ = UCASE$(LEFT$(R$,1))
    IF R$ = "Y" THEN R = 1 : GOTO EndYesNo
    IF R$ = "N" THEN R = 0 : GOTO EndYesNo
        PRINT "Answer Yes or No, Please"
        PRINT
        GOTO YesNo
EndYesNo:
    END SUB
```

Subprograms are invoked with a CALL statement. They must begin with a SUB statement and end with an END SUB statement. The CALL statement names the subprogram and lists values for use in the subprogram. The SUB statement identifies the subprogram name and lists variables for the subprogram to hold the values that come from the main program. In addition, version 2.0 of Microsoft BASIC for the Macintosh requires the keyword STATIC. STATIC causes variables within a subprogram to maintain their values from any previous execution of the subprogram.

The statement

CALL ProcessYesNo(QUESTION$, ANSWER)

passes a string value in QUESTION$ and a numeric value in ANSWER to the subprogram named "ProcessYesNo" and causes the subprogram to be executed.

The statement

SUB ProcessYesNo(A$, R) **STATIC**

identifies the beginning of the subprogram ProcessYesNo. A$ receives the string contents of QUESTION$ and R receives the numeric contents of ANSWER as named in the CALL statement above. The variable lists are simply lined up in the same order in the SUB statement as the CALL statement. The required STATIC keyword is included.

The statement

END SUB

marks the end of a subprogram.

EXIT SUB

We can cause program execution to leave a subprogram at any point and pick up at the statement following the CALL statement. The statement

IF R$ = "N" **THEN** R = 0 : **GOTO** EndYesNo

in Program 5-11 could have used EXIT SUB as follows:

IF R$ = "N" **THEN** R = 0 : **EXIT SUB**

In this case, the line label EndYesNo would be unnecessary.

SHARED

The statement

SHARED NAM1, NETPAY, X, Y

within a subprogram causes the named variables to be shared by the main program and the subprogram in which the SHARED statement appears. These variables are relieved of local status.

Error Checking for Subprograms

BASIC searches all programs for one of seven subprogram errors before executing. The program will not execute if any of the following errors exists:

> Tried To declare a **SUB** within a **SUB**
> **SUB** already defined
> Missing **STATIC** in **SUB** statement
> **EXIT SUB** outside of a subprogram
> **END SUB** outside of a subprogram
> **SUB** without **END SUB**
> **SHARED** outside of a subprogram

More About CALL

The keyword CALL may be omitted. In this case, the parentheses must be left out. The following two statements are equivalent:

> **CALL** Testing(LETTER$, NUM1)
> Testing LETTER$, NUM1

This is why the error "Undefined subprogram" occurs so often. Lots of typographical errors result in lines that look like a subprogram call, especially when we accidentally insert a space in a line label. Occasionally a condition arises in which an error box displays an error message and the CALL statement is outlined as the source of the problem, but the CALL statement is correct. Most likely the error is in the SUB statement.

In a CALL statement, data may be passed to a subprogram not only in variables but also directly as values, as long as they are enclosed in parentheses. For example,

> **CALL** Testing ((4), (A+B), X)

passes 4, the sum of A and B, and the value of X to the subprogram Testing. On the other hand, the subprogram uses those positions in the argument list only to name variables to receive information from the main program. The subprogram cannot directly specify values to be transferred to the main program in an argument list. Instead, when the END SUB statement is executed, whatever values are stored in the variables named in the SUB statement are automatically returned to the corresponding variables named in the CALL statement. In the example above, the only value the subprogram will return to the main program will be the value of the third variable in the SUB statement argument list, which will be held in X in the main program.

No DEF statement may appear within a subprogram. That will generate the "Statement illegal within subprogram" error box. Functions DEFined in the main program are active within subprograms.

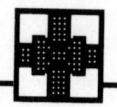

Summary

In addition to subroutines, we now have subprograms at our disposal. They both serve as small segments of larger programs. Subprograms are most useful when they perform jobs needed in many different programs. Subroutines require the keywords GOSUB and RETURN, and subprograms require the SUB... STATIC and END SUB statements. The keyword CALL may be omitted as long as the parentheses around the variable list are also omitted. EXIT SUB and SHARED are also used for subprograms.

Problems for Section 5-7

1. Write a subprogram to process a date in the form YYMMDD. Note that dates in this form can be sorted to arrange in real chronological order. Verify that it could be a real date with a subroutine. Then create a string holding that date in the form YY-Mmm-DD. Example: 751225 becomes 75-Dec-25.

2. Write a subprogram to return the current date in a string with the month name written out, for use in a report. For example, 03-16-1998 becomes March 16, 1998.

3. Write a subprogram to check a string for any nonalphabetic characters. (See the ASCII chart in Appendix D.)

4. Write a subprogram to take a string entered at the keyboard and return it with the first letter of every word capitalized and the rest lowercase.

5. Write a subprogram to allow substitution of one set of characters for another in a string. Get the string from the main program, and the character(s) to be replaced and the replacement from the keyboard.

6. Do the substitution of Problem 5 for every occurrence of the character(s) in the string.

CHAPTER 6

Picture Windows: Using Macintosh Features

Microsoft BASIC provides numerous statements and functions for using many of the Macintosh features. This chapter will introduce windows, pictures, menus, buttons, dialog boxes, and event trapping. Many of these features will be used in future programs as appropriate.

Most of the programs in this chapter will be working with windows, and are oriented toward producing special effects on the screen. For this reason, it will soon be especially apparent that you should clear the desktop just before running a program by clicking the "go-away box" on the List windows and the Command window. Then they will not interfere.

6-1. Windows

Programming is routinely done with three or four windows. The process of writing BASIC programs revolves around the use of two List windows, the Command window, and the output window. Various WINDOW statements and the WINDOW function enable us to write BASIC programs that control windows. Up to four output windows of four different types are available.

WINDOW Statements

An output window is established with a statement of the following form:

WINDOW number, title$, (x1,y1)–(x2,y2), type

Window numbers 1 to 4 are allowed. The default output window is window number 1.

The title is a string that will be displayed in the title bar, if the output window has one (see the discussion on types that follows). If the title is null, "Untitled" will appear in the title bar.

The expression (x1,y1)–(x2,y2) is used to define the boundaries of the window. The x and y values are measured in pixels. Everything that is displayed on the Macintosh screen is made up of pixels. A pixel is the smallest displayable unit. The normal default output window that appears when BASIC is first opened is 491 pixels wide and 254 pixels high. The output window presented when we execute a program by double-clicking the BASIC program icon on the desktop is 491 by 299 pixels. The entire Macintosh screen is 512 pixels wide and 342 pixels high. In all cases the pixel numbering begins with 0. For example, the pixels in the 491 by 254 output window are numbered 0 to 490 from left to right across and 0 to 253 from top to bottom. The pixel numbering for the Macintosh screen begins in the upper left corner of the menu bar, and the pixel numbering within any window begins in the upper left corner of that window.

The default output window that appears when BASIC is started is located with its upper left corner at (2,41) of the Macintosh screen. However, numbering within the window begins in the corner of the window and not in the corner of the screen. So, if we are referring to the screen, the point is called (2,41), but if we are referring to the window, the point is called (0,0).

The expression (x1,y1)–(x2,y2) is universally used to describe rectangles on the Macintosh screen and within windows. It will come up again and again.

There are four types of output windows. Type 1 is the usual output window with a title bar and a size box. This is referred to as a document window. When you double-click on the title bar or the size box, the window fills the screen; do it again, and the window returns to its original size. We can move a document window by dragging the title bar, and we can change its size with the size box in the usual manner. Type 2 is a box with a two-line border. This is the usual dialog box we see often on the Macintosh. Error messages are displayed in such a box. Type 3 has a single-line border. Type 4 has a single-line border with a shadow.

Values of -1 through -4 may be used for window type. Windows with negative types prevent use of the mouse to select anything outside the active window. Any attempt to do so is rewarded with a beep. Many of the dialog boxes displayed by BASIC are of this type.

Each type of output window may be used for display in all of the ways that we have been using the default output window. INPUT statements may request information from the keyboard in any type output window. Type 1 is the only version whose shape and location can be manipulated directly with the mouse. (We can move it by dragging the title bar and change the size with the size box.)

Only the window number in the WINDOW statement is required. If any feature is left off the end of the statement, the value assigned in a previous WINDOW statement for the corresponding window remains in effect. But consider the following WINDOW statement:

WINDOW 4,,,1

In the case where the title is skipped over, BASIC will display "Untitled" in the title bar of a type 1 output window. To get around this, use " " to produce an empty space. If the coordinates of the rectangle are skipped over, BASIC will use the dimensions of the normal default output window that appears when BASIC is started for type 1 windows. For types 2 through 4, the default rectangle is (200,60)–(400,200).

Program 6-1 demonstrates many of the features of output windows.

Program 6-1. Demonstrate output windows.

```
WINDOW 3,"Title bar",(1,41)–(200,72),1
    PRINT "Window No. 3: Type 1"
WINDOW 2,,(211,41)–(410,72),2
    PRINT "Window No. 2: Type 2"
WINDOW 1,,(1,100)–(250,151),4
    PRINT "Window No. 1" : PRINT "Type 4"
WINDOW 4,,(100,80)–(230,250),3
    PRINT "Window No. 4" : PRINT "Type 3"

Select:
    INPUT "Next window"; X% : IF X% = 0 THEN Quit
    IF X% > 0 AND X% < 5 THEN WINDOW X%
    GOTO Select

Quit:
    FOR K = 4 TO 1 STEP -1
        WINDOW CLOSE K
    NEXT K
    WINDOW 1,,,1
    END
```

The first four WINDOW statements create windows. For windows 1, 2, and 4, we skipped over the title because none of them is a type 1 window and no title is needed. In the statement

IF X% > 0 AND X% < 5 THEN WINDOW X%

the window X% is made current and active without changing any of the characteristics established when it was created with the earlier WINDOW statement. Being active means that the window can accept data from the keyboard, as in an INPUT statement, INKEY$, or INPUT$, and it will respond to mouse activity. Being current means that the window shows all display.

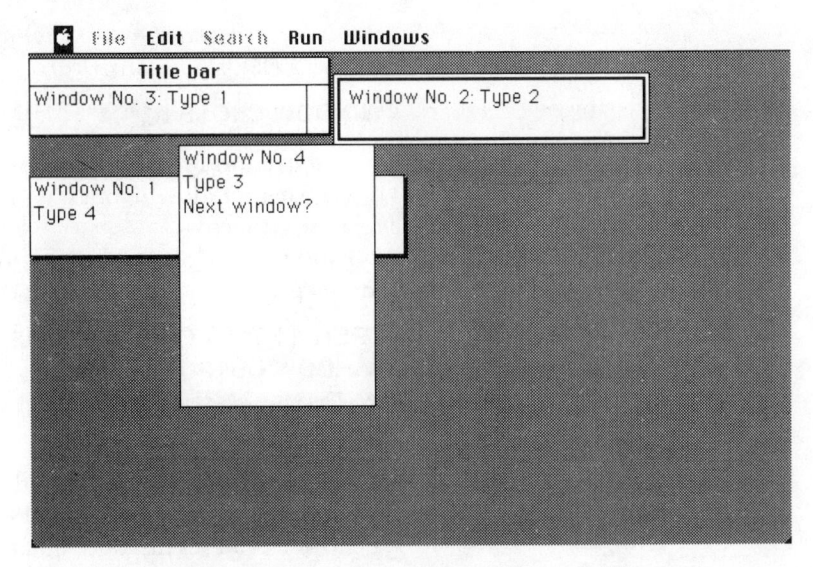

Figure 6-1. Execution of Program 6-1.

It will be worth typing in Program 6-1 to help become familiar with the effects of having several output windows on the screen at the same time. Respond to the "Next window" question with 0 to quit.

Program 6-1 creates one window of each type. Note that window 3 and window 2 are both 199 pixels wide and 31 pixels high, but window number 3 is taller than window number 2. That is because the title bar is outside the window. Windows of every type having the same vertical distance in the window definition have the same interior space available vertically. This is not the case for horizontal distance. Type 1 windows are narrower than the others by 15 pixels. That 15 pixel vertical band is where the size box appears in the lower right corner of the output window.

When an output window is created, it is both current and active. It may be that we want to have INPUT statements processed in one window and a display going on in a different window.

WINDOW OUTPUT n

makes window n the current output window without changing the active window number. To change the active window and retain the current output window, two statements are required. First execute a WINDOW m statement to make m both active and current, then execute a WINDOW OUTPUT n statement to make n current.

When we are done with a window, it may be closed with a WINDOW CLOSE statement.

WINDOW CLOSE n

removes the window numbered n from the screen. WINDOW n will bring back window n, but it will not retain the full display that was formerly there.

A window may also be output to a graphics printer. Once the window is prepared, the following three statements are required:

OPEN "LPT1:" **FOR OUTPUT AS** #n
WINDOW OUTPUT #n
... Display statements here ...
CLOSE #n

OPEN, CLOSE, and LPT1: are treated in more detail in the chapters on files, but for the purposes of WINDOW OUTPUT, it is sufficient to type these statements and make sure that the value of n is consistent.

WINDOW Function

The WINDOW function provides information about output windows.

WINDOW(n)

returns values according to the value of n.

WINDOW(0)   The number of the active output window. If no window is active, 0 is returned.

WINDOW(1)   The number of the current output window to which the next display will go.

WINDOW(2)   The width of the current output window in pixels. Using the WIDTH function to measure the pixel width of a string, we can determine whether a string will fit on one line in the current output window. The default text in Microsoft BASIC version 2.00 begins text display at pixel 2.

WINDOW(3)   The height of the current output window in pixels. Using this and the height of the printed line, we can assure that the display fits entirely within the current output window. The default text in Microsoft BASIC version 2.00 requires 12 pixels for the first line and 16 for the rest.

WINDOW(4)   The x coordinate of the drawing pen in the current output window. This is the horizontal pixel position where the next character will be displayed. The starting point of a character is the lower left corner.

WINDOW(5)   The y coordinate of the drawing pen in the current output window. This is the vertical pixel position where the next character will be displayed.

6-2. Pictures

PICTURE gives us the ability to take a snapshot of an output window. Following this, we may manipulate the image. Pictures can be displayed at any point in an output window and scaled to suit any purpose. We can even save pictures in files on disk. This means we can create a catalog of pictures on disk and use them in any program. Pictures may be text, displays produced by graphics statements and Macintosh Quickdraw ROM routines, or any combination of these.

PICTURE statements

PICTURE ON and PICTURE OFF are used to create a picture without displaying it. Following PICTURE ON and preceding PICTURE OFF, any display that would otherwise appear in an output window is saved in memory as a PICTURE. Once the picture exists, the PICTURE statement may be used to produce the actual display in an output window. For our first example, let's display a message. Study Program 6-2.

Program 6-2. Introduce PICTURE ON, PICTURE OFF, and PICTURE.

```
PICTURE ON
  PRINT "Demonstrate PICTURE"
PICTURE OFF
PICTURE
PICTURE (200,10)
```

In Program 6-2 the PRINT statement between the PICTURE ON and PICTURE OFF statements creates the image that the PICTURE statements use later in the program. The statement

PICTURE

simply displays the image created between the most recent PICTURE ON and PICTURE OFF statement pair. The statement

PICTURE (200,10)

causes the same image to be displayed but beginning at the point (200,10) within the output window. See the result in Figure 6-2.

```
Program 6-2
Demonstrate PICTURE
                    Demonstrate PICTURE
```

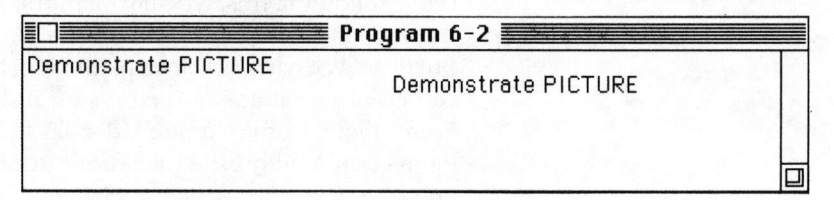

Figure 6-2. Execution of Program 6-2.

Once we have learned some of the graphics statements and the ROM routines, we can use them to create more elaborate images.

The PICTURE statement can use (x1,y1)-(x2,y2) to scale the display. The statement

PICTURE (20,40)-(180,140)

uses (20,40) in the current output window as the upper left corner of the display and uses 160 to scale in the horizontal direction and 100 to scale in the vertical direction. The width of the rectangle in PICTURE is 180 minus 20 and the height is 140 minus 40. Suppose the above picture statement is executed with an output window that is 320 wide and 200 high. The display will be scaled to .5 times normal. The scale is determined according to the ratio of the rectangle mentioned in the PICTURE statement to the dimensions of the output window in which the image is displayed. The dimensions of a rectangle (x1,y1)-(x2,y2) are x2-x1 pixels wide and y2-y1 pixels high. If we want to describe a rectangle beginning at the point (X,Y) that is WIDE pixels wide and HIGH pixels high we would use the following definition:

(X,Y)–(X+WIDE,Y+HIGH)

If we desire an image reduced to half the original size, we simply set WIDE equal to half the width of the window as determined with the WINDOW(2) function and set HIGH equal to half the height of the window as determined with the WINDOW(3) function. Images can be scaled by different values vertically and horizontally to produce stretched or distorted pictures.

It can be an interesting challenge to write expressions that move the rectangle around within a window and change the size of an image to produce a desirable display. Try making the rectangle successively larger or smaller to simulate motion toward or away from the observer. Remember, the WINDOW function can be used to return the width and height of the current window and WIDTH(X$) returns the width of a string in pixels. So, it is possible to assure that messages fall entirely within the borders of an output window.

We have been using the PICTURE statement to display an image created in a PICTURE ON–PICTURE OFF sequence. The PICTURE statement can also take the image from a string variable. The string is assigned with the PICTURE$ function.

PICTURE$

The PICTURE$ function transfers a copy of an image created with PICTURE ON and PICTURE OFF to a string. The string contains all information required for the PICTURE statement to produce the display. This means that we can have several images stored in strings and display them as needed with the PICTURE statement. The statement

X$ = PICTURE$

following a PICTURE ON–PICTURE OFF sequence does the job. The statement

PICTURE, X$

produces the display with no change in size.

Program 6-3 saves one message in A$ and another in B$. Following this, the program displays them in two different windows.

144 Chapter 6: Picture Windows Using Macintosh Features

Program 6-3. Introduce PICTURE$ function.

```
PICTURE ON
  PRINT "First message"
PICTURE OFF
A$ = PICTURE$

PICTURE ON
  PRINT "Second message"
PICTURE OFF
B$ = PICTURE$
WINDOW CLOSE 1

WINDOW 3,"Window 3",(2,41)-(180,150),1
PICTURE, A$

WINDOW 2,"Window 2",(202,41)-(380,150),1
PICTURE, B$
```

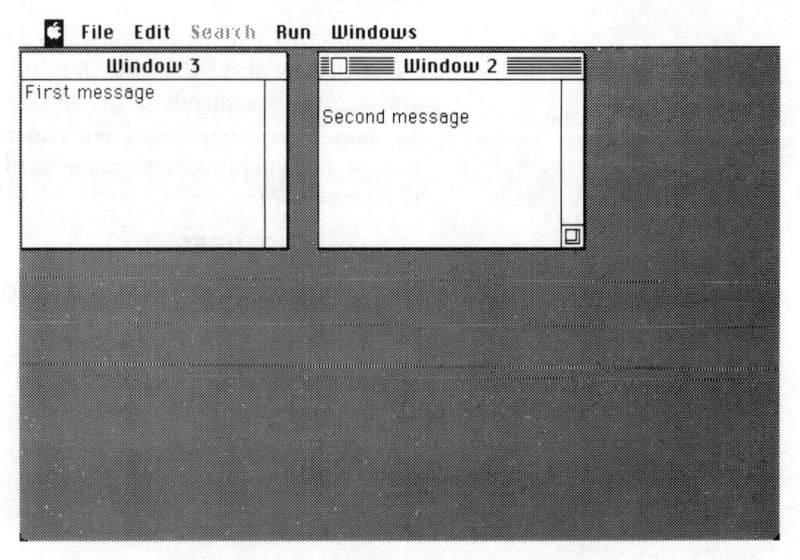

Figure 6-3. Execution of Program 6-3.

Notice that the message in window 2 is displayed on the second line of the window, even though nothing is displayed on the first line. That is because "First message" and "Second message" were created one following the other while the same output window was current. The way to avoid that is to use CLS to clear the screen before the second picture is created.

The PICTURE statement can also specify a rectangle to scale the display or just specify the starting coordinates using one of the following forms:

PICTURE (x1,y1)-(x2,y2), x$
PICTURE (x1,y1), x$

Now that we have the ability to store images in strings, it makes sense to think about saving them in disk files. While sequential files are treated in more detail in Chapter 11, this is a good time to learn enough to do this one job. Once we have an image stored in a string we can save it in a file with just three statements as follows:

OPEN "Save Picture" **FOR OUTPUT AS** #1
PRINT #1, A$
CLOSE #1

where "Save Picture" is the name of the file that will contain the string A$. The OPEN statement makes the file available to the current program. The keyword OUTPUT notifies BASIC that the program will send data out to the file on the disk. We will use the keyword INPUT for a program to bring data from the file on the disk into the program. The PRINT # statement causes A$ to "go out to the file." The CLOSE statement performs the necessary housekeeping for the next program to correctly retrieve the string from the file. In this program segment, #1 designates the file number, or channel. Channels that we open in a program are numbered so that we may keep track of several open files at the same time. To use a different file, simply change the name in the OPEN statement. To use additional files at the same time, use other channels (in the range 1 to 255). We can use the same channel for files opened one after another as long as the CLOSE statement is executed before the next OPEN statement. Program 6-4 just sends a picture string out to a file. The program causes no display.

Program 6-4. Write a picture string to a file.

```
PICTURE ON
  PRINT "Macintosh picture"
PICTURE OFF
A$ = PICTURE$

OPEN "Save Picture" FOR OUTPUT AS #1
PRINT #1, A$
CLOSE #1
```

It requires only three statements to retrieve the picture string from the file "Save Picture." First, open the file for INPUT. Second, input the characters from the file. We need the INPUT$ function for this.

INPUT$(x,#1)

returns x characters from the file on channel #1. In order to do that we need to determine the number of characters in the file. The LOF function is made just for this.

LOF(1)

returns the number of characters in the file on channel #1. So, the statement

A$ = INPUT$(LOF(1), #1)

copies the picture string from the file to the string A$. Now the string is ready for the PICTURE statement. See Program 6-5.

Program 6-5. Retrieve a picture string from a file.

```
OPEN "Save Picture" FOR INPUT AS #1
A$ = INPUT$(LOF(1), #1)
CLOSE #1

WINDOW 2,,(10,50)-(400,250),4
PICTURE, A$
```

It would be a good idea to type in Program 6-4 and Program 6-5 to convince yourself that they work as described. Then experiment with the programs to become more familiar with the various PICTURE features.

Any picture that is displayed on the Macintosh screen can be read into a Microsoft BASIC program. Images can be passed between MacPaint and BASIC using the Macintosh Clipboard. The Clipboard must be named "CLIP:Picture" for this purpose. Suppose you want to display a desktop icon in a BASIC program. This is done in three steps. First, save a screen image to a file by holding down the Command and Shift keys while pressing 3. The first time this is done on any disk, the file "Screen 0" is created. Following this, files up to "Screen 9" are saved. Second, use MacPaint to access the screen image file created in step one. Isolate the picture you want to display with a BASIC program and use Cut or Copy in the Edit menu. Quit MacPaint. Finally, load the picture from the Clipboard with the following three statements:

OPEN "CLIP:Picture" **FOR INPUT AS** #1
A$ = **INPUT$(LOF**(1), #1)
CLOSE #1

You can move a picture from a BASIC program to MacPaint by writing the picture to the Clipboard in a BASIC program as follows:

OPEN "CLIP:Picture" **FOR OUTPUT AS** #1
PRINT #1, A$
CLOSE #1

and then using Paste from the Edit menu in MacPaint. Just make sure that the Clipboard is not overwritten before you get into MacPaint.

SCROLL

The statement

SCROLL (x1,y1)–(x2,y2),x,y

causes the portion of the current output window defined by (x1,y1) –(x2,y2) to be moved x pixels vertically and y pixels horizontally. The scroll rectangle coordinates are measured relative to the current output window. The image is scrolled within the defined rectangle. Once an image has been scrolled outside the defined rectangle, it disappears and cannot be scrolled back. The program would have to explicitly reproduce the image. SCROLL cannot be used to change the scale of an image.

Program 6-6 demonstrates scrolling. The rabbit "runs" about within the inner window. Type the program in and experiment. The picture of the rabbit is produced by pressing Option-Shift-grave-accent. The grave-accent key is the leftmost key in the top row of the keyboard. Once you learn about the graphics features, you will be able to do more with SCROLL.

Program 6-6. Run rabbit Run, using SCROLL.

```
WINDOW 1,,(90,40)–(210,160),2
WINDOW 2,,(100,50)–(200,150),3
LOCATE 2, 4 : PRINT "     🐇    " 'CHR$(217)
X = 32 : Y = 28

BeginScroll:
    DX = INT(RND*21–10) : DY = INT(RND*11–5)
    IF X + DX > 80 OR X + DX < 20 THEN DX = 0
    IF Y + DY > 80 OR Y + DY < 20 THEN DY = 0
    X = X + DX : Y = Y + DY
    SCROLL (5,5)–(95,95),DX,DY
    FOR K = 1 TO 150 : NEXT K 'Delay
    GOTO BeginScroll
```

6-3. Menus

While Microsoft BASIC is running, the menu bar contains five menus in addition to the Macintosh Apple menu. A collection of MENU statements and functions allows us to replace existing menus or add new ones.

A menu is created with a statement of the following form:

MENU number, item number, state, label$

Menu numbers 1 to 10 are allowed, counting from left to right. Think of the Apple as menu 0.

An item number of 0 refers to the entire menu. Item numbers from 1 through 20 refer to items within the menu.

The state of a menu item can range from 0 to 2. A 0 specifies that the item is disabled. A disabled item is indicated by a shaded label. 1 specifies a normal, useable item. 2 specifies a useable item that is displayed with a check mark.

The menu label is a string. For menu item 0 the label serves as the title in the menu bar. It is up to the programmer to worry about whether the titles fit in the menu bar. The other menu item labels are displayed when the menu is activated with the mouse.

Once a menu exists, the state of an item can be changed with a statement of the following form:

MENU number, item number, state

Program 6-7a creates a menu labeled "Appetizer" containing 4 items.

Program 6-7a. Create a menu.

```
MENU 6,0,1, "Appetizer"
MENU 6,1,1, "Stuffed Mushrooms"
MENU 6,2,1, "Soup du Jour"
MENU 6,3,1, "Shrimp Cocktail"
MENU 6,4,1, "none"
```

As soon as the program finishes executing, though, our menu will disappear. The program must provide the opportunity to actually use the menu. A variety of statements and functions is provided for this purpose. First the menu functions.

MENU(0) returns the number of the most recently selected menu. Menus are selected in the usual way by placing the mouse on the title and pressing the mouse button. If no menu has been selected, MENU(0) returns 0. This only applies to menus created by a BASIC program. BASIC programs cannot control the default menus. A selection occurs when an item within the menu is selected. Merely opening the menu doesn't activate MENU(0). After MENU(0) is accessed in a program its value is reset. This means that we can only examine its value once. If the program needs the menu number in more than one place, it must be saved in a variable. For our Appetizer menu, we will poll the menu until a selection has been made. The key to polling is that the BASIC program must continously monitor the activity of interest. This means that BASIC program statements must be executed over and over again to catch the menu activity. Once a selection has been made in a menu and the value of MENU(0) contains the position of the menu in the menu bar, MENU(1) returns the position of the selected item within the menu. Program 6-7b uses polling for a selection in menu 6.

Program 6-7b. Wait for a menu selection.

```
REM ** Wait for a menu selection
Poll:
    SELECTION = MENU(0)
    IF SELECTION <> 6 THEN Poll
    GOSUB Appetizer
```

When the value of MENU(0) is 6 in Program 6-7b the subroutine at Appetizer will be executed.

Whenever a menu title is selected, it is highlighted. As Program 6-7b is written, the title will stay highlighted until another menu is accessed. This serves to remind the user which menu was accessed most recently. The MENU statement restores normal display once the new selection has been processed.

MENU

removes highlighting from a menu label.

This is taken care of in Program 6-7.

Program 6-7. A menu program

```
MENU 6,0,1,"Appetizer"
MENU 6,1,1,"Stuffed Mushrooms"
MENU 6,2,1,"Soup du Jour"
MENU 6,3,1,"Shrimp Cocktail"
MENU 6,4,1,"none"

REM** Wait for a menu selection
Poll:
    SELECTION=MENU(0)
    IF SELECTION <> 6 THEN Poll
    GOSUB Appetizer
    MENU

    PRINT "Your choice:"
    PRINT TAB (9); APPETIZERS$
Key: IF LEN (INKEY$) = 0 THEN Key
END

Appetizer:
    ON MENU(1) GOSUB A1, A2, A3, A4
    RETURN

A1: APPETIZER$ = "Stuffed Mushrooms" : RETURN
A2: APPETIZER$ = "Soup du Jour" : RETURN
A3: APPETIZER$ = "Shrimp Cocktail" : RETURN
A4: APPETIZER$ = "none" : RETURN
```

Notice the statement

    Key: **IF LEN(INKEY$) = 0 THEN** Key

The program will wait until the user presses any key. This keeps the display intact for the user to examine. Once the END statement is executed, the menu bar is restored to the normal one for Microsoft BASIC.

We might want to run a restaurant using the Macintosh. We could put "Breakfast", "Lunch", and "Dinner" on the menu bar. Once a customer has selected the meal, the program needs to display the appropriate menu labels. We can replace any menu with another. A menu can be eliminated with a statement such as the following:

    MENU 8,0,0,""

The menu bar is restored to the default condition with

    MENU RESET

Following this, the normal Microsoft BASIC menus are again available and the menus created in a BASIC program are gone.

MENU and Event Trapping

Polling is a technique for monitoring menu activity using explicit program statements executed repeatedly to determine whether a menu item has been selected. Event trapping is a built-in feature that does the monitoring automatically. It is a lot like setting a mousetrap. A program can "set a trap" and then do other things. When the trap is "sprung" BASIC automatically responds. The following two statements set this up:

    ON MENU GOSUB ProcessMenu
    MENU ON

ON MENU GOSUB is special. Following ON MENU GOSUB and MENU ON, no matter what is happening in the program, if a menu item is selected from a menu created by the BASIC program, execution will be diverted to the subroutine ProcessMenu. Following the RETURN statement execution takes up wherever it was when the interruption took place. And that could be anywhere in the program. It will not necessarily be the statement following the ON MENU GOSUB statement. Program 6-8 demonstrates this.

Program 6-8. Demonstrate ON MENU GOSUB.

```
MENU 6,0,1,"Appetizer"
MENU 6,1,1,"Stuffed Mushrooms"
MENU 6,2,1,"Soup du Jour"
MENU 6,3,1,"Shrimp Cocktail"
MENU 6,4,1,"none"
ON MENU GOSUB ProcessMenu
MENU ON

FOR COUNT = 1 TO 9.99999E+62 : NEXT COUNT
END

ProcessMenu:
    IF MENU(0) = 6 THEN GOSUB Appetizer : MENU
    RETURN

Appetizer:
    ON MENU(1) GOSUB A1, A2, A3, A4
    PRINT COUNT, APPETIZER$
    RETURN

A1: APPETIZER$ = "Stuffed Mushrooms" : RETURN
A2: APPETIZER$ = "Soup du Jour" : RETURN
A3: APPETIZER$ = "Shrimp Cocktail" : RETURN
A4: APPETIZER$ = "none" : RETURN
```

Program 6-8 spends most of its time counting, but if a menu item is selected, BASIC will interrupt its counting to display the selected menu item and the value of COUNT. Figure 6-4 shows the screen after several menu selections, but it is a good idea to type this program in and experiment with it to acquire a better feel for what is going on.

```
        File  Edit  Search  Run  Windows  Appetizer
                                          Stuffed Mushrooms
                              Program     Soup du Jour
    2091      Stuffed Mushrooms           Shrimp Cocktail
    3485      Shrimp Cocktail             none
    6779      none
    11573     Stuffed Mushrooms
    15067     Stuffed Mushrooms
    19161     Shrimp Cocktail
    26355     Soup du Jour
```

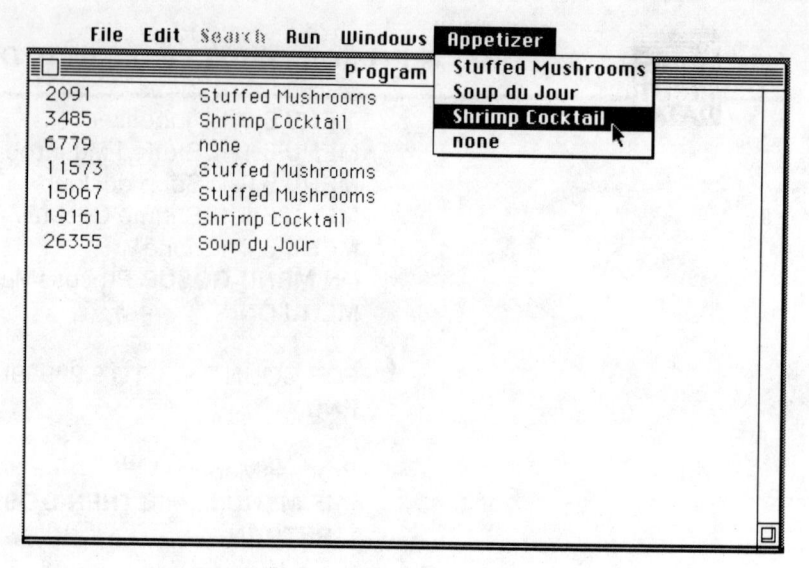

Figure 6-4. Execution of Program 6-8.

It may be desirable to disable menu trapping or turn it off just temporarily.

MENU OFF

disables menu trapping. Following MENU OFF, menu activity will no longer be noticed by the program. Upon executing a MENU ON statement the ON MENU GOSUB will again become effective. If we merely want to delay processing the menu activity until some special process is completed, MENU STOP is the statement to use.

MENU STOP

turns off the GOSUB called for in the ON MENU GOSUB statement, but if a MENU ON statement is executed, BASIC remembers if there was menu activity since the MENU STOP statement was executed.

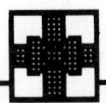

> **Summary**
>
> MENU number, item number, state, label$ creates a menu item. Omitting the menu label changes the state of an existing menu.
>
> MENU RESET restores the menu bar to the Microsoft BASIC default.
>
> MENU removes the highlighting on a menu title in the menu bar.
>
> MENU(0) returns the number of the most recently selected menu.
>
> MENU(1) returns the number of the selected item in the menu reported in MENU(0).
>
> MENU ON enables event trapping for menus.
>
> MENU OFF disables event trapping for menus.
>
> MENU STOP suspends event trapping for menus. A menu event is remembered if a MENU ON statement is subsequently executed.
>
> ON MENU GOSUB ProcessMenu sets up the subroutine to execute when a menu event occurs.

6-4. Buttons

The Macintosh user soon gets used to buttons. Many system messages are displayed on the screen with an OK button. Error messages in BASIC include an OK button. The dialog box for selecting a file using the Open item in the File menu from BASIC contains a number of buttons. Choose PRINT ... in the File menu and lots of buttons appear. We can include buttons in our BASIC program. We use a button by placing the mouse pointer in it and clicking. A button is created with a statement of the following form:

BUTTON number, state, label$, (x1,y1)–(x2,y2), type

Button number is used to identify buttons so that the program can keep track of them. Buttons in different output windows are independent. So, two buttons in the same program may have the same number as long as they go to different output windows.

State is used to display the condition of a button. State 0 means the button is inactive. An inactive button shows up as a dimmed image on the screen. State 1 indicates an active button that has not been selected. A state of 2 indicates an active currently selected button.

Label is a string that will be displayed with the button.

(x1,y1)–(x2,y2) is the familiar method for specifying the corners of a rectangle in an output window. The rectangle needs to be large enough to enclose the label and, for types 2 and 3, the button itself.

Type specifies shape. Type 1 is a rectangle (push button) with rounded corners the size of the rectangle specification and containing the label. Type 2 is a small square (check box) of predetermined size with the label displayed to the right. Type 3 is a small circle (radio button) with the label displayed to the right.

Program 6-9 is a simple program to display every kind of button.

Program 6-9. Display every button.

```
REM ** Display every kind of BUTTON
B = 0
PRINT : PRINT TAB(12); "Type State"
FOR TYPE = 1 TO 3
   FOR STATE = 0 TO 2
      B = B + 1
      PRINT TAB(12); TYPE; " "; STATE
      X$ = "Button" + STR$(B) : Y = (B+TYPE)*16
      BUTTON B,STATE,X$,(10,Y)–(90,Y+15),TYPE
   NEXT STATE
   PRINT
NEXT TYPE
```

Buttons

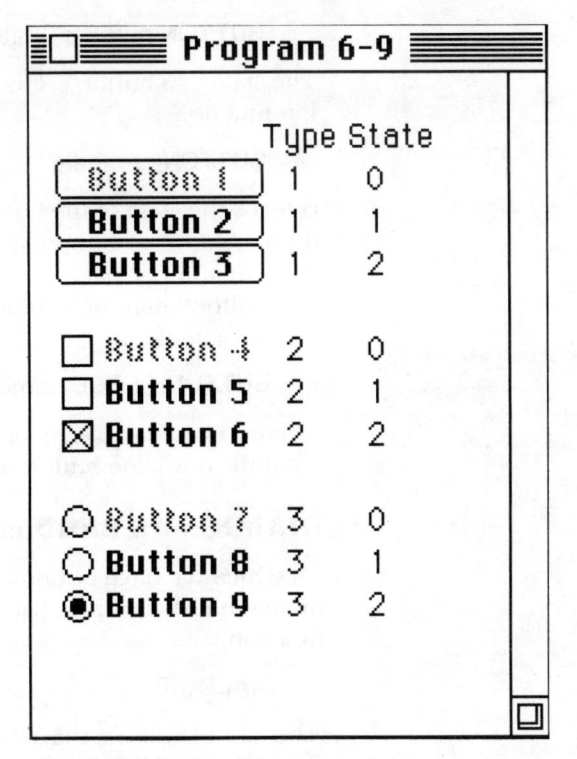

```
╔════════ Program 6-9 ════════╗

                    Type State
    ( Button 1 )     1     0
    ( Button 2 )     1     1
    ( Button 3 )     1     2

    ☐ Button 4       2     0
    ☐ Button 5       2     1
    ☒ Button 6       2     2

    ○ Button 7       3     0
    ○ Button 8       3     1
    ⦿ Button 9       3     2
```

Figure 6-5. Execution of Program 6-9.

Figure 6-5 shows the appearance of every button on the screen. The appearance of an active button changes while the mouse button is held down. Release the mouse button and the appearance returns to normal. A button statement must be executed with a state of 2 for a type 2 button to display the "X" or a type 3 button to display the dot in the middle. Type 1 buttons are the only ones for which we can control the size. Note, however, that for types 2 and 3 the rectangle specified in (x1,y1)–(x2,y2) must be large enough to enclose the label.

PRINT is affected while there is an active button. Printed output is not scrolled in the window. This means that it may be desirable to place text at a specific place on the screen with LOCATE, TAB, and PTAB.

The state of an existing button may be changed with a statement of the following form:

BUTTON number, state

The state of a button set in a button statement is read with the button function.

BUTTON(number)

returns the state of the button number in parentheses. This makes it possible to set button states in one part of a program and read them in another part.

Buttons may be removed from a window with the BUTTON CLOSE statement.

BUTTON CLOSE number

A button can also be removed by executing another button statement for the same button number.

DIALOG and Buttons

Once we have buttons on the screen we need a way to determine which ones have been pressed. This is done with the dialog function.

DIALOG(0)

returns 1 to indicate that a button in the active window has been selected. If the value of DIALOG(0) is 0 then there has been no dialog activity since the last time DIALOG(0) was accessed. Other values report information about other features. DIALOG(0) stores up events in a buffer the way the keyboard stores up keypresses. If DIALOG(0) indicates that a button has been selected the button number is found in DIALOG(1). Dialog activities are reported, oldest first. For button "presses" we are only interested in the situations in which DIALOG(0) = 1. Let's look at a simple demonstration program.

Program 6-10. BUTTON demonstration.

```
WINDOW 2,,(10,29)-(120,44),4
WINDOW 1,,(20,59)-(110,260),2

FOR K = 1 TO 5
   READ A$
   BUTTON K,1,A$,(10,20*K-5)-(75,20*K+10),2
NEXT K
BUTTON 6,1,"Done",(10,170)-(80,190),1

Poll:
     WINDOW OUTPUT 1 : RESTORE
     IF DIALOG(0) <> 1 THEN Poll
     SELECT = DIALOG(1) : IF SELECT = 6 THEN Quit
     FOR K = 1 TO 5
        IF BUTTON(K) <> 1 THEN BUTTON K,1
     NEXT K
     BUTTON SELECT, 2
     WINDOW OUTPUT 2 : FOR K = 1 TO SELECT : READ A$ : NEXT K
     CLS : PRINT "You chose "; A$
     GOTO Poll

Quit: WINDOW CLOSE 2 : WINDOW 1,,,1 : END

DATA First, Second, Third, Fourth, Last
```

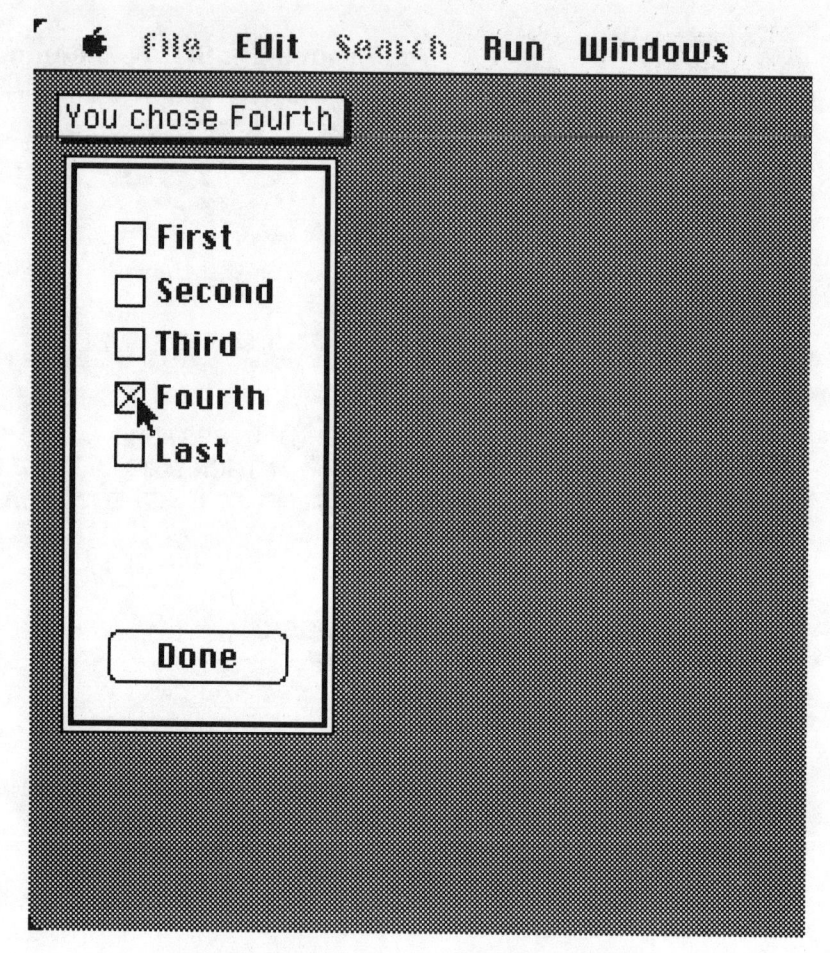

Figure 6-6. Execution of Program 6-10.

6-5. Event trapping

Section 6-3 demonstrated event trapping with menus. In addition to MENU, it is possible to trap BREAK, TIMER, MOUSE, and DIALOG. The concept is the same for these new events as for MENU event trapping. Set up a subroutine to manage the event, include an event ON statement, and an ON event GOSUB statement. Each event is turned on by event ON, turned off by event OFF, and suspended by event STOP. But polling is reasonable for MENU, MOUSE, and DIALOG. The only way to monitor BREAK is through event trapping.

BREAK

A program can monitor ⌘-. from the keyboard or Stop from the Run menu.

ON BREAK GOSUB ProcessEmergencyStop

does it. It is important that such a program provide a way to execute a STOP statement or an END statement. Otherwise, the user will have to turn the computer off. Be cautious about this.

TIMER

Events can be timed during program execution.

ON TIMER (60) **GOSUB** CheckExcessTime

will execute the subroutine at CheckExcessTime every 60 seconds. The number of seconds may range from 1 to 86400.

MOUSE

The click of the mouse button is a trappable event.

ON MOUSE GOSUB DecipherMousePress

monitors the mouse button. If the mouse button is pressed the subroutine is executed. The subroutine can determine the current state of the mouse. MOUSE(0) returns a 1, 2, or 3 to report a single-click, a double-click, or a triple-click since the last access to MOUSE(0). Negative values indicate that the button was still depressed at the time that MOUSE(0) was accessed. The value of MOUSE(0) and MOUSE(1) through MOUSE(6) are refreshed every time MOUSE(0) is returned. MOUSE(1) and MOUSE(2) return the current X and Y pixel coordinates of the mouse cursor in the output window. MOUSE(3) and MOUSE(4) return the X and Y pixel coordinates of the mouse cursor at the beginning of a drag (MOUSE(0) is negative). MOUSE(5) and MOUSE(6) return the X and Y pixel coordinates of the mouse cursor at the end of a drag. The end of the drag could be different from the current mouse position. If the MOUSE(0) function is accessed in rapid succession, the drag distances will be very small.

DIALOG

DIALOG is used to monitor BUTTON, EDIT FIELD, and output windows.

ON DIALOG GOSUB ProcessDialog

will cause the subroutine at ProcessDialog to be executed under a wide variety of conditions. Program 6-10 used polling and DIALOG to monitor BUTTON activity when DIALOG(0) returned a value of 1. Values 2 through 7 are returned for activity involving edit fields, output windows, and additional button features. DIALOG(0) returns values from 0 to 7. See Appendix D for a description of all features of the dialog functions.

CHAPTER 7

Pigeonholes Galore (Arrays)

We have been working with numeric variables for some time now. These variables have been very useful for many programs. We use them in FOR loops and calculations of all kinds. Numeric variables are important in making the computer such a useful tool. Likewise, we have taken advantage of the string variable features of BASIC. The variables we have been using are all classed as simple variables. They hold a single value.

In this chapter we are going to take a quantum leap forward. While we have used a separate variable for each value in the past, we are going to see how to use the variable concept to encompass a large number of values with a single name. We are going to enter the world of the computer array.

Arrays are used for storing information that naturally belongs together. Tax tables, pricing structures, inventory information, and life insurance premium listings are all appropriate for arrays. Often an array is useful for storing information about the workings of the program itself. We may use arrays for storing test scores, temperatures, random numbers, and lists of all kinds. An array might store the days of the week or the months of the year.

7-1. Numbers, Numbers, and More Numbers (Numeric Arrays)

If we were going to store the high temperature for each day of the week we might use SUNDAY, MONDAY, . . . , FRIDAY, and SATURDAY as variables. That would be cumbersome. We would probably prefer to do the necessary calculation by hand. An array variable is a new kind of place to store values. An array may have as many pigeonholes as we need for any problem. (As long as we need only 32768 pigeonholes and the computer has enough memory.) We can designate WEEK to be an array variable to contain values for the seven days of the week. To distinguish the several values stored in any array we use a value written in parentheses following the variable name. The value written in parentheses is called a subscript and each data value stored in the array is called an element. Thus, the temperature for SUNDAY could be stored in

WEEK(1)

In this case WEEK is the array name and one (1) is the subscript. The temperature for Sunday is stored in the element designated as number one. We read WEEK(1) as "WEEK-sub-one". In our example "WEEK-sub-seven" would be used for the temperature on Saturday. We can just as well use WEEK(X) or WEEK(J9).

The first occurrence of any reference to a variable such as WEEK(1) establishes the array named WEEK. BASIC automatically provides eleven elements numbered from 0 through 10. In the next section we will learn how to specify exactly the number of elements we need for each situation.

The benefits of arrays are immediately available to us with no new requirements or keywords to learn. They are just like simple variables but with a special naming convention. We may use BASIC to assign values in all the ways we already know. Assignment (LET), INPUT, and READ all work the same as for simple variables. Array variables are used in calculations and PRINT, LPRINT, PRINT USING, and LPRINT USING statements with ease. We may test the value of an array element in an IF statement.

For our first example let's write a program to read temperatures for a week, calculate the average, and find the highest and lowest temperatures. In order to do this we will set three initial values equal to the temperature of day one. That is, on Sunday the SUM and the HIGH and LOW temperatures are each equal to Sunday's temperature. Then for each of the other days of the week we will perform three tasks. We will add today's temperature to the SUM. We will see whether today's temperature is lower than the current LOW. And we will determine whether today's temperature is higher than the current HIGH. Finally, we must display the results. See Program 7-1.

Numbers, Numbers, and More Numbers

Program 7-1. Find average, highest, and lowest temperatures.

```
REM ** Enter the temperatures in array WEEK
FOR J = 1 TO 7 : READ WEEK(J) : NEXT J
REM ** Set up initial conditions
SUM = WEEK(1) : HIGH = WEEK(1) : LOW = WEEK(1)

REM ** Scan the week's temperatures
FOR J = 2 TO 7
 SUM = SUM + WEEK(J)
 IF WEEK(J) < LOW THEN LOW = WEEK(J)
 IF WEEK(J) > HIGH THEN HIGH = WEEK(J)
NEXT J

PRINT USING "Average temp:          ##.##"; SUM / 7
PRINT "Highest temp:", HIGH
PRINT "Lowest temp:", LOW

DATA 71, 77, 82, 76, 79, 72, 74
```

```
▄▄▄▄▄▄▄▄▄ Program 7-1 ▄▄▄▄▄▄▄▄▄
Average temp:     75.86
Highest temp:     82
Lowest temp:      71
```

Figure 7-1. Execution of Program 7-1.

Using arrays, it was easy to read in all the information that belonged together because it all went in one place, the array WEEK. Here we used a FOR...NEXT loop to go through the array elements one through seven when reading the DATA values in, and used another one to review elements two through seven to do the summing and comparisons.

As is often the case, there are lots of things we might do to change this program. We might want to know on which days the high and low temperatures occurred. We might want to know how many times the temperature increased and decreased. These are left as exercises.

Drawing Random Numbers from a Hat

Suppose we wish to simulate drawing numbers from a hat. We can easily do it with random numbers, provided that we may return each number to the hat before drawing the next one. If we want to simulate drawing without replacement, then we must have a way of keeping track of what has been drawn. Here is an ideal application for an array. We simply set each element of an array equal to 1 and change it to 0 when that element has been selected. If the selected element equals 1 then we know that it is available for use; we use the element number as our random number and set the value to 0. If a selected element is 0 then we know that it is not available for use and we must select again. Let's look at such a program to draw five numbers at random from among ten. See Program 7-2.

Numbers, Numbers, and More Numbers

> **Program 7-2. Drawing five random numbers from among ten.**
>
> ```
> REM ** Drawing five random numbers from among ten
> RANDOMIZE TIMER
>
> REM ** Make all values available
> FOR J = 1 TO 10
>   A(J) = 1 'Value available
> NEXT J
>
> REM ** Select five random values
> FOR J = 1 TO 5
>   DrawValue:
>     RANDOM = INT(RND * 10 + 1)
>     IF A(RANDOM) = 0 THEN DrawValue
>   PRINT RANDOM;
>   A(RANDOM) = 0 'Value unavailable
> NEXT J
> ```

```
┌─────────── Program 7-2 ───────────┐
│ 6   9   3   4   2                 │
│                                   │
│                                   │
└───────────────────────────────────┘
```

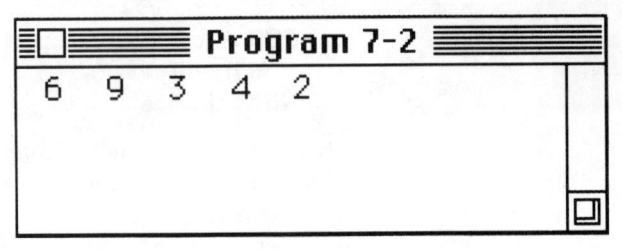

Figure 7-2. Execution of Program 7-2.

From all appearances, our program works just fine. But look at the two lines under DrawValue:

RANDOM = **INT**(**RND** * 10 + 1)
IF A(RANDOM) = 0 **THEN** DrawValue

If the value selected by the RND function has already been used, then the next line requires the computer to draw another random value. Inevitably this is a trial-and-error process. It might be interesting to evaluate how well it does work. One measure of the quality of the program will be the number of unusable random numbers generated: the fewer the better. We can easily insert a counting variable to determine this. This is left as an exercise.

Considering the problem set before us, the trial-and-error method of the above program is not really a serious flaw in design. Drawing five numbers from among ten, or even drawing ten from among ten, does not require major computer resources. However, what happens when we increase the numbers? Suppose we want to draw one hundred from among one hundred? When we draw for the last number, we have a one in a hundred chance of getting it. That could take a while. It is worth investing some effort to eliminate the trial-and-error entirely.

Here is a plan that allows us to use every random number selected. First initialize the elements of the array as follows:

FOR J = 1 **TO** 10
  A(J) = J
NEXT J

This means that each element stores one of the numbers in the range 1 to 10. Next, generate a random number in the range 1 to 10 to select a subscript value in the array. Now display A(SUBSCRIPT), the first random draw, and get ready to draw the next number from among only the nine left. We can replace the number A(SUBSCRIPT), wherever it is in the range, with the element on the very end, A(10). Then we know that A(SUBSCRIPT) has been eliminated from the pool. At this point the number 10 may exist in two places: in the element A(10), where it was originally set up, and in the element A(SUBSCRIPT), the element that happened to be selected (unless SUBSCRIPT happens to equal 10, and that is OK, too). By eliminating A(SUBSCRIPT) from the pool, we may select from among the remaining 9 elements and still include all of the remaining numbers in the next random selection. The second time through, we move A(9) into the selected element. Next, select a random number in the range 1 to 8. We simply repeat the select–display–replace sequence until the desired number of random draws has occurred. Try it with pencil and paper if the process seems complex. Once you master the concept for five numbers, it is easy to make the jump to a hundred or a thousand.

We need to calculate the number of elements remaining. As the draw number (J) goes from 1 to 5, the number of elements remaining goes from 10 to 6. Thus, we can calculate the last element with

LAST = 10 − J + 1

Of course we could just as well use LAST = 11−J, but the form in the line above tells us more about where the numbers are coming from. This makes the program easier to read. See Program 7-3.

Program 7-3. Drawing without replacement efficiently.

```
REM ** Random values without replacement
      'and without trial-and-error.
FOR J = 1 TO 10
   A(J) = J
NEXT J

FOR J = 1 TO 5
   LAST = 10 - J + 1
   SUBSCRIPT = INT(RND * LAST + 1)
   PRINT A(SUBSCRIPT);
   A(SUBSCRIPT) = A(LAST) 'Move last value
NEXT J
END
```

```
============ Program 7-3 ============
 2    6    7    9    5
```

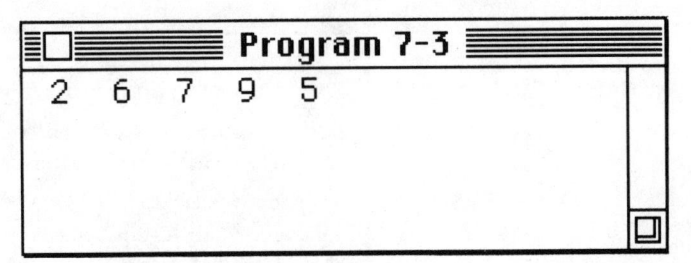

Figure 7-3. Execution of Program 7-3.

Notice that the element is printed with PRINT A(SUBSCRIPT); and then immediately replaced by the current LAST element in the next line. LAST is always the number of active elements in the array. Even if we happen to select the LAST element this method continues to function properly. The LAST element will be assigned to itself. No harm done. You might want to use RANDOMIZE to change the results from one run to the next.

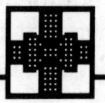

Summary

Now we have a variable that allows us to include several values in a single variable name. X(J) is the Jth element in the array variable X. We may use subscripts from 0 to 10. We often use arrays to store data values that belong in a group.

Problems for Section 7-1

It is a good idea to experiment with arrays to get the feel of how they work. Some of these problems are suggested to provide a chance to learn by doing.

1. Modify the temperature program (7-1) to determine how many times the temperature increased, decreased, and remained unchanged.
2. Modify the temperature program (7-1) to display the days on which the highest and lowest temperatures occurred.
3. Modify the first random number program (7-2) to draw ten numbers from among ten.
4. Change the first random number drawing program (7-2) to count the number of random values that are duplicates.
5. Enter 3, 5, 6, and 17 in one array and 6, −9, 11, −13, and 3 in another. Display all possible pairs by selecting one element from each array. There are 20 pairs.
6. Fill two arrays as in Problem 5. Have the program fill a third array with all elements in either array with no duplicates. Display the resulting array.
7. Fill an 11-element array with random values. Display the largest value and its position in the array.

7-2. A Simple Sort

Computers do a lot of sorting and arranging of data. Whole books are devoted to sorting and searching. In this section we are going to look at a very simple sort and write a program to implement it. Arrays are ideal for jobs like this. We will load an array with ten numbers and arrange them in increasing order. To do this we will check pairs of elements in the array one pair at a time. If they are in the correct order, we simply go to the next pair. If they are not in the correct order, then we want to exchange them. When we have gone all the way through the 10 elements once, we know that the biggest number is already in place at the end because it has proven bigger in every comparison since it was first encountered in the progression. So on the second pass through we need only compare up to the 9th element. And so on.

One way to exchange two values requires an intermediate variable. To exchange A and B, we need three BASIC statements as follows:

```
TEMP = A
A    = B
B    = TEMP
```

The variable TEMP is used to save the value of A while we copy the value of B into it. Then the value that we saved in TEMP can be copied into B. BASIC lets us do that in a special statement.

SWAP A, B

does exactly the same thing. If we check out pairs of numbers that are next to each other in an array named A, the heart of the sort will be the following statement:

IF A(J) > A(J+1) **THEN SWAP** A(J), A(J+1)

We need a routine to read the values into the array, a routine to perform the test of the line above on all necessary pairs, and a routine to display the results.

The values can be read in with a loop that looks for a special value to signal the end of DATA. Let's use −999999.

The routine that checks all necessary pairs simply scans the array from the beginning to the end minus 1, looking at the Jth and J+1st elements. At the end of each scan, we can look at one less pair because we have moved the next largest value to the correct location in the array. Once we have put the correct value in the element numbered 2, the process is guaranteed to be complete. This sort is another process that is easy to follow with pencil and paper for a few numbers. See Program 7-4.

Program 7-4. A simple sort.

```
REM ** A simple sort
REM ** Load numbers to be sorted in array A
N = 0 : READ X
WHILE X <> -999999!
   N = N + 1
   A(N) = X
   READ X
WEND

REM ** Here is the sort
FOR LAST = N-1 TO 2 STEP -1
   FOR J = 1 TO LAST
      IF A(J) > A(J+1) THEN SWAP A(J), A(J+1)
   NEXT J
NEXT LAST

REM ** Sort complete—display
FOR J = 1 TO N
 PRINT A(J);
NEXT J
END

REM ** Test data
DATA 102, 32, -91, 982, 87
DATA 73, 23, -981, 234, 21
DATA -999999
```

```
┌─────────────────── Program 7-4 ───────────────────┐
│ -981  -91   21   23   32   73   87   102  234  982│
│                                                    │
│                                                    │
└────────────────────────────────────────────────────┘
```

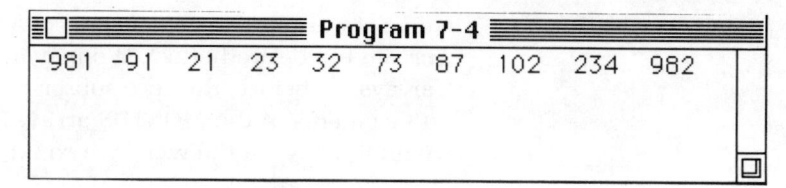

Figure 7-4. Execution of Program 7-4.

This sort is very straightforward. It is also very slow. If we have much data to be sorted, we must turn to more sophisticated methods.

Problems for Section 7-2

1. Notice that the routine of Program 7-4 that does the actual sorting would take the same time for a list that is already in order as for any other. Put in a variable that switches on whenever a SWAP is done. At the end of the inner loop have the program test to see if any SWAP has been done. If no SWAP has been done then the sort is finished. (This will improve execution for some lists, but very little can be done to improve the inherent inefficiency of this type of sort).

2. Change Program 7-4 to arrange in decreasing order.

7-3. Array Sizes and Shapes (DIM)

Suppose we want to deal with data for the 12 months of the year. We would like to have an array with subscripts up to 12. It is easy with DIM.

DIM MONTHS(12)

does the trick. The DIMension statement is executed only once to create the desired effect. We may also use DIM to declare smaller arrays. As before, the zero subscript is available, so we really have 13 elements in the MONTHS array. For our little problem dealing with the days of the week we could use

    DIM WEEK(7)

It is always good programming practice to include every array in a DIM statement. Ideally this statement is among the early statements in the program. This provides important information to anyone reading our program. It is disconcerting to find a statement referring to X(6), or worse yet X(J9), without any clue as to how large the array might be. Even if we want to allow subscripts up to ten, we should state that in a DIM statement. Several arrays may be mentioned in a single DIM statement by separating them with commas.

    DIM WEEK(7), MONTH(12)

takes care of two arrays for us. Arrays are limited to 32768 elements.

Variable DIM

Suppose we have a program in which the dimensions of our arrays might change depending on data handled during execution. We can provide for all situations by using a variable DIM statement. We may use a program segment such as the following:

    INPUT "   Number of weeks:"; W
    INPUT "Number of values per week:"; V
    DIM WEEKS(W), VALUES(V)

If we call for too large an array BASIC will deliver the "Out of memory" error box. If we try to dimension the same array again, regardless of the amount of memory required, we will see the "Duplicate Definition" error box. There is a way around the Duplicate Definition problem.

ERASE

We can eliminate an array and recover the memory it occupies with the ERASE statement.

    ERASE TEST, TEST1

does this for arrays TEST and TEST1. This frees us to redimension any array mentioned in the ERASE statement. Or we might just want the space for some other purpose. An attempt to erase a nonexistent array brings forth an "Illegal function call" error message.

Variable Typing and Memory

If we have a situation in which we need a very large array, and values in the range −32768 to 32767 are sufficient, then we have the option of declaring our array as an integer array just as we did for simple variables.

DIM ARRAY%(900)

The memory saved will be 6 bytes per element for the decimal ($) version of Microsoft BASIC or 5400 bytes for this example and 2 bytes per element or 1800 bytes for the binary (π) version.

On the other hand, we might require up to 6-digit precision in a program using the decimal ($) version, but still need to save room in memory. In this case, we declare a single precision array.

DIM NUMBER!(4000)

does the job. Now the values occupy four bytes each instead of eight.

In a program where several numeric data types are in use, we might want to explicitly declare double precision with a statement such as

DIM TIDBIT#(12)

Such a move will serve to more clearly document what is going on in the program. We can also use DEFINT, DEFSNG, and DEFDBL to declare variable types. The use of the symbols %, !, and #, however, provides a visible indication of the variable type.

Multiple Dimensions

Suppose we want to work with population figures spanning a period of years. Let's look at a table of values for Spokane, Washington.

Table 7-1. Population of Spokane, Washington.

Year	Population
1950	161,271
1960	181,608
1970	170,516
1980	171,300

With such a small table we could actually do a lot of analysis by eye. However, the principles we learn here may be applied to larger amounts of data. We need an array with four rows and two columns. We can easily provide such an array with

DIM CENSUS(4,2)

Up to 255 dimensions are theoretically possible. There are numerous practical limits that we will reach long before 255. Three or four dimensions quickly gobble up computer memory. If we ever access CENSUS with a first subscript larger than 4 or a second subscript larger than 2, we will get "Subscript out of range." On the other hand, if a subscript goes negative, we get "Illegal function call."

Arrays and Subprograms

Some special rules apply for passing arrays to subprograms. The statement that calls a subprogram names an array by listing the array name followed by a pair of parentheses with nothing enclosed. The SUB statement includes the array names with the number of dimensions enclosed in parentheses.

DIM COURSES%(24)

CountCourses COURSES%(),NUMBEROFCOURSES
PRINT NUMBEROFCOURSES
END

SUB CountCourses (A%(1),X) **STATIC**

The array COURSES% is treated as A% within the subprogram. For one-dimensional arrays, placing the number of dimensions in the parentheses in the SUB statement is optional. The number of dimensions must not be named in the calling statement.

In the CENSUS situation we are actually providing an extra row and an extra column because of the automatic zero subscripts. In the interest of simplicity, let's not use the zero subscripts. We'll use OPTION BASE here to eliminate them.

OPTION BASE

When we work with large arrays, the unused zero elements alone can take up a lot of memory. Suppose we look at an array DIMensioned ten by ten by ten. Such an array contains 1,331 elements. Of those, 331 are referenced by at least one zero subscript. If we have no logical use for them, we can save all that space with

OPTION BASE 1

This statement eliminates all elements with a zero subscript. So this ten-by-ten-by-ten array will use only enough memory for 1,000 elements. That is about a 25% saving. And for a ten-by-ten-by-ten-by-ten, the saving is about 32%.

LBOUND and UBOUND

The LBOUND and UBOUND functions return the lowest and highest possible subscripts for an array. This is done with

LOW = **LBOUND**(B,2)
HIGH = **UBOUND**(B,2)

In the example above, B is the array name and 2 causes the functions to return the bounds on the second dimension. For single dimension arrays, the dimension may be omitted. The low value is 0 unless changed by the OPTION BASE statement. The high value is the value declared in the DIM statement. These functions may be useful in some subprograms.

Now back to the census project: What do we do with all this data? We might want to know the years of the largest and smallest populations. Or we might want to know about percentage increases and decreases. Perhaps it would be useful to arrange the years in order of population. But first we must get the data into the array. Perhaps the easiest way is to READ DATA. We will be careful to leave the extra commas out when typing the DATA statements for our program. Commas are used to separate DATA items. Once we have the data in our array we can then put together a program to provide answers to all of our questions. It will be a good idea to develop the program using subroutines for the various processes. See Program 7-5.

Program 7-5. Read and display census data.

```
OPTION BASE 1
DIM CENSUS(4,2)
GOSUB ReadCensusData
GOSUB DisplayCensusData
END

ReadCensusData:
  FOR ROW = 1 TO 4
    FOR COLUMN = 1 TO 2
      READ CENSUS( ROW, COLUMN )
    NEXT COLUMN
  NEXT ROW
  RETURN

DisplayCensusData:
  FOR ROW = 1 TO 4
    FOR COLUMN = 1 TO 2
      PRINT CENSUS( ROW, COLUMN )
    NEXT COLUMN
    PRINT
  NEXT ROW
  RETURN

DATA 1950,161271,  1960,181608
DATA 1970,170516,  1980,171300
```

```
▣▭▭▭▭▭▭ Program 7-5 ▭▭▭▭▭
  1950           161271
  1960           181608
  1970           170516
  1980           171300
```

Figure 7-5. Execution of Program 7-5.

Note how convenient it will be to have the display isolated as a subroutine. Later, when we only want to know which year produced the largest census for Spokane we may simply leave out GOSUB DisplayCensusData. In this way the display routine will be unaffected. We could also include the conventional comma in the population figures with PRINT USING.

Now we are in a position to begin asking questions about the data. Let's find out which census tabulated the greatest population. We need a little routine that scans the array looking for the largest value of CENSUS(J,2). We also need to keep track of the year. The routine will set YEAR to the first year and set LARGE to the population for the first year. Then it will scan the rest of the array to see if any year has a higher population. If one is found, it saves the year in YEAR and the population in LARGE. Program 7-6 lists the relevant changes to Program 7-5.

Program 7-6. Change Program 7-5 to find largest population.

```
OPTION BASE 1
DIM CENSUS(4,2)
GOSUB ReadCensusData
GOSUB FindLargestPop
END

FindLargestPop:
  YEAR = CENSUS(1,1) : LARGE = CENSUS(1,2)
  FOR J = 2 TO 4
    IF CENSUS(J,2) > LARGE THEN YEAR = CENSUS(J,1) : LARGE = CENSUS(J,2)
  NEXT J
  PRINT YEAR, LARGE
  RETURN
```

Look at the line:

IF CENSUS(J,2) > LARGE **THEN** YEAR = CENSUS(J,1) : LARGE = CENSUS(J,2)

If any value in column two is greater than the current value of LARGE, we save the new higher value, along with the year. If the value in column two is less than the current value of LARGE, we proceed directly to the next value in column two. This program will inform us that Spokane had a population high of 181,608 in 1960.

Problems for Section 7-3

Again, it is good to just experiment with arrays. DIMension a two dimensional array and try things. Try three dimensions.

1. Write a program to fill a five-by-seven array with values of your choice. Display the totals column by column. Display the totals row by row.
2. Write a program to fill a five-by-seven array with values of your choice. Display the largest value in each row. Display the largest value in each column.
3. Fill a four-by-eight array with random values in the range from 1 to 100. Display the array. Then multiply each element by −5 and display the result.
4. Draw one hundred numbers from among one hundred using the method of Program 7-2 and then Program 7-3. Compare the time required by using TIMER.

7-4. Words, Words, and More Words (String Arrays)

If we were going to store the high temperature for each day of the week we might also want to store the names of the days of the week. We want Sunday, Monday,... Friday, and Saturday as data. This is easy to do with a string array. Let's look at a little program to display the names of the days of the week.

Program 7-7. Display the days of the week.

```
REM ** Display the days of the week

DIM DAY$(7)
FOR J = 1 TO 7
   READ DAY$(J)
NEXT J

FOR J = 1 TO 7
   PRINT DAY$(J)
NEXT J

DATA Sunday, Monday, Tuesday, Wednesday
DATA Thursday, Friday, Saturday
```

Now it is a simple step to combine the ideas of Programs 7-1 and 7-7 to label the results of the temperature program with the day name.

Once we have the day names in a string array some nice things begin to happen. We have the labels available at all times for display. We also have the flexibility of using the full day name where that is important or using abbreviations where there is little space. We may use

   **LEFT$**(DAY$(J),3)

to display just the first three letters.

String values are listed in DATA statements in the same manner as numeric values. Strings and numerics may be intermixed at will. A string variable may read a numeric value, but a numeric variable cannot read a string value. If you try to do that you will get a "Type mismatch" error box. If it becomes necessary to include a comma or a colon as part of a data item, then surround the entire data item with quotes. Quotes are also required for important leading or trailing spaces.

Problems for Section 7-4

1. Modify Program 7-7 to display only the three letter day name abbreviation in common use.
2. Write a program that stores the months of the year in a string array and displays them as column headers as follows:

   J F M A M J J A S O N D
   a e a p a u u u e c o e
   n b r r y n l g p t v c

3. Write a program that stores the months of the year in a string array and displays them as column headers as follows:

   J F M A M J J A S O N D
   a e a p a u u u e c o e
   n b r r y n l g p t v c

7-5. An Alphabet Game

You're driving along and someone says, "Let's play Alphabet." Everybody in the car tries to find every letter of the alphabet in order on signs along the roadside. Whoever gets to "Z" first wins. We can develop a computer program to do a fair job of simulating that game. Then you may want to expand on it. The program will involve many of the things we have been doing recently. There will be a string array to store the signs. We can use the RND function to help select signs at random. The sign should appear only briefly on the screen to simulate highway driving. During that time the player should have the opportunity to strike a letter key to signify that he or she has spotted the next letter. The computer needs to do some checking and display messages according to the outcome.

For now we may enter the signs in DATA statements. Later we may want to use data files. Since much of what we will be doing in this program has to do with single letters, and many signs have both uppercase and lowercase letters, we will have an opportunity to work with the ASC function and the UCASE$ function. Later, when you have read about controlling text in Chapter 10, you might want to come back and jazz up some of the signs by using different fonts, sizes, and styles on the screen.

An Alphabet Game

This is a big job we have laid out, but it can easily be trimmed down to size by spending a little extra time organizing before we generate any BASIC program statements. Think about the steps in the game in programming terms.

Load the Signs Array

It can be said that once we select our route, the stream of signs has been determined. We may easily simulate this by storing a sequence of signs in a string array. By later selecting signs at random, we may offer the game player different "routes." We may arbitrarily DIMension a string array. Let's use 50 for now. We can just think up a few signs and put them in DATA statements. Later we can put in additional DATA statements if we wish to.

Establish Game Beginning

It is easy to get a game going. We begin with "A" or "a". For simplicity let's use capital "A". Since we will be scanning the alphabet, it will be convenient to think in terms of numeric or ASCII codes. The ASCII code for a capital "A" is easy to find with PRINT ASC("A"). We get 65.

Simulate Random Signs along the Road

Once we have the first letter established, all we need is to generate some random signs. Of course, when we are riding in a car the signs come whizzing by. We can use PICTURE to make the signs appear as if they were coming toward the viewer, simulating the way it looks as we drive along the highway.

Did the Player Spot the Next Letter?

Here we create a routine that allows the player to either enter a letter of the alphabet or not. The easiest way to do that is to use the INKEY$ function to read a single character from the keyboard. BASIC does not display the character entered. If we want to display it, we do that with PRINT. The Return key is not required. If no key has been pressed, then the resulting string is null—that is, it contains no characters. And program execution continues on, unlike with INPUT, which stops to wait for a response at the keyboard no matter what. So the program must "look" at the keyboard to see if a letter has been pressed. If a letter has been pressed, convert it to uppercase with UCASE$. Then this routine should determine that the player did press the next letter in the alphabet. If no key has been pressed then the sign selecting routine should be repeated.

Is the Next Letter on the Sign?

Having displayed a sign and received the next letter in alphabetic sequence, the program should check to be sure that the letter is on the sign. Here again, we need to deal with uppercase and lowercase. If the current letter is on the sign, and the player has not completed the alphabet, then we repeat the sign-generating routine. Otherwise we move on to terminate the game.

The Program

Each of the processes described here is an ideal candidate for a subroutine. This means that we have partitioned the complex problem into manageable tasks. We may concentrate on each smaller task and do the job efficiently. The benefits don't stop there. Once the program has been written and it performs to our satisfaction, we may easily make important modifications by concentrating on a single subroutine rather than pouring through one long stream of program statements. It is going to be a simple job to convert this program later on so that it stores the signs in a data file on disk. Then we can ask each new player to enter a favorite sign that can be saved permanently from run to run. Thus the game will become more and more interesting as more people play it.

To summarize, then, here is a description of the final program.

1. Load the signs array
2. Establish game beginning
3. Simulate random signs along the road
4. Did the player spot the next letter? If not then repeat step 3
5. Is the next letter on the sign? If not "Z" yet, repeat step 3 or else wind up this game

We will handle each of the numbered steps as a subroutine. This summary will serve as the control routine. By retaining each line of the summary as a remark in the program itself we can provide good documentation without further effort. All that remains is for us to make a few decisions about appropriate line labels and variables, and the control routine is complete. Let's name the subroutines LoadSigns, BeginGame, DisplaySigns, CheckPlayer, and CheckLetter. The section of the control routine that will keep displaying new signs and checking the player's response (steps 3 through 5) we'll call GetNextSign.

Now for the variables. Let's use SIGNS$ as the signs array, NUMBEROFSIGNS as the total number of signs, NEXTLETTER as the

ASCII value of the current letter, LETTER as the ASCII value of the letter entered at the keyboard during the play of the game (it will be zero if no key is pressed), and R as the randomly selected position of the current sign in the SIGNS$ array. So SIGNS$(R) contains the current sign. And we won't forget to DIMension SIGNS$. All of this transforms easily into BASIC for a routine to control our game program. See Program 7-8a.

Program 7-8a. Control routine to play Alphabet.

```
DIM SIGNS$(50)
RANDOMIZE TIMER
GOSUB LoadSigns                               'Load the signs array
GOSUB BeginGame                               'Establish game beginning
GetNextSign:
    GOSUB DisplaySigns                        'Simulate random signs along the road
    GOSUB CheckPlayer                         'Did the player spot the next letter?
        IF LETTER = 0 THEN GetNextSign        'If not then repeat step 3
    GOSUB CheckLetter                         'Is the next letter on the sign?
        IF NEXTLETTER < 91 THEN GetNextSign   'If not "Z" yet, repeat step 3
    PRINT "Congratulations, you have made it through the alphabet"
END
```

Now we can concentrate on each of the subroutines. The program will practically write itself. Loading the SIGNS$ array consists of reading data. We provide for a counter and a final data value as a signal that all data has been read. The number of signs read here is returned in NUMBEROFSIGNS. See Program 7-8b.

Program 7-8b. Load the Alphabet game road signs.

```
LoadSigns:
   NUMBEROFSIGNS = 0 : READ A$
   WHILE A$ <> "Done"
      NUMBEROFSIGNS = NUMBEROFSIGNS + 1 : SIGNS$(NUMBEROFSIGNS) = A$
      READ A$
   WEND
   PRINT "There are:"; NUMBEROFSIGNS; "signs in this game."
   GOSUB Delay
   RETURN
```

Note the statement

GOSUB Delay

just before the RETURN statement. We need a delay so that the player has time to read the message in the output window. This should be another subroutine that can be used for all displayed messages. The DATA statements can be added anytime.

Now let's establish the game beginning. This simply consists of initializing NEXTLETTER to the ASCII value for capital A.

Program 7-8c. Start with capital A.

```
BeginGame:
   NEXTLETTER = 65 'Get ready to look for A
   RETURN
```

To simulate the signs along the roadside we need to generate random values from one to the number of signs in the array. It would be nice to have the sign grow larger as it approaches. This can be done using PICTURE in a loop with changing specifications for the corners. Once a sign has been selected at random, the program needs to create a picture by printing the sign between a PICTURE ON and a PICTURE OFF statement. Then the sign can be displayed and replaced repeatedly within a loop. See Program 7-8d.

Program 7-8d. Display a sign.

```
DisplaySigns:
    R = INT(RND * NUMBEROFSIGNS + 1)
    CLS
    PICTURE ON
        PRINT SIGNS$(R)
    PICTURE OFF
    FOR K = 1 TO 250 STEP 30
        PICTURE(1+5*SQR(K),250−K)−(100+4*K,300+K)
        FOR X = 1 TO 100 : NEXT X
        CLS
    NEXT K
    RETURN
```

Next we process the player keyboard input. When the INKEY$ function finds that no key has been pressed, it returns a null string. It is important to know that the ASC function cannot handle a null string. The length of such a string is 0 and can be found with the LEN function.

If a player happens to press several keys or hold a key down until the keyboard repeat takes effect, there will be several characters coming from the keyboard for the INKEY$ function to pick up. Then each new sign will pick another character from the keyboard even though the player has not responded to the current sign. INKEY$ is just picking up characters left over from the previous sign. What we need to do here is take the first character held in the INKEY$ buffer and use it for the game and then read and throw away any others one at a time until there are no more characters. Here is a line that will throw away excess characters:

ClearKey: **IF LEN(INKEY$)** = 1 **THEN** ClearKey

You could first try the program without this line and press several keys for one sign to get a clear idea of what is happening at the keyboard. As long as INKEY$ finds a character in its buffer, its length will be 1. When its length is no longer 1, there are no more characters in the buffer and when the next sign is displayed only the new keypress will be picked up. This method allows us to take only the first letter of any string of characters accidently entered. Then, since the INKEY$ function does not display keyboard input, we will include a PRINT statement to do so.

If a letter has been typed that is not the next one in the alphabet, the program should display a message and keep it on the screen long enough for the player to read. Here is another use for the Delay subroutine. See Program 7-8e.

Program 7-8e. Check keyboard input.

```
CheckPlayer:
    A$ = INKEY$ : IF LEN(A$) = 0 THEN LETTER = 0 : GOTO EndCheckPlayer
    ClearKey: IF LEN(INKEY$) = 1 THEN ClearKey
    PRINT A$; "     ";
    A$ = UCASE$(A$) : LETTER = ASC(A$)
    IF A$ < "A" OR A$ > "Z" THEN CheckPlayer
    IF LETTER = NEXTLETTER THEN EndCheckPlayer
        PRINT "Not the next letter in the alphabet" : GOSUB Delay
        GOTO CheckPlayer
EndCheckPlayer:
RETURN
```

To check if a letter is on a sign, only uppercase need be checked. We need a message for "not found" and one for "found." Here is yet another use for the Delay routine. If the letter is found we need to increment NEXTLETTER to move to the next letter in the alphabet. See Program 7-8f.

Program 7-8f. Check if a letter is on a sign.

```
CheckLetter:
    IF INSTR(UCASE$(SIGNS$(R)), A$) THEN Found ELSE NotFound
    NotFound:
        PRINT "Your letter is not on the sign" : GOSUB Delay
        GOTO EndCheckLetter
    Found:
        PRINT "Good" : GOSUB Delay
        NEXTLETTER = NEXTLETTER + 1
EndCheckLetter:
RETURN
```

And now we come to the delay routine. It is simply a FOR...NEXT loop that does nothing. Here we have set the upper limit at 2500. You might want to change that to suit your own taste.

Program 7-8g. Time delay routine.

Delay: 'Time delay for messages
FOR J = 1 **TO** 2500 : **NEXT** J
RETURN

Finally, we have included a few signs for data.

Program 7-8h. Data for the Alphabet game.

REM ** The signs
DATA Stop, Al's Pizza, Dairy Queen, Burger King
DATA Yield, One Way, This Way Out, Detour
DATA One Show Only Tonight, Exit Only, Entrance Only Please
DATA Florida 2138 mi., Fly United, Jet Set Diner
DATA Give Her a Valentine, Give Him a Valentine
DATA First Avenue, North Side
DATA Done

This concludes the writing of Program 7-8 to play the alphabet game. The program is in 8 pieces. You could type the program from beginning to end and save it in one exercise. But, sometimes it makes sense to save individual subroutines as separate programs on disk. In this case, the complete program can be assembled using MERGE. Load the first routine with a statement such as:

LOAD "Program 8-7a"

typed in the Command window. Following this, type

MERGE "Next Program..."

Each new program named is appended to the end of the program already in memory. Finally, be sure to save the resulting program on disk.

Another method is to type NEW. Then type

MERGE "Program 8-7a"

in the list window. Now you have a one line program. Run it. With the mouse, change the "a" in "8-7a" to "b" and run the result. Successively merge each segment of the program. When the final subroutine is merged, remove the MERGE statement and the program is complete. This requires much less typing than doing it all in the Command window. See Appendix B for more information on LOAD and MERGE.

Here is the complete Alphabet game program.

Program 7-8. The Alphabet game.

```
DIM SIGNS$(50)
RANDOMIZE TIMER
GOSUB LoadSigns                          'Load the signs array
GOSUB BeginGame                          'Establish game beginning
GetNextSign:
   GOSUB DisplaySigns                    'Simulate random signs along the road
   GOSUB CheckPlayer                     'Did the player spot the next letter?
      IF LETTER = 0 THEN GetNextSign     'If not then repeat step 3
   GOSUB CheckLetter                     'Is the next letter on the sign?
      IF NEXTLETTER < 91 THEN GetNextSign 'If not "Z" yet, repeat step 3
   PRINT "Congratulations, you have made it through the alphabet"
END

LoadSigns:
   NUMBEROFSIGNS = 0 : READ A$
   WHILE A$ <> "Done"
      NUMBEROFSIGNS = NUMBEROFSIGNS + 1 : SIGNS$(NUMBEROFSIGNS) = A$
      READ A$
   WEND
   PRINT "There are:"; NUMBEROFSIGNS; "signs in this game."
   GOSUB Delay
   RETURN
```

An Alphabet Game

```
BeginGame:
  NEXTLETTER = 65 'Get ready to look for 'A'
  RETURN

DisplaySigns:
  R = INT(RND * NUMBEROFSIGNS + 1)
  CLS
  PICTURE ON
    PRINT SIGNS$(R)
  PICTURE OFF
  FOR K = 1 TO 250 STEP 30
    PICTURE(1+5*SQR(K),250−K)−(100+4*K,300+K)
    FOR X = 1 TO 100 : NEXT X
    CLS
  NEXT K
  RETURN

CheckPlayer:
  A$ = INKEY$ : IF LEN(A$) = 0 THEN LETTER = 0 : GOTO EndCheckPlayer
  ClearKey: IF LEN(INKEY$) = 1 THEN ClearKey
  PRINT A$; "        ";
  A$ = UCASE$(A$) : LETTER = ASC(A$)
  IF A$ < "A" OR A$ > "Z" THEN CheckPlayer
  IF LETTER = NEXTLETTER THEN EndCheckPlayer
    PRINT "Not the next letter in the alphabet" : GOSUB Delay
    GOTO CheckPlayer
EndCheckPlayer:
  RETURN

CheckLetter:
  IF INSTR(UCASE$(SIGNS$(R)), A$) THEN Found ELSE NotFound
  NotFound:
    PRINT "Your letter is not on the sign" : GOSUB Delay
    GOTO EndCheckLetter
  Found:
    PRINT "Good" : GOSUB Delay
    NEXTLETTER = NEXTLETTER + 1
  EndCheckLetter:
  RETURN

Delay: 'Time delay for messages
  FOR J = 1 TO 2500 : NEXT J
  RETURN
```

```
REM ** The signs
DATA Stop, Al's Pizza, Dairy Queen, Burger King
DATA Yield, One Way, This Way Out, Detour
DATA One Show Only Tonight, Exit Only, Entrance Only Please
DATA Florida 2138 mi., Fly United, Jet Set Diner
DATA Give Her a Valentine, Give Him a Valentine
DATA First Avenue, North Side
DATA Done
```

Now, there are lots of things that you could do to improve this program. You could make the program point out when the player misses signs that have the next letter on them. The program could easily be made to go faster or slower and to change speed at random. Stop at a traffic light or move onto an Interstate. The speed could be made to depend on the length of the sign. The current letter could be displayed in another window. You could do more things with graphics and windows. We have only scratched the surface.

Problems for Section 7-5

Problems 1 through 5 refer to the Alphabet game.
1. Change the Alphabet game to simulate changing speed in the car. Stop at a traffic light. Move onto the Interstate.
2. Make the time a sign stays on the screen proportional to the length of the sign.
3. Give the program the ability to make signs appear with differing probability. Yield could appear often, but Rudy's Diner should appear only once in any one game, (unless we get lost).
4. Write a program to tabulate the frequency of occurrence of the letters in the signs. This information could be used to decide on additional signs to include in the DATA.
5. Arrange the results in Problem 4 in order of frequency of occurrence.
6. Write a program to play Geography. In this game two or more players take turns thinking of place names. Each player must name a place whose first letter matches the last letter of the previous player's place. Have the program add new place names to the array and offer to play additional games. Make the computer a player in a two player game. Names may not be repeated in any one game.

CHAPTER 8

Miscellaneous Applications

Let's write a program to display one month of a calendar, given the month and year. The workings of our calendar are well established. The days of the week have a seven day rotation. The number of days in each month is fixed. The calendar follows a strange pattern, but it is a fixed pattern. The four year rotation for leap year is clear. If we limit ourselves to the twentieth century, we don't have to worry about the 400 year cycle. It is easy to develop this program by going from the big tasks down to the smaller ones.

8-1. A Calendar Program

Given a month and year, we are going to produce a calendar display in the form of Figure 8-1.

```
       Dec     1929
|Sun|Mon|Tue|Wed|Thu|Fri|Sat|
|  1|  2|  3|  4|  5|  6|  7|
|  8|  9| 10| 11| 12| 13| 14|
| 15| 16| 17| 18| 19| 20| 21|
| 22| 23| 24| 25| 26| 27| 28|
| 29| 30| 31|
```

Figure 8-1. One page of a calendar.

We can write a control routine calling for only two subroutines: request data from the keyboard and display the calendar for that month. We start right in with Program 8-1a.

> **Program 8-1a. Calendar control routine.**
>
> **GOSUB** RequestData
> **GOSUB** DisplayCalendar
> **END**

We want a number from 1 to 12 for the month and from 0 to 99 for the year. Let's make sure that values entered are within that range. We might just as well assure that the values passed to the main program are integers, while we are at it. This is easy to do using integer variables. Further, all variables in the program might just as well be integer. Make a note to define all variables as integer. See Program 8-1b.

> **Program 8-1b. Request data for the calendar program.**
>
> RequestData:
>   **INPUT** "Month, Year"; MONTH, YEAR
>   **IF** MONTH < 1 **OR** MONTH > 12 **THEN** RequestData
>   **IF** YEAR < 0 **OR** YEAR > 99 **THEN** RequestData
> **RETURN**

Wow, we are already half done—but not quite. We need to break up the calendar display into several smaller tasks. A few calculations are needed, and we might split the display into two parts. Let's display the title and calendar separately. That sounds like more subroutines. We just keep on breaking the task into manageable pieces. Study Program 8-1c.

Program 8-1c. Calendar display control routine.

DisplayCalendar:
  GOSUB Calculate
  GOSUB DisplayTitle
  GOSUB DisplayDays
  RETURN

The subroutine Calculate will make all the necessary calculations from the month and year entered at the keyboard. As long as we keep the month and year variables intact, another subroutine can easily display the title. In order to display the familiar number grid for a month, we need to know the number of days in the month and the day of the week for the first day. Given those two things, the third subroutine can display the days.

The calculations are next. The leap-year calculation is modular in nature. If the year number is divisible by 4 then it is a leap year (ignoring the 400 year cycle here). If YEAR MOD 4 is 0, then we have a leap year. Remember MOD from Chapter 2?

  IF YEAR **MOD** 4 = 0 **THEN** LEAP = 1 **ELSE** LEAP = 0

This line sets LEAP to 1 for leap year and 0 otherwise.

The days follow a seven-day cycle. This is another modular process. Let's assign 0 to 6 to the day names Sunday through Saturday. If we can just work out the day name for the first of January for any year, then we will be able to work our way through the months. For 365 day years, the day of the week of January 1 advances one day from year to year. Leap years advance one extra day. It turns out that January 1, 1900, fell on a Sunday. So the day of the week of the first of January is the year number adjusted for leap years taken MOD 7. The leap year adjustment should add an extra day every four years beginning with 1901. Therefore, we add 3 to the year number before dividing by 4. Remember, we are accepting year numbers in the range 0 to 99.

  DAY = (YEAR + (YEAR + 3) / 4) **MOD** 7

Upon execution of this line, DAY will be in the range 0 to 6 for the day of the week of January 1 of the current year.

Now we want to know the day name for the first day of the current month. For this we need to know the pattern governing the number of days in each month. Here it is:

Jan	Feb	Mar	Apr	May	Jun	Jul	Aug	Sep	Oct	Nov	Dec
1	2	3	4	5	6	7	8	9	10	11	12
31	28	31	30	31	30	31	31	30	31	30	31

See that the alternation between long and short months changes after July? The number of days in a month is 30 plus 1 for odd numbered months up to the seventh month. For the later months, we add 1 for the even numbered months. This is a perfect place for another MOD calculation. M MOD 2 is 1 for odd numbered months and 0 for even numbered months. For all months after the seventh, we want to change the number that goes into the MOD operator by 1, so that we add a day to the even numbered months instead of the odd numbered months. Adding or subtracting 1 for M > 7 gets us back on the track. In Microsoft BASIC, any expression with an arithmetic operator evaluates to −1 when true and 0 when false. Thus we can use the expression (M > 7) itself to cause a change of 1 for the months after July. All this is done to assign the number of days in the current month to the variable N in the following statement:

N = 30 + ((M + (M > 7)) **MOD** 2)

We need to add this to the day-of-the-week value for the next month as we cycle through the months of the current year to get to the requested month. Note that for January, the value for N must be 0 as we begin to cycle through the months of the year, since there is no previous month. When we come to February, as we cycle through the months of the requested year, we must set N to either 28 or 29 depending on whether this is a leap year or not.

IF M = 2 **THEN** N = 28 + LEAP

Remember, LEAP equals 1 for leap year and 0 otherwise. All this goes to make up the calculations of Program 8-1d.

Program 8-1d. Calendar calculations.

```
Calculate:
        'DAY-DAY of week, 1st of Month
        'N-No. of days in Month
IF YEAR MOD 4 = 0 THEN LEAP = 1 ELSE LEAP = 0
DAY = (YEAR + (YEAR + 3) / 4) MOD 7
N = 0
FOR M = 1 TO MONTH
  DAY = (DAY + N) MOD 7
  N = 30 + ((M + (M>7)) MOD 2)
  IF M = 2 THEN N = 28 + LEAP
NEXT M
RETURN
```

The calendar title comes next. We simply set up a string with all the month names and print the three characters corresponding to the month selected. See Program 8-1e.

Program 8-1e. Display calendar title.

```
DisplayTitle:
  M$ = "JanFebMarAprMayJunJulAugSepOctNovDec"
  PRINT
  PRINT TAB(9); MID$(M$, MONTH*3-2, 3), 1900 + YEAR
  PRINT : PRINT " Sun Mon Tue Wed Thu Fri Sat"
  RETURN
```

Finally, we need to work out the display of the number grid for the month. We are going to display 28, 29, 30, or 31 days as determined by the value of N. That is easy with a FOR loop running from 1 to N. The first day of the month needs to be positioned under the corresponding day name as displayed by Program 8-1e. The program needs to output a blank PRINT whenever it has just displayed a Saturday. See Program 8-1f.

Program 8-1f. Display calendar days.

```
DisplayDays:
  K = DAY
  FOR J = 1 TO N
    PRINT TAB(K*4 + 1 - (J < 10)); J;
    K = (K + 1) MOD 7 : IF K = 0 THEN PRINT
  NEXT J
  PRINT : PRINT
  RETURN
```

We are using TAB to position the display in the correct column. To make it come out right, we are subtracting (J < 10) there. Since the expression (J < 10) is –1 when true, we are tabbing an extra space for one digit values of J. Thus, the subtraction. This lines up the columns nicely for us. Note that while spaces are half the width of digits on the Macintosh screen, TAB reckons in character widths. The display could be dressed up a little by using a small output window for the calendar page.

This program has been designed to be flexible. The control routines of Program 8-1a and 8-1c can be changed to achieve different goals. By breaking up the task into small subroutines, we can easily use them unchanged for other purposes. The problems for this section are intended to clearly demonstrate this concept.

Now we list the program in its entirety.

Program 8-1. The calendar program.

```
DEFINT A-Z
GOSUB RequestData
GOSUB DisplayCalendar
END

RequestData:
  INPUT "Month, Year"; MONTH, YEAR
  IF MONTH < 1 OR MONTH > 12 THEN RequestData
  IF YEAR  < 0 OR YEAR  > 99 THEN RequestData
  RETURN
```

A Calendar Program

```
DisplayCalendar:
  GOSUB Calculate
  GOSUB DisplayTitle
  GOSUB DisplayDays
  RETURN


Calculate:
            'DAY – DAY of the week, 1st of Month
            'N – No. of days in Month
  IF YEAR MOD 4 = 0 THEN LEAP = 1 ELSE LEAP = 0
  DAY = (YEAR + (YEAR + 3) / 4) MOD 7
  N = 0
  FOR M = 1 TO MONTH
    DAY = (DAY + N) MOD 7
    N = 30 + ((M + (M > 7)) MOD 2)
    IF M = 2 THEN N = 28 + LEAP
  NEXT M
  RETURN


DisplayTitle:
  M$ = "JanFebMarAprMayJunJulAugSepOctNovDec"
  PRINT
  PRINT TAB(9); MID$(M$, MONTH*3−2, 3), 1900 + YEAR
  PRINT : PRINT " Sun Mon Tue Wed Thu Fri Sat"
  RETURN

DisplayDays:
  K = DAY
  FOR J = 1 TO N
    PRINT TAB(K*4 + 1 − (J < 10)); J;
    K = (K + 1) MOD 7 : IF K = 0 THEN PRINT
  NEXT J
  PRINT : PRINT
  RETURN
```

Problems for Section 8-1

1. Modify Program 8-1 so that it displays the calendar for an entire year.
2. Modify Program 8-1 so that it displays all calendars for a given month for a range of years.
3. Modify Program 8-1 to display the month and year for every month that has a Friday the thirteenth. Note: If Friday falls on the thirteenth, then what day of the week does the first of the month fall on?
4. Modify Program 8-1 to request a date in the form YYMMDD and display the day of the week for that date.
5. With the year 2000 close at hand, modify Program 8-1 to handle the twenty-first century.
6. Write a subroutine to verify keyboard input for being a valid date. Accept numbers in the form YYMMDD. Get right down to February and leap years.
7. Modify Program 8-1 so that the calendar is displayed in a small output window on an otherwise blank screen. Try using a type 1 window and experiment with window size and position. Try to display the month and year in the title bar.

8-2. The Sieve of Eratosthenes

Eratosthenes, who lived around 240 B.C., worked out a way of detecting prime numbers by eliminating all composite numbers. Composite numbers are numbers that can be formed by multiplying any two other numbers besides zero and one. It goes like this: Write down all the integers. Now, beginning with 2, cross out all multiples of 2 up to the upper limit. Go back to the next uncrossed-out integer and cross out all multiples of it. Repeat this until there are no more numbers to cross out. The remaining numbers are prime.

This is nicely implemented on the computer using an array to "write down" the integers we want. Set all array values to 1. Then begin with 2, leave it, and proceed by crossing out 4, 6, and so on. Next go back to the 3, leave it, and cross out 6, 9, and etc. The crossing out process may be simulated by setting the array value to 0.

This is surprisingly easy to program. We first try it with just 100 elements in our array. If we start out with thousands and we make a programming error, it might be several minutes before the results are displayed. Let's perfect it with the smaller task. After we are sure that it works then we can try larger and larger values until we use all of memory. See Program 8-2.

Program 8-2. Primes using the Sieve of Eratosthenes.

```
WIDTH 60
PRINT "Finding primes using the Sieve of Eratosthenes"
PRINT
UPPER.LIMIT = 100
DIM SIEVE(UPPER.LIMIT)

REM ** Load the array with 1s
FOR J = 1 TO UPPER.LIMIT : SIEVE(J) = 1 : NEXT J

REM ** "Work the sieve"
FOR J1 = 2 TO UPPER.LIMIT
   FOR J2 = 2*J1 TO UPPER.LIMIT STEP J1
      SIEVE( J2 ) = 0
   NEXT J2
NEXT J1

REM ** Display primes only
FOR J1 = 2 TO UPPER.LIMIT
   IF SIEVE( J1 ) = 1 THEN PRINT J1;
NEXT J1
```

Since we may want to run this program with a large value for UPPER.LIMIT, it makes sense to consider efficiency.

Look at this line:

FOR J1 = 2 **TO** UPPER.LIMIT

There is no need to have J1 go past the square root of the UPPER.LIMIT. Any larger values that should be crossed out already have been. Think about what happens in this routine when J1 gets to 4. It will go cross out 8, 16, and so on. But any multiple of 4 is also a multiple of 2. And all multiples of 2 have already been crossed out, including 4. Therefore, there is no need to cross out values if the first element we come to already has been. This test can be carried out with an IF statement. The combination of these two things will result in a saving of execution time.

Problems for Section 8-2

1. Set the UPPER.LIMIT in Program 8-2 at 1000 and run the program. Change the UPPER.LIMIT to SQR(UPPER.LIMIT) and insert a line immediately after this line to test if SIEVE(J1) has already been crossed out. Run the new version and compare the execution time for the two versions. Use TIMER (the number of seconds since midnight).

2. The 128k Mac sometimes limits array size. As written, the Program 8-2 uses 8 bytes for each integer in array SIEVE. First increase the UPPER.LIMIT to the maximum possible size. Then change the program to use an integer array SIEVE%. You should be able to increase the array size by a factor of four.

3. BASIC handles integers faster than double precision numbers. Speed up Program 8-2 by DEFining all variables as INTeger with

   DEFINT A-Z

   Compare execution time for double precision and integer modes.

8-3. Number Bases

Binary Numbering

Computers are not very good at reckoning in our familiar base ten number system. Computers digest everything they do in terms of electrical states. Things are either at a charged state or an uncharged state. With just two states, it makes sense to represent them with 1 and 0. This leads us to the binary, or base two numbering system. The computer doesn't work with different numbers, it just represents them differently. We are very used to working with the decimal, or base ten, numbering system. In base ten, each place represents a power of ten. In binary, each place represents a power of two. When we write 10 in decimal, we mean ten. When we write 10 in binary, we mean two. To write ten in binary, we use 1010. 1010 is $2^3 + 2^1$. In base ten, 1010 is one thousand ten.

Binary arithmetic in base two is very easy. For addition, the result of adding two digits is either 0, 1, or 10.

$$0 + 0 = 0$$
$$1 + 0 = 1$$
$$1 + 1 = 10$$

When adding 1 and 1 there will be a carry into the next place to the left.

Multiplication is also straightforward. When multiplying by 1 the digits shift according to the position of the 1, and when multiplying by 0 the result is 0. The shift when 1 is in the first column on the right is 0 places, for 1 in the second column it is 1 place, for 1 in the third column it is 2 places, and so on. Numbering the columns beginning with 0 makes the shift equal to the column number. Representing each digit by 2 to a power fits in nicely here. The exponent on two will be the same as the column number. Some examples:

$$1 * 101 = 101 \text{ (shift of 0)}$$
$$10 * 101 = 1010 \text{ (shift of 1)}$$
$$1000 * 101 = 101000 \text{ (shift of 3)}$$

Multiplying 2 by 2 in binary looks like this:

```
   10
 * 10
 ----
  100
```

And to multiply 27 by 5, we would write the following:

```
    11011
 *    101
 --------
    11011
    00000
   11011
 --------
 10000111
```

Note that the carry from adding 1 and 1 in column 3 created a "domino effect" by pushing the carry across several columns.

A Binary digIT is called a BIT. Since a single bit isn't always useful, it make sense to group them into packages. One byte is 8 bits. This works out to exactly accommodate numbers in the range 0 to 255.

In any number system each digit of any integer represents an integer power of the base. So the digits in base two represent 1, 2, 4, 8, 16, 32, 64, 128, 256, 512, 1024, and so on in base ten, corresponding to the bit positions 0, 1, 2, 3, 4, 5, 6, 7, 8, 9, 10, and so on in binary.

One disadvantage of the binary number system is that it takes so many digits to represent numbers. For instance, 15 base ten is written as 1111 in binary, and 127 base ten is written 1111111 in binary. Only humans notice how cumbersome this is. Computers are well suited to accessing individual digits to determine their state or to change their state.

In BASIC the largest true integer value is 32767, and the smallest is –32768. That comes out to 65536 numbers. Zero base ten is 0 in binary. And 65535 base ten is 1111111111111111 in binary notation. That is 16 bits. We get 16 bits by grouping two bytes together. But, in practice, that number range is utilized as numbers in the range –32768 to 32767. Values from 0 to 32767 are stored as we would expect. Values from 32768 to 65535 are translated into values in the range –1 to –32768. The 16th bit is used to determine the sign of the number. We'll come back to this later.

It is instructive to write a program to convert base ten numbers to binary notation. A very easy way to start is to use MOD to decide whether the given base ten number is odd or even. If it is odd, then the units digit in the binary number is a 1. If even, then the units binary digit is 0. Next, we "peel off" the binary digit by using integer division to divide by 2 and do the odd/even test on the result. We repeat this until the result is zero.

Program 8-3. Convert base ten to binary.

```
PRINT "Convert base ten numbers to binary format"
PRINT
INPUT "Enter a value"; DECIMAL
GetBit:
  X = DECIMAL MOD 2
  A$ = STR$(X) + A$
  DECIMAL = DECIMAL \ 2
  IF DECIMAL THEN GetBit
  PRINT A$
```

```
┌─────────────────────────────────────────────┐
│ ▭ ≡≡≡≡≡≡≡≡≡  Program 8-3  ≡≡≡≡≡≡≡≡≡         │
│ Convert base ten numbers to binary format   │
│                                             │
│ Enter a value? 8466                         │
│ 1 0 0 0 0 1 0 0 0 1 0 0 1 0                 │
│                                             │
│                                             │
└─────────────────────────────────────────────┘
```

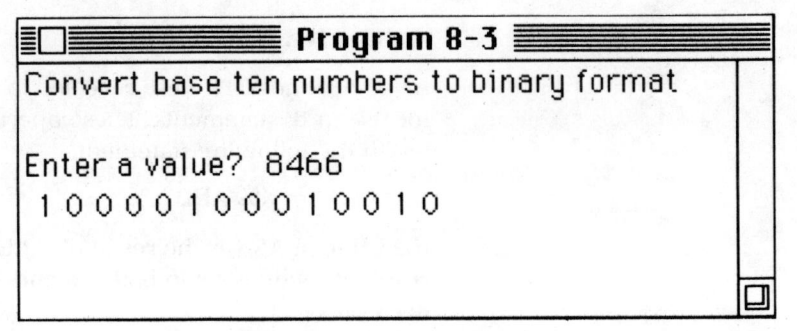

Figure 8-2. Execution of Program 8-3.

In Program 8-3, the line

    IF DECIMAL **THEN** GetBit

performs exactly like

    IF DECIMAL <> 0 **THEN** GetBit

Remember that an expression using a relational operator is evaluated as −1 or 0 according to whether it is true or not true. We can also supply a numeric value in a test to determine when the condition will be evaluated as "true" and when as "not true." A value of 0 stands for not true, and any other value stands for true. In this line, DECIMAL will evaluate as true as long as it is not yet zero. Therefore it is convenient to just use the variable name itself in the IF... THEN test to make BASIC go GetBit until the value of DECIMAL equals zero.

    MOD and integer division are limited to integers. Values entered outside the range −32768 to 32767 will bring forth the "Overflow" error box.

    Program 8-3 does not handle negative numbers. BASIC uses "twos complement" form to store negative integers in the range −1 to −32768. Once we have the binary form of the absolute value of our negative number, the rule to get twos complement is: Change every 0 to a 1, change every 1 to a 0, and add 1 to the result. Let's look at an example. Running Program 8-3 for 32000 gives us

    0 1 1 1 1 1 0 1 0 0 0 0 0 0 0 0

According to the rule we change 1s to 0s, 0s to 1s, and add 1, thus:

    1 0 0 0 0 0 1 0 1 1 1 1 1 1 1 1
                                   + 1
    ─────────────────────────────
    1 0 0 0 0 0 1 1 0 0 0 0 0 0 0 0

This last 16-bit binary display represents −32000.

AND, OR, and NOT

AND, OR, and NOT were revealed in Chapter 3 as logical operators for use in IF statements. These operators deal with integers bit by bit. In the following statement:

AN% = X% **AND** Y%

the value of AN% is the result of setting a bit in AN% only if the corresponding bit is set in both X% and Y%. The value of 19 AND 6 is 2 because

```
    19      =  10011
     6      =    110
  ─────        ─────
19 AND 6    =     10
```

OR sets a bit in the result if the corresponding bit in either argument is set. So, 19 OR 6 is 23. NOT reverses every bit. Thus, NOT 32767 comes out −32768 as shown below:

```
 32767 = 0111111111111111
-32768 = 1000000000000000
```

Hexadecimal Numbering

It doesn't take long working with binary numbers to realize that it would be nice to have some shorthand. Hexadecimal numbering comes to the rescue. This new system has 16 digits. Since our familiar base ten system has only 10 digits, it is necessary to invent 6 new digits. A through F have been selected. Thus, the hexadecimal digits are

0, 1, 2, 3, 4, 5, 6, 7, 8, 9, A, B, C, D, E, and F

Now each place represents an integer power of 16. Here are some example values:

11 hex	17 base ten	10001 binary
1A hex	26 base ten	11010 binary
4FFF hex	16383 base ten	111111111111 binary
8FFF hex	32767 base ten	1111111111111 binary
FFFE hex	65534 base ten	1111110000010110 binary

Clearly, the hex form is very compact. Hex values from 0 to FF exactly correspond to base ten values from 0 to 255. That exactly corresponds to the range of values available in one 8-bit byte.

Fortunately, BASIC handles hex numbers with ease. If we want to know the base ten equivalent for 4F, we just

PRINT &H4F

and instantly we get 79. Hex numbers are expressed in BASIC with the &H prefix. They will be indispensible for working with the QuickDraw graphics routines. (See Chapter 10.) Suppose we want the base ten representation for FEFE. BASIC replies with −258. This assumes that we are interested in strict integer values in the range −32768 to 32767. For values in the range −1 to −32768, we can get a positive result by adding 65536. Here we get 65278. Values greater than FFFF cause an Overflow.

Converting values the other way is just as easy. The HEX$ function is the way to go. To find a hex value for 32676 we simply

PRINT HEX$(32767)

BASIC unselfishly reports 7FFF. Trying to get a hex value for numbers greater than 32767 will also evoke the Overflow error message.

Four binary digits are all that is necessary to express the full range of values from 0 to 15. So, four binary digits are equivalent to a single hex digit. Program 8-4 is a utility program that uses buttons to make it easy to see the relationship between binary and hex notation.

Program 8-4. Practice with binary and hex.

```
WINDOW CLOSE 1 : WINDOW 2,,(40,50)–(240,110),2
FOR X = 1 TO 4
   BUTTON X, 1, "", (31+X*16,35)–(31+X*16+17,50), 2
NEXT X
BUTTON 25, 1, "Quit", (130,35)–(160,51), 1
X$ = "0 0 0 0" : N = 0
LOCATE 2,1 : PRINT "Binary "; X$
LOCATE 1,1 : PRINT "Hex       "; HEX$(N)

Poll:   PROCESS = DIALOG(0) : IF PROCESS <> 1 THEN Poll
        PRESS = DIALOG(1) : IF PRESS = 25 THEN CleanUp
        STATE = BUTTON(PRESS)
        IF STATE = 2 THEN STATE = 1 ELSE STATE = 2
        BUTTON PRESS, STATE
        DIGIT = STATE - 1
        VALUE = 2^(4-PRESS)
        IF DIGIT = 0 THEN D$ = "0" : N = N - VALUE
        IF DIGIT = 1 THEN D$ = "1" : N = N + VALUE
        MID$(X$,(PRESS-1)*3+1,1) = D$
        LOCATE 2,7 : PRINT X$
        LOCATE 1,10 : PRINT HEX$(N)
        GOTO Poll

CleanUp:
   WINDOW CLOSE 2 : WINDOW 1
   END
```

Remember, DIALOG(0) returns the value 1 if a button has been pressed. DIALOG(1) returns the number of the pressed button. BUTTON(number) returns the state of the button.

```
┌─────────────────────────────┐
│  Hex        A               │
│  Binary  1 0 1 0            │
│         ☒ ☐ ☒ ☐    [Quit]   │
└─────────────────────────────┘
```

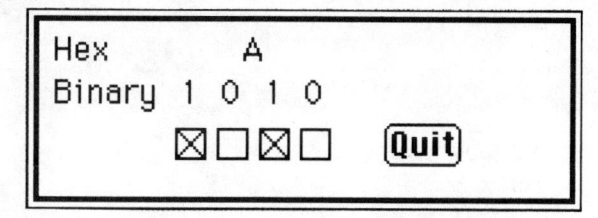

Figure 8-3. Execution of Program 8-4.

Figure 8-3 shows only a single result. To see Program 8-4 in action, you should type the program in and run it. You can repeatedly turn bits on and off by pressing the digit buttons. Use this program to help you gain a better feel for both ways of writing numbers.

Octal Numbering

For completeness here, we introduce the OCT$ function and the &O prefix for octal values. The base eight system is referred to as OCTAL. The digits run from 0 through 7. The use of OCT$ and &O parallels, in every way, the use of HEX$ and &H. The largest octal value allowed in BASIC is 177777, which is equivalent to 65535 in base ten but displays as −1.

Problems for Section 8-3

1. Program 8-3 displays the results with the binary digits separated. Fix this.
2. Program 8-3 uses the convenience of the integer MOD operator and integer division. We might like to see a binary representation of integers greater than 32767. Use ordinary division and the INT function to do this.
3. Write a program to convert binary numbers to base ten form. Accept binary values from the keyboard into a string and process into a BASIC numeric variable.
4. Rewrite Program 8-3 to display twos complement for integers in the range -1 to -32768.
5. Expand Program 8-4 to convert 8 binary digits to 2 hex digits or try 16 binary digits to 4 hex digits.

CHAPTER 9

Graphics

Although many computer applications are centered around numeric manipulations and things like word processing, there is a great deal of interest in computer graphics. Some people are attracted by the ease with which data can be presented in chart form using a computer. Others are attracted to the games aspect. Still others will use graphics merely for the pleasing effects that are possible.

With just one statement we can draw every kind of straight line we'll need for graphics. Variations of the LINE statement create lines, boxes, and solid boxes. Another statement draws every kind of curved line. With the CIRCLE statement we can draw circles, ellipses, arcs, and even outlines shaped like pieces of pie. The PSET statement is used to draw single points. The color of a point in an output window is returned in the POINT function. GET and PUT are used to manipulate graphics images in output windows. The various picture features may be just what is needed to create a special graphics effect. We also have access to the Macintosh QuickDraw routines in Microsoft BASIC. These are covered in Chapter 10.

Once we have produced figures with Microsoft BASIC on the Macintosh, there are many options for what to do next. We may be satisfied just to have produced each masterpiece. We may want to save a program on disk for future use. We may use picture features to save just the image in a disk file.

We may want to preserve the image on paper with the printer. This can be done in several ways. ⌘-Shift-4 sends the currently active window to the Imagewriter, while ⌘-Shift-4 with Caps Lock engaged sends the full screen image out. We can also save the contents of the Macintosh screen on disk with ⌘-Shift-3. Images stored in this way are named Screen 0 through Screen 9. These are MacPaint documents, so you can use MacPaint to work on them later. The BASIC keyword LCOPY causes the screen image to be sent to the printer. This means that we can print the screen at any time during program execution. Do this with great care. You can use up a lot of paper this way.

9-1. Getting Started

The Graphics Screen

The graphics screen is the current output window. Some output window characteristics introduced in Chapter 6 are reviewed here. All graphics coordinates within the output window refer to pixels. The default type 1 output window obtained by clicking on a BASIC program icon on the desktop measures 491 pixels wide by 299 pixels high. The pixel numbering is from 0 to 490 from left to right horizontally and from 0 to 298 from top to bottom vertically. The default type 1 output window obtained by clicking on the Microsoft BASIC icon on the desktop is 491 pixels wide and 254 pixels high. The default type 2, 3, and 4 output windows are 200 pixels by 140 pixels.

Other output windows are created with statements of the form:

WINDOW number, title$, (x1,y2)–(x2,y2), type

Remember that the coordinates specified in the window statement refer to the larger Macintosh screen. Once inside the window, coordinates are relative to the upper left corner of the window. The screen coordinates for the larger default output window are:

(2,41)–(508,340)

for a type 1 window. Remember, the size box vertical bar takes up 15 pixels.

The width and height of the current window are found in WINDOW(2) and WINDOW(3) respectively. Using this information, programs can be written to respond to changes in window size.

Drawing Straight Lines (LINE)

LINE – (0,100)

draws a line in the current output window from the current pen position to the coordinates (0,100). The pen position is the most recent point drawn. The default position after NEW, RUN, and CLS is the center of the output window. This example draws a line from the center to the left edge of the output window 100 pixels from the top.

We can specify both the starting and ending coordinates of a line by using the standard rectangle specification.

LINE (0,0)–(490,253)

draws a diagonal line from the upper left corner to the lower right corner of a 491 by 254 output window. Even if the window has been made smaller, the line is drawn to where the endpoints should be whether or not they are visible. Any integer values may be used in the LINE statement. Other values cause an "Overflow" error box.

Box and BoxFill

How about drawing a box? It does not require four LINE statements to do this. If we specify the beginning corner and the ending corner, the "Box" option does it for us. To make the outline of a box into a solid box, we use "BF", for "BoxFill".

LINE (0,0)–(100,50),,B

draws a box with the upper left corner at (0,0) and the lower right corner at (100,50).

Color

The extra comma before the ",B" in the example above is holding a place for the color specification. To draw in white, use 30. To draw in black, use 33. Black is the default color, so it is often convenient to just omit the number when we want black.

STEP

The STEP option calls for a displacement relative to the most recent point.

LINE (15,50) – **STEP** (20,35),,B

will display a box 20 pixels wide and 35 pixels high with the beginning corner at the point (15,50). STEP may also be used to cause the LINE to begin relative to the last point plotted.

LINE STEP (10,20) − (490,40)

will begin the line 10 pixels to the right and 20 pixels below wherever the last point was plotted and draw toward the upper right corner of the window. The nice feature of this STEP option is that it enables us to think in terms of size. Often we know where we want to put the beginning point of a line, and how long it should be. Using STEP, we do not have to calculate the length added to the starting point in order to specify the ending point. It is just as convenient for drawing boxes. We only have to think about where to put the upper left corner and the dimensions of the box.

Program 9-1 incorporates a variety of possible uses of the LINE statement options.

Program 9-1. Variety of LINE statements.

```
REM ** Box with a border
LINE (50,10) - STEP (100,100),,BF
LINE (60,20) - STEP (80,80),30,B

REM ** Checkerboard
LINE (170,20) - STEP (80,80),,B
FOR X = 170 TO 230 STEP 20
   FOR Y = 20 TO 80 STEP 20
      LINE (X,Y) - STEP (10,10),33,BF
      LINE (X+10,Y+10) - STEP (10,10),33,BF
   NEXT Y
NEXT X

REM ** Grid
FOR K = 270 TO 370 STEP 10
   LINE (K,10)-(K,110)
   LINE (270,K-260)-(370,K-260)
NEXT K
```

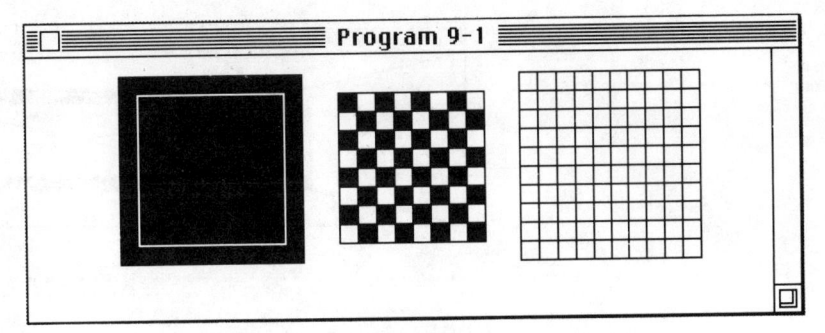

Figure 9-1. Execution of Program 9-1.

As mentioned earlier in this chapter and in Chapter 6, WINDOW(2) and WINDOW(3) return the width and height of the current output window. This makes it easy to write programs with a display that responds to changes in window size. Using a type 1 window we can allow the user to move it and change the size with the mouse and the size box. Program 9-2 is a simple example to demonstrate the technique.

Program 9-2. Demonstrate using WINDOW function to change display.

```
Refresh:
   CLS : WIDE = WINDOW(2) : HIGH = WINDOW(3)
   LINE (.2*WIDE,.2*HIGH)–(.8*WIDE,.8*HIGH),,BF
   LINE (.3*WIDE,.3*HIGH)–(.7*WIDE,.7*HIGH),30,BF
   LINE (0,0)–(WIDE,HIGH)
   LINE (0,HIGH)–(WIDE,0)
   WHILE WIDE = WINDOW(2) AND HIGH = WINDOW(3) : WEND
   GOTO Refresh
```

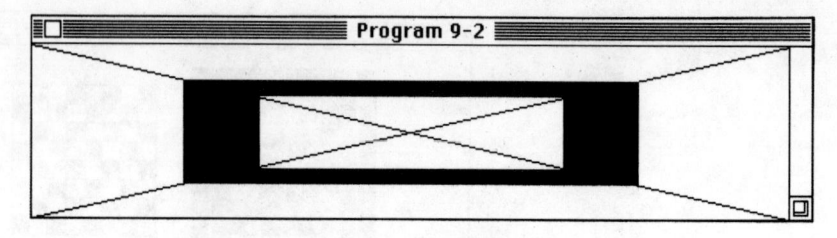

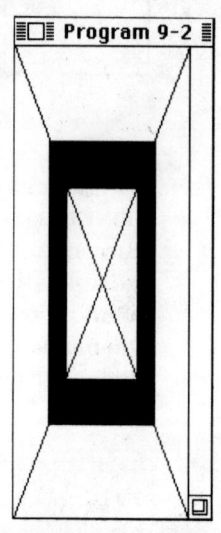

Figure 9-2. Execution of Program 9-2.

Two results are shown in Figure 9-2, but the full effect is possible only if you type the program in and experiment with it.

Drawing Curved Lines (CIRCLE)

The CIRCLE statement also has several options to create a variety of effects. The simplest form of the statement draws a circle of radius R with the center at X,Y.

CIRCLE (X,Y),R

We can also use STEP here to place the center of the circle at a point relative to the current pen position. The color parameter also works in the same way as it does with LINE. 30 is white and 33 is black. So already we have five possible specifications:

CIRCLE STEP (X,Y),Radius,Color

Of these, STEP and Color are optional.

Start and End Angles

We can also specify start and end angles in the CIRCLE statement so we can regulate how much of the full circle is drawn. This is the way to draw a short curved line or any portion of a circle. The angles are measured in radians. The values for the angles may range from -2π to 2π. Remember π is about 3.14159, so decimal values in the range −6.28 to 6.28 are good to use. Suppose a circle uses a start angle of 0 and an end angle of $1/2\pi$, or about 1.57. A quarter of a circle will be drawn traveling counterclockwise, starting level with the X-axis on the right and ending at the top of where the full circle would be. If the start angle is less than the end angle, that's okay. The arc is drawn exactly according to instructions, starting at the start angle and ending at the end angle, always drawing counterclockwise. However, the values from -2π to 0 do not represent negative angles as they are commonly used. Instead, a dash in front of the number causes a line to be drawn from the center of the circle to the (positive) angle specified. This is the way to draw a piece of pie. Program 9-3 demonstrates this feature.

Program 9-3. Positive vs. negative start and end angles.

```
PRINT " Positive Negative"
CIRCLE (35,50),20,33,1/2,6                'One
CIRCLE (90,50),20,33,-1/2,-6              'Two
LOCATE 6, 4 : PRINT "One    Two"

CIRCLE (35,150),20,33,6,1/2               'Three
CIRCLE (90,150),20,33,-6,-1/2             'Four
LOCATE 12, 4 : PRINT "Three    Four"
```

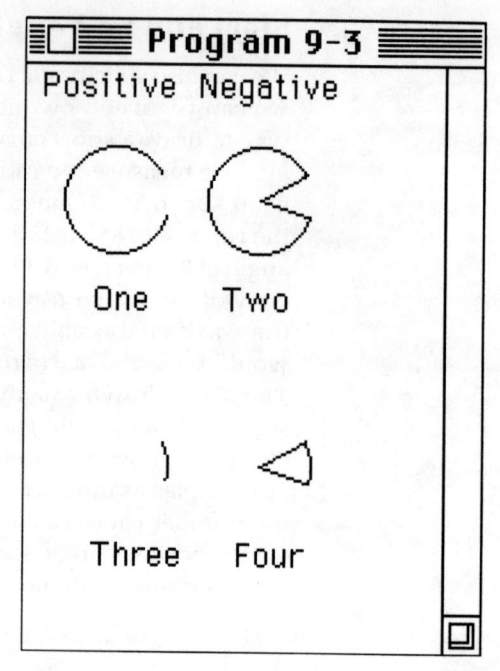

Figure 9-3. Execution of Program 9-3.

Aspect

The final CIRCLE option is the "aspect." We can "squash" the circle into an ellipse of any proportions by specifying an aspect ratio. The aspect ratio is the ratio of the Y radius to the X radius. The default ratio is 1, so the radius is identical in all directions for a regular circle. An aspect ratio of 3 means that the Y radius is three times the X radius, so the ellipse will be tall and thin. An aspect ratio of 1/3 will produce the same shape lying on its side, or a short, squat ellipse. When the aspect ratio is less than one, the radius specified in the CIRCLE statement is used for the X radius. When the ratio is more than one, the radius given is used for the Y radius. In other words, the radius specified will be the larger of the two.

The "B" and "BF" options of the LINE statement are used to draw boxes and to fill boxes. Sometimes it would be nice to fill a circle. The CIRCLE statement does not offer such an option. But, we can easily place a CIRCLE statement in a loop with the radius value going from 0 to the desired radius. Sometimes this "growing" effect is desirable. Changing the limits on the radius variable in the FOR loop can cause the circle to grow toward the center or create a donut.

Experiment with different start and end angles and different aspect ratios to become familiar with the way they affect CIRCLE. Here is a little program to get you started:

```
FOR A = .1 TO 2.5 STEP .1
    CIRCLE (100,150),50,33,,,A
NEXT A
```

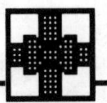

Summary

With only two BASIC statements, we can draw an amazing variety of lines and shapes. We can use as much of the output window as we want for graphics. The computer allows us to draw to points that aren't visible in the window. The columns are numbered from 0 to the upper limit beginning at the left edge of the window. The rows are numbered from 0 to the upper limit beginning at the top of the window. In both the LINE and CIRCLE statements we have several options that draw different shapes depending on how we use them. To draw in white we use 30 as the color specification. Use 33 for black. We select from among the options in the following statements to produce the desired effects:

LINE STEP (X,Y) – **STEP** (X1,Y1),Color,BoxFill
CIRCLE STEP (X,Y),Radius,Color,Begin,Finish,Aspect

Problems for Section 9-1

A few problems are offered here to get you going in your experimentation with graphics. One of the nice things about working with graphics programs is that it is easy to produce dramatic changes in the results with minor changes in program statements. Don't limit yourself. Try new things. You can't damage the computer with a BASIC program.

1. Write a program to draw the outline of a three-dimensional box. You need two squares or rectangles offset a little and four lines connecting the corners.

2. Write a program to show the video game monster drawn with CIRCLE opening and closing its mouth.

3. Display a number of ellipses at random locations with randomly selected shapes.

4. Modify the program for Problem 3 to frame each ellipse in a rectangular box that fits its dimensions.

5. Write a program to draw a bar graph picturing the following temperatures for a nine-day period:

Day	Temp
1	30
2	27
3	26
4	31
5	26
6	30
7	38
8	36
9	34

6. Write a program to simulate stars blinking in the sky. First fill a box (try 100 by 100) to show the night sky. Randomly set the color to either 30 or 33. You'll want more 33's than 30's. Randomly select coordinates within the box. Separate the stars so that we don't end up with some stars obscuring others.

7. Write a program to display donuts.

8. Write a program to display a box with a border 10 pixels thick.

9-2. A Graphic Example (Drawing Dice)

It is easy to program a computer to simulate the roll of a die and display a numeric result. Now that we know about graphics let's display a realistic picture of the die. This will be surprisingly easy to do. We might just as well write a little program to produce graph paper for the job. See Program 9-4.

Program 9-4. Draw graph paper.

```
REM ** Draw graph paper
FOR X = 10 TO 480 STEP 10
    LINE (X,10)–(X,250)
NEXT X
FOR Y = 10 TO 250 STEP 10
    LINE (10,Y)–(480,Y)
NEXT Y
```

Figure 9-4 shows a drawing of the six possible faces of a die on graph paper.

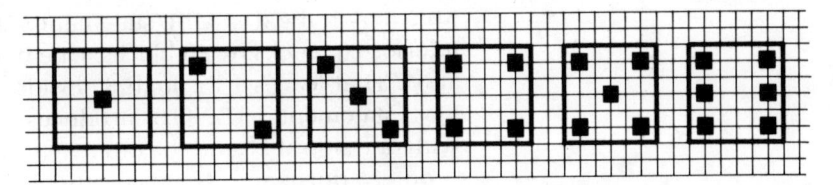

Figure 9-4. The six dice.

They can be represented nicely if we use squares sixty pixels wide and sixty pixels high. Then the dots can be ten by ten pixels.

Now the computer problem separates into two parts. First, we need the die background. And second, we need six different configurations for the dots. Having learned the wondrous things the LINE statement can do, we can now plan how to apply them to draw a die. Let's first draw the "1" face of a die. All we need is a box with a solid block in the middle. Program 9-5 draws a "1" in the upper left corner of the screen:

Chapter 9: Graphics

Program 9-5. Draw the "1" face of a die.

```
REM ** The "1" face on a die
LINE (0,0) - STEP (61,61),,B
LINE (26,26) - STEP (9,9),,BF
```

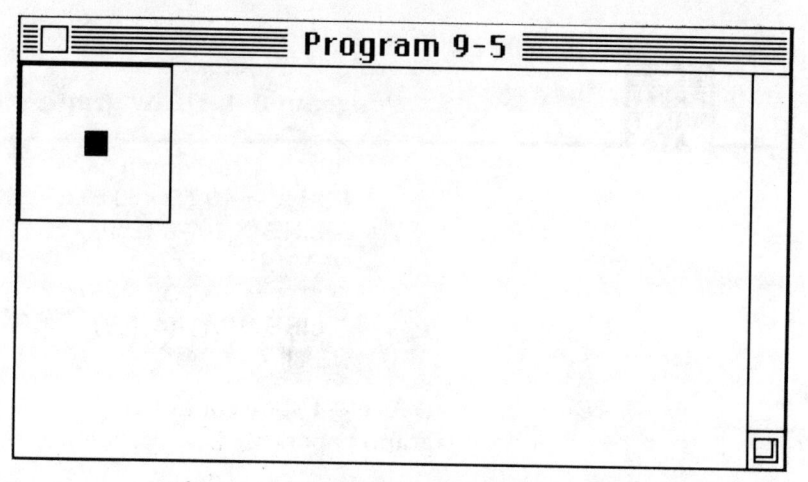

Figure 9-5. Execution of Program 9-5.

Note that in the first LINE statement STEP (61,61) draws a box with interior 60 blocks by 60 blocks. One border is at 0 and the other is at 61. That leaves 1 through 60 inside the box. And in the second LINE statement, STEP (9,9) produces a filled box that is 10 by 10 with one side at 26 and the other at 35, leaving a border around the '1 dot' 25 dots wide. That is pretty nice. How do we get a "3"? Simply add the following two statements and run the new program:

```
LINE (6,6) - STEP (9,9),,BF
LINE (46,46) - STEP (9,9),,BF
```

By properly selecting our coordinates, we may draw any of the six faces.

Wouldn't it be nice to make these dice even more realistic? Real dice usually have round dots. But there's no "F" option to fill in circles, so if we just use CIRCLE we will get outlines of the dots. That's not much better than square ones. Using the FILLROUNDRECT subroutine in Chapter 10 is an option, but we can create our own solid circles, by using a variable for the radius of a circle and putting it in a FOR...NEXT loop. If we make the radius go from 0 to 5, we'll get a solid circle with a radius of 5. Program 9-6 displays a three die using circles for the dots.

Program 9-6. Draw the "3" face of a die with circular dots.

```
REM ** The "3" face of a die
LINE (0,0) – STEP (61,61),,BF
FOR R = 0 TO 5
   CIRCLE (10,10),R
   CIRCLE (30,30),R
   CIRCLE (50,50),R
NEXT R
END
```

It turns out that CIRCLE (X,Y),R creates drawings by taking (X,Y) as the center of the circle and drawing all pixels at a distance of R. The circle crosses the X-axis at X+R and X–R, and it crosses the Y-axis at Y+R and Y–R. That way, drawing a circle with a radius of zero produces a single dot on the screen. The result is a circle with a diameter of 1 more than 2 times R. We simply cannot get circles with a diameter of 10. Our dice will be just fine with 11 pixel dots.

Divide and Conquer (More Dice)

Once we have written a routine to display a die having a particular face value in a particular place, it is hard to be inspired to write a new one to display that same die in another location. And even less exciting to consider displaying five different dice this way. When we find ourselves writing routine after routine, each of which is only a slight variation of another one, programming becomes tedious. It does not need to be that way. The more experience we gain in programming, the more opportunity we will have to utilize what we have already done. Often a current problem is only a slight variation of an old one that we have already solved.

We would like to be able to display a die anywhere on the screen. This is easy with subroutines. All we need to do is make the references to coordinates in the subroutine relative to some fixed point. Program 9-7 uses (X,Y) as the position of the upper left corner of the one die.

Chapter 9: Graphics

> **Program 9-7. Drawing a "1" anywhere in the window.**
>
> ```
> One: 'Display a "1" die
>      LINE (X,Y) - STEP (61,61),,B
>      FOR R = 0 TO 5
>        CIRCLE (X+30,Y+30),R
>      NEXT R
>      RETURN
> ```

We think of

GOSUB One

as "display the one die" without having to think about the actual BASIC statements required to do the display. Just be careful to keep the display visible in the currrent output window.

We can take this even one step further by separating the display of the die background from the display of the dots. Let's think of writing seven subroutines—one to display each of the die faces and one to do the background. All we have to do to create the routine to display the background is remove the dot display statements in Program 9-7.

We will use the variation of GOSUB that allows us to select a subroutine from a list of line labels as follows:

ON N **GOSUB** One,Two,Three,Four,Five,Six

where N is the value for this roll of a die. If N equals 1 then BASIC executes the statement:

GOSUB One

If N equals 3 then BASIC executes the statement:

GOSUB Three

Here are some of the die display routines to get you started:

```
One:
FOR R = 0 TO 5
  CIRCLE (X+30,Y+30),R
NEXT R
RETURN
```

A Graphic Example (Drawing Dice)

```
Two:
FOR R = 0 TO 5
    CIRCLE (X+10,Y+10),R
    CIRCLE (X+50,Y+50),R
NEXT R
RETURN
  .
  .
  .
Six:
FOR R = 0 TO 5
    CIRCLE (X+10,Y+10),R
    CIRCLE (X+10,Y+30),R
    CIRCLE (X+10,Y+50),R
    CIRCLE (X+50,Y+10),R
    CIRCLE (X+50,Y+30),R
    CIRCLE (X+50,Y+50),R
NEXT R
RETURN
```

Now we need to remove the dot-drawing statements from Program 9-7 so it will just draw the die outline. Further, if we simply put in a variable for color, we can use the same routine to erase a die by setting color to 30. This requires adding the color variable to all the circle statements.

```
DieBackground:
    LINE (X,Y) - STEP (61,61),C,B
    RETURN
```

Now the program boils down to two ideas—display a background and display the dots. We set values for N, X, Y, and C and then two statements do the work:

```
Set N, X, Y, and C
GOSUB DieBackground
ON N GOSUB One,Two,Three,Four,Five,Six
```

Problems for Section 9-2

1. Write a program to display a die face showing a "5" in the upper right corner of the graphics window.

2. Write a program to display a random die face in the upper left corner of the window.

3. Display a random die face, leave it for a few seconds and then erase it.

4. Display two dice at random next to each other in the lower left corner.

5. Write a program to display a blinking die. Let it blink 10 times, then leave the display in the window.

6. Display a few dice at random in random locations on the window to simulate physically rolling the dice. Then display a pair of dice at random and leave them in the window.

7. PICTURE could be used to draw dots on dice. First, create a picture with statements such as the following:

   PICTURE ON
   FOR R = 0 **TO** 5
     CIRCLE (5,5),R
   NEXT R
   PICTURE OFF

   Following this, PICTURE (X,Y) will display a dot with the upper left corner at the point (X,Y). Do Problem 6 using PICTURE.

9-3. Drawing from DATA

Let's write a little routine that draws lines using data stored in DATA statements. We can specify any line for black or white with five numbers—one for the color and two for each end of the line. Including a sixth item allows for boxes and solid boxes. This makes the plotting routine very simple indeed. Once we perfect it, we may use it for any drawing by simply changing the data. It is easy to terminate plotting by looking for a data value that would call for a negative color. We need a scheme for "B" and "BF". Let's use "b" for Box, "bf" for BoxFill, and "n" for None. The program ought to be able to accommodate uppercase and lowercase string data.

Program 9-8. Plot line drawings from DATA.

```
PlotLine:
  READ X,Y,X1,Y1,C,B$
  WHILE C > 0
    B$ = UCASE$(B$)
    IF B$ = "B" THEN LINE (X,Y)-(X1,Y1),C,B
    IF B$ = "BF" THEN LINE (X,Y)-(X1,Y1),C,BF
    IF B$ = "N" THEN LINE (X,Y)-(X1,Y1),C
    READ X,Y,X1,Y1,C,B$
  WEND
RETURN
```

Program 9-8 takes care of any kind of line we might need in one simple routine. It is very nice to come upon such a short routine that does so much. The real work in this drawing business is producing the data.

Just for fun let's draw a traffic light at an intersection of two roads. We should do the drawing on cross-section paper so that we can easily read the (X,Y) coordinates for each end of each straight line in the drawing. See Figure 9-6.

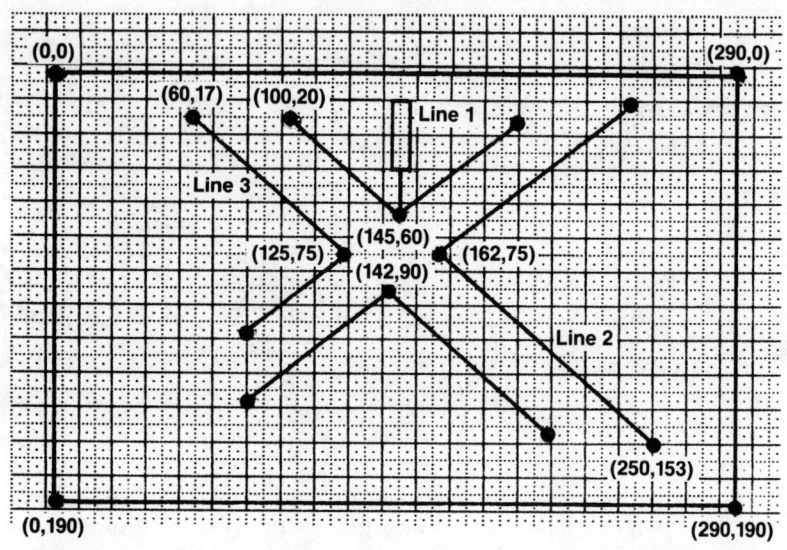

Figure 9-6. Drawing of a traffic light on cross-section paper.

The first three lines are numbered as examples in Figure 9-6. Line 1 is represented by the data 100,20,145,60,33,n. Line 2 is represented by the data 162,75,250,153,33,n. And line 3 is represented by the data 60,17,125,75,33,n. In a similar fashion we obtain the rest of the data shown in Program 9-9a. It is a good idea to separate the data into sensible groups.

Program 9-9a. Draw a traffic light using data statements.

```
REM ** Drawing a Traffic Light
LOCATE 10, 12 : PRINT "A Traffic Light"
GOSUB PlotLine
END

PlotLine:
   READ X,Y,X1,Y1,C,B$
   WHILE C > 0
     B$ = UCASE$(B$)
     IF B$ = "B" THEN LINE (X,Y)–(X1,Y1),C,B
     IF B$ = "BF" THEN LINE (X,Y)–(X1,Y1),C,BF
     IF B$ = "N" THEN LINE (X,Y)–(X1,Y1),C
     READ X,Y,X1,Y1,C,B$
   WEND
   RETURN

REM ** Line data
   ' The road
DATA 100,20,145,60,33,n
DATA 162,75,250,153,33,n
DATA 60,17,125,75,33,n
DATA 142,90,210,151,33,n
DATA 200,19,145,60,33,n
DATA 125,75,80,109,33,n
DATA 245,14,162,76,33,n
DATA 142,90,80,137,33,n

   ' The light standard
DATA 138,8,152,46,33,b
DATA 143,46,145,58,33,n
DATA 147,46,145,58,33,n
DATA 0,0,0,0,–1,n
```

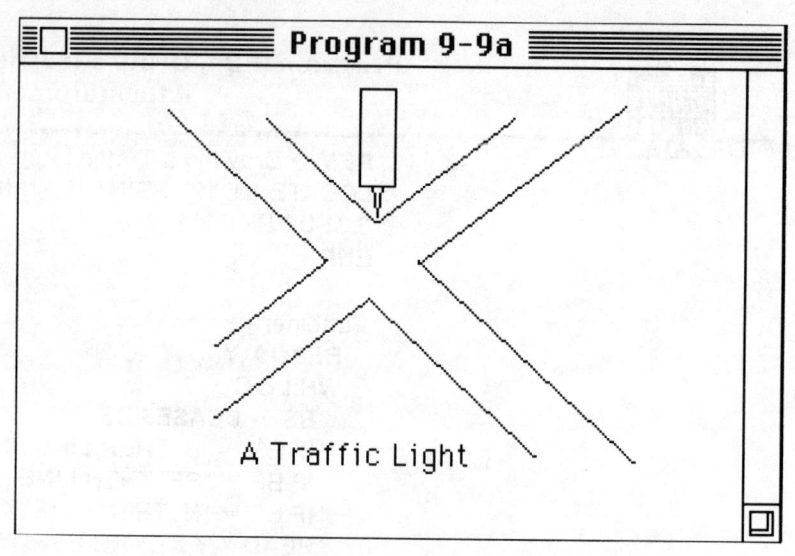

[Screen display showing "Program 9-9a" with an X drawn and label "A Traffic Light"]

Figure 9-7. Execution of Program 9-9a.

Well, this is a good start. But we certainly ought to put in the three lights. All we need is another subroutine. See Program 9-9b.

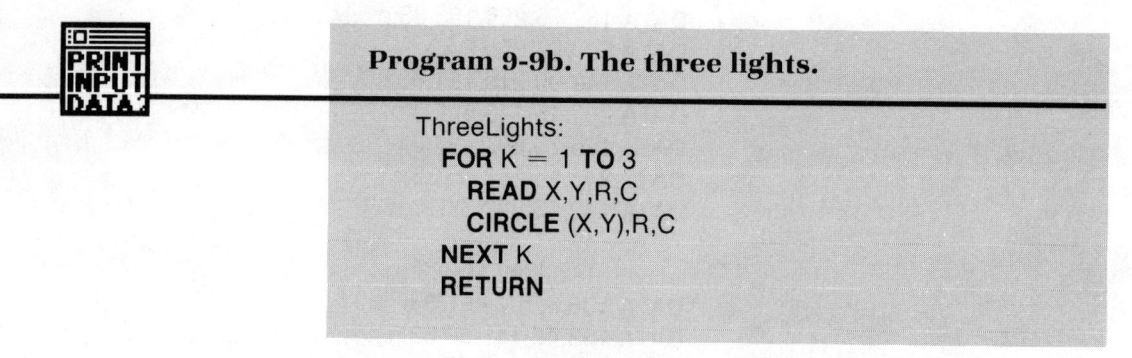

Program 9-9b. The three lights.

```
ThreeLights:
    FOR K = 1 TO 3
        READ X,Y,R,C
        CIRCLE (X,Y),R,C
    NEXT K
    RETURN
```

We need to determine the appropriate data for this latest subroutine. Looking again at our drawing of the traffic light we can see that we should center the three lights at (145,15), (145,27), and (145,39). Just add DATA statements for this.

```
LightsData:
    DATA 145,39,5,33
    DATA 145,27,5,33
    DATA 145,15,5,33
```

Now we need a routine to have the light change at reasonable intervals. It will fill in each circle in turn with black and then with white. Let's do this several times so people have a chance to appreciate our work. This sounds like nested loops—three, in fact. The innermost loop is the one to fill in the circle, drawing circles with several different radii at the same center until it looks like a solid circle. We want to do this for each of three circles and we want to repeat that several times. That means reading the data for the centers of the circles several times, so we will have a chance to use RESTORE here. Remember RESTORE? It stands alone to direct the computer to the first DATA statement in the program the next time it encounters a READ statement. We can also direct it to begin with a specific DATA line with RESTORE linelabel. See Program 9-9c.

Program 9-9c. Change the lights.

```
ChangeLights:
  FOR J1 = 1 TO 5
    RESTORE LightsData
    FOR J2 = 1 TO 3
      READ X,Y,R,C   'Turn light on
      FOR K = 0 TO R−1 : CIRCLE (X,Y),K,C : NEXT K
      FOR K = 1 TO 2500 : NEXT K
      C = 30          'Erase light with white
      FOR K = 0 TO R−1 : CIRCLE (X,Y),K,C : NEXT K
    NEXT J2
  NEXT J1
  RETURN
```

If we put all these pieces together with a control routine, we will have the road intersection along with the changing light. Program 9-9a draws the intersection and the light standard. Program 9-9b along with the three DATA statements following it draws the lights within the light standard. And finally, Program 9-9c controls the light changing process using the same data that Program 9-9b used to draw the lights. Now let's write the control routine. The first three lines come right from Program 9-9a.

Program 9-9d. Control the traffic light program.

```
REM ** Drawing a Traffic Light
LOCATE 10, 12 : PRINT "A Traffic Light"
GOSUB PlotLine
GOSUB ThreeLights
GOSUB ChangeLights
END
```

This completes a sketch of a traffic light at an intersection of two roads.

Since we can't show the changing lights on the printed page, you will have to type in the collection of Programs 9-9a through 9-9d to see it work. Don't forget to type in the LightsData.

There is always room for improvement. This example draws a single traffic light in one spot. Using PICTURE we could draw a traffic light, save it in a string variable and display it anywhere and in any size. The middle light really should stay on for a shorter time than the other two, and all the lights could be made white on black background. Maybe we could draw cars racing around the screen. We might draw a border or use a type -2, -3, or -4 window. We could determine the data for many figures and save it in data files on disk. Then we will have a whole library of figures to use for later graphics applications. There is an amazing variety of possibilities.

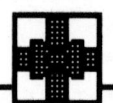

Summary

We have developed a routine that allows us to specify a drawing in terms of a collection of line segments. We can use one CIRCLE statement to draw many figures by storing as many parameters as we like in DATA statements. With LINE, we can supply the endpoints and color the same way, and use some IF tests to determine the "BF" option.

Problems for Section 9-3

The possibilities for drawing figures in the window are literally unlimited. We can only begin to make some suggestions leading you into problems of interest. Let your imagination plunge you into exciting graphics demonstrations.

1. Adjust the data in the traffic light drawing program so that each set of data is calculated in terms of a fixed starting point. Using (X0,Y0) for (100,20), the first three data lines will be

   DATA 0,0,45,40,33,n
   DATA 62,55,150,133,33,n
   DATA −40,−3,25,55,33,n

   Now the control routine can select a variety of starting points and draw the traffic light anywhere in the window with just one plotting subroutine.

2. Supply data to draw a sailboat in the window using the plotting routine of Program 9-9a.

3. Supply data to draw a simple TV set in the window using the plotting routine of Program 9-9a.

4. Write a program that illustrates the raising of a flag on a flagpole. Plotting the flagpole is straightforward. By successively plotting a flag on ever-increasing heights of the pole, the flag will appear to be raised. Note that you must erase the previous flag as you plot each new one.

9-4. More Graphics Features

Controlling Single Points (PSET, PRESET, POINT)

We can display single points in an output window in black or in white and ascertain the color of any point. This gives the programmer absolute control over the display.

PSET

The statement

   PSET (x1,y1)

places a black dot in the current output window at the point (x1,y1). To specify the color, simply add a color value to the statement. Think of it as Point SET. PSET also allows a STEP option to give x1 and y1 relative to the current position of the graphics pen. So,

PSET STEP (x1,y1),Color

first moves the pen x1 horizontally and y1 vertically from the current pen position and then sets the new point to Color. If the point is already set to Color, then there is no change in the appearance of the output window.

PRESET

The statement

PRESET (x1,y1)

sets the dot at the point x1,y1 in the current output window to white. To specify the color, simply add a color value to the statement. Think of it as Point RESET. PRESET also allows a STEP option to give x1 and y1 relative to the current position of the graphics pen. So,

PRESET STEP (x1,y1),Color

first moves the pen x1 horizontally and y1 vertically from the current pen position and then sets the new point to Color. If the point is already set to Color, then there is no change in the appearance of the output window.

PSET and PRESET are simply opposites. If we use the color option, then they are indistinguishable. Both statements allow coordinates outside the current output window. In such a case, of course, nothing happens to change the appearance of the display.

Sometimes, it would be nice to be able to determine the current graphics pen location. This information is especially useful if we are having trouble getting a program to produce the desired display. The STEP option in PSET and PRESET can be used with (0,0). First try

PSET STEP(0,0)

If no point shows up in the window, then the pen must be at a black point. Then try

PRESET STEP(0,0)

You should see a white point. If a single pixel is too small to see, simply use STEP(0,0) and STEP(1,1). Try using these statements in the Command window.

POINT

A statement of the form

COLOR = **POINT**(x1,y1)

uses the POINT function to determine the color of the point (x1,y1) in the current output window. If the point is outside the current output window POINT returns –1. Black comes back as 33 and white is 30, as expected.

Let's write a program that uses the mouse to exercise these latest graphics features. With just three of the mouse functions, we can develop a simple sketching program. MOUSE(0) returns a 0 if the mouse button is not depressed and has not been depressed since the last access of MOUSE(0). Any other value indicates that the mouse button has been pressed. Let's take that to mean the user wants to set the point at the current location of the mouse pointer. The current x-coordinate is returned in MOUSE(1) and the current y-coordinate is returned in MOUSE(2). See Appendix D for additional information on the MOUSE function.

While we are at it, let's offer some options. It would be good to be able to specify which color to use. It would be good to even be able to reverse the color of a point in the window. This could be provided very nicely with a menu. Let's add "Quit" to this menu. It would be nice to display a large window. Since we want to demonstrate drawing in white and black, let's make the program display a black box. Program 9-10 does all of this.

Program 9-10. Making a simple drawing using the mouse.

```
FOR K = 1 TO 5 : MENU K,0,0,"" : NEXT K  'Erase default menus

DIM LABEL$(4)                            'Set up new menu
READ NUMBEROFCHOICES
FOR ITEM = 0 TO NUMBEROFCHOICES – 1
   READ LABEL$(ITEM)
   MENU 6,ITEM,1,LABEL$(ITEM)
NEXT ITEM
ON MENU GOSUB ProcessMenu                'Use event trapping for menu
MENU ON
```

```
WINDOW 1,,(13,31)-(498,327),2
LINE (5,5)-(45,45),,BF

SELECT = 0 : NEWREQUEST = 0
MouseDraw:
   IF NEWREQUEST = 4 THEN Quit
   CLICK = MOUSE(0) : IF CLICK = 0 THEN MouseDraw
   X = MOUSE(1) : Y = MOUSE(2)
   ON NEWREQUEST GOSUB Black, White, Reverse
   GOTO MouseDraw

Black: PSET (X,Y) : RETURN

White: PRESET (X,Y) : RETURN

Reverse:
   IF POINT(X,Y) = 30 THEN PSET (X,Y) ELSE PRESET (X,Y) : RETURN

Quit: MENU RESET : WINDOW 1,,,1 : END

ProcessMenu:
   SELECT = MENU(0) : IF SELECT <> 6 THEN EndProcessMenu
   NEWREQUEST = MENU(1)
   MENU 6,OLDREQUEST,1
   MENU 6,NEWREQUEST,2
   MENU 7,0,1,LABEL$(NEWREQUEST)
   OLDREQUEST = NEWREQUEST
EndProcessMenu:
   RETURN

'Number of choices, followed by the choices
DATA 5
DATA Drawing in, Black, White, Reverse, Quit
```

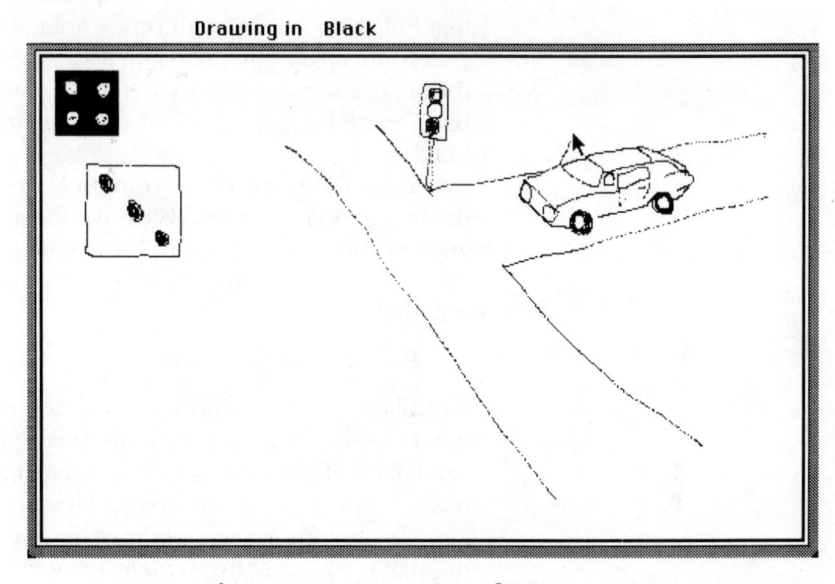

Figure 9-8. Execution of Program 9-10.

GET and PUT

The PICTURE statements and function have been mentioned as a way of manipulating images in an output window. The PICTURE statement causes the figure to be reconstructed on the screen exactly as it was created with BASIC display statements. If the display takes time to create, then picture will reproduce the display in the same time.

GET and PUT are based on the pixel pattern in the output window. GET converts a pixel pattern on the screen to a numeric pattern in an array. PUT creates a screen image based on the numeric pattern in the array created with GET. PUT is very fast and includes several interesting options for producing animation.

GET (x1,y1)–(x2,y2),B%

stores a pixel pattern in the integer array B%. The area stored is defined by the rectangle having one corner at (x1,y1) and the opposite corner at (x2,y2). The rectangle for GET and PUT is used in the same way that it is used for windows and pictures. The number of bytes required is given by the formula

NUMBEROFBYTES = 4 + 2*(**ABS**(x2−x1)+1)*((**ABS**(y2−y1)+16)\16)

If (x1,y1) is always above and to the left of (x2,y2), it is not necessary to use ABS. Since integers are stored in two bytes, the number of integer elements is one half this number. We may use integer, single precision, or double precision arrays as long as they have room for the image we want to save. For an integer array used with GET, B%(0) contains the width of the rectangle and B%(1) contains the height.

With the pattern saved in an array we may use PUT to place the image on the screen. We have the ability to change the appearance of the image in several ways. It is easy to change the dimensions by simply naming two opposite corners of another rectangle.

PUT (x1,y1)–(x2,y2),B%

will place the image on the screen. If we omit the "–(x2,y2)" then the image is simply copied with the upper left corner at (x1,y1). We can specify (x2,y2) to stretch or squash the picture to suit any purpose. The size of the image displayed by PUT is scaled by the relative sizes of the rectangles used for GET and PUT. If a PUT statement of the form shown above is executed a second time, the image stored in B% will disappear and the screen will be restored to its previous appearance.

An "action-verb" may be added to a PUT statement to control the interaction between the image stored in the array and the pixel pattern on the screen.

- PSET draws the new image on the screen replacing the current pixel pattern.
- PRESET first reverses the pattern in the array and then replaces the current screen pixel pattern.
- AND compares the screen to the image in the array. The result is that the pixel on the screen is turned on only if both the screen pixel and the image pixel are on. So an image will disappear on a white screen.
- OR superimposes the image on the screen. The image in the array will disappear on a black screen.
- XOR if a pixel in the array is turned on then the corresponding pixel on the screen is reversed. This makes it possible to restore the screen to a previous appearance by doing a second PUT. This is the default condition for the PUT statement. This is the mode to use for producing animation without disturbing the background. First display an image. Then display it again at the same location and in the same size. Next, display the image in the new location and new size (if desired) and repeat.

Program 9-11 demonstrates some of the features of PUT and GET.

Program 9-11. Demonstrate GET and PUT with screen images.

```
DIM A%(249)
CLS
LOCATE 9, 4
PRINT "Default     PSET     PRESET     OR     XOR"

X = 1 : Y = 1
LINE (1,1)-STEP (60,60),,B
GOSUB Six

GET (1,1)-(62,62),A%
LINE (0,0)-(490,95),,BF
PUT (20,65),A%
PUT (110,65),A%,PSET
PUT (200,65),A%,PRESET
PUT (290,65),A%,OR
PUT (380,65),A%,XOR

LINE (0,155)-(490,160),,BF
LOCATE 15, 25 : PRINT "Change size in PUT";
SIZE = 61
FOR X = 20 TO 380 STEP 90
   PUT (X,170)-(X+SIZE,170+SIZE),A%
   SIZE = SIZE-10
NEXT X
END

Six:
   FOR R = 0 TO 5
      CIRCLE (X+10,Y+10),R
      CIRCLE (X+10,Y+30),R
      CIRCLE (X+10,Y+50),R
      CIRCLE (X+50,Y+10),R
      CIRCLE (X+50,Y+30),R
      CIRCLE (X+50,Y+50),R
   NEXT R
   RETURN
```

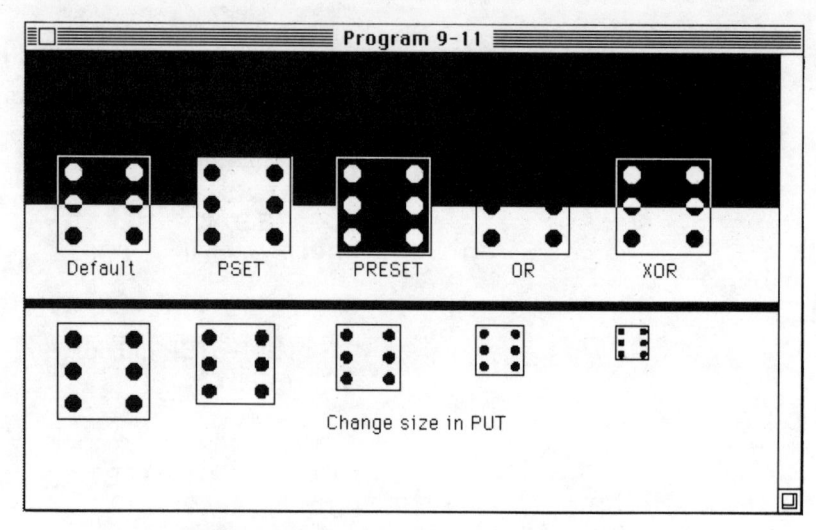

Figure 9-9. Execution of Program 9-11.

Several images can be stored in an array for GET and PUT. It might be interesting to store all six dice in one array. This could be done very nicely in a 250 by 6 array. The GET and PUT statements need to specify the coordinates of the element in the array where the data for each die begins. A%(0,K-1) would specify the starting place for die number K. This can be done with a structure as follows:

```
DIM A%(249,5)
    .
    .
FOR DIE = 1 TO 6
ON DIE GOSUB One, Two, Three, Four, Five, Six
GET (x1,y1)-(x2,y2),A%(0,DIE-1)
NEXT DIE
    .
    .
' a PUT statement to display die number DIE:
PUT (A,B),A%(0,DIE-1) .
```

This technique allows us to display all the dice with the same PUT statement by merely selecting the appropriate subscript value.

As with images stored in strings with PICTURE$, images stored in arrays using GET can be saved in data files. This means that images can be created with one program and used by another one.

The following statements will save an image in a file:

```
OPEN "SAVE IMAGE" FOR OUTPUT AS #1
FOR K = 0 TO NUMBEROFELEMENTS - 1
  PRINT #1, IMAGE%(K)
NEXT K
CLOSE #1
```

Later, another program can access the array IMAGE% with the following statements:

```
OPEN "SAVE IMAGE" FOR INPUT AS #1
FOR K = 0 TO NUMBEROFELEMENTS - 1
  INPUT #1, PICT%(K)
NEXT K
CLOSE #1
```

The program must properly dimension the arrays and do the other bookkeeping. Using this technique, many images can be saved in a file in one or more arrays.

9-5. Graphs from Formulas

Figures that can be described using a formula are easy to graph. There are many examples from mathematics.

Cartesian Coordinates

Let's develop a method for adjusting the X and Y values in the conventional Cartesian coordinate system for plotting in the output window. We would like to place the origin (point (0,0)) near the center of the output window and alter the orientation for Y values so that they are increasing up instead of down. Suppose we specify that the point (XORIGIN,YORIGIN) in the window shall represent the point (0,0) in a Cartesian system. The point (XORIGIN,YORIGIN) can easily be found using the window function as follows:

```
XORIGIN = WINDOW(2)\2 : YORIGIN = WINDOW(3)\2
```

The X conversion is easy. We simply want to move each plotted point to the right. The Y conversion requires that we turn the graph "upside down." So the point:

(X1,Y1)

in the conventional Cartesian coordinate system becomes

(XORIGIN + X1, YORIGIN - Y1)

in the output window. It would be nice to plot the X and Y axes right in the window. A very simple subroutine will do that for us.

Plotting points that fit a formula is straightforward enough. For our first graphs we might do just functions. This is a good application for a DEFined function. We can start with a simple function that graphs as a straight line.

$$Y = 1/3*X + 20$$

We define this function with

DEF FN F(X) = 1/3*X + 20

We need a subroutine that scans all possible values for X and determines if the Y value is in the window. If it is, then the routine should plot the point. If not, then the routine should simply try the next X value. Again the window function will be helpful here. The plotting is a direct application of the PSET statement.

Program 9-12. Plot a function.

```
REM ** Graph a function
DEF FN F(X) = 1/3*X + 20           'Define the function
LOCATE 2, 10 : PRINT "Y = 1/3*X + 20"
XORIGIN = WINDOW(2)\2 : YORIGIN = WINDOW(3)\2
GOSUB PlotAxes
GOSUB PlotFunction
END

PlotFunction:
    FOR X1 = -XORIGIN TO WINDOW(2) - XORIGIN STEP 5
        Y1 = FN F(X1)              'Use the function
        X = XORIGIN +X1 : Y = YORIGIN - Y1
        IF Y < WINDOW(3) AND Y > 0 THEN PSET (X,Y)
    NEXT X1
RETURN

PlotAxes:
    LINE (0,YORIGIN)-(WINDOW(2),YORIGIN)
    LINE (XORIGIN,0)-(XORIGIN,WINDOW(3))
RETURN
```

We might want to move the axes so that the point (0,0) is not in the exact center. This is done by passing the adjusted values of XORIGIN and YORIGIN to the the subroutines that do the plotting. It is worth experimenting with the STEP value of the FOR loop in the function-plotting subroutine to obtain a pleasing display in a reasonable time. The bigger the step, the faster the plotting. It may be desirable to create bolder graphs. This can be done by displaying two points in the window for each plotted point.

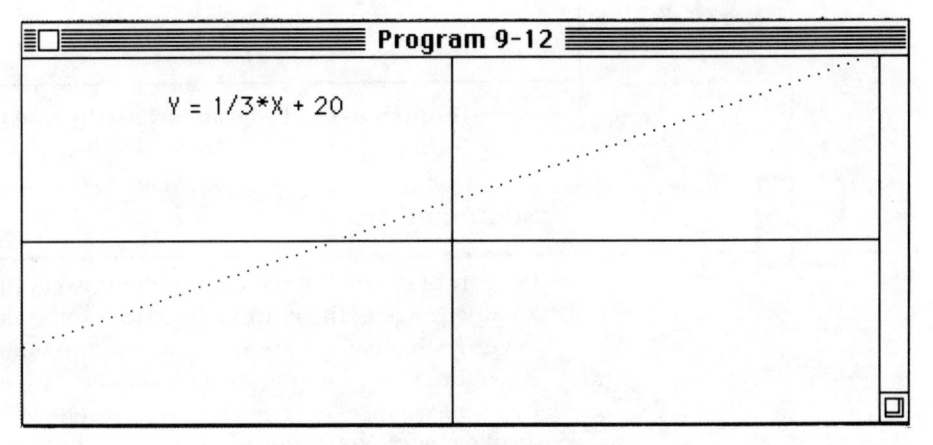

Figure 9-10. Execution of Program 9-12.

Now it is a very simple matter to replace the DEFined function of Program 9-12 with any function of our choice. With a little experimentation we can produce attractive displays without the tedium of arduous calculations. DEFined functions using the trigonometric functions, SIN(X), COS(X), TAN(X), and ATN(X), have great potential for making interesting curves when graphed. Values of Sine are in the range from −1 to +1, so we need to scale up to get values that will show up nicely in the window. A scale factor of 50 will give an idea of what it looks like. The drawing also needs to be stretched out in the horizontal direction to get a smooth curve. Dividing by 30 gives a nice result. Figure 9-11 demonstrates Program 9-12 with

DEF FN F(X) = 50 * **SIN**(X/30)

```
┌─────────────────────────────────────────┐
│▤▭              Program 9-12           ▤│
├─────────────────────────────────────────┤
│       Y = 50 * SIN(X/30)                │
│            ....                ....     │
│          ..    ..            ..    ..   │
│         .        .          .        .  │
│        .          .        .          . │
│───────.────────────.──────.────────────.│
│      .              .    .              │
│                      ....               │
│                                         │
│                                        ▫│
└─────────────────────────────────────────┘
```

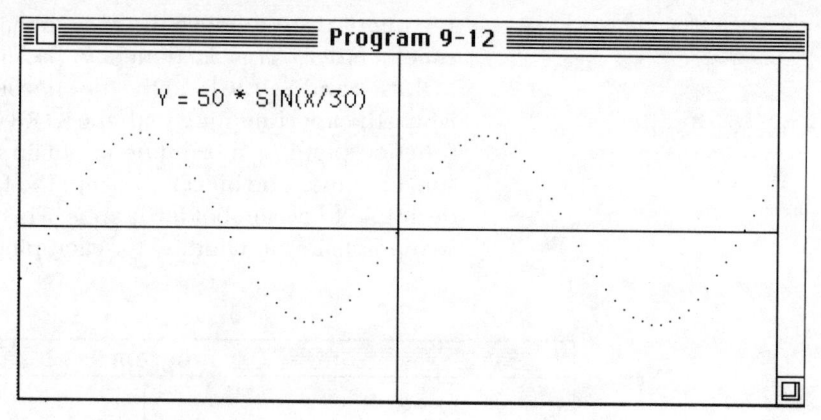

Figure 9-11. Program 9-12 with Sine function.

Summary

We can plot a mathematical function by simply scanning the X-value range in the graphics window and doing a calculation to verify that each point is actually in the window. The PSET statement is used to plot the actual points. By using a DEFined function we have been able to write a generalized program to display functions of our choice. The window functions have been valuable for determining where to place things in the output window.

Problems for Section 9-5

Use Program 9-12 to experiment with graphs. Change the size of the output window using the size box and the mouse. Try types 2, 3, or 4 output windows. Try moving the origin to examine special segments of a graph. Try a bolder display by using PSET with (X,Y) and (X+1,Y).

1. Sometimes we need to experiment with a function. Try to plot $2X^3 - 2X^2 + 3X - 5$. It should be apparent that most of the Y values are off the screen. We can scale the Y dimension down by dividing the value of Y by a large number—say 100000. Try it.

2. Try $X^2 + 50X - 450$. Divide by 100. Even though the scale is distorted we can gain a lot of insight into how a function performs.

9-6. Polar Graphs

Polar equations often produce interesting graphs. One of the reasons we don't draw many polar graphs by hand is that they take too much tedious calculation involving trigonometric functions. We can easily produce the graphs without the tedium by using graphics and letting BASIC do the calculations.

We may use

R = 1 − 2cos(G)

as an example equation. Using sines and cosines we get the X and Y coordinates as follows:

X = R*cos(G)   and   Y = R*sin(G)

where G is the central angle in radians. These two formulas are used to convert from polar coordinates (R,G) (radius central angle) to the (X,Y) coordinates of the cartesian system. To obtain a full graph the central angle must sweep through a full 360 degrees or 2π radians. We can get about 60 points by using STEP .1 in a FOR...NEXT loop since 2π is about 6.3.

Now we have to think about adjusting the X and Y values on the conventional Cartesian coordinate system for plotting in the window. This is exactly the same conversion we carried out in Section 9-5. So the point:

(X1,Y1)

in the conventional Cartesian coordinate system becomes

(XORIGIN + X1, YORIGIN − Y1)

in the graphics window, where the point (XORIGIN,YORIGIN) defines the point on the screen where we want the Cartesian point (0,0) to be located. Again we have shifted to the right and turned the graph upside down.

It would be nice to display a polar axis right in the window with the graph. This is easy to do using XORIGIN, YORIGIN, and WINDOW(2). Placing the polar axis in the window will clearly locate the graph for us.

Once we have a working program, it will be a simple matter to plug in other equations. In this way we can look at dozens of graphs in the time it would take to draw a single graph by hand. It is interesting to watch the figures as they are formed in the window. Drawing a polar graph by hand, like typing a 100-page paper on a portable typewriter, is one of those things everybody ought to do once in a lifetime.

Our program separates nicely into three packages: the control routine, the polar axis plotting routine, and the graph plotting routine.

In the control routine we define the origin and call the polar axis plotting subroutine. For general purposes, the origin will be the center of the output window. Once we see a graph, it may be desirable to move it. Polar graphs plotted true size are usually very small, so we should provide a scaling factor to produce a larger graph. RADIALSCALE takes care of that. In the plotting subroutine we will be arranging for the central angle to range through a full rotation of 2π radians. But we might like to control the step size in the control routine. We can begin with a step size of .1 to get an idea of what these graphs will look like. Finally, we call the plotting subroutine. That is all there is to it. See Program 9-13.

Program 9-13. Draw polar graphs.

```
REM ** Polar Graphing
XORIGIN = WINDOW(2)\2 : YORIGIN = WINDOW(3)\2
GOSUB PlotPolarAxis
RADIALSCALE = 45 : STEPSIZE = .1
GOSUB PlotPolarGraph
END

PlotPolarGraph:
   FOR ANGLE = 0 TO 6.29 STEP STEPSIZE
      RADIUS = 1 - 2 * COS(ANGLE)                 'Get polar radius
      X1 = RADIALSCALE * RADIUS * COS(ANGLE)      'Convert to Cartesian
      Y1 = RADIALSCALE * RADIUS * SIN(ANGLE)
      PSET(XORIGIN + X1,YORIGIN - Y1)             'Plot the point
   NEXT ANGLE
   RETURN

PlotPolarAxis:
   LINE (XORIGIN,YORIGIN)-(WINDOW(2),YORIGIN) : RETURN
```

Inside the FOR...NEXT loop in PlotPolarGraph of Program 9-13, the radius is assigned using the polar equation. The X-value and the Y-value are calculated by converting to cartesian coordinates and implementing the radial scale in one statement each. Finally, PSET does the plotting. It will be a simple matter to graph another polar equation by changing just the line where the radius is assigned. We must be aware that other polar equations may contain points that are outside the window. We can test for out-of-range values and skip the plotting for those points. Further, we must be alert for equations that may cause BASIC to attempt to divide by zero. See Figure 9-12 for a trial run of this program.

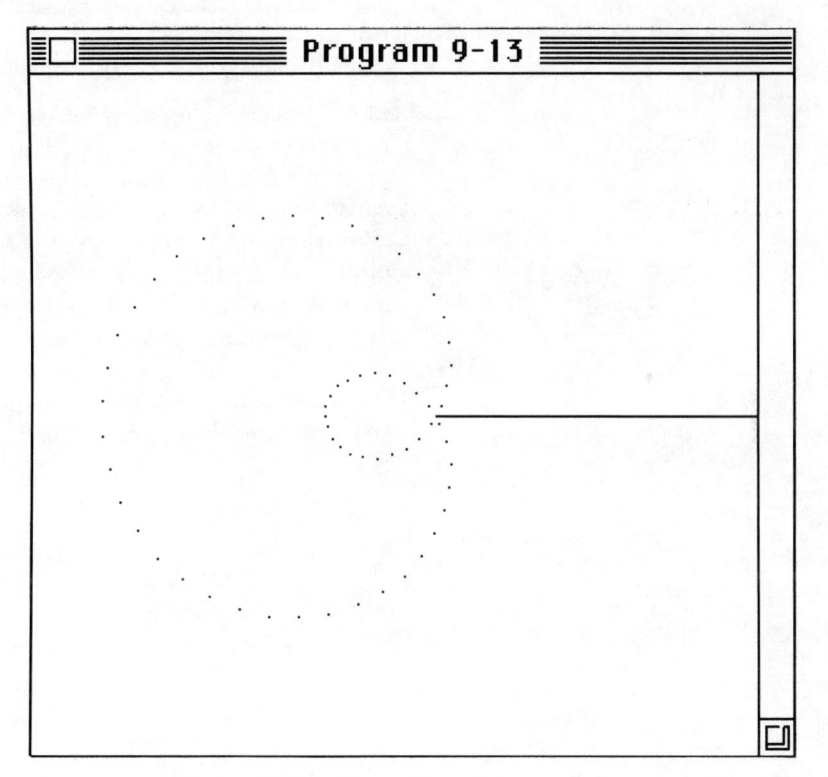

Figure 9-12. Execution of Program 9-13.

Problems for Section 9-6

1. We can easily plot a circle with our polar equation plotting program using the polar equation

   R = 1

   Do this.

2. There are lots of interesting polar graphs. Graph any of the following:

   (a) R = 1 + 2cos(G) − 3sin(G)²   (RSCALE = 30)
   (b) R = 3 + sin(3G)   (RSCALE = 25)
   (c) R = 2 + sin(2G)   (RSCALE = 40)
   (d) R = sin(G) + cos(G)   (RSCALE = 60)

3. Many polar equations produce nice graphs, but they will cause our polar plotting program to fail. Some points will lie outside the graphics window. Some values of G will cause division by zero. We can easily test whether a point is in the window just after it is calculated and before it is plotted. If a point won't be visible don't plot it. If the formula we enter has an indicated division then we can put in a test one line above it. If the current value of G would cause such a zero division, don't even execute the line that uses the formula. Adding these features will enable you to draw graphs for any of the following:

   (a)   Rcos(G) = 1
   (b)   R = 1 + Rcos(G)
   (c)   R = tan(G)
   (d)   R = 2G   (scale = 1 and G ranges from −50 to 50)
   (e)   R = 2/G   (scale = 25 and ranges G from −10 to 10)

CHAPTER 10

Using Macintosh QuickDraw Graphics Routines

Microsoft BASIC for the Macintosh includes a collection of powerful routines that allow us to control numerous graphics features of the Macintosh. The QuickDraw routines are sometimes also called the "Toolbox." These are available with the BASIC keyword CALL.

We can do lots of things with the Mouse pointer or cursor—even determine its shape. Routines are available that control the graphics pen. We can set its size, set its position, and create our own drawing pattern for it. Lines, rectangles, ovals, arcs, and polygons are easy to work with. We can control the appearance of text display in the output window with four TEXT routines. We will design our own output window background pattern.

Many of the QuickDraw routines require numeric information. A special function is provided for just this sort of thing. VARPTR (VARiable PoinTeR) is used to tell BASIC where our numbers are stored in Macintosh memory. The expression

VARPTR(VALUES%(0))

is used by BASIC to determine where in memory the element number zero of the array VALUES% is located. From this, the particular routine we are working with uses as many numbers as it needs. If we have entered the proper numbers in the array VALUES%, it will produce the expected results. In every case we will be working with integer values only.

Some of the QuickDraw routines use values named right in the CALL itself. For instance:

CALL PENSIZE(X, Y)

uses the values of X and Y directly to create a graphics pen X pixels wide and Y pixels high.

As with subprograms we create, the CALL keyword is optional for the Quickdraw routines. If CALL is dropped, then the outer set of parentheses in the statement is also dropped. Thus the size of the pen can also be set with:

PENSIZE X, Y

Remember: LCOPY causes the screen to be copied to the Imagewriter. ⌘-Shift-4 copies the active window. ⌘-Shift-4 with Caps Lock engaged copies the screen. And ⌘-Shift-3 saves the screen as a MacPaint document.

As each new feature is presented, experiment with the programs. Combine features from Chapter 9 with those discussed here. Try things with PICTURE, and GET and PUT.

10-1. Controlling the Mouse Cursor

HIDECURSOR, SHOWCURSOR, OBSCURECURSOR, and INITCURSOR

HIDECURSOR causes the mouse cursor to disappear until a SHOWCURSOR is executed. We can have a little fun with the invisible cursor. But, since we can't see it we have to be careful. Moving the cursor to the top menu bar can activate the menus. Just don't do anything that requires you to respond to a dialog box. Each HIDECURSOR requires a SHOWCURSOR. Alternatively, if we have hidden the cursor many times and want to bring it back immediately, INITCURSOR is the thing to use. You may want to hide the cursor during an exciting graphics performance.

OBSCURECURSOR makes the cursor disappear temporarily. It reappears as soon as the mouse is moved, a SHOWCURSOR is executed, or an INITCURSOR is encountered. OBSCURECURSOR only takes effect if the cursor has been moved since the last OBSCURECURSOR or there has been an INITCURSOR. Further, if we obscure and hide the cursor, then it takes a SHOWCURSOR to undo the HIDECURSOR and an additional action to undo the OBSCURECURSOR. INITCURSOR will undo it all. There must be one SHOWCURSOR for each HIDECURSOR. None of these mouse cursor controls requires any numeric values.

Customizing the Mouse Cursor

The standard Macintosh mouse cursor is an arrow. BASIC includes a routine that lets us draw our own cursor shape. The cursor consists of a block 16 pixels wide and 16 pixels high. All we have to do is draw a shape we like and learn how to translate that figure into data values that the SETCURSOR routine can use.

SETCURSOR VARPTR(APPLE%(0))

is used to implement a new shape. Remember that VARPTR finds the beginning of the array in memory and the routine, then uses as many values as it requires. SETCURSOR depends on 34 integer values found in the array. It is a good idea to use integer arrays for this sort of thing. The first 16 values specify the shape of the cursor. The next 16 values are used to determine how the shape value and the pixel already on the screen interact to produce each pixel in the final display. This group of values is referred to as a data mask. And the last two values specify the exact spot in the cursor that is read as the cursor position. This active position is sometimes referred to as the "hot spot." The Macintosh responds only to the position of this single point in the cursor. For the standard arrow cursor, the active spot is the very tip. Let's take this one step at a time. First we need a shape. How about an apple?

Drawing a shape

It is pretty easy to use FatBits in MacPaint to obtain the drawing of Figure 10-1.

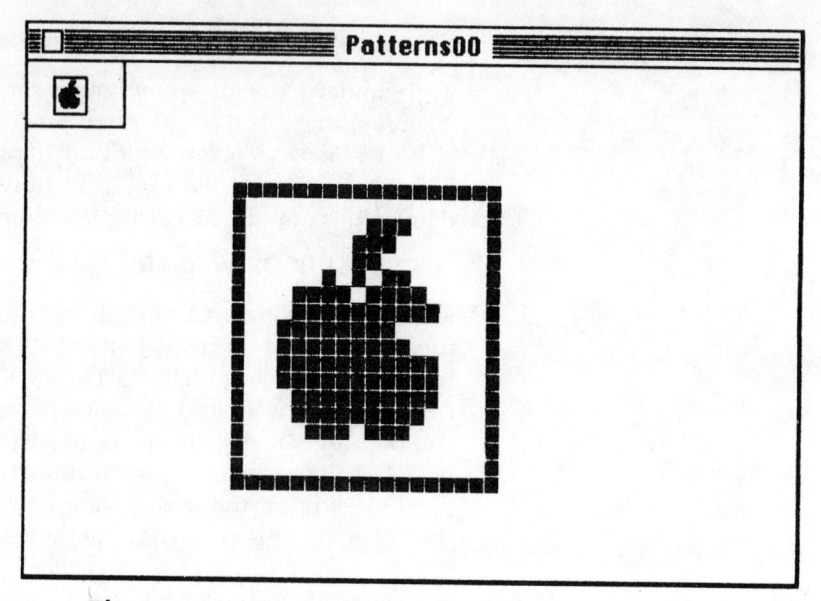

254 Chapter 10: Macintosh QuickDraw Graphics Routines

Figure 10-1. Draw an apple using FatBits in MacPaint.

Now we need to convert the 16 by 16 figure of an apple to 16 integer values for the SETCURSOR routine.

Think of each white block as a zero and each black block as a one. That will give us 16 binary numbers of 16 bits each. See Figure 10-2.

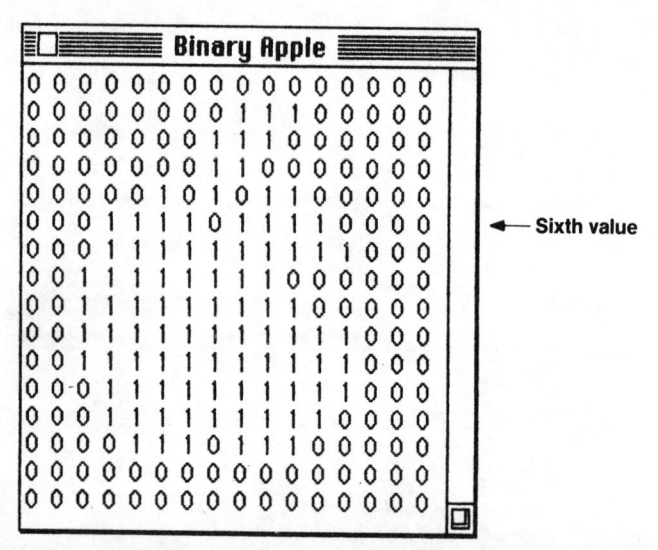

Figure 10-2. The apple converted to ones and zeros.

It's a little tough converting 16-digit binary values into base ten, but converting to hexadecimal is fairly straightforward. We break the 16-digit number into four four-digit numbers. Let's take the sixth value in Figure 10-2 as an example.

0001	1110	1111	0000	in binary
1	E	F	0	in hex

So, 0001111011110000 in binary becomes 1EF0 in hex. We express that as &H1EF0 in the BASIC program.

We can also work directly from the little square blocks of Figure 10-1. Let's use MacPaint again. This time we can draw a binary counter from 0 to 15 and label the values from 0 to F in hex. Then we simply match the four block pattern from the apple in the counter with the corresponding hex digit. This saves having to convert the drawing to zeros and ones. See Figure 10-3.

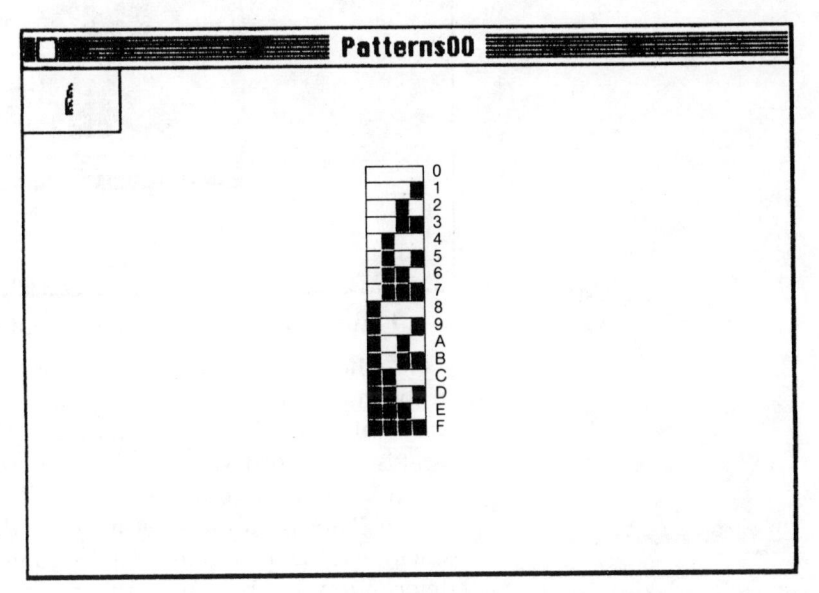

Figure 10-3. A binary counter from 0 to 15.

Following the procedure above for the 16 rows of the drawing will give us the first 16 integer values for the array APPLE%. We simply draw lines marking off each line of blocks in the apple into groups of four blocks.

256 Chapter 10: Macintosh QuickDraw Graphics Routines

Let's use the end of the apple leaf as the hot spot. The hot spot is not a pixel location but at the corner where four pixels come together. In this 16 by 16 block the corners are numbered from 0 to 16. That is, there are 17 of them in each direction. So the upper right corner of the pixel at the end of the leaf is labeled (11,1). That is the spot that the Macintosh will look for whenever we click the mouse.

We put all this together in Figure 10-4.

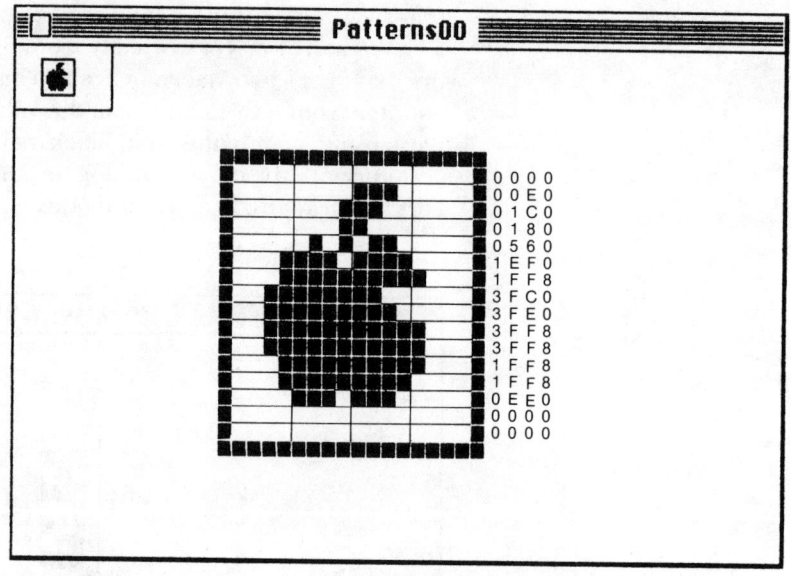

```
0 0 0 0
0 0 E 0
0 1 C 0
0 1 8 0
0 5 6 0
1 E F 0
1 F F 8
3 F C 0
3 F E 0
3 F F 8
3 F F 8
1 F F 8
1 F F 8
0 E E 0
0 0 0 0
0 0 0 0
```

Figure 10-4. Numeric data from mouse cursor drawing.

As mentioned earlier, the values for the position of the active spot in the cursor are the last two values in the array. It turns out that the X-value goes in APPLE%(33) and the Y-value goes in APPLE%(32). That is, in Y,X order rather than X,Y. So, be careful.

It is the mask that determines what actually happens on the screen. There is a mask bit for each data bit in the drawing. The Macintosh ROM routine uses the combination of these two bits to determine what happens at that particular pixel position. Results are produced according to Table 10-1.

Table 10-1. The effect of the mask on the mouse cursor display.

Cursor bit	Mask bit	Result on the screen
0	1	White
1	1	Black
0	0	Retain pixel already on screen
1	0	Reverse pixel already on the screen 0 becomes 1, 1 becomes 0

Look at the second and third lines in Table 10-1. To create a cursor that lets what is already on the screen "show through" any white area in the cursor, we want the mask bit and the cursor bit to be the same. This is easy to do. As we read the data into the first 16 elements of array APPLE%, we simply make the next 16 corresponding elements the same. Now it is time to write Program 10-1.

Program 10-1. Create a new mouse cursor.

```
REM ** Create apple cursor
DIM APPLE%(33)
FOR J = 0 TO 15
   READ APPLE%(J) : APPLE%(J+16) = APPLE%(J)
NEXT J
READ APPLE%(32), APPLE%(33)
SETCURSOR VARPTR(APPLE%(0))

REM ** Demonstrate cursor
WINDOW 1,"Apple Cursor",(2,41)–(508,340),1 'Make output full size
BUTTON 1,1,"Press when done",(140,200)–(360,218),1
BUTTON 2,2,"Not this one",(350,5)–(500,31),2
BUTTON 3,1,"Or this one",(350,40)–(500,57),3
Poll: PROCESS = DIALOG(0) : IF PROCESS <> 1 THEN Poll
      PRESS = DIALOG(1) :    IF PRESS <> 1 THEN Poll

REM ** 16 DATA values for apple mouse cursor
DATA &H0000, &H00E0, &H01C0, &H0180
DATA &H0560, &H1EF0, &H1FF8, &H3FC0
DATA &H3FE0, &H3FF8, &H3FF8, &H1FF8
DATA &H1FF0, &H0EE0, &H0000, &H0000
REM ** The active spot Y, X
DATA 1,11
```

It is a good idea to type in this program and try it. It seems to work as advertised; the background on the screen does show through very nicely. That could present a problem, however, in some situations. Try it on a black background. Enter the following line near the beginning of Program 10-1 and run it.

LINE (0,0)–(100,100),,BF

Now what happens when the cursor moves into the area of the box? It disappears, of course. Let's look at Table 10-1 again. There we see that if the mask is always one (1), we copy the cursor onto the screen obscuring the background in the process. A 16-bit binary number consisting of all 1s is FFFF written in hex notation. Let's try that. Change the fourth line of Program 10-1 to read as follows:

READ APPLE%(J) : APPLE%(J+16) = &HFFFF

Now move the cursor around the screen. It sure shows up in the black box now. Maybe it's too much to have all that white outline. Try &H0000 instead of &HFFFF. We can just have the pixel nearest the active spot set to reverse whatever is already on the screen. First restore the original READ APPLE% line and then put in a statement to turn off the bit that represents the end of the leaf. Look at Figure 10-4. The data for the four bits containing the end of the leaf converts to a hex value of E (that's 14 base ten). Turning off the end of the leaf subtracts 2, leaving C. So, &H00E0 becomes &H00C0.

    READ APPLE%(J) : APPLE%(J+16) = APPLE%(J)
NEXT J
APPLE%(16) = &H00C0

Now run the new version and see that in the black box we get a single white spot. By surrounding the cursor with some mask bits that either reverse or turn off the bit already on the screen, we can create a cursor that seems to shimmer as it moves about. For this, it would be a good idea to create separate DATA for the mask. We can create the effect of passing in front, behind, and through.

    Once the program terminates or we use the Macintosh desk accessories the apple is gone. Back comes the old familiar arrow. Just run the program again and the apple returns.

    INITCURSOR restores the arrow cursor and makes it visible whether or not the old cursor was visible. That could be a problem if we are using a custom-designed cursor because we might not want to bring the arrow back. Just use

INITCURSOR : SETCURSOR VARPTR(APPLE%(0))

This also makes the new cursor visible whether or not it was visible before. Executing this line also clears any excess calls to HIDECURSOR.

10-2. Drawing Lines (LINE and LINETO)

Two routines are available for drawing lines.

LINETO X,Y

draws a line from the current pen position to the pixel (X,Y).

CALL LINE(dX,dY)

draws a line from the current pen position to the point (X+dX,Y+dY), where dX and dY are the relative moves in the X and Y directions. While LINETO draws to absolute pixel positions in the current window, CALL LINE draws to relative positions. Because LINE is also a BASIC keyword, the QuickDraw LINE routine must be called with an explicit CALL. An attempt to leave out CALL and the parentheses constitutes a "Syntax error." This is the only QuickDraw routine that requires the CALL keyword.

Unlike the LINE statement, CALL LINE and LINETO cannot draw boxes. However, like all the QuickDraw routines, they use the graphics pen, which opens up a whole new set of capabilities.

10-3. Controlling the Graphics Pen

Microsoft BASIC includes a collection of routines that control the graphics pen. This is the pen that does all the QuickDraw graphics drawing in the output window. It does not affect the CIRCLE, LINE, PSET, and PRESET statements.

If it hasn't been changed with the size box, the output window is either 491 by 299 (click an application) or 491 by 254 (click BASIC). In any case, remember that these dimensions can be found easily with WINDOW(2) and WINDOW(3). All sizes and coordinates are in pixels. The coordinates for the smaller window are 0 to 490 for X and 0 to 253 for Y. Nothing harmful will happen for values outside this range.

Pen location

Three routines have to do with the location of the pen in the output window. We can determine the pen's current coordinates with GETPEN. MOVETO sets the absolute position of the pen. And MOVE places the pen relative to the current position.

GETPEN

GETPEN VARPTR(POSITION%(0))

causes the X-coordinate of the pen to be entered in the integer array element POSITION%(1) and the Y-coordinate in element POSITION%(0). Note that this is the reverse of the conventional X,Y order in mathematics.

MOVETO

MOVETO X,Y

sets the absolute pixel position of the pen. Nothing appears on the screen, the pen just moves to the point we select. Any called routine begins drawing here.

MOVE

MOVE dX,dY

causes the pen to move dX horizontally and dY vertically relative to the current position. To move up or to the left, simply use a negative value for the corresponding variable. As with MOVETO, nothing appears on the screen. The pen moves only.

Pen Characteristics

Six routines are available for controlling the characteristics of the pen itself. We set the size with PENSIZE. We create our own drawing pattern with PENPAT. The way in which a drawing interacts with figures already on the screen is controlled with PENMODE. HIDEPEN and SHOWPEN hide and show the pen. PENNORMAL restores the pen size, pattern, and mode to the default conditions set by Microsoft BASIC. However, PENNORMAL does not undo HIDEPEN.

PENSIZE

PENSIZE X,Y

makes the pen X pixels wide and Y pixels high. Even though PENSIZE accepts very large values for X and Y, it makes sense to keep them small. All subsequent drawing is done with the new pen size. The normal size is one pixel by one pixel. Giving the pen different dimensions for X and Y can produce interesting results.

Program 10-2 combines the CALL LINE and LINETO routines with different settings of the pen to achieve a variety of effects. You'll learn lots through experimentation.

Program 10-2. Demonstrate some graphics routines.

```
REM ** A house
PENSIZE 15,2 : MOVETO 50,175
CALL LINE (0,-90) : CALL LINE (150,-50)
CALL LINE (30,50)  : CALL LINE (0,90)
LINETO 50,175

REM ** The doorstep
PENSIZE 2,4 : MOVE 120,2
CALL LINE (0,-60) : CALL LINE (30,0)
CALL LINE (0,60)  : CALL LINE (-30,0)

REM ** The chimney
PENSIZE 14,1 : MOVETO 125,60 : CALL LINE (0,-13)
Y = 45
FOR X = 125 TO 1 STEP -12
   FOR ENDANGLE = 5.3 TO 6.3 STEP .1
      CIRCLE (X,Y), 8,, 5.3, ENDANGLE, .6 : GOSUB Slow
   NEXT ENDANGLE
   FOR ENDANGLE = 0 TO 3.6 STEP .1
      CIRCLE (X,Y), 8,, 5.3, ENDANGLE, .6 : GOSUB Slow
   NEXT ENDANGLE
   Y = Y - 3
NEXT X
END

Slow: FOR K = 1 TO 50 : NEXT K : RETURN
```

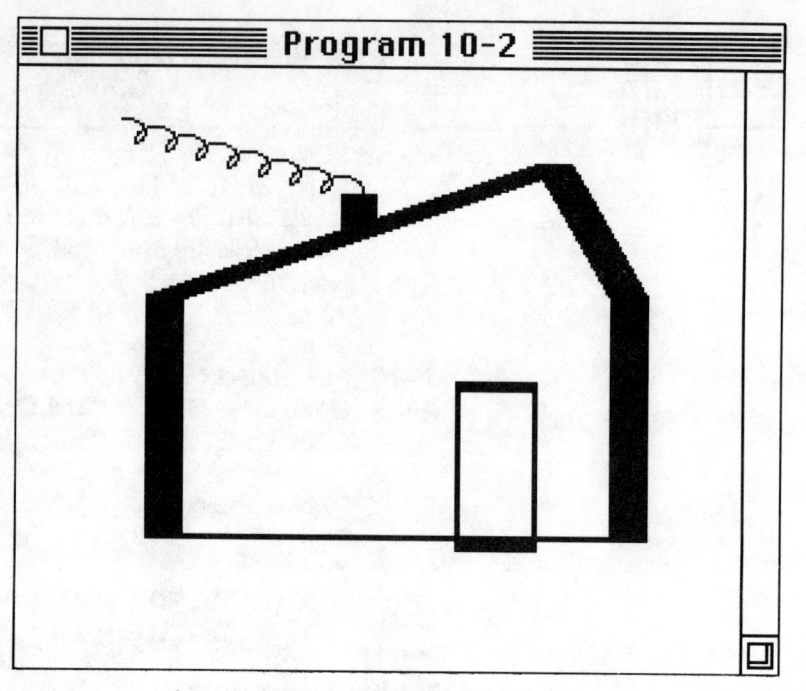

Figure 10-5. Execution of Program 10-2.

PENPAT

The statement

PENPAT VARPTR(PATT%(0))

may be used to create a pattern for the pen to draw. The pattern is based on an 8-pixel by 8-pixel block. The process here is similar to what we did for the mouse cursor. We could draw a pattern on graph paper, use FatBits in MacPaint, or even use the Control Panel to experiment with different arrangements. Once we have a nice pattern it must be converted into integer values in an array for the routine to use. Since integers are expressed by two 8-bit bytes, each element in the array PATT% accommodates two rows of the pattern. Thus we end up with 4 values in elements 0 through 3. Let's use FatBits to draw a pattern in Figure 10-6.

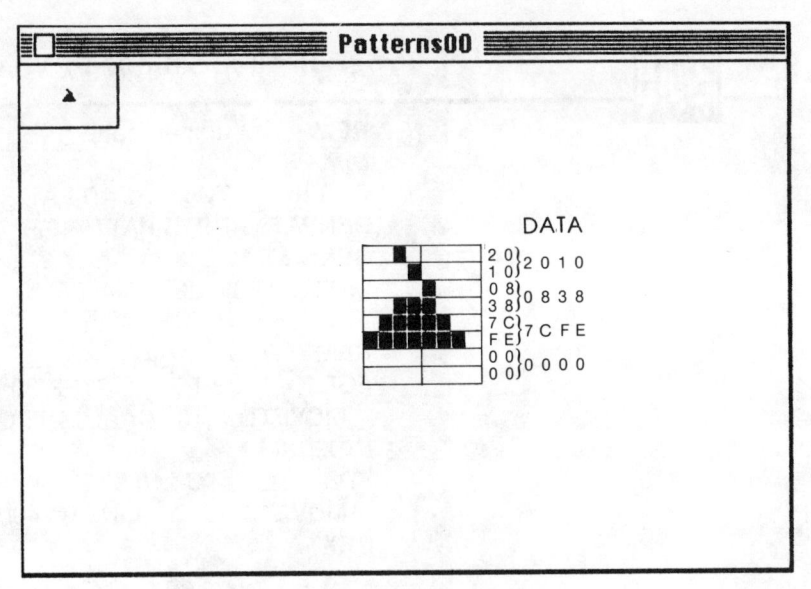

Figure 10-6. Pattern for PENPAT.

Using the little counter of Figure 10-3 that was developed for the mouse cursor, we get the hex values for the array. By rearranging them in pairs we get the integer values. These are the four values that go in PATT%. Simply executing the PENPAT routine will set up the pen with the new pattern. Following this, any graphics drawings will be in the current pen pattern. See Program 10-3. The LINE statement produces the filled box to show what happens with different backgrounds.

Program 10-3. Sample PENPAT.

```
REM ** Set up pen pattern
DIM PATT%(3)
FOR K = 0 TO 3 : READ PATT%(K) : NEXT K
PENPAT VARPTR(PATT%(0))
PENSIZE 12,6
LINE (50,50)–(300,150),,BF

REM ** Draw
FOR X = 100 TO 200 STEP 30
   MOVETO X,10 : CALL LINE (X,230)
NEXT X
FOR Y = 10 TO 210 STEP 30
   MOVETO 100,Y : LINETO 400,Y
NEXT Y

DATA &H2010, &H0838, &H7CFE, &H000
```

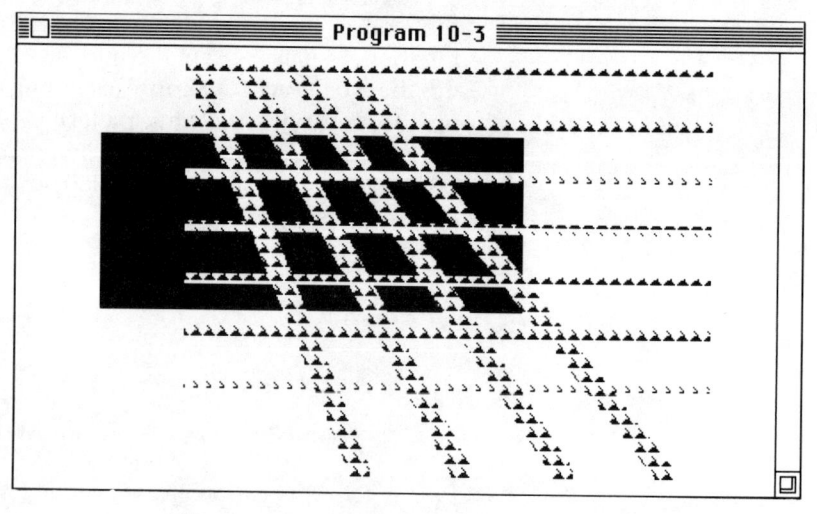

Figure 10-7. Execution of Program 10-3.

This program simply demonstrates the pen drawing with a pattern. Try using this pattern in Program 10-2. You might develop a collection of pattern data, each setting up the pen to draw in a different pattern. Once you have the data, it is a simple matter to use those values in other programs. The pattern data could even be stored in a file.

PENMODE

Notice that the drawing with the pen in Program 10-3 simply replaced whatever was already on the screen. Earlier we saw ways to modify the interaction between a drawing and the existing screen display with the mouse cursor. We have a similar feature for working with the graphics pen. Eight pen modes are available to specify how the pen pattern interacts with what is already on the screen. PENMODE X is used to set a new mode for drawing with the pen. The default condition is that the pen pattern is simply displayed on the screen, replacing what was there. The value 8 is used for this. A value of 9 causes the pen pattern to overlay what is on the screen without changing any screen bits that are already turned on. That is, if a bit in the pen pattern is 0, then the screen is left as it was, and if a bit in the pen pattern is 1, then the bit on the screen is turned to 1 whether it was 1 or 0. See Table 10-2 for a listing of all modes.

Table 10-2. Pen mode values.

Mode	Action
8	Pen pattern replaces screen
9	Pen pattern superimposed on screen A pixel is displayed if the screen or the figure pixel is turned on
10	Pen pattern XORed with screen pattern Screen pixel is turned on only if screen and pen are different
11	Black is changed—if pen value is 1, then the screen is changed to 0. Pen value of 0 is not changed. (BIC) The values 12 through 15 correspond to 8 through 11, except that the pen pattern is inverted before the action takes place.

A picture is worth a thousand words. Let's write a demonstration program to translate Table 10-2 into something that we can see. We need to show images on both a white background and a black one. We need to display all eight modes. And we should label the results. Program 10-4 does all this using the pen pattern from Program 10-3.

Program 10-4. Demonstrate PENMODE.

```
REM ** Demonstrate PENMODE
DIM PATT%(3)
HIDECURSOR

FOR BAND = 0 TO 5
   LINE (75*BAND+25,5)-(75*BAND+50,250),,BF
NEXT BAND

REM ** Establish pen characteristics
FOR K = 0 TO 3 : READ PATT%(K) : NEXT K
PENPAT VARPTR(PATT%(0))

REM ** Display in all modes
MOVETO 455, 11 : PRINT "Mode:";
FOR MODE = 8 TO 15
   Y = (MODE-8)*30+10
   MOVETO 460,Y+15 : PRINT MODE;
   PENMODE MODE
   PENSIZE 20, 20 : MOVETO 5, Y : CALL LINE(0,0)
     PENSIZE 1, 20
     FOR X = 5 TO 425
       MOVETO X, Y : CALL LINE(0,0)        'Display
       MOVETO X+20, Y : CALL LINE(0,0)     'Redisplay at left of block
     NEXT X
NEXT MODE
SHOWCURSOR
END

REM ** Data for PENPAT
DATA &H2010, &H0838, &H7CFE, &H0000
```

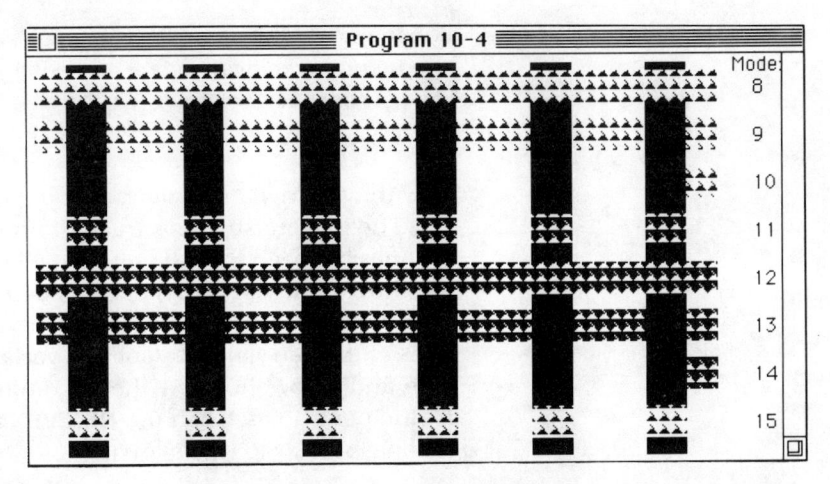

Figure 10-8. Execution of Program 10-4.

Figure 10-8 displays only part of what can be done with different pen modes. You must execute Program 10-4 to see the whole display. The various modes create the effect of one figure going behind, in front of, or through another. You can produce animated figures by selecting the right mode. Notice that modes 10 and 14 are called XOR. This is the same characteristic displayed by the XOR action verb option for the screen PUT statement discussed in Chapter 9. So, displaying a figure in one of these modes and then redisplaying it causes the first figure to disappear as though it had never been displayed. That is, the background is undisturbed. This is the same as using PUT two times with the same figure and position.

Small changes in Program 10-4 produce dramatic changes in the display. For example, try replacing

PENSIZE 1, 20
FOR X = 5 **TO** 425

with the following:

PENSIZE 10, 20
FOR X = 5 **TO** 425 **STEP** 10

With a little experimentation you can select the mode that creates the visual effect you are looking for.

HIDEPEN and SHOWPEN

To make the pen disappear, just use

HIDEPEN

Following this statement, you may still direct the pen to move about and make drawings. They will just not show. The way to get the pen back is to execute

SHOWPEN

Now the pen will draw normally.

The Macintosh keeps track of how many times each of these routines has been used. If you HIDEPEN ten times, then the pen will not show until you SHOWPEN ten times. CLS won't even clear the screen if HIDEPEN is active. Your program will simply have to keep track of the pen status. Establish a variable PENSTATUS that is 0 for hide and 1 for show. At the beginning of the program set it to 1—the pen shows. Then use HIDEPEN and SHOWPEN only in subroutines similar to the following:

Hide.Pen:
   IF PENSTATUS = 1 **THEN HIDEPEN** : PENSTATUS = 0
   RETURN

Show.Pen:
   IF PENSTATUS = 0 **THEN SHOWPEN** : PENSTATUS = 1
   RETURN

Finally, at the end of program execution simply do a GOSUB Show.Pen. There is no INITPEN routine to take care of this.

PENNORMAL

PENNORMAL restores the default conditions for PENSIZE, PENPAT, and PENMODE. But, it will not clear the status of HIDEPEN. You must do that yourself as described earlier. PENNORMAL also does not move the pen or change the appearance of the output window.

10-4. Drawing with Rectangles, Ovals, Arcs, and Polygons

This group offers five kinds of shapes—rectangles, rounded rectangles, ovals, arcs, and polygons. There are five operations that may be performed on each shape—FRAME, PAINT, ERASE, INVERT, and FILL.

FRAME, PAINT, ERASE, INVERT, and FILL

The names of the operations clearly suggest the result. FRAME simply draws the outline of the shape specified. PAINT uses the current pen pattern (see PENPAT Section 10-3) to paint the shape and its interior. ERASE makes the shape disappear by using the background pattern (see BACKPAT Section 10-6) to paint it. INVERT reverses each pixel of the shape. This includes the boundary and the interior points. Each black pixel becomes white and vice versa. FILL fills the shape with a pattern that is defined by an array named in the call.

RECTangle

We can easily draw a rectangle with the following:

FRAMERECT VARPTR(BOUNDS%(0))

where the integer array BOUNDS% contains the locations of the top, left, bottom, and right boundaries, in that order. Beginning with the top side, simply go counterclockwise. It is easy to draw a square by making the difference between top and bottom the same as the difference between right and left. Let's draw a rectangle just inside the output window. See Program 10-5.

Program 10-5. Draw a simple rectangle.

```
DIM BOUNDS%(3)
FOR J = 0 TO 3 : READ BOUNDS%(J) : NEXT J
FRAMERECT VARPTR(BOUNDS%(0))
DATA 10, 10, 43, 80
```

Note the difference between FRAMERECT and "BF" (BoxFill) in the LINE statement. While LINE draws lines only one pixel wide, FRAMERECT uses the current size, mode and pattern of the graphics pen. It might be fun to draw lots of rectangles by changing BOUNDS% in a loop. Once you see the display it is easy to make small changes in the program that produce dramatic changes in the result. See Program 10-6.

Program 10-6. Display numerous rectangles with a FOR loop.

```
DIM BOUNDS%(3)
BOUNDS%(0) = 10 : BOUNDS%(1) = 10
FOR J = 20 TO 200 STEP 10
    BOUNDS%(0) = BOUNDS%(0) + 5
    BOUNDS%(1) = BOUNDS%(1) + 8
    BOUNDS%(2) = J
    BOUNDS%(3) = 2 * J
    FRAMERECT VARPTR(BOUNDS%(0))
NEXT J
```

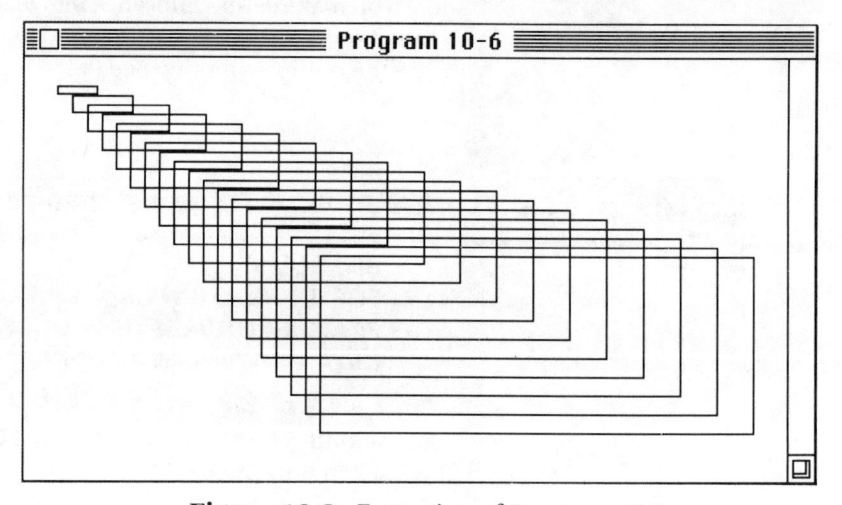

Figure 10-9. Execution of Program 10-6.

PAINT, ERASE, and INVERT take the same form as FRAME.

PAINTRECT VARPTR(BOUNDS%(0))
ERASERECT VARPTR(BOUNDS%(0))
INVERTRECT VARPTR(BOUNDS%(0))

FILL is different. The pattern for FILLRECT must be supplied in an integer array right in the call. The structure for this pattern is just like the structure for PENPAT. Let's make up another pattern. See Figure 10-10.

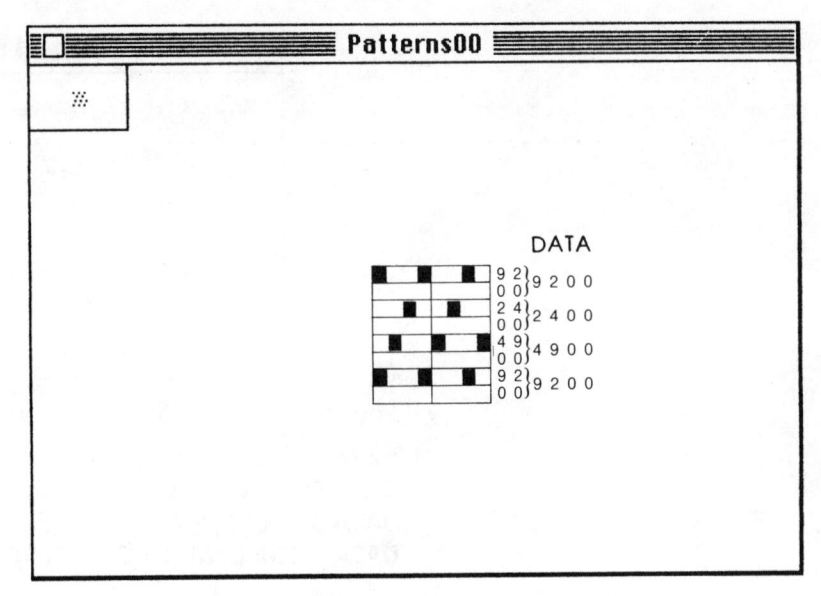

Figure 10-10. Pattern for FILLRECT.

Using the little counter of Figure 10-3 we get the hex values to the right of the pattern in Figure 10-10. We supply this data in a four element integer array to be used in a statement of the following form:

FILLRECT VARPTR(BOUNDS%(0)), **VARPTR**(PATT%(0))

where PATT% contains the values for the pattern we select. We use BOUNDS% from Program 10-5, replace the FRAMERECT statement, and add this pattern data to create Program 10-7.

Program 10-7. FILLRECT with a pattern.

```
DIM BOUNDS%(3), PATT%(3)
FOR J = 0 TO 3 : READ BOUNDS%(J) : NEXT J
FOR J = 0 TO 3 : READ PATT%(J)   : NEXT J
FILLRECT VARPTR(BOUNDS%(0)), VARPTR(PATT%(0))
DATA 10, 10, 43, 80
DATA &H9200, &H2400, &H4900, &H9200
```

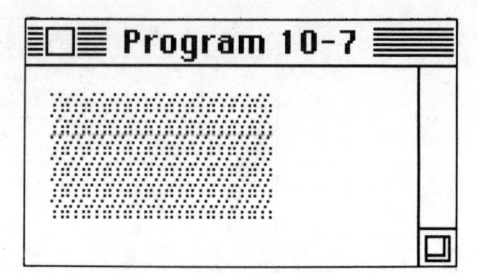

Figure 10-11. Execution of Program 10-7.

Type this one in and try a variety of pattern data. Replace the second line of data with a line such as one of the following:

DATA 1, 1, 1, 1
DATA 511, 511, 511, 511
DATA 511, 0, 511, 0
DATA &H00FE, &H00FE, &H00FE, &H00FE

Design other patterns. Use your own ideas.

The method used so far to obtain these values is straightforward, but somewhat tedious. Why do all that paperwork when there is a powerful computer available? We can use BASIC to experiment with an 8 by 8 pattern on the screen using the mouse. Then we display it as a pattern drawn with the pen, and at the same time print out the hex data for the array. See Program 10-8.

Program 10-8. Produce DATA for 8-by-8 patterns.

```
REM ** Calculate hex values from a pattern
DIM PATT%(3)

WINDOW CLOSE 1
WINDOW 3,,(97,30)–(167,158),3
WINDOW 2,,(167,30)–(389,158),3
BUTTON 1,1,"Quit",(30,100)–(70,118),1

FOR S = 0 TO 3 : PATT%(S) = 0 : NEXT S
X0 = 10 : Y0 = 10 'Starting point in window 2
FOR Y = Y0 TO Y0+80 STEP 20 : LINE(X0,Y)–(X0+80,Y) : NEXT Y 'The
FOR X = X0 TO X0+80 STEP 40 : LINE(X,Y0)–(X,Y0+80) : NEXT X 'Grid
```

Poll:
    WINDOW 2
    PROCESS = **DIALOG**(0) : EVENT = **MOUSE**(0)
    IF PROCESS = 1 **THEN** Quit
    IF EVENT <> 1 **THEN** Poll
    X = **MOUSE**(1) : X1 = (X–X0)\10
    Y = **MOUSE**(2) : Y1 = (Y–Y0)\10
    IF X < X0 **OR** X > X0 + 80 **OR** Y < Y0 **OR** Y > Y0 + 80 **THEN** Poll
    COLOR = **POINT**(X,Y) : **IF** COLOR = 30 **THEN** COLOR = 33 **ELSE** COLOR = 30
    X = 10*(X\10) : Y = 10*(Y\10) : **LINE** (X+1,Y+1)–(X+9,Y+9),COLOR,BF
    S = Y1\2 'Subscript in PATT% array
    BASETEN = 2^(3–(X1 **MOD** 4))
    BASEHEX = BASETEN*16^(3–((Y1 **MOD** 2)*2+X1\4))
    IF BASEHEX = 32768! **THEN** BASEHEX = –32768!
    IF COLOR = 30 **THEN** PATT%(S) = PATT%(S) **AND** (&HFFFF–BASEHEX)
    IF COLOR = 33 **THEN** PATT%(S) = PATT%(S) **OR** BASEHEX
    PENPAT VARPTR(PATT%(0))
    MOVETO 104, 8 : **PENSIZE** 104, 104 : **LINETO** 104, 8
    WINDOW OUTPUT 3
    FOR S = 0 **TO** 3
      X$ = "&H0000" : Y$ = **HEX$**(PATT%(S))
      X$ = **LEFT$**(X$,6–**LEN**(Y$)) + Y$
      MOVETO 10, 25+20*S : **PRINT** X$
    NEXT S
    GOTO Poll

Quit:
  WINDOW CLOSE 2 : **WINDOW CLOSE** 3 : **WINDOW** 1
  END

Figure 10-12. Execution of Program 10-8.

This program will make it easy to develop a variety of patterns to use with PENPAT and FILL. Program 10-8 lets us experiment with patterns in exactly the same way that MacPaint and the Control Panel do, but this program produces the data for the pattern. If you are going to design many mouse cursors, you should develop a similar program for that.

ROUNDRECTangle

A ROUNDRECTangle is a rectangle with rounded corners. We may specify the dimensions of an oval for the shape of the corners. All we need in addition to the values we have been storing in BOUNDS% is values for the width and height of the oval.

FRAMEROUNDRECT VARPTR(BOUNDS%(0)), WIDE, HIGH

is all it takes. Let's write a demonstration program to show a few different rounded rectangles.

Drawing with Rectangles, Ovals, Arcs, and Polygons

Program 10-9. Draw a few sample rounded rectangles.

REM ** Demonstrate FRAMEROUNDRECT
DIM BOUNDS%(3)
FOR K = 10 **TO** 100 **STEP** 10
   BOUNDS%(0) = 110 − K
   BOUNDS%(1) = 240 − 2*K
   BOUNDS%(2) = 110 + K
   BOUNDS%(3) = 240 + 2*K
   WIDE = 100*(K−10)/K
   HIGH = 90*(K−110)/K
   FRAMEROUNDRECT VARPTR(BOUNDS%(0)), WIDE, HIGH
NEXT K

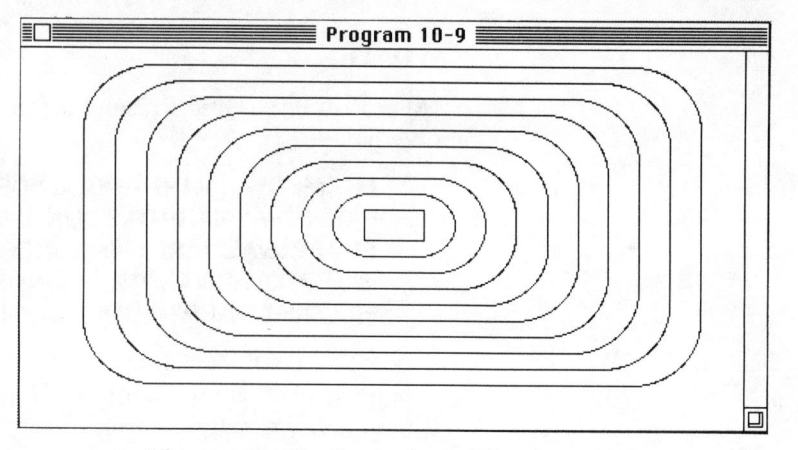

Figure 10-13. Execution of Program 10-9.

PAINT, ERASE, and INVERT are used as follows:

PAINTROUNDRECT VARPTR(BOUNDS%(0)), WIDE, HIGH
ERASEROUNDRECT VARPTR(BOUNDS%(0)), WIDE, HIGH
INVERTROUNDRECT VARPTR(BOUNDS%(0)), WIDE, HIGH

FILLROUNDRECT is exactly analogous to FILLRECT.

FILLROUNDRECT VARPTR(BOUNDS%(0)), WIDE, HIGH, **VARPTR**(PATT%(0))

will draw a rounded rectangle filled with the pattern defined by the values in the array PATT%.

The ROUNDRECT routines are very much like the RECT routines. In fact, with a little thought, we can use ROUNDRECT to produce any drawing made with RECT. All we have to do is make the corners square. We can do that by making the oval width and the oval height equal to zero. Some programmers may find it more convenient to use the RECT calls without the extra two values required by the ROUNDRECT routine. The choice is yours.

OVAL

Microsoft BASIC offers a separate group of routines to draw ovals. We have

FRAMEOVAL VARPTR(BOUNDS%(0))
PAINTOVAL VARPTR(BOUNDS%(0))
ERASEOVAL VARPTR(BOUNDS%(0))
INVERTOVAL VARPTR(BOUNDS%(0))
FILLOVAL VARPTR(BOUNDS%(0)), **VARPTR**(PATT%(0))

These five routines behave just like the equivalent RECT routines. The BOUNDS% array defines the dimensions of the rectangle that the oval will exactly fit into.

Notice that ROUNDRECT can produce any drawing from this latest group, also. If we make the width and height of the oval the same as the width and height of the rectangle that defines the oval, then ROUNDRECT will draw the oval. Remember, too, that the CIRCLE statement can draw ovals using the aspect ratio. But CIRCLE cannot use the characteristics of the pen or use PAINT, ERASE, INVERT, or FILL.

ARC

Another group of routines in this section draws arcs and wedges. This is done by defining the BOUNDS% of the rectangle that the arc would fit into if it were part of an oval, and two angles—one for the beginning of the arc and one for the angle through which the arc will sweep. The angles are measured in degrees with zero being due north or at 12 o'clock. Positive arcs are drawn clockwise from the beginning, and negative arcs are drawn counterclockwise. The five calls look like this:

FRAMEARC VARPTR(BOUNDS%(0)), BEGIN, SWEEP
PAINTARC VARPTR(BOUNDS%(0)), BEGIN, SWEEP
ERASEARC VARPTR(BOUNDS%(0)), BEGIN, SWEEP
INVERTARC VARPTR(BOUNDS%(0)), BEGIN, SWEEP
FILLARC VARPTR(BOUNDS%(0)), BEGIN, SWEEP, **VARPTR**(PATT%(0))

where BOUNDS% and PATT% are exactly the same as for the earlier routines in this section.

POLYGON

The final group of figure drawing calls displays polygons. Given a set of coordinate points, POLY will connect them with straight lines in sequence, just like a dot-to-dot drawing. Here are the five forms for POLY:

FRAMEPOLY VARPTR(VERTEX%(0))
PAINTPOLY VARPTR(VERTEX%(0))
ERASEPOLY VARPTR(VERTEX%(0))
INVERTPOLY VARPTR(VERTEX%(0))
FILLPOLY VARPTR(VERTEX%(0)), **VARPTR**(PATT%(0))

where PATT% stores an 8 by 8 pattern just like the other routines of this section, but VERTEX% is different. The number of bytes in the array VERTEX% is stored in VERTEX%(0). The next four elements are supposed to be the same as elements 0 through 3 in BOUNDS% as we have used it in this section. So, the top goes in VERTEX%(1), the left side goes in VERTEX%(2), the bottom goes in VERTEX%(3), and the right side goes in VERTEX%(4). These boundaries are supposed to contain the polygon. Beginning with element 5 the array VERTEX% stores coordinate pairs for the vertices of a polygon. But, beware, the coordinates must be entered in Y,X order. So, VERTEX%(5) contains the Y coordinate of the first vertex and VERTEX%(6) contains the X coordinate of the first point. Once we have coordinates for a polygon, we know the total number of elements required for the array. Multiply that number by 2 to get the number of bytes and the value of VERTEX%(0).

Program 10-10 demonstrates some of the properties of POLY.

Program 10-10. Demonstrate POLY.

```
READ BYTES
DIM VERTEX%(BYTES/2-1), PATT%(3)
VERTEX%(0) = BYTES
FOR K = 1 TO BYTES/2-1
  READ VERTEX%(K)
NEXT K
FOR K = 0 TO 3 : READ PATT%(K) : NEXT K

FILLPOLY VARPTR(VERTEX%(0)), VARPTR(PATT%(0))
FRAMEPOLY VARPTR(VERTEX%(0))

DATA 38, 0, 0, 300, 600
DATA 10,10, 100,20, 240,100
DATA 120,160, 130,180, 5,120
DATA 10,10

DATA &H0000, &H8888, &HA8D8, &H8800
```

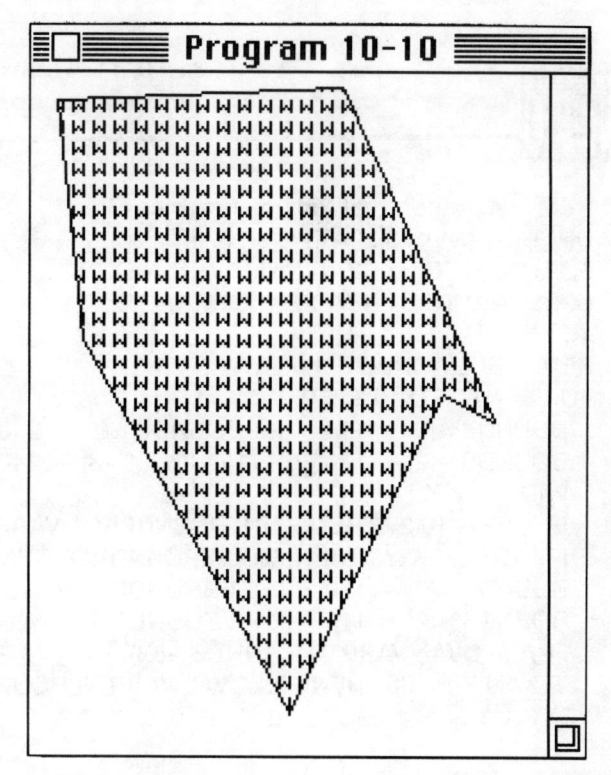

Figure 10-14. Execution of Program 10-10.

A Demonstration Program

Now it is time to present a program that demonstrates a variety of the features discussed in this section. See Program 10-11.

Program 10-11. Demonstrate miscellaneous graphics features.

```
REM ** A potpourri of toolbox graphics
DIM BOUNDS%(3), PATT%(3), PATT1%(3)
FOR K = 0 TO 3 : READ PATT%(K) : NEXT K
FOR K = 0 TO 3 : READ PATT1%(K) : NEXT K

REM ** ROUNDRECT and OVAL
FOR K = 90 TO 10 STEP -10
    BOUNDS%(0) = 110 - K : BOUNDS%(1) = 240 - 2*K
    BOUNDS%(2) = 110 + K : BOUNDS%(3) = 240 + 2*K
    WIDE = 2*K : HIGH = K
    IF K/20 = K\20 THEN PAINTROUNDRECT VARPTR(BOUNDS%(0)), WIDE, HIGH
    IF K/20 <> K\20 THEN ERASEROUNDRECT VARPTR(BOUNDS%(0)), WIDE, HIGH
    BOUNDS%(0) = 110 - 2*K : BOUNDS%(1) = 240 - K
    BOUNDS%(2) = 110 + 2*K : BOUNDS%(3) = 240 + K
    FRAMEOVAL VARPTR(BOUNDS%(0))
    IF K/30 = K\30 THEN FILLOVAL VARPTR(BOUNDS%(0)), VARPTR(PATT%(0))
NEXT K

REM ** ARC and OVAL
FOR K = 1 TO 4
    FOR J = 0 TO 3 : READ BOUNDS%(J) : NEXT J : READ BE, SW
    PAINTARC VARPTR(BOUNDS%(0)), BE, SW
    FOR J = 0 TO 3 : READ BOUNDS%(J) : NEXT J
    FILLOVAL VARPTR(BOUNDS%(0)), VARPTR(PATT1%(0))
NEXT K

DATA &H1234, &H5678, &H9ABC, &HDEF0
DATA &H0018, &H106E, &HFCFC, &HFE6C
DATA -40, -90, 60, 110, 90, 90
DATA 20, 20, 50, 70
DATA 158, -90, 258, 110, 0, 90
DATA 168, 20, 198, 70
DATA -40, 374, 60, 574, 270, -90
DATA 20, 414, 50, 464
DATA 158, 374, 258, 574, 0, -90
DATA 168, 414, 198, 464
```

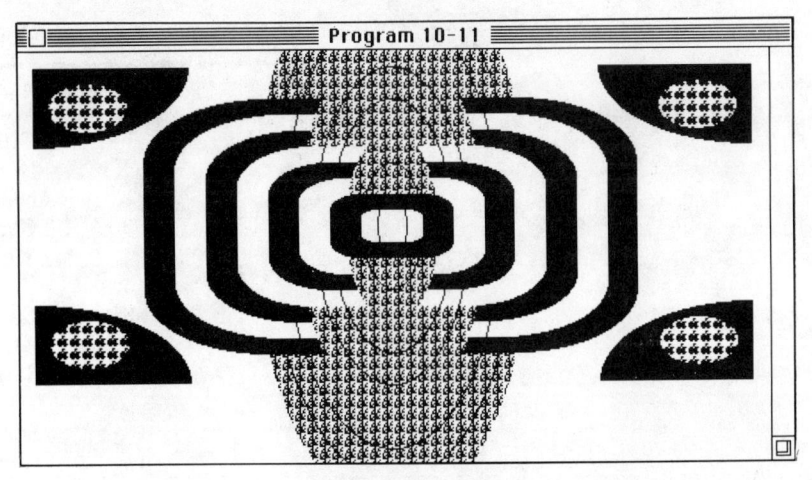

Figure 10-15. Execution of Program 10-11.

10-5. Controlling Text

Four routines are available for controlling text in the output window. Any output to the printer through LPRINT or LLIST is not affected by the routines presented here. Use LCOPY or Command-Shift-4 with or without Caps Lock to save things on paper.

Here are the four routines:

TEXTFONT W
TEXTMODE Y
TEXTFACE X
TEXTSIZE Z

TEXTFONT

The fonts used by Macintosh are all given names of famous cities around the world. They do not correspond to conventional type in the printing industry.

Table 10-3. Text fonts on the Macintosh.

Font Number	Name
0	Chicago*
1	Geneva**
2	New York
3	Geneva
4	Monaco
5	Venice
6	London
7	Athens
8	San Francisco
9	Toronto
10	Seattle
11	Cario

*The default system font is font 0.
**The default font for Microsoft BASIC is Geneva, size 12, plain face, and copy mode.

It is up to you to use the Font Mover to manage the fonts available in your System file. This might be a good time to study the fonts in your system. To see the fonts available on your disk, run the following four line program:

```
FOR F = 0 TO 11
   TEXTFONT F
   PRINT "Display font number"; F
NEXT F
```

If a font is missing from the system, the default font will be used for the display.

TEXTMODE

The actual appearance of text depends on the mode used. The default is 0. In mode 0 the text replaces whatever is already on the screen. Mode 1 causes the text to be superimposed on the screen. Anything already on the screen is unchanged. Mode 2 causes every pixel on the screen where a text pixel should go to be inverted. The screen pixel is XORed with the pixel in the text display. Print the same thing in the same location and it disappears, just like PUT and pen mode 10. Mode 3 is called BIC (for Black Is Changed). In BIC mode all black pixels in the character to be displayed are changed (to white), and white pixels are left unchanged. It is important to match the mode with condition of the screen at the time of the display. A simple demonstration program will illustrate the point. See Program 10-12.

Program 10-12. Demonstrate modes 0 through 3 in TEXTMODE MODE.

```
REM ** Demonstrate text modes
DIM PATT%(3), BOUNDS%(3)
FOR BACKGROUND = 1 TO 2
   FOR J = 0 TO 3 : READ PATT%(J) : NEXT J
   FOR K = 0 TO 3 : READ BOUNDS%(K) : NEXT K
   FILLRECT VARPTR(BOUNDS%(0)), VARPTR(PATT%(0))
NEXT BACKGROUND

LINE (1,8)–(111,78),,BF
LINE (0,7)–(448,79),,B

PRINT
FOR MODE = 0 TO 3
   TEXTMODE MODE
   PRINT "Mode ="; MODE, "Mode ="; MODE
   PRINT "Mode ="; MODE, "Mode ="; MODE
NEXT MODE

TEXTMODE 0 'Restore normal display

DATA &HAA55, &HAA55, &HAA55, &HAA55
DATA 8, 223,78, 334
DATA &H9200, &H2400, &H4900, &H9200
DATA 8, 335, 78, 447
```

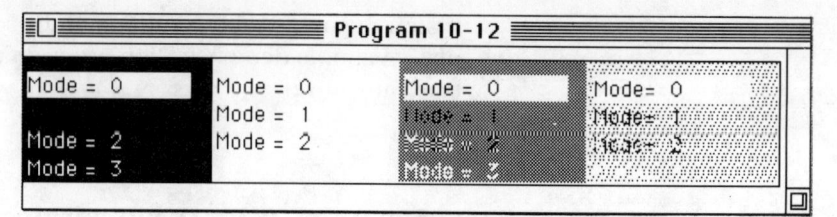

Figure 10-16. Execution of Program 10-12.

Notice that the text display is invisible on the black background for mode 1 and on the white background for mode 3.

TEXTFACE

TEXTFACE has to do with style. Each style is selected by turning a binary bit on. The styles are shown in Table 10-4.

Table 10-4. Text styles.

Bit Position	Bit Value	Style Name
0	1	Bold
1	2	Italic
2	4	Underline
3	8	Outline
4	16	Shadow
5	32	Closer spacing
6	64	Wider spacing

Styles from Table 10-4 can be used together by turning on more than one bit. So, to obtain Bold and Underline we would use 5. The default condition is Plain text, which we may restore with

TEXTFACE 0

For italics, outline, or shadow text, we must use mode 1 or mode 2. This is another place where you will want to experiment a little to determine the best results for your own situation. Different backgrounds have a profound effect on the resulting display.

TEXTSIZE

You may use almost any integer value for TEXTSIZE. Don't try 1 or 128—they cause the Macintosh to crash.

TEXTSIZE 0

returns the size to the default, which is 12 for Geneva. TEXTSIZE 2 is too small to read and TEXTSIZE 127 is too large to fit much on the screen. Sizes somewhere in the range 10 to 20 or 30 are reasonable.

10-6. Controlling the Output Window Background

BACKPAT

BACKPAT VARPTR(PATT%(0)) may be used to fill in the output window with the pattern of your choice. The process for creating a pattern and obtaining the corresponding numeric values is identical to the process for PENPAT and FILL.

Let's use Program 10-8 to do one final pattern.

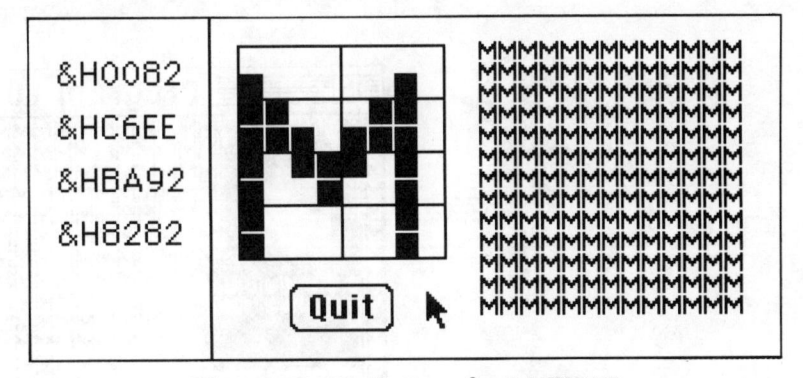

Figure 10-17. Pattern for BACKPAT.

All of the 8 by 8 patterns we have worked with in this chapter are translated into numeric data in the same way. Therefore, they are completely interchangable.

Simply executing the BACKPAT routine will fill in the border with our pattern. In order to fill the entire output window, a CLS statement is required. CLS clears the screen using the pattern established with BACKPAT. Any display in the output window will replace the pattern. See Program 10-13.

Program 10-13. Sample BACKPAT.

```
DIM PATT%(3), BOUNDS%(3)
FOR K = 0 TO 3 : READ PATT%(K) : NEXT K
FOR K = 0 TO 3 : READ BOUNDS%(K) : NEXT K

BACKPAT VARPTR(PATT%(0)) : CLS

LINE (10,10)–(60,60),,BF
LINE (20,20)–(50,50),30,BF
PENSIZE 1, 20 : MOVETO 10, 75 : CALL LINE (60,0)
FRAMEOVAL VARPTR(BOUNDS%(0))

DATA &H0082, &HC6EE. &HBA92, &H8282
DATA 100, 10, 190, 200
```

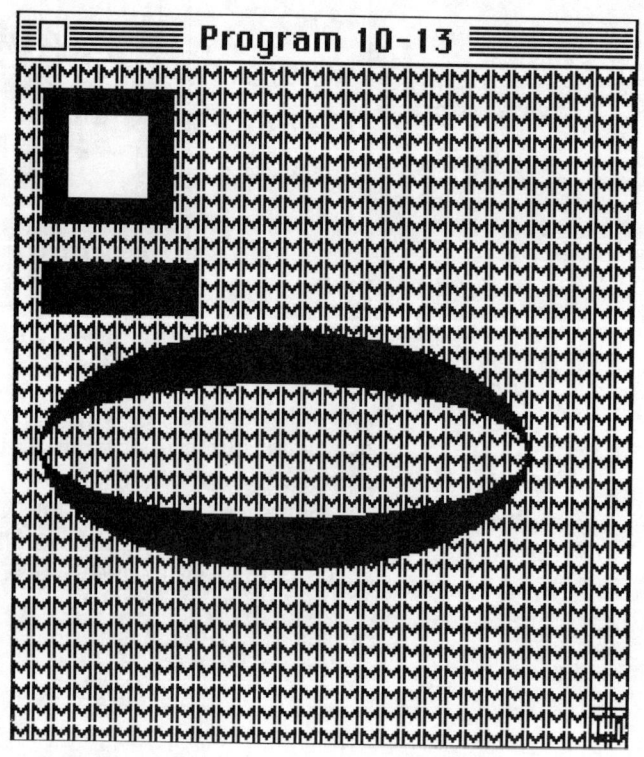

Figure 10-18. Execution of Program 10-13.

We may restore our customized pattern with CLS at any time. NEW does the same thing. To recover the standard white background pattern of BASIC, execute BACKPAT with an array of all zeros and do a CLS.

CHAPTER 11

Files

The disk is at the very heart of the Macintosh. Nearly everything that the Macintosh does is controlled by data and programs stored on a disk. The Finder is a program. Microsoft BASIC is a program. We save BASIC programs on disk with SAVE. We later retrieve them by using the mouse to open them, or by using the LOAD command, as discussed in Appendix A and Appendix B. All data saved on a disk is organized into "disk files." Even programs saved on disk are called files. Figure 11-1 shows the icons for programs and data files for Microsoft BASIC.

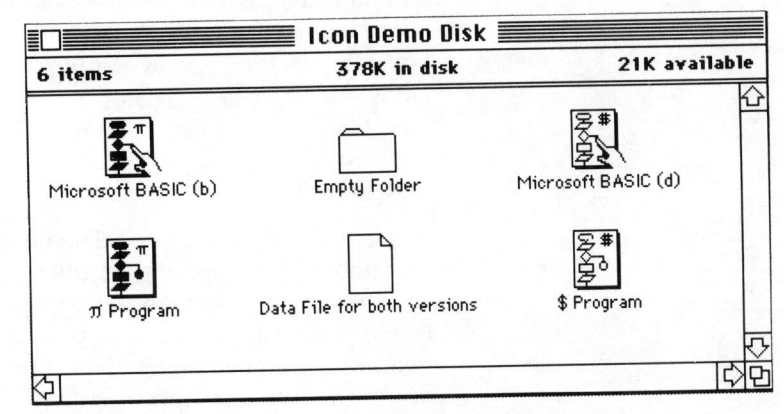

Figure 11-1. File and program icons.

It happens that some files are programs that execute by themselves, some files can be executed by using a language such as BASIC first, some files require other applications, such as MacWrite or MacPaint, and some files are useful only as data. These last are usually called *data files*. In the absence of data files, we have been saving data in DATA statements of programs. (We did look ahead a little for PICTURE and screen GET data.) DATA statements are not practical to update during program execution. With data files we can write a program to manage the data of the file itself and use other programs to obtain information from the file as needed. We can use data from several data files to prepare reports of all kinds.

A data file is just an area of the disk where we may save data. The applications for data files are truly unlimited. We can maintain inventory information, payroll, all kinds of financial information, production records, personnel records, and an endless variety of business-related facts and figures. We use data files for word processing, such as writing letters or writing books (this one is an example). Legal documents of all kinds are prepared using word processing.

In this chapter we will write a few programs as an introduction to data files. We will use relatively small files. The theory and practice of very large files are beyond the scope of this book. As files are required to contain thousands and even millions of data items it becomes necessary to develop special techniques for organizing the data and finding it later.

BASIC data files come in two distinct varieties: sequential access and random access. Data stored in sequential files is similar to data stored in DATA statements of a program. To get to any particular data entry we must read all other data entries that precede the one we want. Random access files are organized into segments that allow us to read any single data entry anywhere in the file directly.

Sequential Access Files

Sequential access files are relatively easy to work with from a programming viewpoint. We simply learn a few new BASIC keywords and think about the continuous stream of data in the file. The catch is that sequential files tend to produce slow-running programs. To make a single change in a data entry of a sequential access file requires that we read and rewrite the entire file. For this reason we avoid sequential access for large files.

Random Access Files

Random access files are slightly more complex to program. But they tend to produce faster results and readily facilitate large files and ones that require frequent updating. Random access does not mean that we go about in an erratic fashion accessing data in the file. It means that we may access data anywhere in the file without regard to where in the file we accessed the last data. We may read the thirty-first entry, change it, and rewrite it without reading any other entry in the file. We simply need to organize the file so that we know where each data item is. Random access files are discussed in the next two chapters.

11-1. Sequential Files

The OPEN, PRINT #, INPUT #, and CLOSE # statements are the four BASIC keywords required to use sequential data files.

OPEN

OPEN establishes a communications channel between the program and the data file on the disk. It creates an area in memory where data items are temporarily held. This is called a file buffer. The file buffer is used to manage the flow of data between the program and the disk file. The program may either output data to the file or input data from the file. A file opened for sequential access cannot do both on a single channel. Data items are output to a file in OUTPUT mode or APPEND mode. Output mode begins at the beginning of the file, while append mode begins at the end of a file. If we are working with a new file, they amount to the same thing. For an existing file, output mode erases any data already in the file and begins at the beginning. Append mode enables us to maintain a sequential file by always adding data to the end of the file.

In addition, we need to select a channel number for the file and give it a name.

OPEN "Sample Data" **FOR OUTPUT AS** #1

opens a file named Sample Data for output on channel number 1 and prepares to enter data in the file at the beginning. We may select any channel number from 1 to 255. All other numbers will cause BASIC to respond with an error box. Variables may be used for the file name and the channel number.

If the file already exists, OPEN simply forms the necessary linkage. If the file does not exist then it can only be opened for output or append. Any attempt to open a new file for input will evoke the "File not found" error box. Once opened for output or append, a file is ready to receive data. This is done with a PRINT # statement.

Here is an alternate form for the OPEN statement:

OPEN "OUTPUT", #1, "Sample Data"

or even

OPEN "O", #1, "Sample Data"

Since BASIC only checks the first letter of the mode in this form of the OPEN statement. You may use "O", "A", and "I" for Output, Append, and Input respectively. The two forms are entirely equivalent. Use the one you like.

PRINT

PRINT #C outputs data to the file buffer on the channel numbered C. Whenever the file buffer fills up, it is then written out to the disk file itself. That is, a copy of the information in the buffer is written out to the disk. And PRINT #C again fills the buffer. Since disk access is slow and memory access is fast, this buffer scheme is used to reduce the time it takes to move data back and forth between a program and a file.

PRINT # performs very much like PRINT.

PRINT #C, A$

places the string A$ in the file followed by a carriage return-line feed (cr-lf). These first examples will simply send string data out to the file, one string to a line. Section 11-5 will examine in detail the procedure for sending several data items out to the file and for mixing string and numeric data.

INPUT

INPUT #C accepts data from the file buffer on the channel numbered C. This is just a different form of the INPUT statement that is used for accepting data from the keyboard. To make a file available for INPUT #, it must first be opened in input mode.

OPEN "Sample Data" **FOR INPUT AS** #1

does the job. The data from the PRINT # example can be read using a single string variable in an INPUT # statement.

INPUT #1, X$

will cause the string written out to the file by the PRINT # statement above to be loaded into string variable X$. It's that simple.

CLOSE

The communications channel between the file and the program is severed with the CLOSE # statement.

CLOSE #1

disconnects the program from the file opened on channel 1. Part of this process may involve transferring all data from the file buffer in memory to the file itself on disk. CLOSE without any file number disconnects all files. It is especially important to close files that have been written to. Failure to do this could result in losing data when the file buffer contains something that hasn't been copied to the file on disk yet.

This problem is of special concern when program execution terminates due to an error condition. In this situation, the file buffer is left hanging. We must issue a CLOSE from the keyboard in the Command window to assure that any data written to the buffer is copied out to the file. Executing an END statement does perform the functions of a CLOSE #, but it is good practice to include an explicit CLOSE # anyway.

STOP, Stop, CONT

The STOP keyword in a program and Stop from the Run menu (⌘-.) leave things in the same condition as an error, so a CLOSE # is not automatic. We may use ⌘-. to interrupt a program during testing. This gives us the opportunity to display the values of variables and decide whether the program is performing satisfactorily. If all is well, then we may resume execution with CONT typed in the Command window. Continue is also an option in the Run menu. We may also insert STOP statements at key points in a program for the same purpose. As with ⌘-., files are still open so we may proceed with CONT. Since a STOP statement also causes the List window to display a box around the STOP keyword itself, this is an important technique for finding trouble spots in a program.

If you get a "Can't continue" error box, it could be that you have edited a line of the program, added a line, or deleted a line. In any of these cases, BASIC has to do its housekeeping to organize the program. In so doing, it simply cannot pick up where it was in the old program.

We have four of the crucial sequential files statements: OPEN, PRINT #, INPUT #, and CLOSE #. With these four statements we can create and use significant sequential files.

A File-Based Alphabet Game

We are ready to convert the little Alphabet program from Chapter 7 so that it works with a file. We already have the program to play the game. Now we need an initialization program to set up a signs file to replace the DATA statements. All we have to do is take the DATA statements from Program 7-8h, write a new control routine, and create a new subroutine that reads DATA and uses PRINT # to write it to a file. Then all the signs for the Alphabet game program will be available in this data file. See Program 11-1.

Program 11-1. Initialize the signs file for Alphabet game.

```
REM ** Write some signs to a file for Alphabet game

OPEN "Signs Data" FOR OUTPUT AS #1
GOSUB MakeSignsFile 'Write the signs to the signs file
CLOSE #1
END


REM ** The signs
DATA Stop, Al's Pizza, Dairy Queen, Burger King
DATA Yield, One Way, This Way Out, Detour
DATA One Show Only Tonight, Exit Only, Entrance Only Please
DATA Florida 2138 mi., Fly United, Jet Set Diner
DATA Give Her a Valentine, Give Him a Valentine
DATA First Avenue, North Side
DATA Done

MakeSignsFile:
  A$ = "Start"
  WHILE A$ <> "Done"
    READ A$
    PRINT #1, A$
  WEND
  RETURN
```

The control routine for initializing the signs file couldn't be simpler. It just opens the file, uses a subroutine to read the signs from DATA statements and write the signs to the Signs Data file, and executes CLOSE #. That's all.

Look at the MakeSignsFile subroutine. Notice that the end-of-data signal word "Done" is written to the file. This means that we can use the LoadSigns subroutine of the original program with very slight changes to read the signs back. When we play the game we will get the data from the file instead of from DATA statements in the program itself. Instead of using READ we want to use INPUT #. The conversion is astonishingly straightforward. See Program 11-2a.

Program 11-2a. Load the Alphabet game road signs.

```
LoadSigns:
   NUMBEROFSIGNS = 0 : INPUT #1, A$
   WHILE A$ <> "Done"
      NUMBEROFSIGNS = NUMBEROFSIGNS + 1 : SIGNS$(NUMBEROFSIGNS) = A$
      INPUT #1, A$
   WEND
   PRINT "There are:"; NUMBEROFSIGNS; "signs in this game."
   GOSUB Delay
RETURN
```

The only change in this subroutine was the replacement of READ A$ with INPUT #1, A$. Nothing more!

Next we need only provide an OPEN before GOSUB LoadSigns and a CLOSE # after. See Program 11-2b.

Program 11-2b. Changed control routine in Alphabet game for files.

```
DIM SIGNS$(50)
RANDOMIZE TIMER
OPEN "Signs Data" FOR INPUT AS #1
GOSUB LoadSigns        'Load the signs array
CLOSE #1
GOSUB BeginGame        'Establish game beginning
GetNextSign:
   GOSUB DisplaySigns  'Simulate random signs along the road
   GOSUB CheckPlayer   'Did the player spot the next letter?
     IF LETTER = 0 THEN GetNextSign 'If not then repeat step 3
   GOSUB CheckLetter   'Is the next letter on the sign?
     IF NEXTLETTER < 91 THEN GetNextSign 'If not "Z" yet repeat step 3
PRINT "Congratulations, you have made it through the alphabet"
END
```

We converted the control routine by adding an OPEN statement and a CLOSE statement. Nothing more is needed in the control routine. Finally, there is the matter of removing the unwanted DATA statements. It is remarkable that we have made such a major conversion with so little programming effort. It pays to organize programs carefully.

Program 11-2. File-based Alphabet game.

```
    DIM SIGNS$(50)
    RANDOMIZE TIMER
    OPEN "Signs Data" FOR INPUT AS #1
    GOSUB LoadSigns        'Load the signs array
    CLOSE #1
    GOSUB BeginGame        'Establish game beginning
GetNextSign:
      GOSUB DisplaySigns   'Simulate random signs along the road
      GOSUB CheckPlayer    'Did the player spot the next letter?
        IF LETTER = 0 THEN GetNextSign 'If not then repeat step 3
      GOSUB CheckLetter    'Is the next letter on the sign?
        IF NEXTLETTER < 91 THEN GetNextSign 'If not "Z" yet repeat step 3
    PRINT "Congratulations, you have made it through the alphabet"
    END

LoadSigns:
    NUMBEROFSIGNS = 0 : INPUT #1, A$
    WHILE A$ <> "Done"
      NUMBEROFSIGNS = NUMBEROFSIGNS + 1 : SIGNS$(NUMBEROFSIGNS) = A$
      INPUT #1, A$
    WEND
    PRINT "There are:"; NUMBEROFSIGNS; "signs in this game."
    GOSUB Delay
    RETURN

BeginGame:
    NEXTLETTER = 65 'Get ready to look for 'A'
    RETURN
```

```
DisplaySigns:
  R = INT(RND * NUMBEROFSIGNS + 1)
  CLS
  PICTURE ON
    PRINT SIGNS$(R)
  PICTURE OFF
  FOR K = 1 TO 250 STEP 30
    PICTURE(1+5*SQR(K),250-K)-(100+4*K,300+K)
    FOR X = 1 TO 100 : NEXT X
    CLS
  NEXT K
  RETURN

CheckPlayer:
  A$ = INKEY$ : IF LEN(A$) = 0 THEN LETTER = 0 : GOTO EndCheckPlayer
  ClearKey: IF LEN(INKEY$) = 1 THEN ClearKey
    PRINT A$; "    ";
    A$ = UCASE$(A$) : LETTER = ASC(A$)
    IF A$ < "A" OR A$ > "Z" THEN CheckPlayer
    IF LETTER = NEXTLETTER THEN EndCheckPlayer
      PRINT "Not the next letter in the alphabet" : GOSUB Delay
      GOTO CheckPlayer
  EndCheckPlayer:
  RETURN

CheckLetter:
  IF INSTR(UCASE$(SIGNS$(R)), A$) THEN Found ELSE NotFound
  Not Found:
    BEEP : PRINT "Your letter is not on the sign" : GOSUB Delay
    GOTO EndCheckLetter
  Found:
    PRINT "Good" : GOSUB Delay
    NEXTLETTER = NEXTLETTER + 1
  EndCheckLetter:
  RETURN

Delay: 'Time delay for messages
  FOR J = 1 TO 2500 : NEXT J
  RETURN
```

Since we have changed none of the game-playing features of this program, it will behave exactly as the last version did.

There are lots of things we could do now to add interest to the program. We could make it tell the player when a letter was on a sign but not identified. We could keep track of the number of times any particular person has played the game. Now that the program is file-based we could ask each player to enter his or her favorite sign. If the entry is not in the file, then the program could add it and rewrite the file. There is a whole world of graphics features that could be used to add interest here.

Problems for Section 11-1

There are lots of games that could be computerized using files to store information. Use your imagination.

1. Modify the Alphabet game program to request a new sign from the keyboard at the beginning of every game. Compare the new sign with those in the array. If it is a new one, add it to the end of the array, open the file for output, and write the array out to the file. Then close the file. Following this, begin the game. Just use the MakeSignsFile subroutine in Program 11-1.

2. Modify Program 11-2 to report each time the player missed the next letter twice.

3. Write a program to tabulate the number of times each letter of the alphabet occurs in the signs file.

4. Add a routine to your program in Problem 3 to arrange the results in order of frequency of occurrence.

5. Write a program to play Geography. In this game, two or more players take turns thinking of place names. Each player must name a place so that the first letter matches the last letter of the previous player's place. Have the program save all new place names in a disk file. No name may be used twice in the same game. Make the computer one player in a two-player game.

11-2. A Program is a File, Too!

When we write useful programs, we save them on disk. Now the program is a file. If the "Text" option is used to save the program, it is accessible to other programs. (See Appendix A.) You may use MacWrite to edit a BASIC program provided you use the "Text" option when saving it in BASIC and the "Text only" option when saving it in MacWrite.

Let's write a little program to simply display a program stored on disk. Then let's think about expanding it to pretty up program listings. Some programmers use lots of colons to include several statements on the same line. This does save computer memory and disk space. The drawback is that too much of this makes programs hard to read. We can break each of those lines up into individual statements and display them separately. But first let's display the program as is. Note that the program we are writing can display any file stored in Text format.

We simply open for input and repeatedly input data from the file, displaying as we go. Let's use this program to display Program 11-2a as the first example. See Program 11-3.

Program 11-3. Display a program from disk.

```
REM ** Display a program from disk
OPEN "Program 11-2a" FOR INPUT AS #1

GetLine:
    INPUT #1, A$
    GOSUB StraightPRINT
    GOTO GetLine

StraightPRINT:
    PRINT A$ : RETURN
```

We have named Program 11-2a in the OPEN statement. Now let's run Program 11-3. See Figure 11-3.

A Program is a File, too!

```
 File  Edit  Search  Run  Windows

LoadSigns:
NUMBEROFSIGNS = 0 : INPUT
A$
WHILE A$ <> "Done"
NUMBEROFSIGNS = NUMBEROFSI
INPUT #1
A$
WEND
PRINT "There are:"; NUMBEROFS
GOSUB Delay
RETURN
```

Input past end   OK

```
List
REM ** Display a program from disk
OPEN "Program 11-2a" FOR INPUT A$

GetLine:
    INPUT #1, A$
    GOSUB StraightPRINT
    GOTO GetLine

StraightPRINT:
    PRINT A$ : RETURN
```

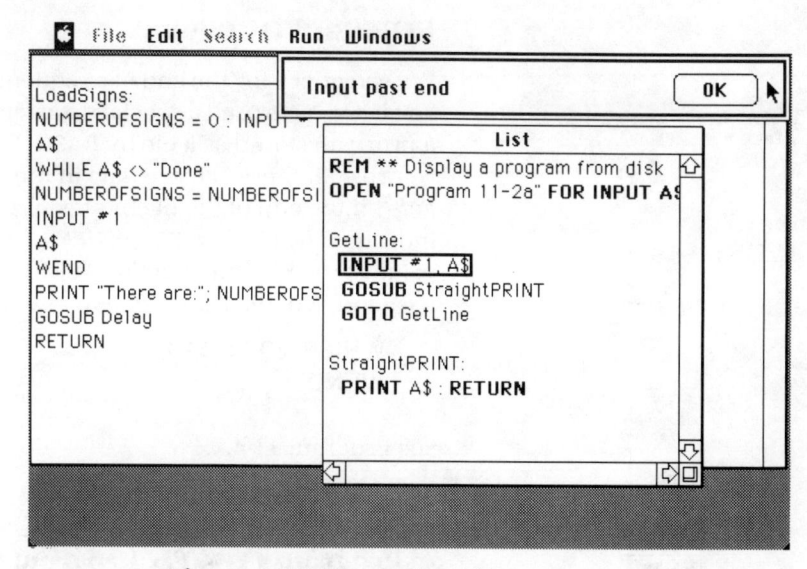

Figure 11-3. Execution of Program 11-3.

Figure 11-3 reveals three serious problems. We can solve all of them easily with new BASIC features. Notice that in each of the INPUT statements, the "A$" is displayed on a second line. That is because there was a comma in the program line. A comma here has the same meaning as a comma entered at the keyboard in response to INPUT. It separates data items from one another. To cure this we need a statement that reads data from the file until a carriage return-line feed is encountered. That way we get the whole program statement. LINE INPUT is made to solve just this kind of problem.

LINE INPUT

LINE INPUT accepts all data on a line up to the cr-lf pair. LINE INPUT #F does it for file #F. All we have to do is change the INPUT # statement to

LINE INPUT #1, A$

LINE INPUT also solves the second problem. Notice that each display line begins at the very left of the output window. That is because the INPUT statement ignores all leading spaces. Fortunately, LINE INPUT includes those spaces in the string.

But what about the third problem? "Input past end" is similar to "Out of DATA." We can use EOF here.

EOF (End Of File)

We can check for the end of a sequential file with the EOF function. So far we have used a special data item to signal the end of data, but a program stored as a file by BASIC has no such easy signal. EOF(F) returns 0 if there is more data in the file on channel number F. We get -1 if the end of the file has been reached. Remember that -1 also indicates "true" in an IF. . . THEN or WHILE test, so we can use the value of the EOF function in a WHILE. . . WEND loop to avoid "Input past end." All we need are two new lines

    WHILE NOT EOF(1)
    WEND

See Program 11-4.

Program 11-4. Fix Program 11-3.

```
REM ** Display a program from disk
OPEN "Program 11-2a" FOR INPUT AS #1
WHILE NOT EOF(1)
    LINE INPUT #1, A$
    GOSUB StraightPRINT
WEND
END

StraightPRINT:
    PRINT A$ : RETURN
```

Executing this program will display Program 11-2a.

Now it's time to work on breaking out multiple statements on a line. We can just add a subroutine to do this. Let's look for space–colon–space. If we just look for the colon, we will break up lines that happen to have colons in quoted strings as well as lines with colons marking multiple statements. In order for this formatting program to be useful, we have to be sure to write all our programs using space–colon–space to separate statements on the same line. Now we add the Format subroutine and change GOSUB StraightPRINT to GOSUB Format. See Program 11-5.

Program 11-5. Format multiple statements in a program.

```
REM ** Display a program from disk
OPEN "Program 11-2a" FOR INPUT AS #1
WHILE NOT EOF(1)
   LINE INPUT #1, A$
   GOSUB Format
WEND
END

StraightPRINT:
   PRINT A$ : RETURN

Format:
   FOR J = 1 TO LEN(A$)
      IF MID$(A$,J,3) <> " : " THEN NextCharacter
         PRINT LEFT$(A$,J-1)
         PRINT TAB(5);
         A$ = MID$(A$,J+1) : GOTO Format
   NextCharacter:
   NEXT J
   PRINT A$
   RETURN
```

The Format subroutine will search a line character by character for the colon-space-colon sequence. If it goes through the loop without finding one, the line is just printed. If it finds one, the program has to display the first part, and then TAB 5 spaces to get ready to display the next part on the next line. It should, however, continue looking on the same line for more space–colon–spaces. We could do this in another subroutine. Or we could adjust the string variable a little bit and use the same routine over again. This line reassigns A$ with everything on the line after the line break:

   A$ = MID$(A$,J+1) : **GOTO** Format

Then back at the beginning of the subroutine, it can be treated exactly as if it were a new program line taken from the file in the LINE INPUT # statement. Now, just for fun, let's save Program 11-5 and use it to display itself. See Figure 11-4.

```
REM **Display a program from disk
OPEN "Program 11-5" FOR INPUT AS #1
WHILE NOT EOF(1)
   LINE INPUT #1,A$
   GOSUB Format
WEND
END

StraightPRINT:
   PRINT A$
   :RETURN

Format:
   FOR J = 1 TO LEN(A$)
     IF MID$(A$,J,3) <> "
: " THEN NextCharacter
     PRINT LEFT$(A$,J-1)
     PRINT TAB(5);
        A$=MID$(A$,J+1)
   : GOTO Format
NextCharacter:
NEXT J
PRINT A$
RETURN
```

Figure 11-4. Execution of Program 11-5.

The program has very nicely rearranged the lines with multiple statements. But look at this line:

```
IF MID$(A$,J,3) <> "
: " THEN NextCharacter
```

The very statement that decides to break statements up has the sequence of characters we are looking for in it. We could easily put in another check to see if the J+3rd character is a quotation mark by comparing to CHR$(34). (See the ASCII chart in Appendix C.) This is left as a problem.

Problems for Section 11-2

1. Add a check in Program 11-5 to fix the improper display of this line:

    IF MID$(A$,J,3) <> "
    : " THEN NextCharacter

2. Modify Program 11-5 to display only lines containing FOR or NEXT statements. Hint: INSTR will be handy here.

11-3. Updating a Sequential File

We have seen how to create a sequential file. If we can read the file contents into an array in memory, we can easily rewrite the file with updated information. Now let's see a more general method for updating a file. We simply open a second file temporarily. Once the changes are made and the new file complete, we eliminate the old file using KILL, and give its name to the new file. The NAME statement is very simple. We just NAME oldfilename AS newfilename. The filenames must be enclosed in quotation marks or must be string expressions.

Let's maintain a list of names in a file. We will write a program that allows us to add a name at the beginning of the file. First, we need to create the file. See Program 11-6.

Program 11-6. Put some names in a file.

```
OPEN "Name List 01 Data" FOR OUTPUT AS #1

N$ = "Begin"
WHILE N$ <> "End"
  READ N$
  PRINT #1, N$
WEND

CLOSE #1
END

DATA Tom, Dick, Harry
DATA End
```

Now we can work on the program to do the actual update. Let's name the temporary file "Name List 01 Temp." See Program 11-7.

Program 11-7. Add a name to a sequential file.

```
REM ** Add a name to a sequential file
OPEN "Name List 01 Data" FOR INPUT AS #1
OPEN "Name List 01 Temp" FOR OUTPUT AS #2

INPUT "Add a name"; N1$
PRINT #2, N1$

N$ = "Begin"
WHILE N$ <> "End"
  INPUT #1, N$ : PRINT #2, N$
WEND

CLOSE #1, #2
KILL "Name List 01 Data"
NAME "Name List 01 Temp" AS "Name List 01 Data"
END
```

This program could be made to do a number of other things. We might want to prevent duplicates from getting into the names file. We might want to keep it alphabetized. We might want to include the ability to delete names. All of these are relatively straightforward tasks. They are left as problems.

We could make slight changes to Program 11-7 to add data at the end of the file. On the other hand, if we always want to add at the end of the file, it is easier to open the file in append mode and skip the temporary file all together.

Problems for Section 11-3

1. Write a program to simply display the names in the names file.
2. Modify Program 11-7 to prevent duplicate names from ever getting into the file. This can be done without an extra pass through the file.
3. Modify Program 11-7 to keep the file alphabetized. Of course, the data in Program 11-6 must be in the right order to begin with.
4. Rewrite Program 11-7 to delete a name.

11-4. Miscellaneous Features and Techniques

FILES$

The FILES$ function allows us to select files with a dialog box in a BASIC program.

X$ = **FILES$**(0, "Enter your choice")

causes the following dialog box to appear:

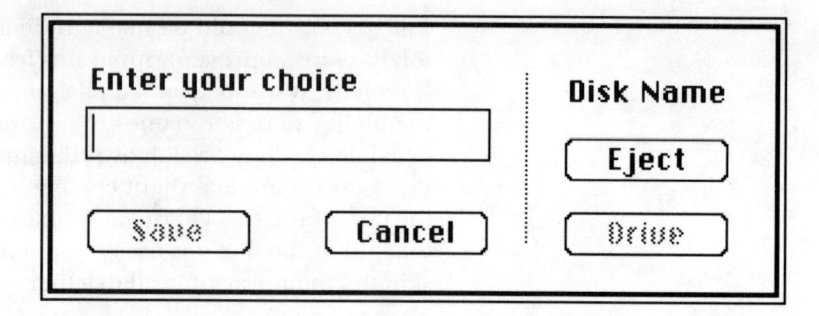

If the file entered already exists, the next dialog box asks if you want to replace the existing file. The FILES$ function will not actually alter the file, but it does put the user off. For existing files, it is better to use the second FILES$ function.

Z$ = **FILES$**(1, type spec)

This form of the FILES$ function produces a dialog box in exactly the same format that Open... in the File menu produces. The "type spec" allows the program to limit the user to a specific collection of files. Each file is assigned a type. BASIC saves all data files as "TEXT". Programs saved in Text format are also type "TEXT". BASIC itself is type "APPL". We assign the type with the NAME statement as follows:

NAME "File Name" **AS** "File Name","type"

It is not necessary to know the old type to assign a new one. In the FILES$ function the type spec string is analyzed four characters at a time. To look for SPECIAL and TEXT, use "SPECIAL TEXT" as the type spec. File types may be more than four characters, but in the FILES$ function we need to add spaces so that the next type in the string begins a group of four characters. Omitting the file spec produces a dialog box that displays every file on the disk.

Both forms of the FILES$ function return the name of the selected file in a string. That string may then be used in a program to open a file. The string contains the name of the disk followed by a colon followed by the file name. The FILES$ function empowers a BASIC program to use the full selection of changing disks and selecting or canceling with very little programming effort. If the user cancels, FILES$ returns a string of zero length.

Commas in PRINT

We might like to group data into sets of several items each. There are times when we want to keep track of several values that belong together in a sequence in the file. It would help to print several values in a single PRINT # statement. In such a case we may use

PRINT #F, X, Y, Z

The result will have the exact configuration that it would have on the screen or the printer. If the value of X is positive, then the leading space that would appear in the output window goes to the file. In other words, when we use commas with PRINT #, the values have comma spacing in the file. Since the default spacing for commas in PRINT is 14, the result will often waste file space. This can be demonstrated by using

LINE INPUT #1, A$

to read the numeric values written to the file with the line above. The display of A$ may be surprising since spaces require a full digit space in a string variable, but when printed in the output window, take only half the space of a digit. A check of LEN(A$) will quickly confirm this. When PRINT displays a numeric value it is followed by a space. On the printer, spaces are the same width as digits.

Even though we sent numeric data out, it can be read back into a string variable. However, we cannot read string data with numeric variables. The rules for using INPUT # and LINE INPUT # to obtain data from a file are the same as for using INPUT and LINE INPUT from the keyboard. Normally the data above can be read with a statement such as

INPUT #1, A, B, C

WIDTH

It may be important to be efficient when using disk space in files, so we ought to tackle this excess space condition. WIDTH # controls line width and comma spacing in a file. This works in the file exactly as it does in the output window.

WIDTH #F, 64, 8

sets the line width to 64 and the comma spacing to 8 characters in file number F.

Semicolon in PRINT

Data can also be compressed in a file by using semicolons to separate the data items in the PRINT # statement. This inserts a space before and after numerics (no space is inserted in front of negative values), and strings are placed right next to each other. This is a help, but there are still limitations on mixing string and numeric data. Both with comma spacing and with semicolon spacing, only a single string is allowed in a PRINT # statement, and if we are mixing it with numeric values, then the string must be the last item in the line. If there is a comma in a string, then it goes out as two strings. PRINT #F, X; Y; A$ is fine, but PRINT #F, X; A$; Y won't work if we use INPUT #G, C; B$; D to read the data back. A string variable in an INPUT # statement reads all the data on the rest of that line as part of the string. In this case B$ will read all the data from A$ on, or the data from both A$ and Y. We can explicitly PRINT # comma delimiters in the file to overcome this problem. There are many more details in this complex topic, but a simpler alternative is available with WRITE #.

WRITE

The WRITE # statement is designed to provide for all possibilities. WRITE # places commas right in the file to separate each data item and surrounds all string items with quotation marks. See Program 11-8.

Program 11-8. Demonstrate WRITE #.

```
OPEN "Test file" FOR OUTPUT AS #1
X = 12.098 : Y = .002 : READ A$
WRITE #1, X, A$, Y
CLOSE #1

OPEN "Test file" FOR INPUT AS #1
LINE INPUT #1, X$
PRINT X$
CLOSE #1

DATA Demonstrate WRITE #
```

Note that we used LINE INPUT # to retrieve the data from the file only for the purpose of demonstrating how WRITE # works here. Normally we would use a statement like INPUT #1, A, B$, C.

```
┌─────────────────────────────────────────┐
│ ▤□▤▤▤▤▤▤▤▤ Program 11-8 ▤▤▤▤▤▤▤▤▤▤▤    │
│ 12.098,"Demonstrate WRITE #",.002       │
│                                         │
│                                         │
│                                      ▫ │
└─────────────────────────────────────────┘
```

Figure 11-5. Execution of Program 11-8.

With the WRITE # statement you can mix strings and numerics in any way that suits your purpose. Further, there's no need to worry when some string data might have commas as part of the data. With WRITE # those commas are safely enclosed within the quotation marks.

Devices (LPT1:, SCRN:, KYBD:, and CLIP:)

With Microsoft BASIC, the printer (LPT1:), the output window (SCRN:), the keyboard (KYBD:), and the Macintosh Clipboard (CLIP:) can be treated as sequential files. They are called devices. Any of these devices may be named in an OPEN statement in an appropriate mode—output for LPT1: and SCRN:, input for KYBD:, and input and output for CLIP:.

LPT1: and SCRN

An ideal application for LPT1: and SCRN: arises when we want a program to display sometimes on the screen and sometimes on the printer. Instead of writing two versions of the program—one with PRINT and the other with LPRINT—we can assign the appropriate device name to a string variable. When DEVICE$ is set to "LPT1:" the display goes to the printer, and when it is set to "SCRN:" the display goes to the screen. Here is a program fragment to demonstrate the point.

```
SetDevice:
    INPUT "LPT1: or SCRN:", DEVICE$
    IF DEVICE$ <> "LPT1:" OR DEVICE$ <> "SCRN:" THEN SetDevice
    OPEN DEVICE$ FOR OUTPUT AS #8
    B$ = "See where the display goes"
    PRINT #8, B$
    CLOSE #8
```

We can even use WIDTH # to control such a display.

KYBD:

We have already looked at a number of options for entering data into a program from the keyboard. We have used INPUT, LINE INPUT, INPUT$, and INKEY$. The first three of these are also available for retrieving data from a file. INPUT # and LINE INPUT # work just as we have seen earlier in this chapter. INPUT$ is used to retrieve a specified number of characters.

INPUT$(N, #F)

waits for N characters from file number F. For the keyboard, this is a good way to make sure that the user types exactly the right number of characters. INPUT$ accepts commas, quotation marks and Return as valid characters. It waits for N characters. Only ⌘-. or Stop will interrupt the process.

CLIP:

Data is moved between BASIC and other applications using the Macintosh Clipboard as a file. This is the same Clipboard that is used by ⌘-X, ⌘-C, and ⌘-V for editing, so be careful.

The LOF function is invaluable for working with the Clipboard.

LOF(F)

returns the number of characters in a sequential file. This means that we can open a file and read the entire contents into a string variable with the following lines:

OPEN "CLIP:" **FOR INPUT AS** #2
A$ = **INPUT$**(LOF(2), #2)
CLOSE #2

The only limitation is that the string must be less than 32768 characters long. This technique is useful for moving a picture between BASIC and MacPaint, for example. For pictures, the CLIP: file must be opened with the name "CLIP:PICTURE."

Double Buffer

We have already covered updating a sequential file by several different commonly used methods. In the Alphabet game we talked about adding a new sign to the array and then rewriting the entire file from the array. We wrote a program that used a temporary file to make a complete copy on the disk. And we mentioned append mode for adding names to the end of a file. For any job that deletes entries, adds entries only to the end of the file, or makes any replacements that do not result in making the file longer (except at the end), here is another method.

OPEN the same file on two different file channels, thus creating the "double buffer." Open it for input on one channel and for output on another. Then transfer the entire file by INPUT #'ing from the input channel and PRINT #'ing to the output channel. Make the necessary changes on the way.

One advantage over creating a second file, killing the old file, and finally renaming the temporary file is that the double buffer method requires no extra disk space. A disadvantage is that additions must come at the end. Let's use the Name List file we created in Program 11-6 for a demonstration.

This example will be a program that lets us add names. It can easily transfer all names up to the "End" marker. Next it will request a name from the keyboard, write it to the file, and finally, write "End" out there. See Program 11-9.

Program 11-9. Double buffer sequential file update.

```
OPEN "Name List 01 Data" FOR INPUT AS #1
OPEN "Name List 01 Data" FOR OUTPUT AS #2

INPUT #1, N$
WHILE N$ <> "End"
   PRINT #2, N$ : PRINT N$
   INPUT #1, N$
WEND

INPUT "Enter a new name"; N1$
PRINT #2, N1$
PRINT #2, N$ 'Be sure End goes out
CLOSE #1, #2
END
```

There are some pitfalls to be avoided with this double buffer business. Whoever runs this program must never exit this INPUT

INPUT "Enter a new name"; N1$

with Stop (⌘-.) from the Run menu. This would result in a file without the "End" marker. The next time we run this program we will get an "Input past end" error box. One other word of caution: Look carefully at the two OPEN statements. It is no accident that we opened for input before we opened for output. When a file is opened for output, BASIC points to the beginning of the file and clears out as much of the file as it reads into the file buffer. By opening for input first, we have caused the first data in the file to be copied to a buffer area in the memory of the computer. Now, no harm is done when the statement

OPEN "Name List 01 Data" **FOR OUTPUT AS** #2

clears it out.

Problems for Section 11-4

1. Write a program to accept characters from KYBD: and write them to the Clipboard.

2. Use FILES$ and provide a menu with four options: New, Open, Kill, and Quit. New should create a file and request a message from the user that is written into the file. Open should ask the user to select a file and display the message previously written there. Kill should kill the selected file after giving the user every opportunity to cancel out. Buttons would be good for this. Quit should quit. First assign some special file type. Then try it with type "TEXT" to dislay BASIC programs from disk.

3. Write a program to read characters from the Clipboard and write them to a disk file.

CHAPTER 12

Random-Access Files

Since entries in a file may vary in length, they may require varying amounts of space. Therefore, there is no way of predicting just where the fifth or the fiftieth entry might begin. Sequential files must always be read from the beginning of the file. When we write to such a file, we must write the entire file. As the file becomes larger and larger, all this takes more and more time.

It takes a little more programming effort to work with random access, but these files tend to produce faster results and readily facilitate large amounts of data. Random access is essential for applications that require frequent updating. It allows us to access data anywhere in the file without reading any other data. We may read, change, or write any entry in the file as an independent action. We simply need to organize each file so that we know where all the data is. And that takes a little planning.

Random-access files are used for all kinds of record keeping. The ability to access any data entry at will is ideal for applications where we will not be processing every entry every time we access the file. Contrast this with the Alphabet game in which every entry in the file must be read with every use of the program. Random-access files are used for name-and-address mailing lists, every conceivable financial accounting function, and stock portfolio management. Recipes, home-management data, and inventory data are all appropriate for random-access files.

In many applications several files are linked together to form a system of files. An order entry might "point" off to a mailing-list file and an inventory file.

In order to access data entries in a file at random (that is, in any sequence), BASIC must be able to calculate the exact location of every entry. This can be done by allocating a fixed amount of disk space to every entry. Thus, if 25 bytes are allowed for each entry, the tenth entry ends with the 250th byte and the eleventh entry begins with the 251st byte. In practice, when the program specifies the entry number, BASIC does the rest.

With sequential files the fundamental unit of storage is the character or byte. With random-access files the fundamental unit of storage is the record. A record is simply a collection of bytes. Think of each record as containing one entry. An entry consists of items that belong together. We might have an inventory file in which an entry contains the part number, price, number on hand, reorder point, and date last received. Those five items make up one entry. If 32 bytes is enough for the items in each entry, then the file may be organized into records that contain just 32 bytes. We decide record size according to the application. It is important to study each application thoroughly and plan effectively how to organize files to manage the data required. We can easily specify the record size we need.

Often a group of programs will be used to handle a file or system of files—one program to enter and delete entries, another to edit entries and perhaps a third to print a nicely formatted report to display all of the data in the file. Additional programs may be used to prepare various other kinds of reports.

A new set of tools is needed to work with random-access files.

12-1. Some Tools

We have a set of new keywords and conditions that enable us to work with random-access files. We can get started with FIELD #, LSET and RSET, PUT #, and GET #. In addition, we will learn new ways to use OPEN. CLOSE # works just the way it did for sequential access files.

OPEN

We open for random access by simply leaving out the mode in an OPEN statement. The default is random access. Further, we may declare the record length in the same statement.

OPEN "Sample Data" **AS** #1 **LEN** = 40

sets up a file named Sample Data for random access on channel 1. As with sequential files, a file channel forms the communications linkage between the program and the file itself on disk. The record size here is 40 bytes. If we don't specify a record length, BASIC automatically makes it 128 bytes. If your Macintosh has enough memory, the record length may be up to 32767.

To set up the same file with the alternate form of the OPEN statement, use the "R" indicator and simply add a comma and the record length at the end of the statement.

OPEN "R", #1, "Sample Data", 40

FIELD

Once a file is opened for random access, the file buffer is established in memory. A FIELD statement is required to describe the layout of the buffer. That is, we need to tell BASIC just how each item in an entry shall be placed in the record. All data in a random-access file must be in string form. Later we will see how to convert numeric values to string values and vice versa.

FIELD #1, 22 **AS** X$, 10 **AS** Y$

defines the buffer as having two strings: X$ and Y$. The X$ string is allocated the first 22 bytes in the buffer and the Y$ string is allocated the next 10 bytes. From this point on X$ and Y$ are special variables that should only be used for file data. The string values must be assigned with LSET and RSET.

Items in sequential files are separated by commas or a carriage return and line feed. In random access files the FIELD statement establishes compartments within each record for each separate data item. The divisions between compartments do not consume any file space.

LSET and RSET

Once the buffer is established in memory and a FIELD statement is used to partition the buffer according to our needs, LSET and RSET cause the data to be copied into the file buffer.

LSET Y$ = "TEST"

loads the string value into the space in the buffer designated as Y$ in the FIELD statement.

LSET differs from LET in two regards. LSET assigns a string value in the file buffer. LET may not be used for this purpose. LET assigns a string value in an area of memory restricted to variable usage. LSET moves the string value into the left end of the string variable and fills the right end with spaces, while LET simply assigns the string value to a string variable. LSET would move "TEST" into Y$ of the FIELD statement above as

"TEST   "

Thus, LSET always creates a string having as many characters as specified in the FIELD statement. It is important to note that we cannot place data in a file buffer with a LET statement.

RSET is analogous to LSET except that the string value is loaded into the right end of the space allocated in the buffer. The left end is filled with spaces. So,

RSET Y$ = "TEST"

will cause Y$ to contain "   TEST".

LSET and RSET may be used to left justify or right justify strings in string variables. If a string variable has not been named in a field statement, the length of the string comes from the most recent assignment. We can use that to our advantage. The statements

X$ = **STRING$**(25,32)
RSET X$ = Y$

will enter the characters of the string Y$ right justified in the string X$. Even if X$ isn't filled with spaces, LSET and RSET put spaces in instead of whatever is there.

PUT

PUT # is the statement we use to copy data from the file buffer in memory to the disk file on the disk. Once the program has finished working on a record in memory, we want it written out to the disk.

PUT #1, 5

will write out the buffer to record number 5 of the file opened on channel number 1. If we omit the record number, PUT # simply writes out to the next record.

GET

GET # is the statement we use to copy data from the disk file on the disk to the file buffer in memory.

GET #6, REC

copies the contents of record number REC of the file opened on channel 6 to the associated file buffer. Note that it really is a copy of the data. The data is not removed from the disk file. If we omit the record number, GET # simply accesses the next record.

CLOSE

The communications established by an OPEN statement are severed with a CLOSE # statement.

>   CLOSE #3

terminates any activity on channel number 3. If we have entered any data into the file on that channel and executed a PUT # statement, CLOSE # will cause the current buffer contents to be written out to the disk.

We may also close several channels.

>   CLOSE #1, #2, #8

closes the three file channels designated in the statement. CLOSE by itself closes all active file channels.

Summary

Once we organize files in records of a fixed size, we may get at any data entry in the file as long as we know where it is. Whether the file contains 50 or a 1000 records, a program can access any data entry directly and quickly.

A few easy-to-remember statements are available to manipulate data in a file to solve problems of our choice. OPEN, FIELD #, LSET and RSET, PUT #, GET #, and CLOSE # are all that we need to get started with random-access files. In the next section we will develop an example, then go into a little more detail and introduce some more tools.

12-2. A Sample Random-Access File

Suppose we are working on an accounting system. We have been assigned the task of creating a file to contain the labels for a chart of accounts. For example, we might designate account number 1 as real estate taxes, number 2 as personal property taxes, number 9 as medical expenses, and 99 as miscellaneous.

With just a little planning, we can do the job. We might call the file "Account Names". Now we need to consider the record size. "Personal property taxes" contains 23 letters. So we need at least 23 bytes per record. We need not include carriage return and line-feed characters in the byte count, as we do with sequential files. But, let's allow 30 characters for good measure.

It is a simple matter to open a file and field the corresponding buffer.

Program 12-1a. OPEN and FIELD the accounts-label file.

```
REM ** Initialize account label file

OPEN "Account Names" AS #1 LEN = 30
FIELD #1, 30 AS X$
```

Since we have only one data item in each file record, it turns out that the record size is the same as this single data item. This is a special situation. The record size is usually the sum of the number of bytes required for all items in an entry. (It could be larger.)

If we limit account numbers to the range from 1 to 99 and we don't need them all, what do we do about the "holes"? Let's label them "Unassigned". We can accomplish this by first doing an LSET to store "Unassigned" in X$ and then doing a PUT # in a loop that runs from 1 to 99. Later, as the need for new labels arises, we can use these values. Note that this is a routine we do only once in the life of the file.

Program 12-1b. Fill accounts-label file with "Unassigned".

```
REM ** Fill each record with "Unassigned"
LSET X$ = "Unassigned"
FOR REC = 1 TO 99
   PUT #1, REC
NEXT REC
```

Notice that we only perform the LSET to load the buffer once. The PUT # operation creates a copy in the file. The buffer remains intact. Thus, we can copy the buffer contents over and over again. Now we have a file with "Unassigned" written to all 99 records.

Finally, we need a routine to write the real account labels to the file. This can be done by reading the labels from data in the program. When each label is written to the file, the "Unassigned" label previously written there will be replaced.

Program 12-1c. Write actual account labels to the file.

```
REM ** Write out actual labels
BeginRead:
    READ N, N$ : IF N$ = "Done" THEN EndRead
    IF N < 1 OR N > 99 THEN PRINT N; "Out of range" : GOTO EndRead
    LSET X$ = N$
    PUT #1, N
    GOTO BeginRead
EndRead:
    CLOSE #1
    END
```

We are providing for "Done" as the signal for end of data. In the line,

IF N < 1 **OR** N > 99 **THEN PRINT** N; "Out of range" : **GOTO** EndRead

we check to see if the account number is within the agreed-upon range. If a value is out of range, we get a little message. We would fix the incorrect data and run the program again. Little checks like this save untold grief later on. Working with files increases the complexity of programming. An error in the data written to a file by one program may later look like a programming error in some other program. A little extra care along the way is worth the effort.

We put this all together with sample data as Program 12-1.

Program 12-1. Initialize an accounts-label file.

```
REM ** Initialize account label file

OPEN "Account Names" AS #1 LEN = 30
FIELD #1, 30 AS X$

REM ** Fill each record with "Unassigned"
LSET X$ = "Unassigned"
FOR REC = 1 TO 99
   PUT #1, REC
NEXT REC

REM ** Write out actual labels
BeginRead:
   READ N, N$ : IF N$ = "Done" THEN EndRead
   IF N < 1 OR N > 99 THEN PRINT N; "Out of range" : GOTO EndRead
      LSET X$ = N$
      PUT #1, N
      GOTO BeginRead
EndRead:
   CLOSE #1
END

DATA 1,  Real estate taxes
DATA 2,  Personal property taxes
DATA 9,  Medical expenses
DATA 99, Miscellaneous
DATA 22, Sewer and water
DATA 38, Cleaning and maintenance
DATA 44, Mortgage interest
DATA 0,  Done
```

It's a good thing that we didn't settle for 23 characters in a record, since "Cleaning and maintenance" requires 24. If LSET encounters a string that is too large for the field, it simply drops the extra characters from the right end.

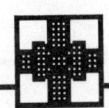

Summary

We have seen most of the basic tools we need for random-access files. With OPEN, FIELD #, LSET, RSET, PUT #, GET #, and CLOSE # we can perform all of the operations required to create and maintain a simple file. It is important to analyze the space requirements of the longest entry so that we allow for large enough records. It is important to execute a CLOSE # statement to copy the final buffer contents to the disk file itself.

Problems for Section 12-2

1. Write a program to print chart-of-account labels. Simply scan the file and print the number and label for all assigned records. Caution: Remember that LSET added spaces to the right when the file was created, so, "Unassigned" has extra spaces.
2. Write a program to allow for adding account labels. Your program should first determine that the account number is actually unassigned. Caution: Remember that LSET added spaces to the right when the file was created, so, "Unassigned" has extra spaces.
3. Write a program to allow renaming account labels. This would be useful when a label is incorrectly spelled due to a typing error, or a more accurate label has been suggested. In practice, accountants don't arbitrarily change account labels.
4. Sometimes it is desirable to have shorter labels for reports that have little space. Change Program 12-1 so that two labels are stored in each record. One label will be the full description and the other will be an abbreviation. Limit abbreviations to eight letters.

12-3. Some More Tools

We have worked with a random-access file using string values only. Obviously there must be some way to handle numeric values. A special set of functions is provided to represent numeric values in string form. These functions provide for compact storage of numeric data. They are the MaKe functions and the ConVert functions. The MaKe functions make strings out of numeric values. The ConVert functions convert string values into numeric values. They differ in important ways from the STR$ and VAL functions.

MKD$

The MKD$ function makes a string out of a double-precision numeric value. The string formed requires eight bytes.

LSET Y$ = **MKD$**(Y9)

does the whole job of loading the string representation of the numeric value of Y9 into the buffer for Y$. We need a companion function to go the other way.

CVD

CVD converts an eight-byte string to a double-precision numeric value.

Z8 = **CVD**(Z$)

does it.

Let's create a file to store the names of the ten largest U. S. cities, their rank, and the percentage growth from 1970 to 1980. Then we can write programs to prepare various reports.

Table 12-1 was prepared from information found in an almanac.

Table 12-1. Ten largest U.S. cities in 1980.

City	Rank	% Growth
Baltimore	9	−13.1
Chicago	2	−10.8
Dallas	7	7.1
Detroit	6	−20.5
Houston	5	29.2
Los Angeles	3	5.5
New York	1	−10.4
Philadelphia	4	−13.4
San Antonio	10	20.1
San Diego	8	25.5

The program will simply open a file and write each data set to a different record. That means we will have to field a record to hold three strings—one for the name of the city, one for the rank, and one for the percentage growth. Let's just use the default double-precision numbers. Philadelphia is the longest city name, with 12 characters. The two numeric values will be converted to two eight-byte strings. That makes the record length 28. We can easily use DATA statements for getting the data into the program. In practice, for larger applications we would have a system of programs. One of those programs would be used to enter data into the file and edit incorrect data already there. For a file with a thousand entries we would not have a thousand DATA statements in a program. The file would be managed directly from the keyboard. See Program 12-2.

Program 12-2. Write ten-largest-cities data to a random-access file.

```
OPEN "Cities Data" AS #1 LEN = 28
FIELD #1, 12 AS CITY$, 8 AS RANK$, 8 AS PERCENT$

FOR K = 1 TO 10
   READ X$, R, G
   LSET CITY$ = X$
   LSET RANK$ = MKD$(R)
   LSET PERCENT$ = MKD$(G)
   PUT #1, K
NEXT K
CLOSE #1
END

DATA Baltimore, 9, -13.1
DATA Chicago, 2, -10.8
DATA Dallas, 7, 7.1
DATA Detroit, 6, -20.5
DATA Houston, 5, 29.2
DATA Los Angeles, 3, 5.5
DATA New York, 1, -10.4
DATA Philadelphia, 4, -13.4
DATA San Antonio, 10, 20.1
DATA San Diego, 8, 25.5
```

We have simplified this project by stating that we will have ten cities. In the next chapter we will develop ways to manage files that have no preset or fixed number of records.

Now that we have the file, one of the easiest tasks we might perform is to simply display the data in a neatly arranged format in the same order in which it appears in the file. This is left as an exercise.

We might want to see the data in the file arranged by rank. An easy scheme will be to form a ten element array that contains the record positions of the appropriate data. Array element 1 will contain the record number of the data for New York and array element 10 will contain the record number of the data for San Antonio. The program will have to first scan the file, build the array, and then access the records in order according to the array just formed for display. See Program 12-3.

Program 12-3. Display cities in rank order.

```
REM ** Display cities in rank order
DIM ARRAY(10)

OPEN "Cities Data" AS #1 LEN = 28
FIELD #1, 12 AS CITY$, 8 AS RANK$, 8 AS PERCENT$

REM ** First load the array with record number
FOR REC = 1 TO 10
   GET #1, REC
   R = CVD(RANK$)
   ARRAY( R ) = REC
NEXT REC

PRINT "City          Rank   % Growth"
FOR K = 1 TO 10
   GET #1, ARRAY( K )
   R = CVD( RANK$ )
   G = CVD( PERCENT$ )
   PRINT CITY$,
   PRINT USING " ##  ###.#"; R, G
NEXT K
CLOSE #1
END
```

Look at this line:

   ARRAY(R) = REC

This program statement loads the array with the record where the city with the appropriate rank will be found in the file. The position in the report is the position in the array and the data value stored in the array is the number of the record in the file. This is easily done with a single dimension array. We have here a very special situation. Most data does not include its own order position as an item. See Figure 12-1.

```
╔═══════════════ Program 12-3 ═══════════════╗
City            Rank      % Growth
New York         1         -10.4
Chicago          2         -10.8
Los Angeles      3           5.5
Philadelphia     4         -13.4
Houston          5          29.2
Detroit          6         -20.5
Dallas           7           7.1
San Diego        8          25.5
Baltimore        9         -13.1
San Antonio     10          20.1
```

Figure 12-1. Execution of Program 12-3.

Because of the Macintosh's proportionally spaced display, the negative numbers are slightly out of line in the output window. Note that if this display is sent to the printer, the problem disappears.

There are two options in PRINT USING that could help us here. We could insert a plus sign in front of "###.#" in the PRINT USING statement to cause BASIC to display plus signs for positive values. The plus sign is the same width as the minus sign, so the problem is fixed. If you don't like having the plus signs displayed, you can insert a minus sign to the right of "###.#". Then only minus signs will be displayed, but they will follow the value. That helps only for the last item in a displayed line. A plus sign following the format string in PRINT USING causes both plus and minus signs to follow the value.

PRINT USING " ##   +###.#"; R, G
PRINT USING " ##   ###.#- "; R, G
PRINT USING " ##   ###.#+"; R, G

It is important to realize that nothing we have done in this program has changed the data in the file. The data has been rearranged on paper only. Writing report-generating programs that do not modify the data file makes all reporting programs totally independent of one another.

MKI$, MKS$, CVI, and CVS

We also have functions to work with integer and single-precision numeric values. MKI$ makes a two-byte string out of an integer numeric. CVI converts it back. MKS$ makes a four-byte string out of a single-precision numeric. The process is reversed with the CVS function. These population tracking programs could just as well have used the single-precision functions for the percent growth and the integer functions for the rank value. That would have saved some space.

MKSBCD$, MKDBCD$, CVSBCD, and CVDBCD

The formats used for single-precision numbers and double-precision numbers are different in the binary version of Microsoft BASIC from the format used in the decimal version. Data written with one version cannot be read directly with the other. To use the binary version to read data written with the decimal version, CVSBCD and CVDBCD are required to convert the file strings to numeric values for the program to use. To use the binary version to write data to a file for a program in the decimal version to read later, MKSBCD$ and MKDBCD$ are required. String and integer data are interchangeable between the two versions of Microsoft BASIC.

Now we have full flexibility to work with all of the data formats available to us. When we are working with files that may grow to hundreds and thousands of records, it becomes important to fit data as compactly as possible.

Multiple Fields

In the chart-of-accounts file in Program 12-1 and in the census data file of Program 12-2, the data structure was uniform throughout the file in each case. Sometimes we would like to store different things in different parts of the same file. We might want to keep records for a baseball team. One segment of the file could be used for the names of the players and their statistics. Another segment might be used to store data pertaining to the season schedule. Yet another segment of the same file could record what players played in what games. And still another could keep track of just what records in the file are storing what kind of information. The records will surely be laid out differently from one segment to the next. We might try opening the same file on a different channel for each segment, but that isn't permitted. When the file is opened on the second channel BASIC issues a "File already open" error box. The solution is to use multiple FIELD statements for the same file on the same channel. The only restriction is that we have to determine the record length according to the largest data entry.

We can use as many FIELD statements as we need. Think of a FIELD statement as a description of how to look at a file record. The record is simply a stream of bytes in a file buffer in the Macintosh memory, but the FIELD statement interprets that stream for us. If we use a different FIELD statement we get a different interpretation. Let's look at an example.

OPEN "Baseball Data" **AS** #5 **LEN** = 64
FIELD #5, 20 **AS** NAMES$, 2 **AS** AGE$, 4 **AS** ERA$, etc.
FIELD #5, 20 **AS** TEAM$, 4 **AS** DATES$, 16 **AS** LOCATION$, etc.
GET #5, REC

At this point, we have record number REC in the file buffer on a channel numbered 5. If we are processing player data, we use the variables NAMES$, AGE$, ERA$, and etc. If we are processing schedule data we use the variables TEAM$, DATES$, LOCATION$, and etc. If the contents of the buffer make sense for schedule data it probably won't make sense for player data. DATES$ uses the same bytes in the buffer as AGE$ plus the first two bytes used by ERA$. They are not the same data—they just use the same bytes in the buffer. Once the FIELD statements have been set up, we don't have to think about FIELD anymore. We simply think in terms of the variables associated with the segment of the file we need.

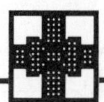

Summary

We have the ability to store numeric data as strings in random-access files using the MaKe (MKI$, MKS$, and MKD$) and ConVert (CVI, CVS, and CVD) functions. Data from the decimal version of BASIC requires CVSBCD and CVDBCD to convert to numeric form for the binary version of BASIC. Data generated in the binary version can be written to a file using MKSBCD$ and MKDBCD$ for the decimal version of BASIC. Strings created with MaKe must also be LSET or RSET into the fielded buffer.

We have seen an example of rearranging data stored in a file for the purpose of producing a report. It was done without changing the file itself. Thus, various reports need not interact.

Multiple FIELD statements may be used to format different parts of a file for different purposes.

Problems for Section 12-3

1. Write a program that simply displays the data in the census file in alphabetic order.

2. Write a program that uses a sorting technique from the chapter on arrays combined with the method used in Program 12-3 to display the cities of Table 12-1 in order of increasing growth.

3. Convert the seive of Eratosthenes program (8-2) to use each record of a file to store one element of the array. Be sure to test your program with a small upper limit before you experiment with large values. Program errors will take longer to detect if you wait a long time before the computer displays the results.

12-4. Mixed Access Files

In some applications it may be desirable to design a file using a mixture of random and sequential access. We may use PUT and GET to position at the desired record and use PRINT # and INPUT # to manipulate the data items within the record. Remember that the use of fielded records results in all string values being filled with spaces to occupy the space allocated. This does not happen in sequentially written records.

With a sequential record we can design for efficient space use. We can calculate the record size from the true maximum space use. Suppose we have an application with several items in each record that fluctuate widely in size. Using a fielded record, we are required to allocate space based on the maximum for each item. Suppose we have a situation in which the maximum for the first item is 35 characters and the maximum for the second item is also 35 characters, but the sum for the first and second items is never more than 50. We can save 16 characters per record by writing sequentially. Remember that a sequential PRINT inserts a cr-lf at the end of the line.

With sequential access we are free to intermix strings and numerics as needed. The only catch is that we must calculate all the characters in the printed form of the numeric value. We could use the MaKe functions to work with numeric values in a file. This would allow us to compress our data into the record. Thus, a number like 9.71208E+20 could be stored in the space of just four characters plus the cr-lf delimiter. We would just use

> X$ = **MKS$**(X9)

and then use PRINT to get the contents of X$ into the file buffer. Of course, we would use the ConVert functions to recover the numeric values from the file later.

CHAPTER 13

Random-Access Address List

Let's develop a program to maintain a name-and-address list, a common need for business and personal use. The idea here is to store the names and addresses in a disk file. Then we may extract those we need for any particular situation. Names may be classified by a code. A business might use B and S for Billing and Shipping addresses. We might set up a personal family mailing-list file using F, W, H, or C to designate friends of family, wife, husband, or children.

In business it is common practice to arrange these names alphabetically or by ZIP code or by business volume. In order to achieve this we would not rearrange the names file itself; instead, we would create a file that contains just a list of the record numbers in the desired order. We might maintain several such lists of record numbers. Then we can easily write a program that will read a list of record numbers from one file and print the corresponding name-and-address data from another file containing the actual data.

13-1. Design the System

Let's organize a program to build the mailing-list data file. There are a number of major tasks involved. One part of the program needs to request the data from the keyboard. Another will write the entry into the file. Another will have to determine where the new entry belongs. Normally, a program to enter names in a file simply requests data for several names, one after another. The program must allow the user to quit entering names. This can be done by testing one of the items for real data. If the item is null, then the user wants to quit. Simply pressing Return with no characters will produce a null string.

We will have to organize the entry itself. We must decide what information belongs in an entry and how many characters to allow for each item. Then we must calculate the necessary record size. Our program must be designed to manage all these things. Probably the most important part of writing the program is deciding how to organize entries within the file.

Design the Files

When we get ready to enter the first name and address, the file is empty. The next name in the file is number 1. After that, we have no idea where the next name goes in the file. We could write a number on a piece of paper to "point" to the next entry number. But then we might just as well keep the names on paper, too. The whole idea is to let the computer do the work. Let's use a file instead of a piece of paper. If we call our working file "Names Data", we can put this information about where the next name goes in a file called "Names Pointer." So when the "Data" file has no names in it, there should be a 1 stored in our little "Pointer" file. We can easily write an initialization program to do this. Then after each new name is entered, the program adds 1 to that value in the "Pointer" file, so the number of the next new entry is always available.

Let's assign each entry its record number as an identification number and include that number as part of the data entry. Thus, the first name in the system is number 1, the second is number 2, and so on. We are beginning to build the system.

Even though we are thinking about a program to enter names in a file, now is the time to think about how names are to be deleted. Let's make deleted records available for new entries by setting up a catalog of available space threaded through the "Data" file itself. We can then place a number in the "Pointer" file that is the record number of the starting point. When an entry is deleted, the program can replace the entry identification number in the deleted record with the record number of the previous starting point (obtained from the "Pointer" file). Replace the beginning number stored in the "Pointer" file with the entry identification number of the deleted entry. The thread has a new starting point. This will leave a trail of deleted record numbers in the "Data" file with the first number of the trail stored in the "Pointer" file. Now we have two numbers there—the next record at the end of the file and the most recently deleted record. When we start up a new file, the next record at the end of the file will be 1 and the most recently deleted record will be 0.

This plan also provides a method for determining whether an entry has been deleted or not. Just read the record. If the identification number equals the record number, then it is real data. If not, then the entry has been deleted and the number is the record number of the previously deleted record. Note that the first deleted record will contain a value of 0. For an example of a file with some deleted records, see Figure 13-1.

Names Pointer

9 {on the end}, 8 {last deleted entry}

Names Data

1	1 Jones John...
2	2 Smith William...
3	3 Hayes Mary...
4	6 {deleted entry}...
5	5 Bradshaw Eleanore...
6	0 {deleted entry (first one)}...
7	7 Hough Hugh...
8	4 {deleted entry}...
9	{never used}

Figure 13-1. Layout of records in use and deleted.

Let's trace the deleted record trail in Figure 13-1. The second number in "Names Pointer" is 8. Look at record 8 of "Names Data." There we find a 4. Look at record 4. There we find a 6. Look at record 6. There we find a 0. Thus the deleted records are 8, 4, and 6. When we finally use record 6 for a new entry, the program should place a 0 in "Names Pointer" where the 8 is now. Following this event, the next new entry will go to new space at the end of the file.

The entry program will look at the two record numbers stored in "Names Pointer" and decide whether to place the new entry at the end of the file or in a record from which a name has been deleted. If the deleted record number is 0 the new name goes on the end. Otherwise it uses the deleted record.

It is important to observe in all this that even though we are designing the program to enter data, it is necessary to thoroughly think through the deleting process. We must design the whole system before actually writing programs for any part of it. Thus we avoid the mistake of having to rewrite programs because of unexpected design changes.

We have entering and deleting pretty well under control. Now how about changing an entry? As long as each name has an identification number, the program can easily read the corresponding record and display each item as it appears, giving the opportunity to make changes in each case. We will also need to periodically print a list of the names with the IDs. It should be relatively easy to write a program to scan the file from beginning to end, displaying the data in each undeleted record. That program can easily select various categories according to the code stored in the code item.

We have thought through four functions of our mailing-list system: enter, delete, change, and display. It is time to move to the next phase.

Design the Data Record Layout

Let's just think of all the things we want to know about each person whose name we want in our mailing list. We can write them down and decide how many characters it will take to store each one in a random-access file. The result is Table 13-1.

Table 13-1. Record layout for mailing-list file.

Data Item	Label	Maximum number of characters	
Identification Number	ID #	2	(32767 limit)
Code	CODE	2	
Last name	LAST	20	
First name	FRST	20	
Address	ADDR	30	
City	CITY	20	
State	STAT	2	
ZIP code	ZIP	5	
Telephone	PHON	17	
		118	

The total comes to 118 characters. We might consider allowing for the four optional digits in the ZIP code, too. If we let the program calculate the total number of characters in the routine that reads the label data in the first place, we won't have to give any further thought to this. The labels are all the same number of characters so that the screen display will be nicely lined up.

Now we are organized to create a mailing list system using computer programs. We know that we will keep track of what file records are in use and what ones are available. We know how all the address data will look in a file record. We are well prepared to begin writing the programs.

13-2. Write the Programs

Start an Address List

We have mentioned the need to initialize the "Pointer" file once to prepare it for entering data. Let's do that first. We'll identify new space at the end of the file with the file variable NEWID$ and deleted old space embedded within the file with the file variable OLDID$. If we limit the mailing list to 32767 names, we can use integers with the MKI$ and CVI functions. See Program 13-1.

Program 13-1. Initialize mailing-list "Pointer" file.

```
REM ** Initialize Pointer file
FILENAME$ = "Names"
OPEN FILENAME$ + " Pointer" AS #1 LEN = 4
FIELD #1, 2 AS NEWID$, 2 AS OLDID$
LSET NEWID$ = MKI$(1)
LSET OLDID$ = MKI$(0)
PUT #1, 1
CLOSE #1
END
```

Once this program has been run, we may count on "Names Pointer" to contain a 1 and a 0. Of course, we must assure that this program is never run again. Life can be quite complete without ever having to reconstruct a file system with a bad "Pointer" file. Of course, it is a good idea to maintain copies of any data system on extra disks. With good data backup, it is easy to avoid such a catastrophe.

Entering Addresses

If we are careful about listing all of the things we discussed in Section 13-1 we will have the structure of the control routine for our data entry program. Once we have the control routine, we may concentrate on a single subroutine at a time. The following shows the list of steps for the name-and-address entry program.

1. Read data labels and limits
2. Read available-space parameters (Pointer file)
3. OPEN the Data file
4. Display next available ID and request data
   Terminate on null LAST name
5. Prepare available space
6. Write entry in Data file
7. Write available-space info to Pointer file
   Do it again (repeat step 4)

Each of the numbered tasks listed can be accomplished with a subroutine. Some of those subroutines will also be used by the other programs that we will be writing for our name-and-address system.

To terminate on null LAST name, we need to provide a way for the data requesting routine to send back a signal to quit. "Do it again" will simply direct the program to repeat the steps beginning with number 4. See Program 13-2a.

Program 13-2a. Control routine for mailing-list program.

```
REM ** Control routine for mailing-list entry program
  GOSUB ReadLabels     'Read data labels and limits
  GOSUB ReadPointer    'Read available-space parameters (Pointer file)
  GOSUB OpenDataFile   'OPEN the Data file
Begin:
  GOSUB RequestEntry   'Display next available ID and request data
  IF QUIT = 1 THEN CLOSE : END  'Terminate on null LAST name
  GOSUB PrepareSpace   'Prepare available space
  GOSUB WriteData      'Write entry in Data file
  GOSUB WritePointer   'Write available-space info to Pointer file
  GOTO Begin           'Do it again (repeat step 4)
```

We have called seven subroutines and used two control statements in our main routine of Program 13-2a. The IF statement requires that the value of QUIT be set to 1 if the user desires to QUIT. Any other value may be used for an entry that is to be placed in the file. The final line simply uses a GOTO to repeat the request for another new entry. We will now write the subroutines, one at a time.

We read the data labels at ReadLabels. We could ask the eight questions in eight statements using INPUT with prompt. For each of the eight inputs we could have a statement that checks to see if the entry is too long. That would require many program statements and would be tedious to write and difficult to change. Wouldn't it be a better idea to put the prompt labels and the maximum field sizes in DATA statements and read them into two arrays? Of course it would. Later, major changes in the program can be made with simple changes in the DATA statements. Our DATA statements will come directly from the labels and character limits in Table 13-1. We can read the data into arrays with a FOR . . . NEXT loop. Here is where the program totals up the number of characters for the random file record length. See Program 13-2b.

Program 13-2b. Read data labels for mailing-list program.

```
ReadLabels:
  READ NUMBEROFITEMS
  RLENGTH = 0
  FOR ITEM = 1 TO NUMBEROFITEMS
    READ LABEL$(ITEM), L(ITEM) 'L array is item length
    RLENGTH = RLENGTH + L(ITEM)
  NEXT ITEM
  RETURN

REM ** DATA – labels and limits
DATA    9
DATA    ID #,     2
DATA    CODE,     2
DATA    LAST,     20
DATA    FRST,     20
DATA    ADDR,     30
DATA    CITY,     20
DATA    STAT,     2
DATA    "ZIP",    5
DATA    PHON,     17
```

In Program 13-2b, NUMBEROFITEMS is the number of data items in an entry. The labels are stored in the LABEL$ array and the maximum numbers of characters are stored in the L array. The completed program should include a DIMension statement to provide for the LABEL$ and L arrays.

The subroutine to read the available-space parameters is very simple. It just reads the two values placed there, first by the initialization program and later by another subroutine of the mailing-list entry program. See Program 13-2c.

Program 13-2c. Read available space in mailing-list program.

```
ReadPointer:
    OPEN FILENAME$ + " Pointer" AS #1 LEN = 4
    FIELD #1, 2 AS NEWID$, 2 AS OLDID$
    GET #1, 1
    NS = CVI(NEWID$)
    DS = CVI(OLDID$)
    RETURN
```

In Program 13-2c we have chosen to carry new space in the variable NS and deleted space in DS.

Before we may access any data in the "Data" file, we must open and field it. We have already taken care of the record length in variable RLENGTH of Program 13-2b. Let's create a string array for the file to match a string array we will be using to accept data from the keyboard. The FIELD statement must provide for all nine elements of the array. The following is a possible FIELD statement:

```
FIELD #2, L(1) AS FILEDATA$(1), L(2) AS FILEDATA$(2),
         L(3) AS FILEDATA$(3), L(4) AS FILEDATA$(4),
         L(5) AS FILEDATA$(5), L(6) AS FILEDATA$(6),
         L(7) AS FILEDATA$(7), L(8) AS FILEDATA$(8),
         L(9) AS FILEDATA$(9)
```

This statement will correctly arrange the data in the file, but it is a little cumbersome. We would have to remember to change this statement if we use the program for a mailing list with a different number of items in an entry. Here is a better way:

```
      X = 0
      FOR J = 1 TO NUMBEROFITEMS
        FIELD #2, X AS D9$, L(J) AS FILEDATA$(J)
        X = X + L(J)
      NEXT J
```

This FIELD statement simply adds the next array element on the end of the record each time through the FOR loop. D9$ is used to skip over the space in the record already allocated to the earlier array elements. Just make sure that D9$ is never used with LSET or RSET in this program. The FOR loop uses NUMBEROFITEMS as the upper limit. We have a FIELD statement that is easy to read and doesn't have to be changed to accommodate changes in labels and limits. See Program 13-2d.

Program 13-2d. OPEN and FIELD the mailing-list data file.

```
OpenDataFile:
    OPEN FILENAME$ + " Data" AS #2 LEN = RLENGTH
    X = 0
    FOR J = 1 TO NUMBEROFITEMS
      FIELD #2, X AS D9$, L(J) AS FILEDATA$(J)
      X = X + L(J)
    NEXT J
    RETURN
```

We write the subroutine once, and that takes care of it.

Now it is time to display the next available ID and request data. We said we would do this at RequestEntry. Since we have planned carefully, this will be very straightforward. The first job here is to determine the next actual available space. This is easily done with an IF...THEN...ELSE. We handle the label display and the data request with a FOR...NEXT loop. See Program 13-2e.

Program 13-2e. Handle keyboard data entry for mailing-list program.

```
RequestEntry:
   IF DS = 0 THEN ID = NS ELSE ID = DS
   PRINT : PRINT LABEL$(1); ": "; ID
   FOR ITEM = 2 TO NUMBEROFITEMS
      PRINT LABEL$(ITEM);
      Ask: INPUT X$
            IF ITEM = 3 AND LEN(X$) = 0 THEN QUIT = 1 : GOTO EndRequest
            IF LEN(X$) <= L(ITEM) THEN GoodValue
            PRINT "Too long – Reenter" : PRINT " : "; : GOTO Ask
      GoodValue:
      KEYDATA$(ITEM) = X$
   NEXT ITEM
QUIT = 0
EndRequest: RETURN
```

Note in

IF ITEM = 3 **AND LEN**(X$) = 0 **THEN** QUIT = 1 : **GOTO** EndRequest

we set QUIT to 1 if the response to the request for LAST name is of zero length. The length will be zero when the user responds only with the Return key. Otherwise, QUIT is set to 0 before EndRequest:. We created an array KEYDATA$ to accept keyboard data. Later we will transfer it to file data in FILEDATA$. We must include the KEYDATA$ and FILEDATA$ arrays in the DIMension statement in the completed program.

Next, we must prepare available space. What we do here depends on whether we are going to replace a deleted entry or write a new record. If we are going to use a new record, we simply add 1 to the New Space variable and RETURN. If we are going to write this data to a previously deleted record then we must retrieve the record number that was written there when the deletion occurred. That number is essential for correctly maintaining the available-space catalog. Remember that from Figure 13-1?

Program 13-2f. Prepare available space for mailing-list file.

```
PrepareSpace:
    IF DS = 0 THEN NS = NS + 1 ELSE GET #2, DS : DS = CVI(FILEDATA$(1))
    RETURN
```

Note that in this subroutine either new space changes or deleted space changes, but never both.

Once the available space situation is taken care of, we may actually write the entry to the file. We use LSET to place the value of ID into FILEDATA$(1) and then move all keyboard data from KEYDATA$ to FILEDATA$ as well. Finally, we use PUT to write the data into record number ID.

Program 13-2g. Write a data entry in the mailing-list program.

```
WriteData:
    LSET FILEDATA$(1) = MKI$(ID)
    FOR ITEM = 2 TO NUMBEROFITEMS
        LSET FILEDATA$(ITEM) = KEYDATA$(ITEM)
    NEXT ITEM
    PUT #2, ID
    RETURN
```

We must provide the subroutine that writes the available-space parameters to the "Pointer" file. This is exactly like the initialization program except that we must write NS and DS. See Program 13-2h.

Program 13-2h. Write available-space parameters in mailing-list program.

```
WritePointer:
    LSET NEWID$ = MKI$(NS)
    LSET OLDID$ = MKI$(DS)
    PUT #1, 1
    RETURN
```

Finally, in order for all of this to happen, we must include the file name in FILENAME$, and the appropriate dimensioning statement. Since we want to use MKI$ and CVI for handling numeric data in the data file, we need to declare NS and DS as integer variables. We might just as well declare all numeric variables as integer. See Program 13-2i.

Program 13-2i. Program parameters for mailing-list program.

```
REM ** Mailing-list program
DEFINT A-Z
FILENAME$ = "Names"
DIM LABEL$(9), L(9), FILEDATA$(9), KEYDATA$(9)
```

This makes it very easy to work on a different mailing list with the same field lengths by simply changing FILENAME$. This would be just the place for the FILES$(1) function.

   X$ = **FILES$**(1, "MAIL")

produces a dialog box that allows the user to search for all files that are of type "MAIL" and offers to select one of them.

We list the complete program here for your convenience.

Program 13-2. Entering names in a mailing-list file.

```
REM ** Mailing-list program
DEFINT A-Z
FILENAME$ = "Names"
DIM LABEL$(9), L(9), FILEDATA$(9), KEYDATA$(9)

REM ** Control routine for mailing-list entry program
GOSUB ReadLabels      'Read data labels and limits
GOSUB ReadPointer     'Read available-space parameters (Pointer file)
GOSUB OpenDataFile    'OPEN the Data file
Begin:
  GOSUB RequestEntry  'Display next available ID and request data
    IF QUIT = 1 THEN CLOSE : END 'Terminate on null LAST name
  GOSUB PrepareSpace  'Prepare available space
  GOSUB WriteData     'Write entry in Data file
  GOSUB WritePointer  'Write available-space info to Pointer file
  GOTO Begin          'Do it again (repeat step 4)

ReadLabels:
  READ NUMBEROFITEMS
  RLENGTH = 0
  FOR ITEM = 1 TO NUMBEROFITEMS
    READ LABEL$(ITEM), L(ITEM) 'L array is item length
    RLENGTH = RLENGTH + L(ITEM)
  NEXT ITEM
  RETURN

  REM ** DATA – labels and limits
  DATA   9
  DATA   ID #,     2
  DATA   CODE,     2
  DATA   LAST,    20
  DATA   FRST,    20
  DATA   ADDR,    30
  DATA   CITY,    20
  DATA   STAT,     2
  DATA   "ZIP",    5
  DATA   PHON,    17
```

```
ReadPointer:
  OPEN FILENAME$ + " Pointer" AS #1 LEN = 4
  FIELD #1, 2 AS NEWID$, 2 AS OLDID$
  GET #1, 1
  NS = CVI(NEWID$)
  DS = CVI(OLDID$)
  RETURN

OpenDataFile:
  OPEN FILENAME$ + " Data" AS #2 LEN = RLENGTH
  X = 0
  FOR J = 1 TO NUMBEROFITEMS
    FIELD #2, X AS D9$, L(J) AS FILEDATA$(J)
    X = X + L(J)
  NEXT J
  RETURN


RequestEntry:
  IF DS = 0 THEN ID = NS ELSE ID = DS
  PRINT : PRINT LABEL$(1); ": "; ID
  FOR ITEM = 2 TO NUMBEROFITEMS
    PRINT LABEL$(ITEM);
    Ask: INPUT X$
        IF ITEM = 3 AND LEN(X$) = 0 THEN QUIT = 1 : GOTO EndRequest
        IF LEN(X$) <= L(ITEM) THEN GoodValue
        PRINT "Too long – Reenter" : PRINT " : "; : GOTO Ask
GoodValue:
    KEYDATA$(ITEM) = X$
  NEXT ITEM
  QUIT = 0
  EndRequest: RETURN

PrepareSpace:
  IF DS = 0 THEN NS = NS + 1 ELSE GET #2, DS : DS = CVI(FILEDATA$(1))
  RETURN

WriteData:
  LSET FILEDATA$(1) = MKI$(ID)
  FOR ITEM = 2 TO NUMBEROFITEMS
    LSET FILEDATA$(ITEM) = KEYDATA$(ITEM)
  NEXT ITEM
  PUT #2, ID
  RETURN
```

```
WritePointer:
    LSET NEWID$ = MKI$(NS)
    LSET OLDID$ = MKI$(DS)
    PUT #1, 1
    RETURN
```

This program is intended to be a simple example of a workable mailing-list data entry program. Using the preceding discussion and some of the routines of this program you should be able to develop programs to delete entries, change entries, and print mailing labels. The benefits of doing things this way are tremendous. With all of the information about the mailing list stored in a file, this one program can be used to process many different mailing lists.

There are many areas in which this program can be made more flexible. We might use FILES$(1) to request the mailing-list file name from the program operator. We might eliminate the DATA statements from the program by placing that data in the "Pointer" file along with the data already there. As the program stands, it can handle different labels and different item lengths. We only have to change the DIM statement to enable this program to handle mailing lists with more items per entry. Even this can be managed with the variable DIM feature. We will soon find that we have to write a program to manage the companion file that contains all of this nice information. That is a small price to pay. When we can change the behavior of a program by changing data in a file, we approach data-base-management capabilities. One goal for programmers is to create programs that can handle many tasks without changing the program itself.

Programming for the delete and change functions can be handled by either writing separate programs or by including the new subroutines right in Program 13-2. We could even provide a menu that lets the user select which function is desired.

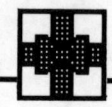

Summary

Once we organize files in records of a fixed size we may get at any data entry in the file as long as we know where it is. We have designed a mailing-list system. We have written the program to enter data into this file using keyboard interaction. Arrays have been used to good advantage to provide a flexible system. We must simply change the name of the file in one line of our program to work with a different mailing list. By changing only a few DATA statements we can even dramatically change the mailing-list file itself. This experience has pointed the way to concepts that will allow us to store the characteristics of a mailing-list system in yet another file.

Problems for Section 13-2

1. Incorporate a delete routine in the name-and-address entry program.

2. Write a program to edit data in the mailing-list file. Use the file management subroutines from Program 13-2. Display each item and ask if the user wants to make a change.

3. Write a program to display all data from the file for names having a specified code. Use the file management subroutines from Program 13-2.

4. Write a program that will print mailing-address labels. Set the program up so that it requests up to ten ID numbers from the keyboard and then prints all of the labels. Use the file management subroutines from Program 13-2. (The next step would be to have the program read the list of IDs from another file prepared by yet another program.)

5. Modify our mailing-list system by placing the labels and item limits in the "Pointer" file. Have the program request the file name from the keyboard. You will have to write a little program to write the data to the "Pointer" file in the first place. To do this you can field the same file three ways. Thus, different records may be used for different purposes. Here is one possible set of FIELD statements.

```
REM ** OPEN the Pointer file
InitPtr:
    OPEN FILENAME$ + " Pointer" AS #1 LEN = 6
    FIELD #1, 2 AS NEWID$, 2 AS OLDID$
    FIELD #1, 2 AS NUMBEROFITEMS$
    FIELD #1, 4 AS LA$, 2 AS LE$
    RETURN
```

13-3. Enhancing the Data Entry Program

Program 13-2 sets up a mailing list. Now let's use some more of the Macintosh features. We can dress up the program by using windows, edit fields, and buttons. Using these features, we may take advantage of the tremendous power of the Macintosh. This can be done without changing any of the structure of the program we have already written. Once again we will reap the benefits of developing programs in segments. We only have to change the RequestEntry subroutine and manage the windows at the beginning and the end of the program. You may find that it helps to experiment and watch the results. When a program produces a pleasing appearance and behaves well, use it that way.

We should establish the window for data entry early in the program. The following two statements immediately after the DIM statement in Program 13-2 set the window up.

WINDOW CLOSE 1
WINDOW 2,,(50,41)–(350,260),–2

Simply closing window 1 at the beginning enables our program to restore it to the same position and dimensions at the end. Using any window 2 through 4 makes this possible. If this program is going to be used after other programs have left a variety of windows on the screen, then we should close them all. But, if every program cleaned up at the end, then we wouldn't have to worry about that. Again, it is a good idea to clear the desktop by clicking the go-away boxes on the List windows and the Command window before running programs with windows.

At the end of program execution, all that has to be changed is what happens in the control routine when QUIT = 1. The following line does it:

IF QUIT = 1 **THEN CLOSE : WINDOW CLOSE** 2 **: WINDOW** 1 **: END**

The RequestEntry subroutine will still ask the same questions and return the entered data in the same form as the version used in Program 13-2, but we have the opportunity to present a professional looking screen. Let's use buttons to allow the user to "Enter" or "Quit" at any time. This means that the program will not have to test for a null entry. Using EDIT FIELD for data input makes it easy to display fields that give a visual indication of the maximum length of the item.

An edit field is an area in an output window that has the same powerful built-in editing features provided by the dialog box that allows the user to enter a program name. This is done with a statement of the following form:

EDIT FIELD number,a$,(x1,y1)–(x2,y2),type,justify

Edit fields are numbered just the way the buttons are numbered. The string a$ will be displayed in the edit field. If the string is null, the display will match the window background pattern. If the string contains characters, they will appear highlighted in the field until the next EDIT FIELD statement is executed. (x1,y1)–(x2,y2) is the now familiar format for specifying a rectangle. There are four edit field types: Types 1 and 2 use the rectangle specification to draw a box around the field, and types 3 and 4 display no box. Types 2 and 4 allow Return in the field, but 1 and 3 do not. Finally, justify values 1, 2, and 3 produce left, center, and right justification of the string within the field, respectively. Only the edit field number is required. All other specifications are optional. However, the string a$ and the rectangle specification must either be used or not used together.

The EDIT$ function returns the current string contents of an edit field. The statement

X$ = **EDIT$**(1)

assigns the contents of edit field number 1 to the string X$.

Once several edit fields have been displayed, the mouse and the DIALOG function may be used to move about from field to field. DIALOG(0) = 2 indicates that the mouse has been clicked in an edit field. The field number is found in DIALOG(2). If the value of DIALOG(0) equals 6, that means the Return key has been pressed in a type 1 or type 3 edit field. It is up to your program to determine which field is active at that time.

A statement of the following form may be used to close an edit field:

EDIT FIELD CLOSE number

Displaying a prompt and managing an edit field are independent. So, we can get away from the cryptic labels of Program 13-2.

The following DATA will make the screen more readable:

DATA 9
DATA ID #, 2
DATA Code, 2
DATA Last, 20
DATA First, 20
DATA Addr, 30
DATA City, 20
DATA State, 2
DATA ZIP, 5
DATA Phone, 17

Now, we come to the RequestEntry subroutine itself. The subroutine will set up the edit fields with the prompts and establish the "Enter" and "Quit" buttons. Following this the edit fields must be monitored. The user may move from one field to the next by pressing Return or the user may move to any other field by clicking on it with the mouse. Our program needs to know the difference. Whenever the user clicks the mouse on one of the buttons the program must react. If the user clicked on "Enter" then the program must verify that no items have too many characters. Program 13-3 takes care of everything.

Program 13-3. Program 13-2e with EDIT FIELD.

```
RequestEntry:
  IF DS = 0 THEN ID = NS ELSE ID = DS
  CLS
  MOVETO 2, 20 : PRINT LABEL$(1); ": "; ID
  FOR ITEM = 2 TO NUMBEROFITEMS
    X = ITEM*20
    MOVETO 2, X : PRINT LABEL$(ITEM)
    EDIT FIELD ITEM,"",(50,X-13)-(52+8*L(ITEM), X+2),1,1
  NEXT ITEM
  BUTTON 1,1,"Enter",(50,190)-(100,206),1
  BUTTON 2,1,"Quit",(150,190)-(200,206),1
  ITEM = 2
```

```
BeginEntry:
  EDIT FIELD ITEM
  Poll: PROCESS = DIALOG(0) : IF PROCESS = 0 THEN Poll
    IF PROCESS = 6 THEN NextEditField
    IF PROCESS = 2 THEN NewEditField
    IF PROCESS = 1 THEN EndEntry
    GOTO Poll

NextEditField:
  ITEM = ITEM + 1
  IF ITEM > NUMBEROFITEMS THEN ITEM = NUMBEROFITEMS
  GOTO BeginEntry

NewEditField:
  ITEM = DIALOG(2)
  GOTO BeginEntry

EndEntry:
  PRESS = DIALOG(1)
  IF PRESS = 2 THEN QUIT = 1 : GOTO EndRequest
  IF PRESS = 1 THEN QUIT = 0
  FOR ITEM = 2 TO NUMBEROFITEMS
    KEYDATA$(ITEM) = EDIT$(ITEM)
    IF LEN(KEYDATA$(ITEM)) <= L(ITEM) THEN VerifyNext
    X = ITEM*20
    EDIT FIELD ITEM,KEYDATA$(ITEM),(50,X-13)-(52+8*L(ITEM), X+2),1,1
    GOTO BeginEntry
  VerifyNext: NEXT ITEM

EndRequest: RETURN
```

Program 13-3 gives the user total flexibility to enter item data and then examine the entry before deciding to use the mouse to select "Enter." If an entry is too long, NewEditField highlights the faulty item. The user can even go back to an earlier item in the list at any time before even typing all the items in.

Note that NextEditField stays at the last item when the user presses Return following the last item. All others cause the next edit field to become active following the Return key. The control routine should control the output window for RequestEntry.

```
┌─────────────────────────────────────────┐
│ ▤▤▤▤▤▤     Demo EDIT FIELD     ▤▤▤▤▤▤  │
│ ID #   3                                │
│ Code  [ ]                               │
│ Last  [                    ]            │
│ First [                    ]            │
│ Addr  [                        ]        │
│ City  [                  ]              │
│ State [ ]                               │
│ ZIP   [     ]                           │
│ Phone [              ]                  │
│                                         │
│     ( Enter )      ( Quit )             │
└─────────────────────────────────────────┘
```

Figure 13-2. Show edit fields of Program 13-3.

A next step in developing a complete mailing-list system might be to create a menu listing all of the available options. Such a menu could be either pulled down or made up of buttons to click with the mouse. The various options might all be in the same program or could be accessed through the CHAIN statement. (See Appendix B.)

Problems for Section 13-3

Use edit fields and buttons for working with data and making decisions about quitting and entering or deleting data where appropriate.

1. Incorporate a delete routine in the name-and-address entry program.
2. Write a program to edit data in the mailing-list file. Use the file management subroutines from Program 13-2. Use separate windows to request the next ID to edit and to perform the actual edit.

APPENDIX A

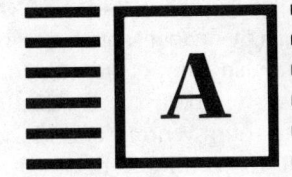

The Microsoft BASIC Menu Bar

The Apple Menu

The Apple menu is the standard menu that contains the Macintosh desk accessories. The About Microsoft BASIC . . . option displays the version number and date of release. If we are working along and want to keep track of the time, we can access the Macintosh Alarm Clock through this menu and place it on the desktop. It remains there even while hidden by BASIC windows. Click on the close box to put it away.

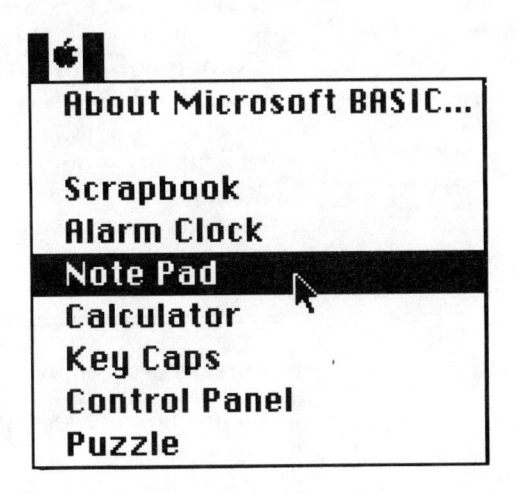

```
About Microsoft BASIC...

Scrapbook
Alarm Clock
Note Pad
Calculator
Key Caps
Control Panel
Puzzle
```

Any of these desk accessories can be opened and used while in BASIC. You can use the Scrapbook to save routines that you use very often. They will be instantly available. Keep notes in the Note Pad and refer to them when needed. Leave notes for a fellow Macintosh user. All this is done without more than a brief pause while still in BASIC.

File

The File options all have to do with managing program files. They do not affect data files. See Appendix B for a complete discussion of dealing with files on disk.

NEW prepares the BASIC work area for a new program. The NEW keyword can also be typed in the Command window. If you are working on a program with a name, then the program is erased and the title of the output window is changed to Untitled. But if you have made changes to the program or the title is Untitled, then you get the following dialog box:

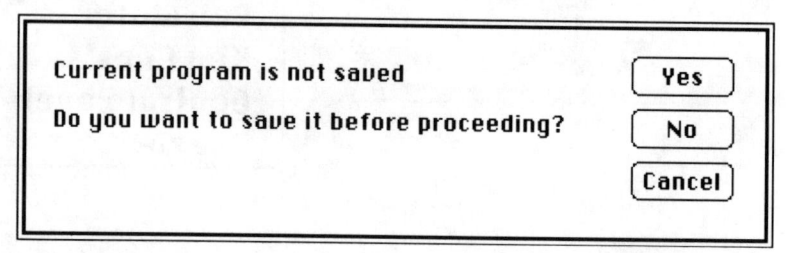

Figure A-1. Offering to save the current program.

If you respond No, then the program is erased from memory. An unsaved program is gone forever. A program that has already been saved on disk is gone from memory, but is still in its original form on disk. You may decide not to save the changes made in the current session if you have just been tinkering and want to keep the original. If you Cancel, then you are back where you were. If you say Yes, then BASIC asks for a file name as shown in Figure A-2.

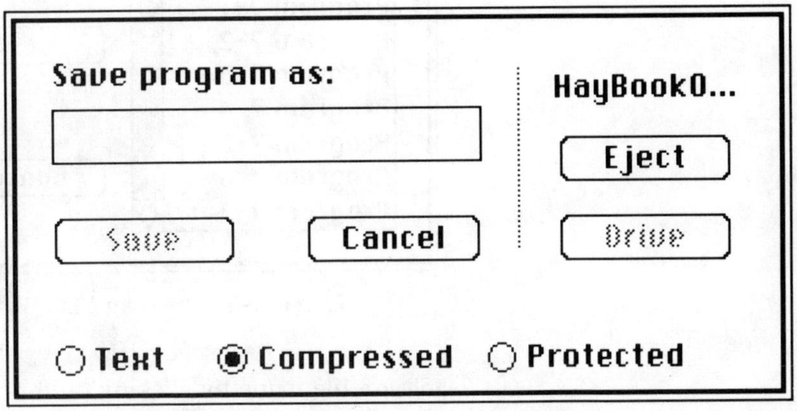

Save program as: HayBook0...

[Save] [Cancel]   [Eject] [Drive]

◯ Text   ⦿ Compressed   ◯ Protected

Figure A-2. Name dialog for saving programs.

Any name that fits in the name box is OK. BASIC allows up to 255 characters, but don't try it! Only 12 to 15 characters are displayed by some BASIC features, and the icons on the desk top will be impossible to deal with.

After we have entered a file name in the file name dialog box, BASIC checks to determine if we have a file with that name already on this disk. If we do, another dialog box lets us either replace it or cancel with Yes or No.

Saving with the Text option allows us to edit the program with a word processor. Programs saved in Text format can also be merged into other programs later. (See Appendix B.) The Compressed format does not allow the use of MERGE, but takes less space on the disk. Protected format encodes the program so that it can only be run later. A protected program will not show up in the List window and cannot be edited. Be absolutely certain that you have an unprotected copy to work with. Click the format you like, enter your program name, and click OK, or press Return to continue with the Save process.

We can request a program from the disk by using Open in the File menu or typing the keyword LOAD in the Command window. We first have the opportunity to save the current program. Then we get the dialog box of Figure A-3 allowing us to choose from all the files on the disk.

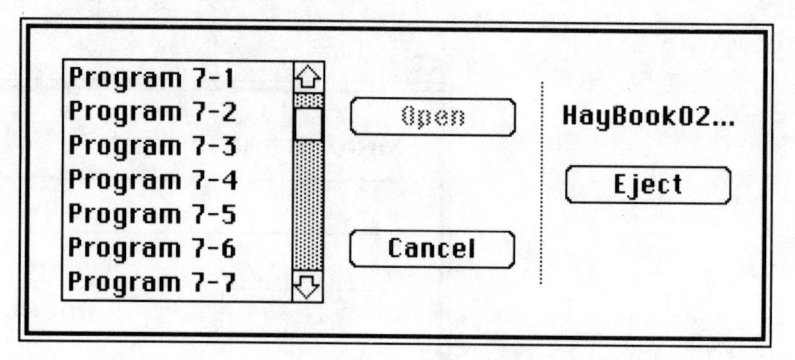

```
┌─────────────────────────────────────────────┐
│  Program 7-1  ↑                             │
│  Program 7-2      ┌──────┐    HayBook02...  │
│  Program 7-3      │ Open │                  │
│  Program 7-4      └──────┘    ┌──────┐      │
│  Program 7-5                  │ Eject│      │
│  Program 7-6      ┌──────┐    └──────┘      │
│  Program 7-7  ↓   │Cancel│                  │
│                   └──────┘                  │
└─────────────────────────────────────────────┘
```

Figure A-3. Open and LOAD file name dialog box.

Select a file name by clicking on the file name and then click the Open button, or just double-click the file name. If the file doesn't exist, then we get an error box reporting "File not found." Click OK or press Return and try again. It is a good idea to keep file names on the short side so they can be seen in the scroll window.

If you have a second disk drive, you may click on the Drive button to change to the other drive and choose from the files on the disk there. The eject button allows you to eject either disk and insert another. You can also use programs on more than one disk from Microsoft BASIC, even if you have only the internal drive for your Macintosh.

Programs may also be opened with the LOAD "file name" statement in the Command window. To load a program from a disk in the external drive, simply add the name of the disk in front of the program name with a colon separating the disk name and the program name. So, to use a program named "Taxes" on a disk named "Year 2001", simply use the program name—"Year 2001:Taxes". The disk name may be referred to as the volume name. If the disk is not in the drive at the time, Microsoft BASIC will instruct you to change disks.

Close will put away the currently active window. It behaves just like a click on the close box.

Save is used to save a program with its current name. In this case the program is saved without any opportunity to check the name unless it is Untitled. In the case of an Untitled program, we get a dialog box requesting the filename and offering a choice of save formats as in Figure A-2.

Save As. . . from the menu and the keyword SAVE typed in the Command window always produce the save dialog box of Figure A-2.

Print . . . sends a copy of the program to the Imagewriter. It is printed on paper exactly as it appears in the List window, including the boldface style for keywords. Typing LLIST in the Command window also prints the program listing on paper, but in plain, small type.

If you are done with BASIC for the moment, then you can use Quit from the menu or type SYSTEM in the Command window. If you are working on a new program or have edited an old one, then a dialog box offers the chance to save it as shown in Figure A-1.

Edit

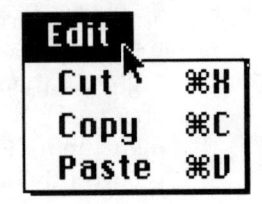

The Edit menu is available whenever either the Command window or a List window is active. For Cut or Copy, select the text to be cut or copied using the mouse cursor to highlight it. This is done by dragging over all the characters or doing a Shift-click. Then, with the mouse, select Cut (⌘-X) or Copy (⌘-C) from the Edit menu.

Once a selection has been cut or copied, it stays on the Clipboard until another Cut or Copy. We may then Paste it at any point in any program line, or even a desk accessory, such as the Note Pad or the Scrapbook. Of course, text can be transferred in the other direction as well, from an accessory to BASIC. Simply click the point of insertion and select Paste (⌘-V) from the menu.

Search

```
Search
Find...          ⌘F
Find Next        ⌘N
Find Selected Text
Find Label
Find the Cursor
Replace...
```

The Search menu adds a variety of convenient editing features. The Find... and Replace... options use dialog boxes to obtain the text to work with. All the others (except Find Cursor) use whatever text is currently selected in the List window. If there is nothing selected, these menu items are not available.

Find... (⌘-F) provides a dialog box in which to type the characters to search for. Clicking the Find Next button causes the List window to scroll to the next occurrence of the characters and highlight them. The Find Next (⌘-N) menu option Finds whatever characters have been most recently used in any of the Search menu items. Find Selected Text does the same thing with whatever is currently highlighted in the List window. Find Label also works with text that is selected in the List window. It adds a colon to whatever characters are selected and scrolls to that line label. This is useful for finding lines that are referred to but not visible in the List window. It is very helpful for detecting duplicate line labels. To automatically scroll to the position of the insertion point, use Find Cursor. Replace... provides a dialog box requesting the text to be replaced and the lines that will replace it. There are two additional options. It is possible to replace all occurrences in the program or verify each replacement or do both or neither. To verify, the occurrence is highlighted and another box offers the choice of doing the substitution or not.

Run

```
Run
Start      ⌘R
Stop       ⌘.
Continue
Suspend    ⌘S
Trace On
Step       ⌘T
```

The Run menu contains commands that influence program execution. Start (⌘-R) runs the program currently in memory. This is the same as typing RUN in the Command window. Stop (⌘-.) halts execution and displays the "Program Stopped" message. As soon as the mouse is moved, the most recently active window is again made active. If we have stopped a program with Stop (⌘-.) in the menu or with a STOP statement in a program, the Continue option is available. Choosing Continue from the menu and typing CONT in the Command window perform the same function. Under certain circumstances the program can't continue. For example, if we have entered or edited any program line, an error results.

Suspend (⌘-S) suspends program execution temporarily. Activating a menu with the mouse also suspends program execution. We may want to do this to keep some output on the screen while we study it. Continue will restart the program. Pressing any key except ⌘-S does the same thing.

Trace On causes the List window to display a box around the current line during program execution. The List window must be visible for us to see the results. This can be a useful tool for finding serious errors in programs that seem to get "hung up" without any results. We can follow the path of a program while it is running this way. Once Trace On has been selected, the menu shows the option Trace Off in its place. The TRON and TROFF statements achieve the same effects, either in a program or in the Command window. Trace On and Trace Off from the menu can be activated while a program is running.

Step (⌘-T) executes one statement of a program at a time. As with Trace On, the List window displays a box around the line just executed. This is very valuable for detecting errors because it reveals exactly what each statement does. After a statement is executed, choose Step again to go on to the next statement.

Windows

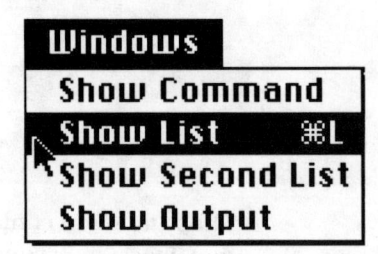

```
Windows
Show Command
Show List        ⌘L
Show Second List
Show Output
```

The Windows menu allows us to activate any of four windows at any time: the Command window, the List window, the output window, or a Second List window. The Second List window may be used to show a different part of the same program to avoid having to scroll up and down a long program in one window. The Second List window may also be used for all editing processes. Characters can be Cut or Copied and Pasted between List windows in either direction. Any window showing on the screen but not currently active can be made active by clicking inside it. The List window is also activated by a ⌘-L or by typing LIST in the Command window.

APPENDIX B

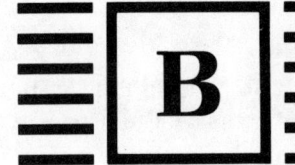

Using the Disk

This appendix covers the keyboard commands used to manage files on the disk using Microsoft BASIC. The File menu and the use of the mouse to manage files on the disk are covered in Appendix A. Once programs are saved on disk, we may use the Macintosh Finder to rearrange things by moving icons around on the desktop. Some applications lend themselves to arranging programs in filefolders. Don't hesitate to put folders within folders.

The keywords associated with managing files are SAVE, FILES, LOAD, RUN, MERGE, CHAIN, COMMON, KILL, and NAME. All of these directives allow us to designate a disk other than the current one.

Program Names (and File Names, Too!)

File names are limited to 255 characters. In practice, short names (eight to ten characters long) are workable. They fit in the window of the Open... dialog box and are not too hard to remember when typing in the Command window. If we are using a disk other than the current one, we add the disk name in front of the program name, separating the two with a colon. So program "Math work" on disk "Current year" is designated as "Current year:Math work". The disk "Current year" must be on the Macintosh desktop before Microsoft BASIC is opened. We may place the disks in the same drive one after the other or in two different drives. They are referred to as internal and external drives, but the Macintosh keeps track of all that.

SAVE

Suppose we have just put the finishing touches on one of the eggs programs. We can save the program on disk with the following:

SAVE "Eggs"

We may mix uppercase and lowercase letters. Be warned, though, that "Eggs" and "EGGS" may not be used at the same time on the same disk. If we first save "Eggs" and then save "EGGS", "EGGS" will replace "Eggs". There will be no dialog box to help us.

If we simply type SAVE without a program name, then we get a dialog box requesting a program name and format. (We'll cover format soon; or see Appendix A.) BASIC checks to see that there are no conflicting names. If there is a file of that name already on the disk, we get a chance to change it. After a little disk activity, BASIC will return to await our next command.

File Formats

There are three formats for programs stored on disk by Microsoft BASIC: ASCII (also called Text), Binary (also called Compressed), and Protected. The Eggs program mentioned earlier would be saved in binary format by our first command. This format is usable only by BASIC, but it saves disk space for large programs and loads and saves faster.

Programs must be saved in Text format for MERGE to work. Each character is stored as a single character using a standard coding method. Using this format the word PRINT is stored as five characters, whereas PRINT may be stored in the space of a single character using Binary format. It is a simple matter to save a program in ASCII format.

SAVE "Eggs",A

does the job.

Sometimes we have a program that we want to let other people use, but we don't want them to be able to read the BASIC code. We may protect our program with

SAVE "Eggs",P

We have to be careful with this one. This program file cannnot be listed or edited. It is necessary to save such a program in an unprotected format as well. If we try to list a program saved in protected format, we will be greeted with an "Illegal function call" error box. Most things we might try to do to change the program are greeted with the same message.

We go merrily along writing and saving programs, and one day we get the message "Too many opened files." It means just that. The disk has room for just so many files, and eventually we reach that point. To see the directory of files on the disk, simply use the FILES command (see below). We may use KILL (see below) to eliminate junk programs, and use SAVE again.

If we find that we cannot part with any programs on this disk, then we can switch disks only if there is another disk on the Macintosh desktop already or we have two drives. What else can happen? Well, if we work with very long programs or files that contain a lot of data, we might see the "Disk full" message. That means just what it says. There is no more room no matter what. Again, determine what can be erased from the disk to make room. It may happen that you see the "Disk full" message when there is still available space. In that case, you have too many files.

FILES

The FILES command causes the names of the files on the current disk to be displayed in the output window. Even if files are stored in folders, each file on the disk is listed by its own name. Folders are not listed. We can check if a particular file is on the disk with

FILES "Special Program"

If the file is there, it will be listed; otherwise, an error box reports "File not found." Press Return and proceed.

LOAD

Any program SAVEd is easily brought back with LOAD.

LOAD "Eggs"

loads a copy of the program into memory from disk. To execute the program, we just issue the RUN statement. Alternatively, we could run the program directly with

LOAD "Eggs",R

The "R" option causes the program to execute as soon as it is loaded. It is important to know that the "R" option keeps data files open. This command can be included within another program. So, we may move from program to program under program control. A loaded program replaces any program already in memory.

We may want to load programs from more than one disk without leaving BASIC. For a program named "Write Checks" on a disk named "Accounting", simply use the following statement:

LOAD "Accounting:Write Checks"

If the disk named "Accounting" is not in either drive, BASIC will request that it be inserted. If that disk has never been in either drive, an "Unknown Volume" error box appears. That is not a problem. We can eject the external disk with ⌘-Shift-2, or the internal disk with ⌘-Shift-1, insert the disk of interest, and try LOAD again.

RUN

This statement may also be used to directly execute a program stored on disk.

RUN "Eggs"

will replace any program in memory and execute "Eggs" stored on disk. Note that the "R" option to keep files open, described under LOAD, may also be used with RUN "program".

MERGE

As we develop more and more programs, we will discover that routines written for one program exactly fit for another. We can use MERGE to incorporate BASIC statements stored in a file on disk with BASIC statements stored in computer memory. The program on disk must have been saved in ASCII format.

MERGE "Eggs1"

will append the statements from Eggs1 on disk to the program residing in memory at the time.

We may want to merge programs from more than one disk. For a program named "Write Checks" on a disk named "Accounting", simply use the following statement:

MERGE "Accounting:Write Checks"

If the disk named "Accounting" is not in either drive, BASIC will request that it be inserted. If that disk has never been in either drive, an "Unknown Volume" error box appears. We can eject the external disk with ⌘-Shift-2, or the internal disk with ⌘-Shift-1, insert the disk of interest, and try MERGE again.

CHAIN

The CHAIN statement provides a variety of options for programs to transfer to other programs. In its simplest form CHAIN is just like LOAD with the ,R option. It may be used in a program.

CHAIN "PROCESS01"

keeps data files open and causes program PROCESS01 to replace the current program and execute. Variable values are not preserved. Additional options allow us to chain to a particular line in the new program and preserve the values of all the variables. The line label referred to must be a number or an expression that equals a number.

CHAIN "PROCESS03",210,**ALL**

If the line number option is omitted and the ALL option is included, then we need both commas.

The MERGE and DELETE options allow us to bring in subroutines and remove sections of a program while it is running. This allows tremendous flexibility in programming.

CHAIN MERGE P$, L1, **ALL**, **DELETE** ReadData-EndProcess

deletes all the lines between ReadData and EndProcess, including these two, merges program P$, preserves variable values, and continues execution at line L1.

COMMON

The COMMON statement may be used in a program to preserve only specified variables for a chained program.

COMMON X,Y,NEXTONE$,ARRAY02

placed near the beginning of a program will pass the values of these variables to the program named in a CHAIN statement later on.

KILL

In addition to using the trash can in the Macintosh Finder, we can erase old unwanted files from disk right in BASIC. The KILL statement does it:

KILL "Eggs"

Needless to say, KILL should be used with great care. There is no easy way to "UNKILL" a file.

NAME

We may change the name of a file stored on disk with the NAME statement.

NAME "Eggs" **AS** "Hamneggs"

changes the name of the Eggs program to Hamneggs. While SAVE can wipe out an old program, NAME will report "File already exists" to save us a lot of trouble. If we really want to replace the old program, we use KILL and NAME again.

File Types

File types are not the same as file formats. The format has to do with the way BASIC actually encodes the file for disk storage, and the type is simply a way of classifying what kind of file it is. BASIC automatically saves all programs as type "TEXT". Applications like MacPaint or BASIC are type "APPL" on disk. We may designate our files as any type with the NAME command.

NAME "Payroll Namelist" **AS** "Payroll Namelist01", "PDAT"

gives the file a new name and changes the type to "PDAT". Now if we have a collection of files containing payroll data, we can use the FILES$(1) function in programs to allow the user to choose from files of that particular type. (See Appendix D.)

A$ = **FILES$**(1, "PDAT")

will produce a dialog box similar to the one used for Open . . . and LOAD, offering only PDAT files. The user has the opportunity to select one. The selected file name is returned in FILES$.

APPENDIX C

ASCII and Special Character Chart

ASCII Chart

The ASCII codes 128 to 255 are essentially a repeat of codes 0 to 127. Any display sent to the printer using LLIST or LPRINT will have the same appearance as the ASCII chart.

0	NUL	18	⌘-R	36	$	54	6	72	H	90	Z	109	m
1	⌘-A	19	⌘-S	37	%	55	7	73	I	91	[	110	n
2	⌘-B	20	⌘-T	38	&	56	8	74	J	92	\	111	o
3	⌘-C	21	⌘-U	39	'	57	9	75	K	93	]	112	p
4	⌘-D	22	⌘-V	40	(	58	:	76	L	94	^	113	q
5	⌘-E	23	⌘-W	41	)	59	;	77	M	95	_	114	r
6	⌘-F	24	⌘-X	42	*	60	<	78	N	96	`	115	s
7	⌘-G	25	⌘-Y	43	+	61	=	79	O	97	a	116	t
8	⌘-H	26	⌘-Z	44	,	62	>	80	P	98	b	117	u
9	⌘-I	27	ESC	45	-	63	?	81	Q	99	c	118	v
10	⌘-J	28	FS	46	.	64	@	82	R	100	d	119	w
11	⌘-K	29	GS	47	/	65	A	83	S	101	e	120	x
12	⌘-L	30	RS	48	0	66	B	84	T	102	f	121	y
13	⌘-M	31	US	49	1	67	C	85	U	103	g	122	z
14	⌘-N	32	SPACE	50	2	68	D	86	V	104	h	123	{
15	⌘-O	33	!	51	3	69	E	87	W	105	i	124	|
16	⌘-P	34	"	52	4	70	F	88	X	106	j	125	}
17	⌘-Q	35	#	53	5	71	G	89	Y	107	k	126	~
										108	l	127	DEL

Fig. C-1 ASCII Character Codes Chart

Appendix C

The key at the lower left of the Macintosh keyboard is labeled with a ⌘ and is referred to as the Command key.

Command-. (period) brings program execution to a halt.
Command-C copies to the Clipboard
Command-F does a Find in the Search menu
Command-G produces a bell-like sound.
Command-H is the backspace character
Command-L displays the List window
Command-M generates the Return character (cr).
Command-N finds the next occurance in the Search menu
Command-R Runs a BASIC program
Command-S suspends program execution. Any key resumes.
Command-T Causes BASIC to execute the next step
Command-V does a Paste from the Clipboard
Command-X does a Cut to the Clipboard
Command-Shift-1 ejects the disk in the internal drive.
Command-Shift-2 ejects the disk in the external drive.
Command-Shift-3 saves the current screen to a disk file.
    Up to 10 screens will be saved automatically named Screen 0 through 9.
    Action begins when the mouse button is released.
Command-Shift-4 dumps the active screen to the printer.
    Action begins when the mouse button is released.
Command-Caps Lock-Shift-4 dumps the full screen to the printer.
    Action begins when the mouse button is released.

128	Ä	139	ã	150	ñ	161	°	172	¨	183	Σ	194	¬	205	Õ
129	Å	140	å	151	ó	162	¢	173	≠	184	Π	195	√	206	Œ
130	Ç	141	ç	152	ò	163	£	174	Æ	185	π	196	ƒ	207	œ
131	É	142	é	153	ô	164	§	175	Ø	186	∫	197	≈	208	–
132	Ñ	143	è	154	ö	165	•	176	∞	187	ª	198	∆	209	—
133	Ö	144	ê	155	õ	166	¶	177	±	188	º	199	«	210	"
134	Ü	145	ë	156	ú	167	ß	178	≤	189	Ω	200	»	211	"
135	á	146	í	157	ù	168	®	179	≥	190	æ	201	…	212	'
136	à	147	ì	158	û	169	©	180	¥	191	ø	202		213	'
137	â	148	î	159	ü	170	™	181	µ	192	¿	203	À	214	÷
138	ä	149	ï	160	†	171	´	182	∂	193	¡	204	Ã	215	◊
														216	ÿ

Fig. C-2 Special Character Codes Chart

APPENDIX D

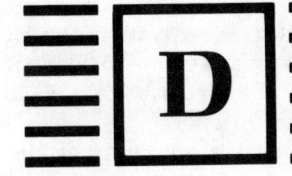

Microsoft BASIC Functions

A function in BASIC is a built-in process that returns a value. Some functions return numeric values and others return string values. Some out-of-range values may produce the "Illegal function call" error box. Others may produce the "Overflow" error box. Some functions, such as DATE$, require no argument. Several functions, such as POS(i), require an argument, but the value of the argument has no effect on the value returned.

Some keywords used for functions are also used for statements in Microsoft BASIC. These are indicated with an asterisk (*).

ABS(z)   Absolute value of z.
ASC(z$)   ASCII function: Returns the numeric code used for managing characters.
ATN(z)   The angle whose Tan is z: ATN returns values in the range $-\pi/2$ to $+\pi/2$ radians. The decimal ($) version of Microsoft BASIC performs this calculation using double precision. The binary (π) version of Microsoft BASIC produces single-precision or double-precision values to match the precision of the argument of the function.
BUTTON(z)*   The state of the button numbered z:
    0   inactive and dimmed
    1   active, not selected
    2   active, selected
CDBL(z)   Converts z to double precision.
CHR$(z)   The string character having ASCII value z.
CINT(z)   Converts z to integer portion of z.
COS(z)   Cosine of z: z is in radians. The decimal ($) version of

Microsoft BASIC performs this calculation using double precision. The binary (π) version of Microsoft BASIC produces single-precision or double-precision values to match the precision of the argument of the function.

CSNG(z)   Converts to single precision form of z.

CSRLIN   Line number of the pen in the output window relative to the top of the output window.

CVI(x$), **CVS**(y$), **CVD**(z$)   Convert string form of numeric values stored in random-access files to numeric form. CVI converts a 2-byte string, CVS converts a 4-byte string, and CVD converts an 8-byte string. (For reading files in one version of Microsoft BASIC written with the other version, see CVSBCD, CVDBCD, MKSBCD$, and MKDBCD$.)

CVSBCD(y$), **CVDBCD**(z$)   Convert string form of numeric single-precision and double-precision values read from a file written with the decimal ($) version of Microsoft BASIC into numeric form for the binary (π) version. String and integer forms are the same in both versions.

DATE$*   The current date according to the Macintosh clock. The date is in the form mm-dd-19yy.

DIALOG(i)*   Provides information about windows, buttons, and edit fields. Activity is stored in a buffer so that the oldest activity is returned first. DIALOG(0) returns the status of 7 activities, including those in the functions DIALOG(1) through DIALOG(5).

> **DIALOG**(0) = 0:   No activity.
>
> **DIALOG**(0) = 1:   A button has been selected. The button number is returned by the function DIALOG(1).
>
> **DIALOG**(0) = 2:   The mouse has been used to change edit fields. By keeping track of the current edit field, the program can determine when the change has occurred and verify the earlier edit field before accepting an entry. The number of the new selected edit field is returned in DIALOG(2).
>
> **DIALOG**(0) = 3:   The mouse has been clicked on the inactive output window returned in DIALOG(3). This selection does not make the window active. A window statement must be executed to do that.
>
> **DIALOG**(0) = 4:   The go-away (or close) box of an output window returned in DIALOG(4) has been clicked with the mouse.
>
> **DIALOG**(0) = 5:   The output window returned in DIALOG(5) has been overwritten.
>
> **DIALOG**(0) = 6:   The Return key has been pressed in a window containing a button or an edit field that doesn't allow Return.
>
> **DIALOG**(0) = 7:   The Tab key has been pressed in an output window with an edit field. Some applications take this as the signal to proceed.

EDIT$(i)   Returns the string in EDIT FIELD number i in the current output window.

EOF(i)   The end-of-file status of the file numbered i:
   −1 end of file
   0 not end of file

ERR, ERL   ERR returns the error number of last error that has occurred. See the Microsoft BASIC manual for a listing of error numbers and descriptions. ERL returns the line number on which the error took place. If there are no line numbers in the program, ERL is set to 65535.

EXP(z)   Raise e (2.718281828459. . .) to the zth power.

**FILES$**(i, a$)   Produces a dialog box and returns a file name according to the value of i.

The statement

NEWNAME$ = **FILES$**(0, PROMPT$)

creates a standard Macintosh dialog box that uses the string in PROMPT$ to request a file name, which is returned in NEWNAME$. If a file exists with the same name, BASIC displays another dialog box asking if the user wishes to replace the existing file. A "yes" response does not actually do the replacement; the FILES$ function only returns the file name string. This form of the function is recommended for accessing new files only.

In the statement

SELECTED$ = **FILES$**(1, TYPE$)

TYPE$ is a string containing four-character file types. Microsoft BASIC labels every file as type "TEXT." Applications such as Microsoft BASIC and MacPaint are assigned file type "APPL." The dialog box displays all files of the type(s) designated in TYPE$ and allows the user to select one of them, which is returned in FILES$. Several file types may be mentioned in TYPE$. The FILES$ function requires an exact match. So, it is recommended that file types be all uppercase. A four-character file type can be assigned to a file using the NAME statement. (See Appendix B.)

FIX(z)   Removes the decimal part of z.

FRE(i)   Returns information about use and availability of various segments of memory.

   i = −1 returns the number of free bytes in the heap. The heap is used by Microsoft BASIC for various segments of BASIC that are read into memory as they are required by each program.

   i, −2 returns the number of bytes never used by the stack. The stack is used by Microsoft BASIC to keep track of information for managing the execution of BASIC programs, such as FOR. . .NEXT loops and GOSUBS.

   For i, any other value, or FRE(""), returns the number of free bytes in the data segment of memory. The data segment stores the program itself and string and numeric data.

HEX$(z)   The value of x expressed in hexadecimal notation.

**INKEY$**   Returns a character typed at the keyboard in an active output window. Note that several keystrokes may accumulate and must be read through several references to INKEY$. The characters are not displayed.

**INPUT$**(i, #j)   Returns i string characters from file number j. If #j is omitted, the characters are read from the keyboard. INPUT$ waits until the specified number of characters has been entered. This function is especially useful for retrieving special characters from a sequential file. INPUT$ accepts all characters with the single exception of ⌘-. .

INSTR(i,a$,b$)   The position of the first character at which the string b$ is found embedded in a$ with the search beginning at the ith character of a$. If i is omitted, INSTR begins the search at the first character of a$.

INT(z)   Returns the greatest integer less than or equal to z.

LBOUND(i,j)   Lower bound for a dimension of an array. i is the array name without parentheses. j is the dimension of interest. For one-dimensional arrays, j is omitted. LBOUND is either 0 or 1 depending on whether OPTION BASE is 0 or 1. The most likely application for LBOUND and its companion UBOUND is within subprograms.

**LEFT$**(a$,i)   The leftmost i characters in a$.

LEN(a$)   The number of characters in a$.

LOC(i)   If i is the number of a random-access file, LOC(i) returns the number of the last record read or written. For sequential files, LOC(i) calculates an equivalent current record number—dividing the number of bytes read or written by the file buffer size. For devices CLIP: and COM1:, LOC(i) returns the number of characters ready for input. For device KYBD:, LOC(i) returns 1 as long as there is at least one character in the keyboard buffer.

LOF(i)   The length of a file in bytes. For files opened for SCRN:, KYBD:, and LPT1:, LOF(i) returns 0.

LOG(z)   The natural (base e) log of z. The decimal ($) version of Microsoft BASIC performs this calculation using double precision. The binary (π) version of Microsoft BASIC produces single-precision or double- precision values to match the precision of the argument of the function.

LPOS(a)   The character position of the line printer within the current line. The value of a has no effect on the function.

MENU(i)*   MENU(0) is the number of the last menu heading selected from the current menu bar. MENU(1) is the number of the last item selected under the currently selected menu bar heading.

**MID$**(a$,i,j)*   Isolates j characters in string a$ beginning at character number i. If j is omitted, MID$(a$,i) returns from the ith character to the end of the string.

MKI$**(i), **MKS$(y), **MKD$**(z) Convert numeric values to string form for storing in a random-access file.

    MKI$(i)   Converts an integer value to a 2-byte string.

    MKS$(y)   Converts a single precision value to a 4-byte string. This 4-byte string is different for the binary and decimal versions of Microsoft BASIC (see CVSBCD and MKSBCD$).

    MKD$(z)   Converts a double-precision value to an 8-byte string. This 8-byte string is different for the binary and decimal versions of Microsoft BASIC (see CVDBCD and MKDBCD$).

MKSBCD$**(y), **MKDBCD$(z) Convert numeric values to string form for storing in a random-access file, and convert numeric values in a binary (π) version Microsoft BASIC program to a form that can be read from a file with a decimal ($) version Microsoft BASIC program and utilized with CVS and CVD.

    MKSBCD$(y)   Converts a single-precision value to a 4-byte string.

    MKDBCD$(z)   Converts a double-precision value to an 8-byte string.

MOUSE(i)   Provides information about the mouse according to the value of i.

    MOUSE(0) = 0:   The mouse button is not down and hasn't been since the last reference to MOUSE(0).

    MOUSE(0) = 1:   A single click has occurred since the last reference to MOUSE(0) and the mouse button has been released.

    MOUSE(0) = 2:   A double click has occurred since the last reference to MOUSE(0) and the mouse button has been released.

    MOUSE(0) = 3:   A triple click has occurred since the last reference to MOUSE(0) and the mouse button has been released.

    MOUSE(0) = −1:   A single click has occurred since the last reference to MOUSE(0) and the mouse button is still down.

    MOUSE(0) = −2:   A double click has occurred since the last reference to MOUSE(0) and the mouse button is still down.

    MOUSE(0) = −3:   A triple click has occurred since the last reference to MOUSE(0) and the mouse button is still down.

MOUSE(0) also updates three pairs of coordinates relating to the mouse cursor. They are returned by MOUSE functions 1 through 6. MOUSE(1) and MOUSE(2) return the x and y coordinates of the mouse cursor at the time of the last reference to MOUSE(0). MOUSE(3) and MOUSE(4) return the x and y coordinates of the mouse cursor at the time of the last press of the mouse button preceeding the last reference to MOUSE(0). MOUSE(5) and MOUSE(6) return the x and y coordinates of the mouse cursor at the time of the last release of the mouse button since the last reference to MOUSE(0) or the coordinates at the time of the reference to MOUSE(0) if the mouse button has not been released in that time. MOUSE(3) and MOUSE(4) are used to establish the beginning of a drag and MOUSE(5) and MOUSE(6) are used to establish the end of a drag.

OCT$(z)   The value of z expressed in octal notation.

PEEK(i)   Reads a byte value from an absolute memory address.

PICTURE$ A string consisting of a display for the output window created between PICTURE ON and PICTURE OFF. This string can be saved in a disk file and thus may be retrieved later. It may be displayed in an output window with the PICTURE statement.

POINT(x, y)   Reads the color value of a pixel at coordinates (x,y). White is 30, black is 33, and outside the window is –1.

POS(i)   The current horizontal position of the pen in the output window measured in units the width of a digit. The value of i has no effect on the value returned.

PTAB(i)   Causes the next display to begin at pixel i of the current line in the output window. PTAB(i) must be used in a PRINT statement. PTAB(i) positions the pen absolutely regardless of the previous position of the pen on the line.

**RIGHT$**(a$,i)   The rightmost i characters in a$.

RND(i)   A random number between 0 and 1. While the numbers returned are random, the results are repeated with each execution of the same program. If i = 0, the value returned is the last number generated. If i is a positive value, RND(i) returns the next number in the sequence. If i is negative, the sequence begins at the same place for the same value of i. The RANDOMIZE statement is used to change the results from one execution to the next.

SGN(i)   1, 0, or –1 as the value of i is positive, zero, or negative.

SIN(z)   Sine of z: z is in radians. The decimal ($) version of Microsoft BASIC performs this calculation using double precision. The binary (π) version of Microsoft BASIC produces single-precision or double-precision values to match the precision of the argument of the function.

SPACE$(i)   String of i spaces.

SPC(i)   In a PRINT or LPRINT statement, causes i spaces to be output.

SQR(z)   Square root of z. The decimal ($) version of Microsoft BASIC performs this calculation using double precision. The binary (π) version of Microsoft BASIC produces single-precision or double-precision values to match the precision of the argument of the function.

STR$(z)   String of characters representing the number z as they would be displayed by a PRINT statement. Positive values are preceded by a space. Negative values are preceded by a minus sign.

STRING$**(i,j), **STRING$(i,a$)   String of i characters. STRING$(i,j) uses the character whose ASCII value is j. STRING$(i,a$) uses the first character of a$.

TAB(i)   Causes the next display to begin at character position i of the current line in the output window. TAB(i) must be used in a PRINT or LPRINT statement. TAB(i) positions the pen on the current line only if i places the display to the right of the current position. If i calls for display to the left of the current pen position, TAB moves to position i of the next line.

TAN(z)   Tangent of z: z is in radians. The decimal ($) version of Microsoft BASIC performs this calculation using double precision. The binary (π) version of Microsoft BASIC produces single-precision or double- precision values to match the precision of the argument of the function.)

TIME$*   The time in the form hh:mm:ss. A 24-hour clock is used according to the Macintosh Alarm Clock.

TIMER*   Number of seconds since midnight according to the Macintosh Alarm Clock.

UBOUND(i,j)   Upper bound for a dimension of an array. i is the array name without parentheses. j is the dimension of interest. For one-dimensional arrays, j is omitted. UBOUND is the value stated in the DIM statement. For example,

$$X = \mathbf{UBOUND}(SCORES,2)$$

returns the upper dimension of the second subscript in the array SCORES.

**UCASE$**(a$)   Converts all characters of a$ to uppercase. The contents of a$ remain unchanged by UCASE$.

VAL(a$)   Converts a$ to a numeric value. The conversion is carried out until the function encounters the first character that could not be part of a numeric value.

VARPTR(a)   The address in memory of the first byte of the data in variable a. Usually used for assembly language routines or Macintosh ROM Routines.

WIDTH(a$)   The width of the string a$ in pixels. This information aids in formatting string display in output windows.

WINDOW(i)   Provides information about windows depending on the value of i.

> **WINDOW**(0):   The number of the currently active output window. If no window is active, 0 is returned.
>
> **WINDOW**(1):   The number of the current output window to which the next display will go.
>
> **WINDOW**(2):   The width of the current output window in pixels.
>
> **WINDOW**(3):   The height of the current output window in pixels.
>
> **WINDOW**(4):   The x coordinate of the drawing pen in the current output window.
>
> **WINDOW**(5):   The y coordinate of the drawing pen in the current output window.

APPENDIX E

Listing of Programs

Program 1-1.   The first program.
Program 1-2.   A two-line program.
Program 1-3.   Practice printing messages.
Program 1-4.   Changing Program 1-3.
Program 1-5.   Paste the line somewhere else.
Program 1-6.   Cutting two lines from Program 1-5.
Program 1-7.   Two PRINT statements display on a single line.
Program 1-8.   Include the space this time.
Program 1-9.   Calculate hours in the year.
Program 1-10. Labeling a calculated result.
Program 1-11. Demonstrate simple calculations.
Program 2-1.   Calculate egg values.
Program 2-2.   Label egg values.
Program 2-3.   First program with variables.
Program 2-4.   Introduce READ and DATA.
Program 2-5.   Demonstrate the INPUT statement.
Program 2-6.   Making the eggs program more flexible.
Program 2-7.   Demonstrate string variable.
Program 2-8.   Demonstrate string READ.
Program 2-9.   READ a comma into a string variable.
Program 2-10. String concatenation.
Program 3-1.   Our first counting program.
Program 3-2.   Counting "out loud" this time.
Program 3-3.   Counting from 1 to 7.

Program 3-4.	Counting from 1 to 7 with COUNT = COUNT + 1.
Program 3-5.	Bouncing a steel ball.
Program 3-6.	Program 3-5 with comma spacing.
Program 3-7a.	Instructions segment.
Program 3-7b.	Keyboard entry segment.
Program 3-7c.	Program segment to calculate and display average.
Program 3-7.	Calculate test score average.
Program 3-8.	An hourly digital clock.
Program 3-9.	Program 3-8 with added features.
Program 4-1.	Counting with FOR and NEXT.
Program 4-1a.	Displaying 1 to 50 with semicolon in PRINT.
Program 4-2.	Counting by twos with STEP.
Program 4-3.	Bouncing a steel ball with FOR and NEXT.
Program 4-4.	Calculate the distance for a bouncing ball.
Program 4-5.	Calculate compound interest.
Program 4-6.	Display Fibonacci numbers.
Program 4-7.	Digital clock with nested loops.
Program 4-8.	Compound interest for several years.
Program 4-9.	Display Pythagorean triples using FOR loops.
Program 4-10.	Display Pythagorean triples using WHILE.
Program 5-1.	Display some square roots.
Program 5-2.	Find factor pairs.
Program 5-3.	Demonstrate LEFT$, MID$, and RIGHT$.
Program 5-4.	Demonstrate INSTR.
Program 5-5.	Demonstrate random numbers.
Program 5-6.	Flip a coin ten times.
Program 5-7.	Roll a die five times.
Program 5-8.	Demonstrate rounding with DEF FN.
Program 5-9.	Defined string function.
Program 5-10.	Subroutine to process yes-no answers.
Program 5-11.	Subprogram to process yes-no answers.
Program 6-1.	Demonstrate output windows.
Program 6-2.	Introduce PICTURE ON, PICTURE OFF, and PICTURE.
Program 6-3.	Introduce PICTURE$ function.
Program 6-4.	Write a picture string to a file.
Program 6-5.	Retrieve a picture string from a file.
Program 6-6.	Run rabbit Run, using SCROLL.
Program 6-7a.	Create a menu.
Program 6-7b.	Wait for a menu selection.

Appendix E

Program 6-7.	A menu program.
Program 6-8.	Demonstrate ON MENU GOSUB.
Program 6-9.	Display every button.
Program 6-10.	BUTTON demonstration.
Program 7-1.	Find average, highest, and lowest temperatures.
Program 7-2.	Drawing five random numbers from among ten.
Program 7-3.	Drawing without replacement efficiently.
Program 7-4.	A simple sort.
Program 7-5.	Read and display census data.
Program 7-6.	Change Program 7-5 to find largest population.
Program 7-7.	Display the days of the week.
Program 7-8a.	Control routine to play Alphabet.
Program 7-8b.	Load the Alphabet game road signs.
Program 7-8c.	Start with capital "A."
Program 7-8d.	Display a sign.
Program 7-8e.	Check keyboard input.
Program 7-8f.	Check if a letter is on a sign.
Program 7-8g.	Time delay routine.
Program 7-8h.	Data for the Alphabet game.
Program 7-8.	The Alphabet game.
Program 8-1a.	Calendar control routine.
Program 8-1b.	Request data for the calendar program.
Program 8-1c.	Calendar display control routine.
Program 8-1d.	Calendar calculations.
Program 8-1e.	Display calendar title.
Program 8-1f.	Display calendar days.
Program 8-1.	The calendar program.
Program 8-2.	Primes using the Sieve of Eratosthenes.
Program 8-3.	Convert base ten to binary.
Program 8-4.	Practice with binary and hex.
Program 9-1.	Variety of LINE statements.
Program 9-2.	Demonstrate using WINDOW function to change display.
Program 9-3.	Positive vs. negative start and end angles.
Program 9-4.	Draw graph paper.
Program 9-5.	Draw the "1" face of a die.
Program 9-6.	Draw the "3" face of a die with circular dots.
Program 9-7.	Drawing a "1" anywhere in the window.
Program 9-8.	Plot line drawings from DATA.
Program 9-9a.	Draw a traffic light using data statements.
Program 9-9b.	The three lights.

Program 9-9c.   Change the lights.
Program 9-9d.   Control the traffic light program.
Program 9-10.   Making a simple drawing using the mouse.
Program 9-11.   Demonstrate GET and PUT with screen images.
Program 9-12.   Plot a function.
Program 9-13.   Draw polar graphs.
Program 10-1.   Create a new mouse cursor.
Program 10-2.   Demonstrate some graphics routines.
Program 10-3.   Sample PENPAT.
Program 10-4.   Demonstrate PENMODE.
Program 10-5.   Draw a simple rectangle.
Program 10-6.   Display numerous rectangles with a FOR loop.
Program 10-7.   FILLRECT with a pattern.
Program 10-8.   Produce DATA for 8 by 8 patterns.
Program 10-9.   Draw a few sample rounded rectangles.
Program 10-10. Demonstrate POLY.
Program 10-11. Demonstrate miscellaneous graphics features.
Program 10-12. Demonstrate modes 0 through 3 in TEXTMODE MODE.
Program 10-13. Sample BACKPAT.
Program 11-1.   Initialize the signs file for Alphabet game.
Program 11-2a. Load the Alphabet game road signs.
Program 11-2b. Changed control routine in Alphabet game for files.
Program 11-2.   File-based Alphabet game.
Program 11-3.   Display a program from disk.
Program 11-4.   Fix Program 11-3.
Program 11-5.   Format multiple statements in a program.
Program 11-6.   Put some names in a file.
Program 11-7.   Add a name to a sequential file.
Program 11-8.   Demonstrate WRITE #.
Program 11-9.   Double buffer sequential file update.
Program 12-1a. OPEN and FIELD the accounts-label file.
Program 12-1b. Fill accounts-label file with "Unassigned".
Program 12-1c. Write actual account labels to the file.
Program 12-1.   Initialize an accounts-label file.
Program 12-2.   Write ten-largest-cities data to random-access file.
Program 12-3.   Display cities in rank order.
Program 13-1.   Initialize mailing-list "Pointer" file.

Program 13-2a. Control routine for mailing-list program.
Program 13-2b. Read data labels for mailing-list program.
Program 13-2c. Read available space in mailing-list program.
Program 13-2d. OPEN and FIELD the mailing-list data file.
Program 13-2e. Handle keyboard data entry for mailing-list program.
Program 13-2f. Prepare available space for mailing-list file.
Program 13-2g. Write a data entry in the mailing-list program.
Program 13-2h. Write available-space parameters in mailing-list program.
Program 13-2i. Program parameters for mailing-list program.
Program 13-2. Entering names in a mailing-list file.
Program 13-3. Program 13-2e with EDIT FIELD.

APPENDIX F

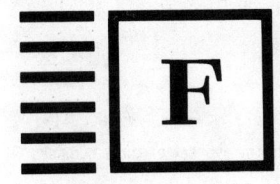

Solution Programs for Even-Numbered Problems

Chapter 1
Section 1-1
Problem No. 2

PRINT "Programming is fun."
PRINT "The computer will solve problems for us."

Programming is fun. The computer will solve problems for us.

Section 1-2
Problem No. 2

PRINT (78 + 89 + 82) / 3

83

Problem No. 4

PRINT "I am 15 years, 3 months, and 2 days old."
PRINT "That makes approximately:";
PRINT ((365*15 + 3*30 + 2)+4) * 24, "Hours"
PRINT "We added 4 for 4 leap years."
PRINT "We could have added 1 or 2 more for the 31 day months."

I am 15 years, 3 months, and 2 days old.
That makes approximately: 133704 Hours
We added 4 for 4 leap years."
We could have added 1 or 2 more for the 31 day months."

Problem No. 6

PRINT 283.4 + 658 + 385.8 + 17

1344.2

385

Chapter 2
Section 2-1
Problem No. 2

```
PRINT "I will calculate the average of three numbers."
PRINT
PRINT "Enter your three numbers:";
INPUT A, B, C
PRINT "The average is:"; (A + B + C) / 3
```

I will calculate the average of three numbers

Enter your three numbers:? 43,56,12
The average is: 37

Problem No. 4

```
PRINT "I will calculate simple interest."
PRINT
PRINT "Interest rate in percent";
INPUT RATE
PRINT "  Dollar amount of loan";
INPUT AMOUNT
PRINT
PRINT "     Interest is $"; RATE * AMOUNT / 100
PRINT "      Amount is $";
PRINT RATE * AMOUNT / 100 + AMOUNT
```

I will calculate simple interest.

Interest rate in percent? 12.81
  Dollar amount of loan? 1000

     Interest is $ 128.1
      Amount is $ 1128.1

Section 2-2
Problem No. 2

```
READ A, B, C, D, E
LET N = A/B + B/C
LET D = D/E + A/B
PRINT N / D
DATA 2, 3, 4, 5, 6
```

.94444444444447

Problem No. 4

```
PRINT "Demonstrate the MOD operator"
PRINT
PRINT "Enter two numbers (A,B)";
INPUT A, B
PRINT "A MOD B ="; A MOD B
```

Demonstrate the MOD operator

Enter two numbers (A,B)? 5,7
A MOD B = 5

Demonstrate the MOD operator

Enter two numbers (A,B)? 7,5
A MOD B = 2

387 Appendix F

Section 2-3
Problem No. 2

```
READ A0$, A1$, A2$, A3$, A4$, A5$, A6$
PRINT A0$
PRINT A1$
PRINT A2$
PRINT A3$
PRINT A4$
PRINT A5$
PRINT A6$
DATA Sunday, Monday, Tuesday, Wednesday
DATA Thursday, Friday, Saturday
```

```
Sunday
Monday
Tuesday
Wednesday
Thursday
Friday
Saturday
```

Problem No. 4

```
PRINT "Enter anything -";
INPUT A$
PRINT
PRINT "You entered <"; A$; ">"
```

Enter anything -? Macintosh

You entered <Macintosh>

Problem No. 6

```
READ WE, WL, WM, WS
PRINT "Enter prices in cents"
PRINT "Extra large, Large, Medium, Small"
INPUT PE, PL, PM, PS
PRINT
PRINT USING "Extra large ##.###"; PE/WE
PRINT USING "      Large ##.###"; PL/WL
PRINT USING "     Medium ##.###"; PM/WM
PRINT USING "      Small ##.###"; PS/WS
DATA 27, 24, 21, 18
```

Enter prices in cents
Extra large, Large, Medium, Small
? 100,95,87,72

```
Extra large  3.704
      Large  3.958
     Medium  4.143
      Small  4.000
```

Chapter 3
Section 3-1
Problem No. 2

```
COUNT = 1
Counting:
  IF COUNT > 19 THEN EndCount
  PRINT COUNT
  COUNT = COUNT + 1
  GOTO Counting
EndCount:
  PRINT "Done"
```

1
2
3
4
5
6
7
8
9
10
11
12
13
14
15
16
17
18
19
Done

Problem No. 4

```
COUNT = 1
TOTAL = 0
Counting:
 IF COUNT > 100 THEN EndCount
   TOTAL = TOTAL + COUNT
   COUNT = COUNT + 1
    GOTO Counting
EndCount:
 PRINT TOTAL
```

5050

Problem No. 6

```
COUNT = 10
Counting:
 IF COUNT < -10 THEN EndCount
 PRINT COUNT
 COUNT = COUNT - 1
 GOTO Counting
EndCount:
PRINT "Done"
```

```
10
9
8
7
6
5
4
3
2
1
0
-1
-2
-3
-4
-5
-6
-7
-8
-9
-10
Done
```

Section 3-2
Problem No. 2

```
PRINT "Bounce", "Height"
HEIGHT = 10
OLD.HEIGHT = HEIGHT
COUNT = 1
DISTANCE = 0

Bouncing:
  DISTANCE = DISTANCE + HEIGHT
  HEIGHT = HEIGHT * .9
  DISTANCE = DISTANCE + HEIGHT
  PRINT COUNT, HEIGHT
  IF HEIGHT * .9 < OLD.HEIGHT / 2 THEN AllDone
    COUNT = COUNT + 1
    GOTO Bouncing
AllDone:
  PRINT COUNT; "Bounces"
  PRINT DISTANCE; "Meters - total distance"
```

```
Bounce      Height
1           9
2           8.1
3           7.29
4           6.561
5           5.9049
6           5.31441
6 Bounces
89.02621 Meters - total distance
```

Problem No. 4

```
PRINT "Enter cents:";
INPUT CENTS
CheckForDone:
  IF CENTS = 0 THEN AllDone
  NextCoin:
    READ COIN, COIN$
    NUMBER = CENTS \ COIN 'Note integer division
    IF NUMBER = 0 THEN NextCoin
    PRINT NUMBER; COIN$
    CENTS = CENTS - NUMBER * COIN
    GOTO CheckForDone
AllDone:
  PRINT "Done"

DATA 50, Half dollars
DATA 25, Quarters
DATA 10, Dimes
DATA  5, Nickels
DATA  1, Pennies

Enter cents:? 91
 1 Half dollars
 1 Quarters
 1 Dimes
 1 Nickels
 1 Pennies
Done
```

Section 3-3
Problem No. 2

```
REM ** Display passing hours 12-hour and 24-hour
HOUR = 24

SetHour:
  HOUR = HOUR MOD 24 + 1
  HOUR1 = HOUR : IF HOUR >12 THEN HOUR1 = HOUR - 12
  PRINT PTAB(1); HOUR;
  PRINT PTAB(30); HOUR1;
  IF HOUR = 12 THEN PRINT "noon";
  IF HOUR = 24 THEN PRINT "midnight";
  IF HOUR < 12 THEN PRINT "am   ";
  IF HOUR < 24 AND HOUR > 12 THEN PRINT "pm";

X = 1
Delay:
  X = X + 1 : IF X < 200 THEN Delay ELSE SetHour
```

Chapter 4

Section 4-1

Problem No. 2

```
FOR COUNT = 93 TO 80 STEP -2
 PRINT COUNT;
NEXT COUNT

93 91 89 87 85 83 81
```

Problem No. 4

```
FOR COUNT = 1 TO 15
 PRINT COUNT, 1 / COUNT
NEXT COUNT

 1              1
 2              .5
 3              .33333333333333
 4              .25
 5              .2
 6              .16666666666667
 7              .14285714285714
 8              .125
 9              .11111111111111
 10             .1
 11             .090909090909091
 12             .083333333333333
 13             .076923076923077
 14             .071428571428571
 15             .066666666666667
```

Problem No. 6

```
FOR COUNT = 1 TO 11
 PRINT COUNT, COUNT / 11
NEXT COUNT

01234567890123456
 1              .090909090909091
 2              .18181818181818
 3              .27272727272727
 4              .36363636363636
 5              .45454545454545
 6              .54545454545455
 7              .63636363636364
 8              .72727272727273
 9              .81818181818182
 10             .90909090909091
 11             1
```

Section 4-2
Problem No. 2

```
A = 0 : B = 0 : FIB = 1
FOR COUNT = 1 TO 20
  PRINT USING "### -> #####"; COUNT, FIB
  A = B : B = FIB : FIB = A + B
NEXT COUNT
```

```
 1 ->     1
 2 ->     1
 3 ->     2
 4 ->     3
 5 ->     5
 6 ->     8
 7 ->    13
 8 ->    21
 9 ->    34
10 ->    55
11 ->    89
12 ->   144
13 ->   233
14 ->   377
15 ->   610
16 ->   987
17 ->  1597
18 ->  2584
19 ->  4181
20 ->  6765
```

Problem No. 4

```
PRINT "The twelve days of Christmas"
PRINT
GIFTS = 0
TODAY = 0
FOR DAY = 1 TO 12
  TODAY = TODAY + DAY
  GIFTS = GIFTS + TODAY
NEXT DAY
PRINT GIFTS; "Gifts"
PRINT
PRINT "The last gift would go back one day"
PRINT "short of a year later."
```

The twelve days of Christmas

364 Gifts

The last gift would go back one day
short of a year later.

Appendix F

Section 4-3
Problem No. 2

```
PRINT "Fibonacci numbers:"
B = 0 : FIB = 1
FOR J = 1 TO 10
  PRINT FIB,
  X = FIB * FIB
   A = B : B = FIB : FIB = A + B
   PRINT X, A * FIB, X - A * FIB
NEXT J
```

Fibonacci numbers:

1	1	0	1
1	1	2	-1
2	4	3	1
3	9	10	-1
5	25	24	1
8	64	65	-1
13	169	168	1
21	441	442	-1
34	1156	1155	1
55	3025	3026	-1

Section 4-4
Problem No. 2

```
REM ** Display a multiplication table
FOR ROW = 1 TO 10
  FOR COLUMN = 1 TO 10
    NUMBER = ROW * COLUMN
    PRINT USING " ###"; NUMBER;
  NEXT COLUMN
  PRINT
NEXT ROW
```

```
  1   2   3   4   5   6   7   8   9  10
  2   4   6   8  10  12  14  16  18  20
  3   6   9  12  15  18  21  24  27  30
  4   8  12  16  20  24  28  32  36  40
  5  10  15  20  25  30  35  40  45  50
  6  12  18  24  30  36  42  48  54  60
  7  14  21  28  35  42  49  46  63  70
  8  16  24  32  40  48  56  64  72  80
  9  18  27  36  45  54  63  72  81  90
 10  20  30  40  50  60  70  80  90 100
```

Chapter 5
Section 5-1
Problem No. 2

```
FOR N = 1 TO 20
  ROOT = SQR(N)
  PRINT USING "### ##.#"; N, ROOT
NEXT N
```

```
 1   1.0
 2   1.4
 3   1.7
 4   2.0
 5   2.2
 6   2.4
 7   2.6
 8   2.8
 9   3.0
10   3.2
11   3.3
12   3.5
13   3.6
14   3.7
15   3.9
16   4.0
17   4.1
18   4.2
19   4.4
20   4.5
```

Problem No. 4

```
RequestDate:
  INPUT "Enter a date in the form YYMMDD"; DATE
  IF DATE = 0 THEN END
  YEAR  = INT(DATE / 10000)
  MONTH = INT( (DATE - YEAR*10000) / 100 )
  DAY   = DATE - YEAR*10000 - MONTH*100

  REM ** Let's validate the entered value
  IF YEAR  < 0  THEN BadYear
  IF YEAR  > 99 THEN BadYear
  IF MONTH < 1  THEN BadMonth
  IF MONTH > 12 THEN BadMonth
  IF DAY   < 1  THEN BadDay
  IF DAY   > 31 THEN BadDay
  PRINT YEAR; MONTH; DAY
END

REM ** Error messages
BadYear:   PRINT "Bad year"  : PRINT : GOTO RequestDate
BadMonth:  PRINT "Bad month" : PRINT : GOTO RequestDate
BadDay:    PRINT "Bad day"   : PRINT : GOTO RequestDate
```

```
Enter a date in the form YYMMDD? 490212
 49  2  12

Enter a date in the form YYMMDD? 322104
Bad month

Enter a date in the form YYMMDD? 321204
 32  12  4
```

Appendix F

Section 5-2
Problem No. 2

```
CLS
B$ = SPACE$(89)
READ M$
WHILE M$ <> "Done"
  FOR J = 1 TO LEN(M$)
    FOR T = 1 TO 10 : NEXT T 'For timing
    B$ = RIGHT$(B$,68) + MID$(M$,J,1)
    PRINT PTAB(1); B$;
  NEXT J
  READ M$
WEND

DATA "Here we go, writing messages across the Macintosh screen"
DATA " looking just like the computerized billboard"
DATA " at the ball park."
DATA "
DATA "Done"
```

Problem No. 4

```
REM ** What day is this?
WEEK$ = "SUNMONTUEWEDTHUFRISAT"
RequestDay:
  INPUT "Day"; DAY$
  IF LEN(DAY$) = 0 THEN END
  DAY$ = LEFT$(DAY$,3) '3 characters to match
  P    = INSTR(WEEK$,DAY$)
  IF P = 0 THEN PRINT "Not found" : GOTO RequestDay
  PRINT "Day number"; P \ 3 + 1
```

```
Weekday? January
Not found
Weekday? TUESDAY
Day number 3
```

Problem No. 6

```
REM ** What day is this?
DAYNAMES$ = "Sunday   Monday   Tuesday  Wednesday"
  DAYNAMES$ = DAYNAMES$ + "Thursday Friday   Saturday "
WEEK$ = "SUNMONTUEWEDTHUFRISAT"
RequestDay:
  INPUT "Day"; DAY$
  IF LEN(DAY$) = 0 THEN END
  DAY$ = LEFT$(DAY$,3) '3 characters to match
  P    = INSTR(WEEK$,DAY$)
  IF P = 0 THEN PRINT "Not found" : GOTO RequestDay
  DAYNUMBER = P\3
  PRINT "Day number"; DAYNUMBER + 1
  PRINT MID$(DAYNAMES$,DAYNUMBER*9+1,9)
```

```
Day? MONDAY
Day number 2
Monday
```

Problem No. 8

```
MONTH$ = "JanFebMarAprMayJunJulAugSepOctNovDec"

RequestDate:
   INPUT "Enter a date in the form YYMMDD"; DATE
   IF DATE = 0 THEN END
   YEAR  = INT(DATE / 10000)
   MONTH = INT( (DATE - YEAR*10000) / 100 )
   DAY   = DATE - YEAR*10000 - MONTH*100

   REM ** Let's validate the entered value
   IF YEAR  < 0  THEN BadYear
   IF YEAR  > 99 THEN BadYear
   IF MONTH < 1  THEN BadMonth
   IF MONTH > 12 THEN BadMonth
   IF DAY   < 1  THEN BadDay
   IF DAY   > 31 THEN BadDay

   Y$ = MID$(STR$(YEAR),2) : IF YEAR < 10 THEN Y$ = "0" + Y$
   D$ = MID$(STR$(DAY ),2) : IF DAY  < 10 THEN D$ = "0" + D$
   M$ = MID$(MONTH$,MONTH*3 - 2,3)
   PRINT Y$; "-"; M$; "-"; D$
   END

REM ** Error messages
BadYear:   PRINT "Bad year"  : PRINT : GOTO RequestDate
BadMonth:  PRINT "Bad month" : PRINT : GOTO RequestDate
BadDay:    PRINT "Bad day"   : PRINT : GOTO RequestDate

Enter a date in the form YYMMDD? 851231
85-Dec-31
```

Section 5-3
Problem No. 2

```
FOR I = 1 TO 200
   COIN = INT( RND*2 )
   IF COIN = 0 THEN HEADS = HEADS + 1
   IF COIN = 1 THEN TAILS = TAILS + 1
NEXT I
PRINT HEADS; "Heads"
PRINT TAILS; "Tails"

99 Heads
101 Tails
```

Section 5-4
Problem No. 2

```
REM ** Convert from Fanrenheit to centigrade
DEF FNC(X) = (X - 32) * 5 / 9
```

Problem No. 4

```
DEF FN DAY$(D%) = MID$(WEEK$, D%*9 + 1, 9)
```

Section 5-6
Problem No. 2

```
MONTH$ = "JanFebMarAprMayJunJulAugSepOctNovDec"
GetDate:
  INPUT "Enter a date in the form YY/MM/DD"; DATE.$
  IF LEN(DATE.$) = 0 THEN END
  GOSUB VerifyDate
  IF ERROR.MESSAGE$ <> "Ok" THEN PRINT ERROR.MESSAGE$ : GOTO GetDate
  GOSUB FormDateString
  PRINT NEW.DATE$
  END

VerifyDate:
  ERROR.MESSAGE$ = "Ok"
  DAY   = VAL(RIGHT$(DATE.$,2 ))
  IF DAY  < 1 OR DAY  > 31 THEN ERROR.MESSAGE$ = "Bad day"
  MONTH = VAL(MID$  (DATE.$,4,2))
  IF MONTH < 1 OR MONTH > 12 THEN ERROR.MESSAGE$ = "Bad month"
  YEAR  = VAL(LEFT$ (DATE.$,2 ))
  IF YEAR  < 0 OR YEAR  > 99 THEN ERROR.MESSAGE$ = "Bad year"
  IF LEN(DATE.$) <> 8       THEN ERROR.MESSAGE$ = "Bad date"
  RETURN

FormDateString:
  Y$ = MID$(STR$(YEAR),2) : IF YEAR < 10 THEN Y$ = "0" + Y$
  M$ = MID$(MONTH$,MONTH*3 - 2,3)
  D$ = MID$(STR$(DAY ),2) : IF DAY  < 10 THEN D$ = "0" + D$
  NEW.DATE$ = Y$ + "-" + M$ + "-" + D$
  RETURN


Enter a date in the form YY/MM/DD? 77/02/14
77 -Feb-14
```

Section 5-7
Problem No. 2

```
GetDate:
  INPUT "Enter a date in the form mm-dd-yyyy"; DATE.$
  IF LEN(DATE.$) = 0 THEN END
  DATE DATE.$, NEW.DATE$, E$
  IF E$ <> "Ok" THEN PRINT E$ : GOTO GetDate
  PRINT NEW.DATE$
  END

  SUB DATE(A$,B$,E$) STATIC
  MONTH$ = " January February  March   April    May   June   July"
  MONTH$ = MONTH$ + "  AugustSeptember October November December"
  GOSUB VerifyDate
  IF E$ = "Ok" THEN GOSUB FormDateString
  EXIT SUB

VerifyDate:
  E$ = "Ok"
  DAY   = VAL(MID$(A$,4,2))
  IF DAY  < 1 OR DAY  > 31 THEN E$ = "Bad day"
  MONTH = VAL(LEFT$(A$,2))
  IF MONTH < 1 OR MONTH > 12 THEN E$ = "Bad month"
  YEAR  = VAL(MID$ (A$,7))
  IF LEN(A$) < 8      THEN E$ = "Bad date"
  RETURN
```

```
FormDateString:
  Y$ = MID$(STR$(YEAR),2) : IF YEAR < 10 THEN Y$ = "0" + Y$
        IF YEAR < 100 THEN Y$ = "19" + Y$
  M$ = MID$(MONTH$,MONTH*9 - 8,9)
  D$ = MID$(STR$(DAY ),2) : IF DAY  < 10 THEN D$ = "0" + D$
  B$ = M$ + " " + D$ + ", " + Y$
  RETURN

END SUB


Enter a date in the form mm-dd-yyyy?  03-31-88
   March 31, 1988
```

Problem No. 4

```
Request:
  INPUT "Enter several words"; X$ : IF UCASE$(X$) = "QUIT" THEN END
  FirstCap X$, R$
  PRINT "Becomes:  "; R$
  GOTO Request

REM ** Subprogram to capitalize first letter of each word
SUB FirstCap(WordIn$, WordOut$) STATIC
  WordOut$ = UCASE$(WordIn$)
  FOR J = 2 TO LEN(WordOut$)
   X9 = ASC(MID$(WordOut$,J,1))
   IF X9 < 65 OR X9 > 90 THEN NextLetter
   IF ASC(MID$(WordOut$,J-1,1)) = 32 THEN NextLetter
     MID$(WordOut$,J,1) = CHR$(X9+32)
  NextLetter:
   NEXT J
END SUB


Enter several words?  Now is the best time for this
Becomes:  Now Is The Best Time For This
Enter several words?  quit
```

Problem No. 6

```
INPUT "Enter the message:", MESSAGE$
Verify:
  PRINT
  PRINT MESSAGE$
  INPUT "Do you want to substitute anything"; ANS$
  IF ASC(UCASE$(ANS$)) <> 89 THEN END
  Substitute MESSAGE$
  GOTO Verify

SUB Substitute(A$) STATIC
  INPUT "Replace:", NO1$
  P = INSTR(A$,NO1$)
  IF P <> 0 THEN INPUT "With:", NO2$
    WHILE P <> 0
      A$ = LEFT$(A$,P-1) + NO2$ + MID$(A$,P+LEN(NO1$))
      P = INSTR(P+1,A$,NO1$)
    WEND
END SUB
```

Enter a message: this is a dull message

this is a dull message
Do you want to substitute anything? y
Replace: is
With: ixx
Thixx ixx a dull message
Do you want to substitute anything? n

Chapter 7
Section 7-1
Problem No. 2

```
WEEK$ = "SunMonTueWedThuFriSat"
REM ** Enter the temperatures in array WEEK
FOR J = 1 TO 7 : READ WEEK(J) : NEXT J

REM ** Set up initial conditions
SUM = WEEK(1) : HIGH = WEEK(1) : LOW = WEEK(1)
LOW.DAY = 1 : HIGH.DAY = 1

REM ** Scan the week's temperatures
FOR J = 2 TO 7
 SUM = SUM + WEEK(J)
 IF WEEK(J) < LOW THEN LOW = WEEK(J) : LOW.DAY = J
 IF WEEK(J) > HIGH THEN HIGH = WEEK(J) : HIGH.DAY = J
NEXT J
PRINT "Average temp:"; SUM / 7
PRINT "Highest temp:"; HIGH
PRINT " Lowest temp:"; LOW
PRINT " Highest day: "; MID$(WEEK$,HIGH.DAY*3 - 2, 3)
PRINT "  Lowest day: "; MID$(WEEK$,LOW.DAY*3 - 2, 3)

DATA 71, 77, 82, 76, 79, 72, 74
END
```

Average temp: 75.857142857143
Highest temp: 82
 Lowest temp: 71
 Highest day: Tue
  Lowest day: Sun

Problem No. 4

```
RANDOMIZE TIMER
REM ** Drawing five random numbers from among ten

REM ** Make all values available
FOR J = 1 TO 10
 A(J) = 1 'Value available
NEXT J
DUPLICATE = 0

REM ** Select five random values
FOR J = 1 TO 5
 Draw: RANDOM = INT(RND * 10 + 1)
 IF A(RANDOM) = 0 THEN DUPLICATE = DUPLICATE + 1 : GOTO Draw
 PRINT RANDOM;
 A(RANDOM) = 0 'Value unavailable
NEXT J
PRINT : PRINT DUPLICATE; "Duplicates"
```

```
3  1  4  5  8
7 Duplicates

6  5  8  10  7
6 Duplicates
```

Problem No. 6

```
REM ** Read the arrays
READ N1
FOR K = 1 TO N1 : READ A(K) : NEXT K

READ N2
FOR K = 1 TO N2 : READ B(K) : NEXT K

REM ** Load the third array
FOR J = 1 TO N1 : C(J) = A(J) : NEXT J : N3 = N1
FOR K = 1 TO N2
 FOR J = 1 TO N3
  IF C(J) = B(K) THEN Skip
 NEXT J
 N3 = N3 + 1 : C(N3) = B(K)
Skip: NEXT K

FOR J = 1 TO N3 : PRINT C(J); : NEXT J
END

DATA 4, 3, 5, 6, 17
DATA 5, 6, -9, 11, -13, 3

  3  5  6  17  -9  11  -13
```

Section 7-2

Problem No. 2

```
Replace
IF A(J) > A(J+1) THEN SWAP A(J), A(J+1)
with
IF A(J) < A(J+1) THEN SWAP A(J), A(J+1)
```

Section 7-3

Problem No. 2

```
REM ** Experimenting with a 5 by 7 array
FOR ROW = 1 TO 5
 FOR COLUMN = 1 TO 7
  A(ROW, COLUMN) = INT(RND*150)
 NEXT COLUMN
NEXT ROW
GOSUB LargeRows
PRINT : PRINT
GOSUB LargeColumns
END

LargeColumns:
 FOR COLUMN = 1 TO 7
  LARGEST = A(1, COLUMN)
  FOR ROW = 2 TO 5
   IF A(ROW, COLUMN) > LARGEST THEN LARGEST = A(ROW, COLUMN)
  NEXT ROW
  PRINT LARGEST; "Largest for column"; COLUMN
 NEXT COLUMN
RETURN
```

```
LargeRows:
FOR ROW = 1 TO 5
LARGEST = A(ROW, 1)
 FOR COLUMN = 1 TO 7
  IF A(ROW, COLUMN) > LARGEST THEN LARGEST = A(ROW, COLUMN)
 NEXT COLUMN
 PRINT LARGEST; "Largest for row"; ROW
NEXT ROW
RETURN
```

```
118 Largest for row 1
147 Largest for row 2
143 Largest for row 3
130 Largest for row 4
117 Largest for row 5


143 Largest for column 1
147 Largest for column 2
135 Largest for column 3
117 Largest for column 4
 83 Largest for column 5
145 Largest for column 6
136 Largest for column 7
```

Problem No. 4

```
RANDOMIZE TIMER
DIM A(100)

TIME1 = TIMER : GOSUB WithTrialandError
 PRINT "Trial and error took:"; TIMER - TIME1

TIME1 = TIMER : GOSUB NoTrialandError
 PRINT "No trial and error took:"; TIMER - TIME1

END

NoTrialandError:
FOR J = 1 TO 100 : A(J) = J : NEXT J

FOR J = 1 TO 100
 LAST = 100 - J + 1
 SUBSCRIPT = INT(RND * LAST + 1)
 A(SUBSCRIPT) = A(LAST)
NEXT J
RETURN

WithTrialandError:
FOR J = 1 TO 100 : A(J) = J : NEXT J

FOR J = 1 TO 100
 Draw: RANDOM = INT(RND * 100 + 1) : IF A(RANDOM) = 0 THEN Draw
 A(RANDOM) = 0 'Value unavailable
NEXT J
RETURN

Trial and error took: 6
No trial and error took: 2
```

Section 7-4
Problem No. 2

```
MONTH$ = "JanFebMarAprMayJunJulAugSepOctNovDec"
FOR R = 1 TO 3
 FOR M = 1 TO 12
  PRINT PTAB(8*3*M-16); MID$(MONTH$,3*M-3+R,1);
 NEXT M
 PRINT
NEXT R
```

```
J  F  M  A  M  J  J  A  S  O  N  D
a  e  a  p  a  u  u  u  e  c  o  e
n  b  r  r  y  n  l  g  p  t  v  c
```

Section 7-5
Problem No. 2

```
'In the DisplaySigns routine replace
FOR X = 1 TO 100 : NEXT X
'with something like:
FOR X = 1 TO LEN(SIGNS$(R)) : NEXT X
'adjust to suit.
```

Problem No. 4

```
REM ** Tabulate frequency of letters on signs
DIM ALPHA(26)
GOSUB Tabulate
GOSUB Display
END

Tabulate:
 READ A$
 WHILE A$ <> "Done" : A$ = UCASE$(A$)
  FOR K = 1 TO LEN(A$)
   B$ = MID$(A$,K,1) : X = ASC(B$)
   IF X > 64 AND X < 91 THEN ALPHA(X-64) = ALPHA(X-64) + 1
  NEXT K
  READ A$
 WEND
 RETURN

Display:
 WIDTH 60
 FOR K = 1 TO 26
  PRINT CHR$(K+64); " "; ALPHA(K),
 NEXT K
 RETURN

REM ** The signs
DATA Stop, Al's Pizza, Dairy Queen, Burger King
DATA Yield, One Way, This Way Out, Detour
DATA One Show Only Tonight, Exit Only, Entrance Only Please
DATA Florida 2138 mi., Fly United, Jet Set Diner
DATA Give Her a Valentine, Give Him a Valentine
DATA First Avenue, North Side
DATA Done
```

403 Appendix F

A	13	B	1	C	1	D	7
E	26	F	3	G	5	H	6
I	18	J	1	K	1	L	10
M	2	N	18	O	12	P	3
Q	1	R	10	S	8	T	15
U	6	V	5	W	3	X	1
Y	8	Z	2				

Problem No. 6

```
REM ** Arrange signs tabulation according to frequency
DIM ALPHA(26), ASCII(26)
GOSUB Tabulate
GOSUB Arrange
GOSUB Display
END

Tabulate:
 READ A$
 WHILE A$ <> "Done" : A$ = UCASE$(A$)
  FOR K = 1 TO LEN(A$)
   B$ = MID$(A$,K,1) : X = ASC(B$)
   IF X > 64 AND X < 91 THEN ALPHA(X-64) = ALPHA(X-64) + 1
  NEXT K
  READ A$
 WEND
 RETURN

Display:
 WIDTH 60
 FOR K = 1 TO 26
  PRINT CHR$(ASCII(K)); " "; ALPHA(K),
 NEXT K
 RETURN

Arrange:
 FOR K = 1 TO 26 : ASCII(K) = K + 64 : NEXT K
 FOR K = 1 TO 25
  FOR J = K + 1 TO 26
   IF ALPHA(K) >= ALPHA(J) THEN NextLetter
   SWAP ALPHA(K), ALPHA(J) : SWAP ASCII(K), ASCII(J)
 NextLetter: NEXT J
 NEXT K
 RETURN

REM ** The signs
DATA Stop, Al's Pizza, Dairy Queen, Burger King
DATA Yield, One Way, This Way Out, Detour
DATA One Show Only Tonight, Exit Only, Entrance Only Please
DATA Florida 2138 mi., Fly United, Jet Set Diner
DATA Give Her a Valentine, Give Him a Valentine
DATA First Avenue, North Side
DATA Done
```

E	26	I	18	N	18	T	15
A	13	O	12	R	10	L	10
S	8	Y	8	D	7	U	6
H	6	V	5	G	5	F	3
W	3	P	3	M	2	Z	2
B	1	Q	1	C	1	X	1
J	1	K	1				

Chapter 8
Section 8-1
Problem No. 2

```
REM ** Replace control routine and RequestData as follows:
DEFINT A-Z
GOSUB RequestData
FOR YEAR = YEAR1 TO YEAR2
GOSUB DisplayCalendar
NEXT YEAR
END

RequestData:
  INPUT "What Month"; MONTH
  IF MONTH < 1 OR MONTH > 12 THEN RequestData
  INPUT "Range of years from,to"; YEAR1, YEAR2
  IF YEAR1 < 0 OR YEAR1 > 99 THEN RequestData
  IF YEAR2 < 0 OR YEAR2 > 99 THEN RequestData
  IF YEAR1 > YEAR2 THEN RequestDAta
RETURN
```

```
             What month? 5
Range of years from, to? 36,37

    May    1936

Sun Mon Tue Wed Thu Fri Sat

                     1   2
 3   4   5   6   7   8   9
10  11  12  13  14  15  16
17  18  19  20  21  22  23
24  25  26  27  28  29  30
31


    May    1937

Sun Mon Tue Wed Thu Fri Sat

                             1
 2   3   4   5   6   7   8
 9  10  11  12  13  14  15
16  17  18  19  20  21  22
23  24  25  26  27  28  29
30  31
```

Appendix F

Problem No. 4

```
GOSUB GetDate : IF DATE = 0 THEN END
GOSUB Display
END

Calculate:
    KDAY - 1st of Month
    N - No. of days in Month
LEAP = 0 : IF YEAR MOD 4 = 0 THEN LEAP = 1
KDAY = (YEAR + INT((YEAR + 3) / 4)) MOD 7
N = 0
FOR M = 1 TO MONTH
 KDAY = (KDAY + N) MOD 7
 N = 30 + ((M + (M > 7)) MOD 2)
 IF M = 2 THEN N = 28 + LEAP
NEXT M
RETURN

VerifyDate:
ERROR.MESSAGE$ = "Ok"
YEAR  = INT(DATE / 10000)
MONTH = INT( (DATE - YEAR*10000) / 100 )
DAY   = DATE - YEAR*10000 - MONTH*100
IF DAY   < 1 OR DAY   > 31 THEN ERROR.MESSAGE$ = "Bad day"
IF MONTH < 1 OR MONTH > 12 THEN ERROR.MESSAGE$ = "Bad month"
IF YEAR  < 0 OR YEAR  > 99 THEN ERROR.MESSAGE$ = "Bad year"
RETURN

GetDate:
INPUT "Enter a date in the form YYMMDD"; DATE
IF DATE = 0 THEN Leave
GOSUB VerifyDate
IF ERROR.MESSAGE$ <> "Ok" THEN PRINT ERROR.MESSAGE$ : GOTO GetDate
Leave: RETURN

Display:
WEEK$ = "SunMonTueWedThuFriSat"
GOSUB Calculate
KDAY = ( KDAY + DAY - 1 ) MOD 7
X = KDAY * 3 + 1
PRINT
PRINT "Your date falls on "; MID$(WEEK$, X, 3)
RETURN
```

Enter a date in the form YYMMDD? 891301
Bad month
Enter a date in the form YYMMDD? 880101

Your date falls on Fri

Problem No. 6

```
MONTH$ = "JanFebMarAprMayJunJulAugSepOctNovDec"
GetDate: INPUT "Enter a date in the form YYMMDD"; DATE
 IF DATE = 0 THEN END
 GOSUB VerifyDate
 IF ERROR.MESSAGE$ <> "Ok" THEN PRINT ERROR.MESSAGE$ : GOTO GetDate
 GOSUB FormDateString : PRINT NEW.DATE$
 END

Calculate:
     KDAY - 1st of Month
     N - No. of days in Month
LEAP = 0 : IF YEAR MOD 4 = 0 THEN LEAP = 1
KDAY = (YEAR + INT((YEAR + 3) / 4)) MOD 7
N = 0
FOR M = 1 TO MONTH
 KDAY = (KDAY + N) MOD 7
 N = 30 + ((M + (M > 7)) MOD 2)
 IF M = 2 THEN N = 28 + LEAP
NEXT M
RETURN

VerifyDate:
ERROR.MESSAGE$ = "Ok"
YEAR  = INT(DATE / 10000)
MONTH = INT( (DATE - YEAR*10000) / 100 )
DAY   = DATE - YEAR*10000 - MONTH*100
IF MONTH < 1 OR MONTH > 12 THEN ERROR.MESSAGE$ = "Bad month"
IF YEAR  < 0 OR YEAR  > 99 THEN ERROR.MESSAGE$ = "Bad year"
GOSUB Calculate
IF DAY   < 1 OR DAY   > N  THEN ERROR.MESSAGE$ = "Bad day"
RETURN

FormDateString:
 Y$ = MID$(STR$(YEAR),2) : IF YEAR < 10 THEN Y$ = "0" + Y$
 M$ = MID$(MONTH$,MONTH*3 - 2,3)
 D$ = MID$(STR$(DAY ),2) : IF DAY  < 10 THEN D$ = "0" + D$
 NEW.DATE$ = Y$ + "-" + M$ + "-" + D$
 RETURN

Enter a date in the form YYMMDD? 890132
Bad day
Enter a date in the form YYMMDD? 880101
88-Jan-01
```

Appendix F

Section 8-3
Problem No. 2

```
PRINT "Convert base ten numbers to binary format"
PRINT

INPUT "Enter a value"; DECIMAL
NextDigit: X = DECIMAL - INT(DECIMAL/2)*2
 A$ = STR$(X) + A$
 DECIMAL = INT(DECIMAL/2)
 IF DECIMAL THEN NextDigit
PRINT A$
```

Convert base ten numbers to binary format

Enter a value? 32768
 1 0 0 0 0 0 0 0 0 0 0 0 0 0 0 0

Problem No. 4

```
PRINT "Convert negative numbers to two's complement form"
PRINT

Keyboard:
INPUT "Enter a negative number in base ten form"; TEN
IF TEN > -1 THEN Keyboard
DECIMAL = ABS(TEN)
GetDigits:
  X = DECIMAL MOD 2
  A$ = RIGHT$(STR$(X),1) + A$
  DECIMAL = DECIMAL \ 2
  IF DECIMAL THEN GetDigits
AddZeros: A$ = "0" + A$ : IF LEN(A$) < 16 THEN AddZeros
PRINT "Binary form of "; ABS(TEN); "is ", A$
REM ** 1's to 0's and vice versa
FOR J1 = 1 TO LEN(A$)
  X$ = MID$(A$,J1,1)
  IF X$ = "0" THEN MID$(A$,J1,1) = "1" : ELSE MID$(A$,J1,1) = "0"
NEXT J1

REM ** Add 1
FOR J1 = LEN(A$) TO 1 STEP -1
  X$ = MID$(A$,J1,1)
  IF X$ = "0" THEN MID$(A$,J1,1) = "1" : GOTO Display
  MID$(A$,J1,1) = "0"
NEXT J1

Display:
PRINT "Two's complement form is", A$
```

Convert negative numbers to two's complement form

Enter a negative number in base ten form? 0
Enter a negative number in base ten form? -1
Binary form of 1 is   0000000000000001
Two's complement form is   1111111111111111

Chapter 9
Section 9-1
Problem No. 2

```
REM ** Video game monster opening and closing
X = 100 : Y = 100
WHILE 4=4
 FOR K = 1 TO 2
  READ A, B, C
  FOR RAD = A TO B STEP C
   X = X + 1 : IF X > 490 THEN X = 0
   Y = Y + 1 : IF Y > 253 THEN Y = 0
   B = 0 - RAD : E = RAD - 6.29
   CIRCLE (X,Y),12,33,B,E
   CIRCLE (X1,Y1),12,30,B1,E1
   X1 = X : Y1 = Y : B1 = B : E1 = E
  NEXT RAD
 NEXT K
 RESTORE
WEND
DATA 0, .6, .1
DATA .6, 0, -.9
```

Problem No. 4

```
RANDOMIZE TIMER
REM ** Random ellipses
FOR K = 1 TO 15
 RADIUS = RND*50 : ASPECT = RND*3
 X = RND*(WINDOW(2)-2*RADIUS) + RADIUS
 Y = RND*(WINDOW(3)-2*RADIUS) + RADIUS
 CIRCLE (X,Y),RADIUS,,,,ASPECT
 XRADIUS = RADIUS : YRADIUS = RADIUS
 IF ASPECT < 1 THEN YRADIUS = RADIUS*ASPECT
 IF ASPECT > 1 THEN XRADIUS = RADIUS/ASPECT
 LINE (X-XRADIUS,Y-YRADIUS) - (X+XRADIUS,Y+YRADIUS),,B
NEXT K
```

Problem No. 6

```
WINDOW 1,,(100,100)-(210,210),-2
REM ** Blinking stars
LINE (5,5) - (105,105),,BF
 WHILE 1=1
  X = RND*97 : Y = RND*97
  X = 6*(X\6)+5 : Y = 6*(Y\6)+5
  C = INT(RND*147) : IF C < 10 THEN COLOR = 30 ELSE COLOR = 33
  LINE (X,Y)-(X+2,Y+2),COLOR,BF
 WEND
```

Problem No. 8

```
REM ** Box with 10 pixel border
FOR K = 0 TO 9
 LINE (20+K,30+K) - (100-K,210-K),,B
NEXT K
```

Section 9-2
Problem No. 2
```
RANDOMIZE TIMER
X = 1 : Y = 1
GOSUB SelectDie
GOSUB DisplayOutline
GOSUB DisplayDots
END

SelectDie:
 NUM = INT(RND*6 + 1)
 RETURN

DisplayDots:
 ON NUM GOSUB One,Two,Three,Four,Five,Six
 RETURN

DisplayOutline:
 LINE (X,Y) - STEP (61,61),,B
 RETURN

One:
 FOR R = 0 TO 5
  CIRCLE (X+30,Y+30),R
 NEXT R
 RETURN

Two:
 FOR R = 0 TO 5
  CIRCLE (X+10,Y+10),R
  CIRCLE (X+50,Y+50),R
 NEXT R
 RETURN

Three:
 FOR R = 0 TO 5
  CIRCLE (X+10,Y+10),R
  CIRCLE (X+30,Y+30),R
  CIRCLE (X+50,Y+50),R
 NEXT R
 RETURN

Four:
 FOR R = 0 TO 5
  CIRCLE (X+10,Y+10),R
  CIRCLE (X+50,Y+10),R
  CIRCLE (X+50,Y+50),R
  CIRCLE (X+10,Y+50),R
 NEXT R
 RETURN

Five:
 FOR R = 0 TO 5
  CIRCLE (X+10,Y+10),R
  CIRCLE (X+50,Y+10),R
  CIRCLE (X+50,Y+50),R
  CIRCLE (X+10,Y+50),R
  CIRCLE (X+30,Y+30),R
 NEXT R
 RETURN
```

Six:
```
  FOR R = 0 TO 5
    CIRCLE (X+10,Y+10),R
    CIRCLE (X+10,Y+30),R
    CIRCLE (X+10,Y+50),R
    CIRCLE (X+50,Y+10),R
    CIRCLE (X+50,Y+30),R
    CIRCLE (X+50,Y+50),R
  NEXT R
  RETURN
```

Problem No. 4

```
REM ** Replace control routine in 9-2-2 above with:
RANDOMIZE TIMER
X = 5 : Y =150
GOSUB SelectDie : GOSUB DisplayOutline : GOSUB DisplayDots
X = 75 : Y = 150
GOSUB SelectDie : GOSUB DisplayOutline : GOSUB DisplayDots
END
```

Problem No. 6

```
REM ** Replace the control routine in 9-2-2 above with:
RANDOMIZE TIMER
FOR K = 1 TO 20
  X = RND*420 : Y = RND*150
  GOSUB SelectDie
  GOSUB DisplayOutline
  GOSUB DisplayDots
  IF K < 19 THEN LINE (X,Y) - STEP (61,61),30,BF
NEXT K
END
```

Section 9-3
Problem No. 2

```
REM ** A Sailboat
DATA 30,40,40,50,33,n
DATA 30,40,30,52,33,n
DATA 30,50,40,50,33,n
DATA 26,52,46,52,33,n
DATA 26,52,28,56,33,n
DATA 28,56,44,56,33,n
DATA 44,56,46,52,33,n
DATA 0,0,0,0,-1,n
```

Problem No. 4

```
DEFINT A-Z

REM ** Raise the flag
X = 155
REM ** The flagpole
LINE (X-2,10) - (X-2,230)
FOR Y = 180 TO 20 STEP -20
  IF Y > 100 THEN X = X + 3 ELSE X = X - 2
  LINE (X,Y) - (X+70,Y+38),,B

  REM ** The stripes
  FOR Y1 = 0 TO 36 STEP 6
    LINE (X,Y+Y1) - (X+70,Y+Y1+2),33,BF      'Red stripe
    IF Y1 = 36 THEN NextStripe
    LINE (X+1,Y+Y1+3) - (X+70-1,Y+Y1+5),30,BF  'White stripe
  NextStripe: NEXT Y1
```

```
REM ** The field for the stars
LINE (X,Y) - (X+31,Y+20),33,BF

REM ** The stars 6 across and 5 down
FOR X1 = 3 TO 28 STEP 5
  FOR Y1 = 2 TO 18 STEP 4
    CIRCLE (X+X1,Y+Y1),0,30
  NEXT Y1
NEXT X1

REM ** The rest of the stars 5 across and 4 down
FOR X1 = 5 TO 25 STEP 5
  FOR Y1 = 4 TO 16 STEP 4
    CIRCLE (X+X1,Y+Y1),0,30
  NEXT Y1
NEXT X1
  IF Y = 20 THEN LINE (X,Y) - (X-2,10),33     'The rope
  IF Y = 20 THEN LINE (X,Y+39) - (X-2,200),33  'more rope
  FOR K = 1 TO 250 : NEXT K
  IF Y > 20 THEN LINE (X,Y) - (X+70,Y+39),30,BF 'Erase the flag
NEXT Y
X$ = INPUT$(1)
```

Section 9-5
Problem No. 2

```
REM ** Simply use the following function in Program 9-12
DEF FNF(X) = (X^2+50*X-450)/100
```

Section 9-6
Problem No. 2

```
REM ** Simply replace lines in Program 9-13 as follows:
a)
RADIAL SCALE = 30 : STEPSIZE = .1
RADIUS = 1 - 2 * COS(ANGLE) - 3 * SIN(ANGLE)^2

b)
RADIALSCALE = 25 : STEPSIZE = .1
RADIUS = 3 + SIN(3*ANGLE)

c)
RADIALSCALE = 40 : STEPSIZE = .1
RADIUS = 2 + SIN(2*ANGLE)

d)
RADIALSCALE = 60 : STEPSIZE = .1
RADIUS = SIN(ANGLE) + COS(ANGLE)
```

Chapter 11
Section 11-1
Problem No. 2

```
REM ** New or changed lines are indicated with '***
DIM SIGNS$(50)
RANDOMIZE TIMER
OPEN "Signs Data" FOR INPUT AS #1
GOSUB LoadSigns                 'Load the signs array
CLOSE #1
GOSUB BeginGame                 'Establish game beginning
GetNextSign:
  GOSUB DisplaySigns            'Simulate random signs along the road
  GOSUB CheckPlayer             'Did the player spot the next letter?
  IF LETTER = 0 AND TIMES < 2 THEN GetNextSign '***
  IF LETTER > 0 THEN GOSUB CheckLetter '***
  IF TIMES < 2 THEN CheckDone '***
  PRINT "You missed "; CHR$(NEXTLETTER); " twice" : GOSUB Delay '***
  NEXTLETTER = NEXTLETTER + 1 '***
  TIMES = 0 '***
  CheckDone: '***
    IF NEXTLETTER < 91 THEN GetNextSign  'If not "Z" yet, repeat step 3
    PRINT "Congratulations, you have made it through the alphabet!"
END

LoadSigns:
  NUMBEROFSIGNS = 0 : INPUT #1, A$
  WHILE A$ <> "Done"
    NUMBEROFSIGNS = NUMBEROFSIGNS + 1 : SIGNS$(NUMBEROFSIGNS) = A$
    INPUT #1, A$
  WEND
  PRINT "There are:"; NUMBEROFSIGNS; "signs in this game."
  GOSUB Delay
  RETURN

BeginGame:
  NEXTLETTER = 65 'Get ready to look for 'A'
  TIMES = 0 '***
  RETURN

DisplaySigns:
  R = INT(RND * NUMBEROFSIGNS + 1)
  GOSUB CountMissed '***
  CLS
    PICTURE ON
  PRINT SIGNS$(R)
  PICTURE OFF
  FOR K = 1 TO 250 STEP 30
    PICTURE(1+5*SQR(K),250-K)-(100+4*K,300+K)
    FOR X = 1 TO 100 : NEXT X
    CLS
  NEXT K
  RETURN
```

```
CheckPlayer:
  A$ = INKEY$ : IF LEN(A$) = 0 THEN LETTER = 0 : GOTO EndCheckPlayer
  ClearKey: IF LEN(INKEY$) = 1 THEN ClearKey
    PRINT A$; " ";
    A$ = UCASE$(A$) : LETTER = ASC(A$)
    IF A$ < "A" OR A$ > "Z" THEN CheckPlayer
    IF LETTER = NEXTLETTER THEN EndCheckPlayer
      PRINT "Not the next letter in the alphabet" : GOSUB Delay
    GOTO CheckPlayer
EndCheckPlayer:
RETURN

CheckLetter:
  IF INSTR(UCASE$(SIGNS$(R)), A$) THEN Found ELSE NotFound
  NotFound:
    BEEP : PRINT "Your letter is not on the sign" : GOSUB Delay
    GOTO EndCheckLetter
  Found:
    PRINT "Good" : GOSUB Delay
    NEXTLETTER = NEXTLETTER + 1
    TIMES = 0 '***
EndCheckLetter:
RETURN

Delay: 'Time delay for messages
  FOR J = 1 TO 2500 : NEXT J
RETURN

CountMissed: '***
  IF INSTR(UCASE$(SIGNS$(R)), CHR$(NEXTLETTER)) THEN TIMES = TIMES + 1 '***
RETURN '***
```

Problem No. 4

```
REM ** Arrange signs tabulation according to frequency
DIM ALPHA(26), ASCII(26)
OPEN "Signs Data" FOR INPUT AS #1
GOSUB Tabulate
CLOSE #1
GOSUB Arrange
GOSUB Display
END

Tabulate:
  INPUT #1, A$
  WHILE A$ <> "Done" : A$ = UCASE$(A$)
    FOR K = 1 TO LEN(A$)
      B$ = MID$(A$,K,1) : X = ASC(B$)
      IF X > 64 AND X < 91 THEN ALPHA(X-64) = ALPHA(X-64) + 1
    NEXT K
    INPUT #1, A$
  WEND
RETURN

Display:
  WIDTH 60
  FOR K = 1 TO 26
    PRINT CHR$(ASCII(K)); " "; ALPHA(K),
  NEXT K
RETURN
```

Arrange:
```
FOR K = 1 TO 26 : ASCII(K) = K + 64 : NEXT K
FOR K = 1 TO 25
 FOR J = K + 1 TO 26
  IF ALPHA(K) >= ALPHA(J) THEN NextLetter
  SWAP ALPHA(K), ALPHA(J) : SWAP ASCII(K), ASCII(J)
 NextLetter: NEXT J
NEXT K
RETURN
```

E	26	I	18	N	18	T	15
A	13	O	12	R	10	L	10
S	8	Y	8	D	7	U	6
H	6	V	5	G	5	F	3
W	3	P	3	M	2	Z	2
B	1	Q	1	C	1	X	1
J	1	K	1				

Section 11-2
Problem No. 2

```
REM ** Display a program from disk
OPEN "Program 11-5" FOR INPUT AS #1
PRINT "Some other statements will appear..."
WHILE NOT EOF(1)
 LINE INPUT #1, A$
 GOSUB Format
WEND
END

StraightPRINT:
 PRINT A$ : RETURN

Format:
 IF INSTR(A$,"FOR") = 0 AND INSTR(A$,"NEXT") = 0 THEN LeaveHere
 FOR J = 1 TO LEN(A$)
  IF MID$(A$,J,3) <> " : " THEN NextCharacter
   PRINT LEFT$(A$,J-1)
   PRINT TAB(5);
   A$ = MID$(A$,J+1) : GOTO Format
 NextCharacter:
 NEXT J
 PRINT A$
 LeaveHere: RETURN
```

```
Some other statements will appear...
OPEN "Program 11-2a" FOR INPUT AS #1
 FOR J = 1 TO LEN(A$)
 NEXT J
```

Section 11-3
Problem No. 2

```
REM ** Add a name to a sequential file
OPEN "Name List 01 Data" FOR INPUT AS #1
OPEN "Name List 01 Temp" FOR OUTPUT AS #2

INPUT "Add a name"; N1$
PRINT #2, N1$
```

Appendix F

```
    N$ = "Begin"
    WHILE N$ <> "End"
      ReadName: INPUT #1, N$
        IF N$ = N1$ THEN PRINT N$; " Duplicate" : GOTO ReadName
        PRINT #2, N$
    WEND

    CLOSE #1, #2
    KILL "Name List 01 Data"
    NAME "Name List 01 Temp" AS "Name List 01 Data"
    END
```

Problem No. 4

```
    REM ** Add a name to a sequential file
    OPEN "Name List 01 Data" FOR INPUT AS #1
    OPEN "Name List 01 Temp" FOR OUTPUT AS #2

    INPUT "Delete a name"; N1$
    PRINT #2, N1$

    N$ = "Begin"
    WHILE N$ <> "End"
      ReadName: INPUT #1, N$
        IF N$ = N1$ THEN PRINT N$; "Deleted" : GOTO ReadName
        PRINT #2, N$
    WEND

    CLOSE #1, #2
    KILL "Name List 01 Data"
    NAME "Name List 01 Temp" AS "Name List 01 Data"
    END
```

Section 11-4
Problem No. 2

```
    REM ** File name selection routine
    MENU 1,0,1,"File"
    MENU 1,1,1,"New"
    MENU 1,2,1,"Open"
    MENU 1,3,1,"Kill"
    MENU 1,4,1,"Quit"
    FOR M = 2 TO 5 : MENU M,0,1,"" : NEXT M

    MenuSelect:
      WHILE MENU(0) = 0 : WEND
      CLS : MENU
      ON MENU(1) GOSUB NewFile, OpenFile, KillFile, EndProgram
      GOTO MenuSelect

    NewFile:
      PROMPT$ = "New output file name:"
      X$ = FILES$(0, PROMPT$) : IF LEN(X$) = 0 THEN LeaveNewFile
      OPEN X$ FOR OUTPUT AS #2
        CLS
        INPUT "Enter a message"; MESSAGE$
        PRINT #2, MESSAGE$
        CLOSE #2
        NAME X$ AS X$, "SPEC"
        CLS
      LeaveNewFile: RETURN
```

```
OpenFile:
 TYPE$ = "SPEC"
 X$ = FILES$(1, TYPE$) : IF LEN(X$) = 0 THEN LeaveOpenFile
 OPEN X$ FOR INPUT AS #3
 A$ = INPUT$(LOF(3), #3)
 CLOSE #3
 PRINT A$
LeaveOpenFile: RETURN

KillFile:
 TYPE$ = "SPEC"
 X$ = FILES$(1, TYPE$) : IF LEN(X$) = 0 THEN LeaveKillFile
 WINDOW 4,, (300,41)-(490,85), 2
 X = INSTR(X$,":")
 PRINT "Kill "; MID$(X$,X+1) .
 BUTTON 1, 1, "No way", (100,20)-(180,35), 1
 BUTTON 2, 1, "Ok", (20,20)-(40,35), 1
 WHILE DIALOG(0) <> 1 : WEND
 IF DIALOG(1) = 2 THEN KILL X$
 WINDOW CLOSE 4
LeaveKillFile: RETURN

EndProgram:
 MENU RESET
 CLS
 END
 RETURN
```

Chapter 12

Section 12-2
Problem No. 2

```
OPEN "Account Names" AS #1 LEN = 30
FIELD #1, 30 AS X$

Request:
 INPUT "New Acct#, Label"; N, A$
 IF N > 0 AND N < 100 THEN WriteFile
  PRINT "Acct# out of range" : GOTO Request
 IF LEN(A$) < 31 THEN WriteFile
  PRINT "Label exceeds 30 characters" : GOTO Request

WriteFile:
 GET #1, N
 IF LEFT$(X$,10) <> "Unassigned" THEN PRINT N; "In use" : GOTO Request
 LSET X$ = A$
 PUT #1, N
 CLOSE #1
 END
```

Problem No. 4

```
REM ** Initialize account label file
OPEN "Account Names" AS #1 LEN = 38
FIELD #1, 30 AS X$, 8 AS Y$

REM ** Fill each record with "Unassigned"
LSET X$ = "Unassigned" : LSET Y$ = "Unassign"
FOR REC = 1 TO 99
  PUT #1, REC
NEXT REC

REM ** Write out actual labels
BeginRead:
  READ N, N$, A$ : IF N$ = "Done" THEN EndRead
  IF N < 1 OR N > 99 THEN PRINT N; "Out of range" : GOTO EndRead
    LSET X$ = N$ : LSET Y$ = A$
    PUT #1, N
    GOTO BeginRead
EndRead: CLOSE #1 : END

DATA 1,  Real estate taxes, R.E. tax
DATA 2,  Personal property taxes, P.P. tax
DATA 9,  Medical expenses, Medical
DATA 99, Miscellaneous, Misc
DATA 22, Sewer and water, S and W
DATA 38, Cleaning and maintenance, Maint
DATA 44, Mortgage interest, Mortgage
DATA 0,  Done, Done
```

Section 12-3
Problem No. 2

```
REM ** Display cities in rank order
DIM ARRAY (10), POSITION(10)

OPEN "Cities Data" AS #1 LEN = 28
FIELD #1, 12 AS CITY$, 8 AS RANK$, 8 AS PERCENT$

FOR REC = 1 TO 10
  GET #1, REC
  G = CVD(PERCENT$)
  ARRAY( REC ) = G
  POSITION(REC) = REC
NEXT REC

GOSUB Arrange

PRINT "City           Rank    % Growth"
FOR K = 1 TO 10
  GET #1, POSITION( K )
  R = CVD( RANK$ )
  G = CVD( PERCENT$ )
  PRINT CITY$,
  PRINT USING " ##       ###.#"; R, G
NEXT K
CLOSE #1
END
```

```
Arrange:
  FOR LAST = 1 TO 9
    FOR J = 1 TO LAST
      IF ARRAY(J) <= ARRAY(J+1) THEN NextCity
        SWAP ARRAY(J), ARRAY(J+1)
        SWAP POSITION(J), POSITION(J+1)
    NextCity: NEXT J
  NEXT LAST
  RETURN
```

City	Rank	% Growth
Detroit	6	-20.5
Baltimore	9	-13.1
Chicago	2	-10.8
New York	1	-10.4
Philadelphia	4	-13.4
Los Angeles	3	5.5
Dallas	7	7.1
San Antonio	10	20.1
San Diego	8	25.5
Houston	5	29.2

Chapter 13
Section 13-2
Problem No. 2

```
REM ** Mailing-list program
DEFINT A-Z
FILENAME$ = "Names"
DIM LABEL$(9), L(9), FILEDATA$(9), KEYDATA$(9)

REM ** Control routine for mailing-list Editing
GOSUB ReadLabels    'Read data labels and limits
GOSUB ReadPointer   'Read available-space parameters ( Pointer file)
GOSUB OpenDataFile
Begin:
  GOSUB RequestID
  IF ID = 0 THEN CLOSE : END  'Terminate on zero ID
  GOSUB EditEntry
  GOTO Begin          'Do it again (repeat step 4)

ReadLabels:
  READ NUMBEROFITEMS
  RLENGTH = 0
  FOR ITEM = 1 TO NUMBEROFITEMS
    READ LABEL$(ITEM), L(ITEM)  'L array is item length
    RLENGTH = RLENGTH + L(ITEM)
  NEXT ITEM
RETURN

REM ** DATA - labels and limits
DATA 9
DATA ID  ,   2
DATA CODE,   2
DATA LAST,  20
DATA FRST,  20
DATA ADDR,  30
DATA CITY,  20
DATA STAT,   2
DATA "ZIP ", 5
DATA PHON,  17
```

Appendix F

```
ReadPointer:
  OPEN FILENAME$ + " Pointer" AS #1 LEN = 4
    FIELD #1, 2 AS NEWID$, 2 AS OLDID$
  GET #1, 1
NS = CVI(NEWID$)
DS = CVI(OLDID$)
RETURN

OpenDataFile:
  OPEN FILENAME$ + " Data" AS #2 LEN = RLENGTH
  X = 0
  FOR J = 1 TO NUMBEROFITEMS
    FIELD #2, X AS D9$, L(J) AS FILEDATA$(J)
    X = X + L(J)
  NEXT J
  RETURN

RequestID:
  PRINT : INPUT "Edit ID#"; ID : IF ID = 0 THEN QuitRequest
  IF !D >= NS OR ID < 1 THEN PRINT "Non-Existent ID" : GOTO RequestID
  QuitRequest: RETURN

EditEntry:
  GET #2, ID : X = CVI(FILEDATA$(1))
  IF X <> ID THEN PRINT "Has been deleted" : GOTO EditEntry
  FOR ITEM = 2 TO NUMBEROFITEMS
    PRINT LABEL$(ITEM); ": "; FILEDATA$(ITEM);
   Ok: PRINT"   Ok"; : AN$ = UCASE$(INPUT$(1)) : PRINT AN$
     IF AN$ <> "Y" AND AN$ <> "N" THEN PRINT "'Y' or 'N' please" : GOTO Ok
     IF AN$ = "Y" THEN NextItem
    Ask: INPUT "   : "; KEYDATA$(ITEM)
      IF LEN(KEYDATA$(ITEM)) > L(ITEM) THEN PRINT "Too long" : GOTO Ask
      LSET FILEDATA$(ITEM) = KEYDATA$(ITEM)
NextItem: NEXT ITEM
  PUT #2, ID
```

Problem No. 4

```
REM ** Mailing-list program
DEFINT A-Z
FILENAME$ = "Names"
DIM LABEL$(9), L(9), FILEDATA$(9), KEYDATA$(9), IDS(10)

REM ** Control routine for mailing-list Print labels
GOSUB ReadLabels      'Read data labels and limits
GOSUB ReadPointer     'Read available-space parameters ( Pointer file)
GOSUB OpenDataFile    'OPEN the Data file
Begin:
  GOSUB RequestIDs    'Get up to 10 IDs
  IF NUMBEROFIDS = 0 THEN CLOSE : END 'Terminate on no IDs
  GOSUB Display       'Print labels
  GOTO Begin          'Do it again (repeat step 4)

ReadLabels:
  READ NUMBEROFITEMS
  RLENGTH = 0
  FOR ITEM = 1 TO NUMBEROFITEMS
    READ LABEL$(ITEM), L(ITEM)  'L array is item length
    RLENGTH = RLENGTH + L(ITEM)
  NEXT ITEM
  RETURN
```

Appendix F

```
REM ** DATA - labels and limits
DATA 9
DATA ID #,    2
DATA CODE,    2
DATA LAST,    20
DATA FRST,    20
DATA ADDR,    30
DATA CITY,    20
DATA STAT,    2
DATA "ZIP ",  5
DATA PHON,    17

ReadPointer:
 OPEN FILENAME$ + " Pointer" AS #1 LEN = 4
 FIELD #1, 2 AS NEWID$, 2 AS OLDID$
 GET #1, 1
 NS = CVI(NEWID$)
 DS = CVI(OLDID$)
 RETURN

OpenDataFile:
 OPEN FILENAME$ + " Data" AS #2 LEN = RLENGTH
 X = 0
 FOR J = 1 TO NUMBEROFITEMS
   FIELD #2, X AS D9$, L(J) AS FILEDATA$(J)
   X = X + L(J)
 NEXT J
 RETURN

RequestIDs:
 IF NS = 1 THEN PRINT "No names in the file" : GOTO EndRequest
 NUMBEROFIDS = 0
 FOR R = 1 TO 10
   IDS(R) = 0


 Ok:  INPUT "ID"; ID : IF ID = 0 THEN EndRequest
   IF ID < 1 OR ID >= NS THEN PRINT "Out of range" : GOTO Ok
   GET #2, ID : X = CVI(FILEDATA$(1))
   IF ID <> X THEN PRINT "Deleted" : GOTO Ok
   IDS(R) = ID
   NUMBEROFIDS = R
 NEXT R
 EndRequest: RETURN

Display:
 FOR R = 1 TO NUMBEROFIDS
   GET #2, IDS(R)
   PRINT FILEDATA$(4); " "; FILEDATA$(3)
   PRINT FILEDATA$(5)
   PRINT FILEDATA$(6); " "; FILEDATA$(7); " "; FILEDATA$(8)
   PRINT : PRINT : PRINT
 NEXT R
 RETURN
```

Appendix F

Section 13-3
Problem No. 2

```
REM ** Mailing-list program
DEFINT A-Z
FILENAME$ = "Names"
DIM LABEL$(9), L(9), FILEDATA$(9), KEYDATA$(9)
WINDOW CLOSE 1
WINDOW 2,,(50,41)-(350,260), -2
WINDOW 3,,(359,41)-(508,105), -3

REM ** Control routine for mailing-list Editing
GOSUB ReadLabels      'Read data labels and limits
GOSUB ReadPointer     'Read available-space parameters (.POINTER file)
GOSUB OpenDataFile    'OPEN the .DATA file
Begin:
  GOSUB RequestID     'Get and verify ID
  IF ID = 0 THEN CLOSE : WINDOW CLOSE 2 : WINDOW CLOSE 3 : WINDOW 1 : END
  GOSUB EditEntry     'Display data - make changes
  GOSUB WriteData     'Write entry in .DATA file
  GOTO Begin          'Do it again (repeat step 4)

ReadLabels:
READ NUMBEROFITEMS
RLENGTH = 0
FOR ITEM = 1 TO NUMBEROFITEMS
  READ LABEL$(ITEM), L(ITEM)  'L array is item length
  RLENGTH = RLENGTH + L(ITEM)
NEXT ITEM
RETURN

REM ** DATA - labels and limits
DATA 9
DATA ID #,  2
DATA Code,  2
DATA Last,  20
DATA First, 20
DATA Addr,  30
DATA City,  20
DATA State, 2
DATA ZIP,   5
DATA Phone, 17

RequestID:
  WINDOW 3
  INPUT "ID to edit"; ID : IF ID = 0 THEN LeaveRequestID
  IF ID >= NS OR ID < 1 THEN PRINT "Non-existent ID" : GOTO RequestID
  GET #2, ID : X = CVI(FILEDATA$(1))
  IF X <> ID THEN PRINT "Has been deleted" : GOTO RequestID
  FOR ITEM = 2 TO NUMBEROFITEMS
    FOR L9 = LEN(FILEDATA$(ITEM)) TO 1 STEP -1
    IF MID$(FILEDATA$(ITEM),L9,1) = CHR$(32) THEN NEXT L9
    KEYDATA$(ITEM) = LEFT$(FILEDATA$(ITEM),L9)
  NEXT ITEM
  LeaveRequestID: RETURN

ReadPointer:
  OPEN FILENAME$ + ".Pointer" AS #1 LEN = 4
  FIELD #1, 2 AS NEWID$, 2 AS OLDID$
  GET #1, 1
  NS = CVI(NEWID$)
  DS = CVI(OLDID$)
  RETURN
```

```
OpenDataFile:
  OPEN FILENAME$ + " Data" AS #2 LEN = RLENGTH
  X = 0
  FOR J = 1 TO NUMBEROFITEMS
    FIELD #2, X AS D9$, L(J) AS FILEDATA$(J)
    X = X + L(J)
  NEXT J
  RETURN


EditEntry:
  WINDOW 2 : CLS
  MOVETO 2, 20 : PRINT LABEL$(1); ": "; ID
  FOR ITEM = 2 TO NUMBEROFITEMS
    X = ITEM*20
    MOVETO 2, ITEM*20 : PRINT LABEL$(ITEM)
    EDIT FIELD ITEM,KEYDATA$(ITEM), (50,X-13)-(53+8*L(ITEM),X+2),1 ,1
  NEXT ITEM
  BUTTON 1,1,"Enter",(50,190)-(100,206),1
  ITEM = 2
  BeginEntry:
    EDIT FIELD ITEM
      Poll: PROCESS = DIALOG(0) : IF PROCESS = 0 THEN Poll
      IF PROCESS = 6 THEN NextEditField
      IF PROCESS = 2 THEN NewEditField
      IF PROCESS = 1 THEN EndEntry
      GOTO Poll

NextEditField:
  ITEM = ITEM + 1 : IF ITEM > NUMBEROFITEMS THEN ITEM = NUMBEROFITEMS
  GOTO BeginEntry

NewEditField:
  ITEM = DIALOG(2)
  GOTO BeginEntry

EndEntry:
  FOR ITEM = 2 TO NUMBEROFITEMS
    KEYDATA$(ITEM) = EDIT$(ITEM)
    IF LEN(KEYDATA$(ITEM)) <= L(ITEM) THEN VerifyNext
    X = ITEM*20
    EDIT FIELD ITEM,KEYDATA$(ITEM), (50,X-13)-(52+8*L(ITEM),X+2),1 ,1
    GOTO BeginEntry
  VerifyNext:
  NEXT ITEM
  FOR ITEM = 2 TO NUMBEROFITEMS
    X = ITEM*20
    EDIT FIELD ITEM,"", (50,X-13)-(52+8*L(ITEM),X+2),1 ,1
  NEXT ITEM
  RETURN

WriteData:
  LSET FILEDATA$(1) = MKI$(ID)
  FOR ITEM = 2 TO NUMBEROFITEMS
    LSET FILEDATA$(ITEM) = KEYDATA$(ITEM)
  NEXT ITEM
  PUT #2, ID
  RETURN
```

Index

Symbols

+	Addition, 20
*	Asterisk, 19
⌘	Command key, 3
⌘-X	Cut, 11
/	Division, 20
$	Dollar sign, 34–35
⌘-E	Eject, 3
>	Greater than, 53
<	Less than, 53
⌘-L	List, 7
π	Microsoft BASIC b, 1
$	Microsoft BASIC d, 1
<>	Not equal to, 53
#	Number sign, 33, 34
⌘-V	Paste, 12
%	Percent, 34
⌘-4	Printing, 22–23
⌘-R	Run, 5, 6
;	Semicolon, 13–15
⌘-.	Stop, 68
–	Subtraction, 20
⌘-S	Suspend, 82
∧	To the power, 39

ABS, 114
Absolute value, 114
Access files:
    mixed, 322
    random, 291
    sequential, 290
Account labels, 321
Adding strings, 45–47
AllDone, 66
Alphabet game, 182–192
AND, 72
Apostrophe, 85–86
Apple menu, 355–356
Arcs:
    drawing with, 268, 276–277
Arithmetic operators, 39–42
Arrays, 163
Array sizes, 173–180
ASC, 106
ASCII Value, 106
Aspect, 220–221
Assignment statement, 28–29
Available space, 340

BACKPAT, 285-287
Base ten number system, 204

BASIC:
    getting out of, 3
BASIC Windows, 6
    command window, 6–7
    list window, 7–9
    output window, 6
    second list window, 6
BF option, 234
Binary digit, 205
Binary numbering, 204–207
BIT, 205
BLUEONES, 101–102
Bouncing simulation, 83–84
Box, 215
BoxFill, 215
BREAK, 161
Buttons, 155–158
    and DIALOG, 158–159
    displaying, 156–157
BUTTON:
    demonstration, 159

Calculations, 18–21
Calendar control routine, 196
Calendar display control
    routine, 197

Calendar program, 195–201
CALL, 129–130, 131–132
Cartesian coordinates, 243–245
CHAIN, 369
Chart-of-accounts file, 329
CHR$, 107
CHR$( ), 23
CIRCLE, 213
CLIP:, 312
CLOSE #, 293
CLOSE #:
    random access files, 318–319
Close box, 7
Color, 215
Command-S, 82
Command window, 6–7
Commas, 35, 78–79
Comma spacing, 57–58
COMMON, 369
Compound interest, 92
Computer graphics, 213
Concantenation, 45–47
CONT, 293–294
Control routine, 185
Controlling single points, 235–242
Controlling text, 281-285
Converting to binary, 206–207
Converting to numeric, 108
Converting to string, 107
Converting to uppercase, 110–111
Copy, 7
COUNT, 54
Counter value, 55
Counting out loud, 52
Counting programs, 49–50
Counting variables, 55
Counting with STEP, 76–77
Creating menus, 149–150
Curved line statements, 213
Cut, 7
Cut, Copy, and Paste, 10–13
CVD, 324–328
CVDBCD, 329
CVI, 329
CVS, 329
CVSBCD, 329

DATA, 30–32
Data entry program, 349–353
Data record layout, 336–337
Data types, 47
DATE$, 111
Decimal digits:
    removal of, 103
DEFDBL, 124–125
Deferred execution, 7
DEFINT, 124–125
DEF FN, 119–123
DEFSNG, 124–125
DEFSTR, 124–125
DELETE Begin, 50–51
Designing files, 334–336
Designing record layout, 336–337
Designing systems, 333–337
Devices, 311
D-format, 66
DIALOG, 158–159
Digital clocks, 91–92
DIM, 173–180
    arrays, 176
    multiple dimensions, 175–176
    subprograms, 176
Disk icon, 2
Displaying messages, 3
Domino effect, 205
Double buffer, 312–314
Double-precision random values, 114
Drawing curved lines, 218
Drawing dice, 223–225
Drawing from DATA, 228–229
Drawing lines:
    LINETO, 259
Drawing polar graphs, 248
Drawing random numbers, 166–167
Drawing straight lines, 215

Edit menu, 359
Eject, 3
E-format, 66
END, 3, 67

End angles, 219
EndCount, 53
End Of File, 302–304
Enhancing programs, 349–353
Entering data, 338–347
EOF, 302–304
ERASE, 174–175, 268–269
Eratosthenes, 202
Error checking, 131
Establishing game, 183
Event trapping, 152–154, 160–162
EXIT SUB, 130
EXP, 119
Exponentiation, 41

Factor pairs, 104
Factors, 104
FatBits, 253
Fibonacci numbers, 90
FIELD#, 317
File-based game, 294-299
File formats, 366–367
File menu, 2, 356–359
File names, 365
FILES, 367
Files:
    random access, 291
    sequential access, 290, 291
FILES$, 307–308
FILLROUNDRECT, 224
Finder, 2, 289
FIX, 103
Flexibility, 329
FOR, 75–76
FOR loops, 96
FRAME, 268–269
FRE, 118
Free memory, 118
Functions, 101

GET:
    manipulating graphics, 213
GET#:
    random access files, 318–319
GetBit, 207

Index

GETPEN, 259–260
Graphics pen:
    controlling, 259–268
Graphics screen, 214
Graphs from formulas, 243–246
Greatest integer, 103
"Go-away box," 7, 135
GOSUB, 125–127
GOTO, 50–52
    evils of, 52

Hexadecimal numbering, 208–211
HEX$, 209
HIDECURSOR, 252
HIDEPEN, 267–268

IF statement, 53
IF...THEN, 53–56, 67
Immediate execution, 7
INITCURSOR, 252
INKEY$, 106–107
INPUT, 30–32
INPUT features, 45
INPUT$, 107
INPUT #, 292–293
INSTR, 109–110
Instructions, 60, 61
Instructions segment, 62
Instructions to BASIC, 4
INT, 103
Integer division, 40–41
Interest:
    calculating, 88–90
INVERT, 268–269

Language features, 101
Labels:
    nonnumber, 50
LBOUND, 177–180
LCOPY, 22
LEFT$, 108
LEN, 106
Length of string, 106
LET, 28–29

LINE, 213
LINE INPUT, 301
Line labels, 50–52
Lineprinter, 22
Line statements, 213
    variety, 216
LINETO, 259
LIST window, 7–9
List window, 4
    editing, 7
LLIST, 22
LOAD, 367–368
Load, 63
Loading array, 183
Local variables, 101
LOCATE, 99
Logical operators, 72
    AND, 208
    NOT, 208
    OR, 208
Loop maker, 55
Loop variable, 76
LPRINT, 22
LPT1:, 311
LSET:
    random access files, 317–318
LSET vs. RSET, 317

Macintosh Control Panel, 3
Managing files, 365
Mask bit, 256–257
Menu Bars, 355–362
MENU, 152–154
Menus, 2, 148–152
    Apple, 355–356
    creating, 149
    edit, 359
    file, 356–359
    pull-down, 2
    run, 361–362
    search, 360
    selecting, 150–152
    window, 362
MERGE, 63, 64–66, 368
Microsoft BASIC disk:
    open, 2

Microsoft BASICs,
    binary (b), 1
    decimal (d), 1
MID$, 108–109
Mini-program, 101
Miscellaneous functions, 114–119
Mixed access files, 322
Mixing data types, 47
MKD$, 324
MKDBCD$, 329
MKI$, 329
MKS$, 329
MKSBCD$, 329
MODular authmetic, 40–41
MOUSE, 161
Mouse Cursor:
    controlling, 252–259
    creating, 257
    customizing, 253
MOVETO, 259, 260
Multiple dimensions, 175–176
Multiple fields, 329–330
Multiple INPUT, 35–37
Multiple READ, 35–37
Multiple statements, 72
Multiplication, 19

NAME, 370
"Names pointer," 334
Nested loops, 91–93
NET.PAY, 34
NEW, 9
NEXT, 75–76
NOT, 72
Number bases, 204–211
Numeric arrays, 163–166
Numeric functions:
    programmer-defined, 119–122
Numeric variables, 27–28
Number pigeonholes, 27–28

OBSCURECURSOR, 252
Octal numbering, 211
OLDLIST, 28
OLD.LIST, 28

Index

ON N GOSUB, 128
OPEN, 63
    random access files, 316–317
Operations:
    order of, 38
Optional LET, 29–30
OPTION BASE, 176–177
OR, 72
Output window, 6
Output window background:
    controlling, 285–287
Ovals:
    drawing with, 268, 276
Overflow errors, 108

PAINT, 268–269
Parenthesis, 21
Partitioning work, 101
Paste, 7
Pen location, 259
PENMODE, 265–267
PENPAT, 262–265
PENSIZE, 252, 260
Pictures, 141–148
PICTURE statements, 141–143
    GET, 239–243
    PUT, 240–243
PICTURE$, 143–147
Planning, 60
Plotting a function, 244
POINT, 213, 237–238
"Pointer" file, 334–335
Point statements, 213
Polar graphs, 247–249
Polygons:
    drawing with, 268–277
Powers:
    raising to, 39
PRESET, 236
Prime numbers, 202–204
PRINT, 3
PRINT #, 292
PRINT#:
    commas, 308–309
    semicolon, 309–310
PrintAverage, 63

Printing, 22–23
PRINT Messages, 4
PRINT USING, 32–33, 35
Program documentation, 61
Programmer-defined functions, 119–123
Programming, 3
Programming repertoire, 101
Program looks, 55
Program names, 365
Program parameters, 344
Proportional spacing, 26
PSET, 235-236
PTAB, 70–71
PTAB (X), 98
Pull-down menus, 2
PUT:
    manipulating graphics, 213
PUT#:
    random access files, 318
Pythagorean triples, 95-98
    FOR loops, 96–97
    WHILE, 97–98

QuickDraw routines, 213
Quit, 3

Random access files:
    sample of, 319–322
RANDOMIZE, 118
Random numbers, 114–117
READ, 30–32
READ and DATA, 30
Reading available space, 340
Record keeping:
    random access files, 315
Records, 316
Rectangles:
    drawing with, 268–269
Relational operators, 53
Release and Cut, 13
REMark, 61–63
Removing decimal digits, 103
Replace, 22
Requesting data, 196
Requesting scores, 60

RESTORE, 37
Results of program, 60–61
RIGHT$, 108–109
RND, 114–117
RND(X) 117
ROUND RECTangle, 274–276
RSET:
    random access files, 317–318
RUN a program, 4–6
Run menu, 361–362

Save, 3
SCRN:, 311
SCROLL, 147–148
Search menu, 360
Seconds Since Midnight, 118
Semicolon, 13–15, 78–79
Sequential access files, 290, 291–299
Sequential file:
    adding names, 306
    open, 291–292
    updating, 305–307
Sequential file update:
    double buffer, 313
SGN, 114
SHARED, 131
SHIFT-6, 39
Show Command, 6
SHOWCURSOR, 252
Show List, 7
SHOWPEN, 267–268
Sieve of Eratosthenes, 202–204
Sign, 114
Simulation, 183
Soft tone, 16
Sorting data, 171–173
SPACE$, 111
Spacing, 26
SQR, 102–103
Square root, 102–103
Start angles, 219
STEP, 76–78, 215
STOP, 3, 68
STR$, 107
String arrays, 180–181

Index

String concatenation, 46–47
String functions, 106–112
    programmer-defined, 122–123
String length, 106
String of characters, 111
String of spaces, 111
Strings:
    addition of, 45–47
String segments, 108–109
String READ, 44
String variables, 43–44
String width, 106
STRING$, 111
SUB, 129–130
Subprograms, 101
    CALL, 129–130
    SUB, 129–130
Subroutines, 101
Substring:
    finding, 109–110
Suspend, 82
Syntax error, 16
SYSTEM, 3

TAB, 98–99
TAB(X), 98
TAX, 28
TEMP, 54
TEXTFONT, 281–282
TEXTMODE, 282–284
TEXT routines, 251
TEXTSIZE, 284
TIME$, 112
Time delay routine, 189
TIMER, 118, 161
"Toolbox," 251
Trigonometric functions, 119

UBOUND, 177–180
UCASE$, 110–111
"Unassigned," 320–321
Undefined subprogram, 16
Untitled, 6
Updating sequential files, 305–307

VAL, 108
Values:
    entering, 30–31
    labelling, 26–27
Variable DIM, 174
Variables, 28
    string, 43–44
Variable type indicators, 125
Variable typing, 124–125, 175

WAGES, 28
WEND, 75
WHILE, 75
WIDTH, 78–80
WIDTH#, 309
WINDOW functions, 140–141
Window menu, 362
Windows, 135
WINDOW statements, 136–140
Word pigeonholes, 43–44
WRITE#, 310–311
Writing programs, 337–347

XOR, 240